The Amphibian Visual System

A Multidisciplinary Approach

CONTRIBUTORS

W. Frank Blair
J.-P. Ewert
Katherine V. Fite
James Gordon
Ursula Grüsser-Cornehls
Werner Himstedt
Donald C. Hood
David Ingle
M. J. Keating
C. Kennard
George W. Nace
Frank Scalia

The Amphibian Visual System

A Multidisciplinary Approach

EDITED BY

KATHERINE V. FITE

Psychology Department
University of Massachusetts at Amherst
Amherst, Massachusetts

ACADEMIC PRESS   New York San Francisco London   1976

A Subsidiary of Harcourt Brace Jovanovich, Publishers

ACADEMIC PRESS, INC.
111 Fifth Avenue, New York, New York 10003

United Kingdom Edition published by
ACADEMIC PRESS, INC. (LONDON) LTD.
24/28 Oval Road, London NW1

Library of Congress Cataloging in Publication Data

Main entry under title:

The Amphibian visual system.

    Bibliography: p.
    Includes index.
    1.   Amphibians–Physiology.   2.   Amphibians–
Behavior.   3.   Vision.   I.   Fite, Katherine V.
QL669.2.A46   597'.6'04823   76-10016
ISBN 0–12–257450–8

**To Lorrin Riggs,
for all his students**

Contents

1 Amphibians, Their Evolutionary History, Taxonomy, and Ecological Adaptations
W. Frank Blair

2 Anatomy and Physiology of the Frog Retina
James Gordon and Donald C. Hood

3 Central Visual Pathways in the Frog
Katherine V. Fite and Frank Scalia

4   Spatial Vision in Anurans
David Ingle

5   The Visual System of the Toad: Behavioral and Physiological Studies on a Pattern Recognition System
J.-P. Ewert

6   The Urodele Visual System
Ursula Grüsser-Cornehls and Werner Himstedt

7   The Amphibian Visual System as a Model for Developmental Neurobiology
M. J. Keating and C. Kennard

8   Standards for Laboratory Amphibians
George W. Nace

List of Contributors

Numbers in parentheses indicate the pages on which the authors' contributions begin.

W. Frank Blair (1), Department of Zoology, The University of Texas, Austin, Texas

J.-P. Ewert (141), Arbeitsgruppe Neuro-Ethologie, University of Kassel, Kassel-Oberzwehren, Germany

Katherine V. Fite (87), Psychology Department, University of Massachusetts at Amherst, Amherst, Massachusetts

James Gordon (29), Department of Psychology, Hunter College, CUNY, New York, and the Rockefeller University, New York, New York

Ursula Grüsser-Cornehls (203), Physiologisches Institut, Berlin, Germany

Werner Himstedt (203), Fachbereich Biologie-Zoologie, Technische Hochschule, Darmstadt, Germany

Donald C. Hood (29), Department of Psychology, Columbia University, New York, New York

David Ingle (119), Laboratory of Neuropsychology, McLean Hospital, Belmont, Massachusetts

M. J. Keating (267), Division of Developmental Biology, National Institute for Medical Research, Mill Hill, London, England

C. Kennard (267), Division of Developmental Biology, National Institute for Medical Research, Mill Hill, London, England

George W. Nace (317), Division of Biological Sciences, University of Michigan, Ann Arbor, Michigan

Frank Scalia (87), Department of Anatomy, Downstate Medical Center, Brooklyn, New York

Preface

The past two decades have yielded rapid and even spectacular progress in the natural sciences, often as the result of a degree of individual specialization and technological refinement not previously achieved in biological laboratories. In particular, the advent of microelectrode recording techniques, electron microscopy, microspectrophotometry, as well as degenerating-fiber and bouton stains have enabled major advances in knowledge concerning the structural and functional substrates of vision in both vertebrate and invertebrate species. The quantity of information presently available challenges even the most determined of scholars who attempt to master its outlines. It is not surprising, therefore, that with increasing frequency the need arises for a compendium of summary and review articles bound together by a common theme which sets forth the major issues, data, and theoretical schemata which guide and stimulate research—a volume that can serve as a multiauthored "progress report" to the scientific community at large. Increasingly, the trend is toward interdisciplinary or multidisciplinary collaborations of this type, integrative in nature, which may represent important sources of new insights.

This volume is primarily multidisciplinary in scope. Its focus is on the amphibian visual system which has been the subject of numerous investigations across a broad range of disciplines within experimental biology. The choice of amphibians was made for many reasons: abundance, convenience, ectothermy, their relative biological and behavioral simplicity, and dependence on vision, and phylogenetically the fact that amphibians occupy an intermediate position between aquatic and terrestrial vertebrates. As Herrick (1948) pointed out, the transition from aquatic to terrestrial life was one of the major critical periods in vertebrate evolution; and, in a sense, the majority of amphibia "recapitulate" such a crucial transition with each new generation. Further,

> It is probable that none of the existing Amphibia are primitive in the sense of survival of the original transitional forms and that the urodeles are not only aberrant, but in some cases retrograde . . . yet the organization of their nervous systems is generalized along very primitive lines and these brains seem to me to be more instructive as types ancestral to mammals than any others that might be chosen (Herrick, 1948, p. 16).

In their search for generalities, however, experimental biologists have often used (perhaps unintentionally) a typological nomenclature, referring to "the amphibian" or "the frog," a practice which has frequently ignored or obscured genera and species differences, many of which may be related to important structural and functional differences. The first chapter in this volume is, therefore, devoted to a survey of the evolutionary history and of the major taxonomic and ecological characteristics which distinguish the many species of extant amphibia, only a few of which have been studied by visual scientists.

Subsequent chapters are devoted to anatomic, physiological, developmental, and behavioral data relating to the visual system of urodeles and anurans, with an emphasis on the extent to which amphibian visual systems have been used as models for various aspects of vertebrate vision. As will inevitably become apparent, the story is not complete, and perhaps one of the most useful functions this book can serve is to reveal more clearly the existing gaps and discontinuities. For example, there is a major hiatus with regard to ethology and the behavioral ecology of amphibians and their visually guided behaviors as they occur in Nature. Where it exists, such information has been included. In Chapter 8 some important standards for laboratory amphibians and the crucial problem of species identification in neurobiological research are briefly described.

Finally, a word of thanks is due each of the contributors, whose individual and collective efforts have helped to make this volume a reality.

Katherine V. Fite

1

Amphibians, Their Evolutionary History, Taxonomy, and Ecological Adaptations

W. Frank Blair

PAST HISTORY OF THE AMPHIBIA

Modern amphibians group into three distinctive evolutionary lines, each of which has its own general set of adaptations for existence. The urodeles have retained the generalized tetrapod body form except for some aquatic-adapted types. They have maintained relatively small body size through their history. They have tended to emphasize chemoreceptors to provide information about their environment. The caecilians represent a highly specialized line of fossorially adapted amphibians that are characterized by a legless, vermiform body shape. The anurans have departed strikingly from the tetrapod body pattern in evolving saltatorial

1

locomotion and alterations of skeleton and body form to accompany this adaptation. They have emphasized vision to provide environmental information and have evolved vocalization for intrapopulational communication.

The fossil record of much of the early history of these lower tetrapods is very incomplete. This means that the affinities among these presently distinct lines are debatable, with the result that various classificatory schemes to portray their relationships have been advanced (e.g., Noble, 1931; Parsons and Williams, 1963; Reig, 1964; Romer, 1966).

The earliest definite amphibians appear in late Devonian sediments in Greenland that are something over 280 million years old. These Ichthyostegalia measured up to more than a meter in length and still carried various characters reminiscent of their origin from crossopterygian fish (Romer, 1966).

Two principal types of amphibians existed during much of the last 80 million years of the Paleozoic Era. Those classified as the subclass Labyrinthodontia achieved great diversity and were, in some instances, much larger in size than any modern amphibian, with some reaching more than 4 meters in length. A broad, heavily roofed and flattened skull with the head proportionately large relative to the body size evolved in this line. The amphibians classified as the subclass Lepospondyli were much less numerous and diverse and were more modest in size. The two lines differed in mode of vertebra formation. Lepospondyls disappeared before the end of the Paleozoic, some 200 million years ago. The Labyrinthodontia survived an additional 35 million years or so, through the Triassic Period of the Mesozoic Era.

A major gap in the fossil record exists between these primitive Paleozoic amphibians and the three modern groups. This gap seems likely to be the result of lesser likelihood of fossilization as the amphibian became reduced in size and as the evolutionary trend toward reduced ossification of the skeleton set in. Because of this gap, the affinities of the three modern orders are uncertain.

Many workers (e.g., Colbert, 1955) have considered the Anura to be derived from the Labyrinthodontia and the Apoda and Urodela to be descended from the Lepospondyli. Romer (1966) has avoided the issue because of the gap in the fossil record and has classified the modern orders in the subclass Lissamphibia, without trying to align them with their Paleozoic precursors. A summary of the earliest known fossils of living families of amphibians is given in Table 1.

The Apoda were unknown as fossils until recently, when a single vertebra was described from the Paleocene of Brazil (Estes and Wake, 1972).

Table 1 Earliest Fossil Records for Living Families of Amphibians[a]

Families	Oldest known fossil Geological period	Oldest known fossil Approximate age (millions of years)	Source
Apoda			
Caeciliidae	Paleocene	55	Estes and Wake, 1972
Urodela			
Cryptobranchidae	Oligocene	30	Estes, 1970a
Sirenidae	Cretaceous	70	Estes, 1970a
Proteidae	Pliocene	5	Estes, 1970a
Salamandridae	Paleocene	65	Estes, 1970a
Amphiumidae	Cretaceous	70	Estes, 1970a
Ambystomatidae	Paleocene?	65	Estes, 1970a
Plethodontidae	Pliocene	5	Estes, 1970a
Anura			
Ascaphidae	Jurassic	150	Estes and Reig, 1973
Discoglossidae	Jurassic	130	Estes and Reig, 1973
Pipidae	Cretaceous	130	Estes and Reig, 1973
Rhinophrynidae	Paleocene	70	Estes and Reig, 1973
Pelobatidae	Cretaceous?	130?	Estes and Reig, 1973
Pelodytidae	Miocene	20	Estes and Reig, 1973
Leptodactylidae	Paleocene	70	Estes and Reig, 1973
Bufonidae	Paleocene	70	Estes and Reig, 1973
Ceratophrynidae	Miocene	20	Estes and Reig, 1973
Hylidae	Paleocene	70	Estes and Reig, 1973
Ranidae	Oligocene	30	Estes and Reig, 1973
Microhylidae	Miocene	20	Estes and Reig, 1973

[a] Estimates of age are my own gross approximations and should be considered reliable only within the time limits of the particular geological period.

All fossil urodeles are from the land masses of the Northern Hemisphere. At least two of the modern families of urodeles (Amphiumidae and Sirenidae) were in existence in North America in the late Cretaceous, more than 70 million years ago (Estes, 1970a). The Salamandridae appear somewhat later in Paleocene rocks of Eurasia and still later in Oligocene sediments of North America. Probable Ambystomatidae were found in the Paleocene strata of North America. The Cryptobranchidae appear in Eurasian deposits in the Oligocene and in North America in the Miocene. The presently most successful family, the Plethodontidae, is known only back to the Pliocene of North America.

The earliest known frog is *Triadobatrachus* from the Triassic of Madagascar. The significance of various skeletal features, including the presence of caudal vertebrae, and even the likelihood of this form being in the line of ancestry of modern frogs have been debated (see Estes and Reig, 1973). *Triadobatrachus* has been classified in its own order, the Proanura. All other fossil and living frogs are classified in the order Anura.

The early history of anuran evolution remains unknown, since there is a gap of about 40 million years between *Triadobatrachus* and the first known early Jurassic frog, *Vieraella*, from Argentina (Estes and Reig, 1973). A few other Mesozoic frogs are known, and recent finds have added materially to our knowledge of the Cenozoic history of the most important extant families (Estes, 1970a; Estes and Reig, 1973). *Vieraella* and the late Jurassic *Notobatrachus*, also from Argentina, belong to the primitive family Ascaphidae, still present as the relict *Liopelma* in New Zealand, *Ascaphus* of North America, although some (Savage, 1973) would place the relict genera in separate families. The family Discoglossidae dates back about 130 million years to the late Jurassic or early Cretaceous of Europe and questionably to the late Cretaceous of North America.

The extant Pipidae are known from remarkably well-preserved fossils from the early Cretaceous of Israel (Nevo, 1968) and from the late Cretaceous of both South America and Africa (Estes and Reig, 1973), continents where the family is known from the Paleocene.

Probable members of the family Pelobatidae are known from the Cretaceous of North America and certain ones from the Eocene (Estes, 1970b). The Pelodytidae are known from the Miocene of North America (Estes and Reig, 1973). Oldest known members of the large and important families Leptodactylidae, Bufonidae, and Hylidae are from the Paleocene of Brazil (Estes and Reig, 1973). The large, successful family Ranidae is known with certainty only back to the Oligocene and the Microhylidae only to the Miocene (Estes and Reig, 1973).

In summary, three of the most primitive living families of anurans (Ascaphidae, Discoglossidae, and Pipidae) have evolutionary histories of roughly 130 million or more years. These exist today in mostly relictual distributions. A fourth very primitive family (Rhinophrynidae), with a known history of about 70 million years, is also relictual, with a single living species. Three of the modern, highly successful families (Leptodactylidae, Bufonidae, and Hylidae), as well as the less numerous Pelobatidae, are now known to have histories of at least 70 million years. The Ranidae, Microhylidae, and Pelodytidae have known histories of the order of 20–30 million years, and one suspects that the Microhylidae at least eventually will be found to go back much further.

RELATIONSHIPS AND BIOGEOGRAPHY OF LIVING AMPHIBIANS

The three orders of living amphibians differ greatly in their patterns of geographic distribution and in their success as measured by the diversity of living types and by the fraction of the earth's surface that the group has been able to colonize. The following discussion draws heavily on Porter's (1972) excellent summarization of amphibian taxonomy.

Apoda

The Apoda (without feet) are the least successful of the amphibians as judged by the criteria just cited. These caecilians are restricted to the world's tropics and subtropics. Only four families are recognized. Two, the Cacciliidae with 19 genera and Ichthyophiidae with 4 genera, occur in both Old and New World tropics or subtropics. The four genera of the Typhlonectidae are restricted to South America. The Scolecomorphidae, with one genus, are found only in Africa. Caecilians are either highly fossorial and hence restricted to relatively moist environments, or they are aquatic, as in the Typhlonectidae.

In view of the virtually nonexistent fossil record, it is impossible to trace the past biogeographic history of the Apoda. The present distribution fits a Gondwanaland origin prior to the breakup of the southern landmass, but this would require the origin of the Apodans much earlier than the fossil record now positively proves. The one fossil caecilian, *Apodops* from the Paleocene of Brazil, most closely resembles an extant African form, which is consistent with such a history, but does not prove it (Estes and Wake, 1972).

Urodela

Living urodeles with eight living families, show much greater diversity than do living caecilians. The history of the urodeles has been linked mostly with the northern continents. In the Old World, only one family (Salamandridae) enters North Africa; in the New World, only one family (Plethodontidae) enters South America, where it penetrates deep into the Amazon forest. Main adaptive strategies that are evident in the evolution of the urodeles include neoteny (retention of larval characters) and paedogenesis (breeding as larval forms). Urodeles as a group are generally associated with moist environments, but these modifications of the life history have permitted some taxa to inhabit relatively arid regions.

Two families of partially metamorphosed aquatic urodeles with eel-like bodies are found only in the southeastern United States. The two genera (*Siren* and *Pseudobranchus*) of the Sirenidae have vestigial fore-legs and no hindlegs. *Amphiuma*, the sole member of the family Am-phiumidae, has two pairs of vestigial legs. These families represent parallel adaptations to aquatic life.

The only other strictly North American family is the Ambystomatidae with four genera. A significant feature of these salamanders is the occurrence of neoteny and even paedogenesis in local populations. It is probably this attribute that permits one of the species, *Ambystoma tigrinum*, to occupy the largest range of any salamander, with a distribution from Canada to Mexico and over most of the United States. All three of these endemic families appear to have been limited to North America through their entire history (Estes, 1970a).

The family Hynobiidae, with five genera, is limited to Asia. The aquatic, semimetamorphosed salamanders of the family Cryptobran-chidae have a relict distribution, with one genus *Andrias* and two species, in China and Japan, and one species, *Cryptobranchus allenganiensis*, in the eastern United States. The family Proteidae also has a highly disjunct distribution, with one European species (*Proteus anguineus*) of blind, unpigmented cave salamander and the aquatic, partially metamorphosed genus *Necturus* in the eastern United States.

The newts, family Salamandridae, are generalized salamanders with 15 genera and a distribution from North America across Eurasia to North Africa. In North America, the distribution of the family is bicentric, with *Notopthalmus* in the forested East and *Taricha* along the Pacific coast. The dry interior of the continent has no member of the family today. The salamandrids are seemingly a group with Eurasian origins that entered North America by way of the Bering land bridge, probably in early Oligocene (Estes, 1970a). The broad disjunction of North America genera is attributable to the general drying of the continental interior through the latter parts of the Tertiary and to the present.

The lungless salamanders, family Plethodontidae, are by far the largest and most diverse family with some 23 genera, which include about two-thirds of all the species of urodeles. The evolution of the plethodon-tids has been well studied by Dunn (1926) and more recently by Wake (1966). The Appalachian region of the eastern United States has been a major center for plenthodontid differentiation and dispersal. There has also been extensive speciation of plethodontids in the Neotropics. There is the same isolation of eastern-forest taxa and Pacific coast taxa by the arid interior that pertains for salamandrids. In this instance, though, relict populations (Edwards Plateau of Texas, mountain tops in New

Mexico) attest to past distributions when Cenozoic climates were more favorable.

This family has one remarkable example of disjunction. The genus *Hydromantes* occurs only on California mountains in North America and has one species on the island of Sardinia and another on mountains of southern Europe. Wake (1966) has suggested a crossing to Eurasia by way of the Bering land bridge in the early Tertiary and subsequent disappearance of all but the relict populations.

Ecologically, and with respect to modifications of the life history, the plethodontids are more diverse than any other urodele family. Neoteny is common. Some, like *Typhlomolge* and *Haideotriton*, are completely aquatic, paedogenic, and limited to subterranean waters. Many are unspecialized, having a metamorphosis from aquatic larva to terrestrial adult. Many have eliminated the larval stage and show direct terrestrial development. Some are arboreal. Plethodontids occur in a diversity of environments ranging from forested midlatitudes through cold Andean páramo to tropical rain forest.

Anura

The anurans are by far the most successful of the living orders of amphibians. Representatives of this group occur on virtually every land area of the globe that is habitable by an amphibian. Living anurans are classified in some 20 families, the exact number depending on whose classification one follows. Genera of living anurans number about 250.

Many details of the classification and biogeographical relationships of this large and successful group of amphibians remain controversial. No two classifications agree in all respects, even at the level of delimiting families. The classification by Noble (1931) based on adult morphology and generally followed for many years has been greatly modified in recent years. Orton's (1953) work on larval characters was of major significance toward improving the classification. Savage (1973) has presented a classification incorporating Orton's evidence and providing the most exhaustive modern treatment of anuran relationship and biogeography. The broadest aspects of anuran classification and biogeography can be summarized in the space available here. Orton (1953) recognized four groups of anuran families, and Savage (1973) has treated these as four suborders.

Group I

Group I (suborder Xenoanura) has two families, the primitive Pipidae and Rhinophrynidae. The larvae have paired spiracles and simple mouth parts. Pipids occur today in South America and Africa, and there is no evidence that they ever reached northern continents. A Gondwanaland origin prior to the separation of the two continents is suggested. The family Rhinophrynidae is represented by a single relict species in Mexico and Central America, although it had a much wider distribution in western North America in the Cenozoic (Estes, 1970a).

Group II

Group II anurans (suborder Ecoptanura) have larvae with a single midventral spiracle and simple mouth parts. The family Microhylidae is a large, diverse assemblage of some 56 genera of mainly tropical anurans. Savage (1973) suggests a Gondwanaland origin. Representatives occur today in Africa south of the Sahara, Madagascar, the Southeastern Asian region, and South America through Central America to southeastern North America. African arboreal derivatives of this group with intercalary cartilages are sometimes treated as a separate family, the Phrynomeridae.

Group III

Group III (suborder Lemmanura) has two families, the Ascaphidae and the Discoglossidae. The larvae, except in *Liopelma* of New Zealand, which has direct development, have a single median spiracle and complex mouth parts with horny beaks and keratinized labial "teeth" in transverse rows. The adults have vestigial free ribs on the anteriormost vertebrae. The ascaphid genera, *Ascaphus* and *Liopelma,* are unique among modern anurans in having nine presacral vertebrae. The relict *Ascaphus* of northwestern North America and *Liopelma* of New Zealand are widely disjunct today. However, the presence of the family in the Mesozoic of South America (*Vieraella* of early Jurassic and *Notobatrachus* of late Jurassic) provides geographical intermediates. The family Discoglossidae has four Old World genera, the Eurasian *Bombina,* European *Alytes,* European and North African *Discoglossus,* and the Philippine *Barbourula.*

Group IV

Group IV (suborder Acosmanura) contains the great majority of living anurans and has the most complex biogeography. In the larva, the single spiracle is deflected to the left and there are complex mouth parts. The family Pelobatidae seems to be the oldest in this group. Its history has been mainly northern with both fossil and living species on the northern landmasses. The exception is the subfamily Megophryinae, which occurs today in southeastern Asia. These have been suggested as ancestral to the large Southern Hemisphere family Leptodactylidae (Lynch, 1971, p. 213). Savage (1973) has argued against this. Megophryine pelobatids are known from the early Tertiary of both North America and Europe (Estes, 1970b). Karyological similarities between *Pelobates* of Europe and *Ceratophrys* (Morescalchi, 1967), a South American genus sometimes classified as a leptodactylid and sometimes in a separate family, support the idea of a pelobatid origin for the leptodactylids. Similarities in vocalization as well as in the karyotype between the pelobatids (*Scaphiopus*) of North America and South American Ceratophrynidae (Bogart, 1971) provide an even more intriguing suggestion of affinity between pelobatids and ceratophrynids.

The European genus *Pelodytes* is sometimes put in the Pelobatidae and sometimes in its own family, the Pelodytidae. As mentioned earlier, this family was in North America in the Miocene (Estes and Reig, 1973).

The family Leptodactylidae is a huge, diverse assemblage of more than 50 genera with a distribution primarily in the Southern Hemisphere. It also appears to be ancestral to other major families of modern anurans (see Hecht, 1963). The present distribution and fossil record are indicative of a Gondwanaland origin. There is a single genus, *Heleophryne*, in South Africa [the author does not agree with Savage (1973) in placing this in a separate family]. Seventeen genera are recognized in the Australo-Papuan region (Lynch, 1971) where leptodactylids comprise a major element in the anuran fauna. There are some 37 genera in South America, where adaptive radiation of this family has filled a wide diversity of ecological niches. The family presently ranges into southern North America, with three genera reaching Texas, but not beyond.

The family Ceratophrynidae of South America, with two living genera, is a derivative of the Leptodactylidae and is treated as a subfamily of the Leptodactylidae by Lynch (1971).

The family Bufonidae and its highly successful genus *Bufo* are nearly cosmopolitan except for the Australian region, where *Bufo* has been introduced. Thirteen genera are currently recognized (Tihen, 1960; McDiarmid, 1971), but only *Bufo* is widely distributed. Evidence is good that this family originated from leptodactylids (Reig, 1972). The southern origin of the Bufonidae now seems clearly established, but whether this came before or after the breakup of Gonwanaland remains unclear. Savage (1973) has suggested an origin on western Gondwanaland after its separation from eastern Gondwanaland. However, there is evidence

(Blair, 1972; Bogart, 1972) that the genus *Bufo*, from which the other genera are apparently derived, originated in South America and that some elements at least moved through the northern continents, by utilizing the Bering land bridge. The family Brachycephalidae, to which the South America bufonid genera other than *Bufo* were formerly assigned, as now restricted, contains only a single Brazilian species (McDiarmid, 1971).

The family Hylidae is a large, primarily neotropical assemblage of some 32 genera, and like the bufonids appears to have evolved from leptodactylid ancestors in South America, where the greatest diversity is found. This family is lacking in Africa and Eurasia except for one small element, the *Hyla arborea* complex, that has North American affinities and that apparently used the Bering land bridge to Asia and has now reached North Africa. Hylids occur as an important element in the fauna of Australia and New Guinea. [The author does not accept Savage's (1973) creation of a separate family (Pelodryadidae) for these hylids and is dubious about Tyler's (1971) removing them from the genus *Hyla* and putting them in a separate genus *Litoria*.]

The South American Pseudidae with two genera are close to and clearly evolved from the Hylidae, in which family they are included by some (see Barrio, 1970a). The Centrolenidae is another small South American family with two genera that is close to the Hylidae and is sometimes included there.

The small neotropical family Dendrobatidae with three genera was treated as a subfamily of the Ranidae by Goin and Goin (1962), and Porter (1972) has followed this. However, Lynch (1971, 1973) allies the dendrobatids with his bufonoid group and proposes a leptodactylid ancestry. The karyotypes also suggests derivation from leptodactylids (Bogart, 1970, 1973), which is biogeographically sensible.

Relationships of the Rhinodermatidae with a single Chilean species, are obscure; it seems nearest to the Leptodactylidae, but there are similarities to bufonids (Lynch, 1971).

The anurans that comprise the greatest bulk of the African fauna and that of the Asian tropics are among the least understood with respect to phylogeny, and the variance in their classification reflects this. There are three main groups, which are treated by current workers as either families or subfamilies. The author agrees with Liem (1970) in treating them as families. The highly diverse family Ranidae, with some 33 genera, has undergone extensive radiation in Africa. Only the genus *Rana* has reached the New World, presumably by way of the Bering land bridge. While there has been considerable speciation of *Rana* in North America, only one species, *Rana palmipes,* represents the penetration of the genus into the northern half of South America. The other two families are characterized by arboreal habits and by intercalary cartilages in the digits and appear to have evolved from ranids. The family Hyperoliidae, with 14 genera, is primarily African, but occurs on Madagascar and the Seychelles Islands. The Rhacophoridae, with 14 genera, are primarily Asiatic, but are also in Africa and on Madagascar.

ANURAN ADAPTATION

Within the limits of their unique body plan, the anurans have evolved a diversity of modes of existence and have made themselves a part of many kinds of ecosystems. Main features of anuran body form relate to the saltatorial locomotion of these amphibians. The fusion of caudal vertebrae into a urostyle that is incorporated in the body, the lack of an external neck, the shortened and usually ribless set of presacral vertebrae, and the enlarged hind legs are the principal morphological features of this saltatorial adaptation. As in other amphibians, a skin that is highly permeable to the passage of water and the physiological conditions of heterothermy are significant in setting patterns of ecological adaptation and of biogeographical limits. In the following sections, some of the principal adaptations that have evolved within the limits of the anuran pattern will be discussed and some unanswered questions with respect to these adaptations will be pointed out.

Major Adaptive Patterns

The anurans have evolved a few major adaptations with respect to the medium in which they live and with respect to how they relate to major features of their ecosystem. The principal patterns are (1) terrestrial surface dwelling, (2) terrestrial fossorial habit, (3) arboreal habit, (4) aquaticism, and (5) littoral habit.

Terrestrial Surface Dwellers

Two main patterns are seen in terrestrial surface-dwelling anurans. Some are relatively short-legged walkers or hoppers rather than jumpers and are protected from predator attack by venomous skin secretions. These secretions may be concentrated in specialized glands such as the parotoid glands of bufonids or sometimes also in comparable glands on the legs, as in *Bufo alvarius* of the Sonoran Desert. In other terrestrial hoppers, highly potent venoms may be secreted by glands scattered throughout the skin, as, for example, in the neotropical Dendrobatidae or in *Scaphiopus* of North America. Bright coloration of the dendrobatids is generally regarded as warning coloration in these highly venomous anurans. *Leptodactylus laticeps* of the Argentine Chaco has extremely venomous secretions (Cei, 1949), and it is brilliantly colored by comparison with the usual *Leptodactylus* color pattern (see Color Plate, 1, facing p. 28).

Not all terrestrial hoppers and walkers are gaudily colored; many show patterns of concealing coloration. This is exemplified by the dead leaf pattern of the toads of the *Bufo guttatus* group, which live on the floor of the neotropical rain forest. The alternative escape pattern among terrestrial anurans is to be a long-legged leaper, and thus actively depart the vicinity. This pattern is exemplified in many ranids, especially *Rana*, and is paralleled in the leptodactylid genus *Leptodactylus*.

Terrestrial Fossorial Types

Some terrestrial anurans seek shelter and protection from desiccation by entering the burrows of mammals or other burrow makers. The gopher frog (*Rana areolata*) uses the burrows of the Florida gopher tortoise and, elsewhere in its range, crayfish or mammal burrows. The Chacoan vizcacha, a large burrowing rodent, provides refuge for several terrestrial anurans, including *Leptodactylus bufonius*, *L. laticeps*, and *Ceratophrys ornata* (Cei, 1949, 1955).

Many terrestrial anurans, however, are capable of burying themselves in the soil. The most common structure for accomplishing this is the modified metatarsal tubercle or "spade" that has evolved in many taxa of anurans, ranging from such primitive types as *Rhinophrynus* to such advanced types as the ranid *Pyxicephalus* of Africa. This may characterize whole genera or families (*Scaphiopus*, Ceratophrynidae) or some species of a genus, e.g., *Bufo cognatus*. Even arboreally adapted types may evolve this fossorial habit and mechanism. For example, the African *Leptopelis bocogei*, a member of an arboreal hyperoliid genus has gone this route (Stewart, 1967), as has the North American hylid genus *Pternohyla* (Trueb, 1970).

The metatarsal spade permits these burrowing anurans to sit on the substrate and work their way downward by lateral movements of the hindfeet. The African ranid *Hemisus* uses a different method of burrowing. This frog burrows head first, pushing the pointed, horny nose, spadelike, into the ground with up-and-down movements and digging away the soil with the front feet (Wager, 1965).

Arboreal Habit

Arboreal anurans have evolved several times, with the principal families being the primarily New World Hylidae and the Old World Rhacophoridae and Hyperoliidae. Principal aspects of the arboreal adaptation are (1) suction cups on the tips of the toes, (2) generally small body size, and (3) frequently the ability to undergo rapid gray-green color change. Most are agile hoppers, but some, such as the hylid *Phyllomedusa,* tend to be clamberers rather than jumpers. Many of the arboreal frogs descend to the ground to breed in rain pools in accordance with the generalized anuran pattern of reproduction. Others, in the tropical rain forest, are completely arboreal, breeding in the water that has been trapped in bromeliads or tree holes and never leaving the forest canopy. As mentioned earlier, some members of arboreal groups have left the trees for other kinds of existence. The United States hylid genera *Acris* and *Pseudacris* are examples.

Aquaticism

Anurans show a wide variance in the degree of dependence on water as a habitat. Some are more or less aquatic; others have become so specialized for this type of existence as to be obligately aquatic. Principal features of aquatic anurans are a smooth skin and strong webbing of the hindfeet. Aquaticism dates far back in known anuran history, as the pipids described by Nevo (1968) from the early Cretaceous were specialized in such ways as to indicate that they were aquatic. As Nevo has suggested, the pipids seem to have been aquatic throughout their history, as the three living genera (*Pipa* of South America and *Xenopus* and *Hymenochirus* of Africa) are the most obligately aquatic of all living anurans.

Representatives of the oldest lineages among the Leptodactylidae also show a high degree of aquaticism. These are the Chilean *Calyptocephalella* (=*Caudiverbera*) and the Andean genera *Telmatobius* and *Eupsophus.* The recently discovered Australian genus *Rheobatrachus,* described as one of the most primitive living leptodactylids, is also aquatic (Liem, 1973). Ranid frogs such as the genera *Rana* and the African *Ptychadena* show various degrees of aquaticism. *Rana grylio* of the southeastern United States is highly aquatic, as is *R. goliath* of Africa; *R. clamitans* of eastern North America is less so. Various species of *Bufo* have evolved semiaquaticism as an adaptation that permits them to exist in arid regions. *Bufo alvarius* of the Sonoran Desert is an example. The small South American family Pseudidae is comprised of three aquatic species (see Gallardo, 1961), which are seemingly derived from the arboreal Hylidae. *Hyla* (= *Litoria*) *aurea* of Australia is an aquatic hylid that has been compared ecologically to the American *Rana clamitans* (Moore, 1961).

Littoral Habit

The interface between land and water is a logical milieu for the evolution of a distinctive anuran way of life. The frog spends much time sitting on the bank. It forages for food both on land and in the water. When approached by a terrestrial predator, it leaps into the water. Principal adaptive features are long legs and good leaping ability, the smooth skin and webbed feet of aquatically adapted anurans, and, in some at least, social interactions that result in the spacing of individuals in this essentially linear environment.

Two rather distinctive ecological niches for anurans in the littoral habitat may be identified in various taxa and on various continents. These may be called the cricket frog niche and the leopard frog niche. They are exemplified by the hylid genus *Acris* of eastern North America and by the leopard frogs of the *Rana pipiens* complex. Milstead (1972) has attempted to quantify the cricket frog niche and has identified occupants of this niche on five continents. These are *Acris* in North America, the leptodactylid *Pseudopaludicola falcipes* in South America, the ranids *Phrynobatrachus ukingensis* and *P. natalensis* in Africa, a leptodactylid *Crinia signifera* in Australia, and a ranid *Rana limnocharis* in India. The leopard frog niche is occupied by species of *Rana* within the broad geographic range of that genus and by other ranids, e.g., *Ptychadena,* in Africa. This niche in South America is occupied by species of *Leptodactylus* The widely distributed *L. ocellatus* group (see Cei, 1962a) of South America is in many ways comparable to the *Rana pipiens* complex of North America.

Body Size

Living amphibians exhibit smaller body size than is found in any other class of living vertebrates. Among anurans, the maximum size is attained by the aquatic *Rana goliath* of Africa, which reaches a length of about 25 cm. Why there should be this upper limit on anuran body size, and why, up to this limit, there should be such enormous variation in body size are complex, intriguing, and largely unanswered questions. Physiological problems of water and temperature must be important in moist-skinned heterotherms occupying a diversity of physical and biotic environments. However, their relative importance versus such things as predator or prey size has yet to be determined. It is possible that size, in some instances, could be related to selection that acts to reinforce the isolating mechanism of mating call (Blair, 1955).

The range of variation in size may be very great within a single genus. The largest *Bufo* is *B. blombergi* of the Colombian rain forest, which reaches 20 cm in snout–vent length; but *B. holdridgei*, which is apparently a member of the same species group (Blair, 1972), reaches only about 30 mm. Some species of neotropical *Hyla* exceed 100 mm in length; the smallest is *H. ocularis* of the southeastern United States, with a length of up to 18 mm. Furthermore, there seem to be no clear ecological correlates of size. *Bufo paracnemis* of the arid Argentine Chaco and Brazilian Caatinga, with females the size of dinner plates and males up to 19 cm in length, approximates the size of *B. blombergi*, which lives in the humid rain forest of eastern Colombia.

Color and Color Pattern

While a great deal is known about the structural and physiological bases for color, color pattern, and color change in anurans, there is relatively less known about the ecological significance of these phenomena. Some broad generalizations are possible, but numerous questions remain unanswered.

Generalizations

Truly terrestrial anurans of xeric (arid) and subxeric regions tend to be plain in pattern and tend to match the substrate. This general color matching of the substrate is comparable to that which has been found in other ground-living vertebrates. For example, *Bufo americanus* is brightly colored and patterned in the northeastern part of its range in eastern Canada, but in the southwestern part of its range in eastern Oklahoma, it is much more drab and patternless in keeping with the more drab substrate of this more xeric environment. *Bufo microscaphus*, another member of this group, which lives on desert soils near permanent water in the Southwest, is even paler.

Countershading, with the underparts the palest, is another phenomenon common to anurans and other terrestrial vertebrates. Rare exceptions to this are seen in the brilliant orange underparts of the quite distantly related discoglossid *Bombina* of Eurasia and bufonid *Melanophryniscus* of South America, both of which have the "unken reflex" where the back is arched to expose the bright underparts when the animal is disturbed. As mentioned earlier, the ability to change from gray to green relates to arboreal life. This is presumably a system providing concealment as the individual moves from gray trunk to green vegetation.

Aposematic (warning) coloring in anurans with highly potent skin secretions has been mentioned earlier. Additionally, however, some tropical forest frogs show gaudy color patterns that seemingly have no relation to their venomosity. A striking example is provided by the Amazonian *Hyla leucophyllata* which has a dorsal pattern of rich yellow and brown (see color plate in Lutz, 1973). One asks, does this bright coloration cause this frog to resemble some commonplace object such as an abundant flower, or fungus, or tropical fruit and hence render it inconspicuous in its environment? Only one example of mimicry of another species of frog has been suggested in anurans (Nelson and Miller, 1971). This involves a South American leptodactylid, *Lithodytes lineatus*, and the venomous dendrobatid *Phyllobates femoralis*. Similarities include similar dorsal coloration and similar flash colors.

Flash colors on the rear of the femur are typical of the arboreal families, and are found in some terrestrial types. These are exposed when the frog jumps, startling the potential predator, and disappear when it comes to rest. Some species such as *Hyperolius marmoratus* also have bright-colored underparts that are exposed during the jump (see Stewart, 1967). The Amazonian *Hyla marmorata* has bright orange underparts and toe webs, which are spread during the jump. The dorsum has a lichen pattern; after showing its flash colors during the jump, the animal blends perfectly once it comes to rest on a tree trunk.

In the leptodactylid genus *Pleurodema*, there is a pair of eyespots. These have been interpreted as a misdirect signal that is of value in making a predator think the frog is headed in the opposite direction to the one in which it will jump (Cei, 1962b).

Polychromatism

Polychromatism is erratic in its appearance among anuran taxa, and the ecological basis for high variability in color and color pattern in some anuran populations is obscure. In *Bufo*, the most striking instances are found among tropical toads (e.g., *B. canaliferus* and *B. coniferus* of Central America and *B. typhonius* of the neotropical rain forest). *Rhinoderma darwini*, a forest-floor inhabitant of the southern Chilean forest, is also strikingly polychromatic. One possibility is that this polymorphism is significant to the survival of the individual and of the species in magnifying the task of predators in becoming conditioned to a fixed image of the species. Infrequency of polychromatism in terrestrial, xeric-adapted anurans suggests that blending into the background is a better mechanism than this in open environments.

In simpler genetic systems, where a few distinct morphs are involved, the polymorphism might be maintained in the population in adapting for concealment on seasonally changing features of the substrate as suggested for *Acris crepitans* by Pyburn (1961). However, no explanation has been offered for the red-gray dimorphism of several members of the *Bufo americanus* group of toads or in the very distantly related *B. regularis* group.

Sexual Dimorphism

Aside from the existence of a colored vocal sac in males of many species, anuran males and females from the same species population tend to differ little in color and color pattern. This implies little need for visual recognition of the sexes and is consistent with the general dependence on vocal signals rather than visual cues for mate attraction. However, there are some notable exceptions. The most extreme example of sexual dimorphism among anurans is found in *Bufo periglenes*, a montane-forest toad of Costa Rica. The male is bright orange and without patterning; the female is blue to black with a pattern of scarlet spots. This species is apparently voiceless and diurnal reproductive activity has been observed (Savage, 1966). Thus, it seems likely that the striking sexual dimorphism does function to provide identification as to sex. Less striking, but very obvious, sexual dimorphism is characteristic of the toads of the "narrow-skulled line" of Blair (1972). These are mostly montane toads, and most New World representatives have lost the mating call. Dimorphism is conspicuous in the primarily Andean spinulosus group, especially *B. variegatus*, the North American boreas group, especially in the high montane *B. canorus*, and in the Eurasian *B. bufo* and *B. viridis* of this evolutionary line, although these latter retain the mating call.

Not all sexual differences in color pattern can be explained this easily. In some highly vocal, nocturnal-breeding species (e.g., *Scaphiopus couchi*), there are distinct sexual differences in color pattern, with, in this example, less patterning in the male. The significance is unknown.

REPRODUCTIVE STRATEGIES

The generalized pattern of anuran reproduction is retained in many taxa, but it has also been modified in various, often parallel, ways in the various anuran families. In this generalized mode, reproductive activity is stimulated by environmental changes, frequently by the incidence of rainfall. Males proceed to the breeding pools and emit the species-specific mating call, which attracts reproductively ready females. After amplexus, the eggs are laid in water. Following a developmental, hatching, and larval stage in which rates are temperature influenced and which are evolutionarily adjusted to local conditions (i.e., slower development in permanent water, more rapid development in temporary pool breeders), the anuran metamorphoses and begins its life on land.

A significant feature of this generalized pattern is the apparent necessity of producing a huge number of eggs to ensure the simple replacement of the parental pair in the population. In an average-sized toad like *Bufo valliceps*, for example, some 25,000 eggs are laid by a single female. Modifications of the generalized pattern are mostly in the direction of specializations that permit a reduction in the number of zygotes. The most important of these are (1) production of foam nests, (2) elimination of the larval stage, with direct development on land, and (3) care of young.

Foam Nests

One mechanism that permits reduction in the number of eggs is the deposition of the eggs in a foam nest that is produced by whipping up a gelatinous secretion during amplexus. Foam nests are produced in some genera of rhacophorids and in some genera of leptodactylids, which gives these anuran groups high versatility with regard to reproductive specialization.

The rhacophorids show considerable diversity in nest specialization as summarized by Liem (1970). The typical pattern found in *Rhacophorus*, *Polypedates*, *Chirixalus*, and *Chiromantis* involves placing the foam nest on leaves over water. The larvae hatch and fall into the water where they continue an aquatic existence. However, two species of *Polypedates* lay their eggs in foam under stones in water. One species of *Rhacophorus* is known to place its nest in underground burrows. *Thaloderma* places its nests with 4 to 8 eggs in tree holes. *Hazelia* also uses tree holes, but produces a gelatinous mass rather than foam. *Philautus* lays the eggs on leaves, but without foam or gelatinous mass. One species of *Rhacophorus* has direct development on land, with the eggs being guarded by the female.

Foam nests are characteristic of the South American leptodactylid genera *Leptodactylus*, *Pleurodema*, and *Physalaemus* and in six genera of Australian leptodactylids. Evolution of the foam nest in *Leptodactylus* has been discussed by Heyer (1969); its evolution in Australian leptodactylids has been discussed by Martin (1967). There are parallels in the evolution of foam nesting in the two groups. *Physalaemus, Pleuro-*

dema, and some *Leptodactylus* float the nest on the surface of the water. Other *Leptodactylus* place the foam nest in pits or burrows that they dig near water. Development begins in the burrow, but subsequent floods liberate the larvae for an aquatic existence. In a third type of specialization, the larvae metamorphose within the nest without a free larval stage. Among the Australian foam nest builders, *Limnodynastes, Lechriodus,* and *Adelotus* float the nests on water. *Heleioporus* lays eggs in burrows; the larvae hatch when the burrows are flooded and have a normal aquatic life. *Kyrannus* lays its eggs in moist soil or sphagnum and lacks a free-swimming larva. The same is probably true of *Philoria.* Selective factors proposed by Heyer (1969) for the change from surface-floating nest to burrow nest on land are (1) reduction of predation, (2) reduction of larval competition, and (3) reduced danger of desiccation.

Various Other Adaptations

In addition to the foam-nesting rhacophorids which place their nests above later so that the larvae can fall into it, some hyperoliids, the centrolenids, and some hylids lay their eggs above water. In the hyperoliid genera, *Hyperolius* and *Phylictimantis,* the eggs are deposited in a gelatinous mass above water (Liem, 1970). In *Afrixalus* of the same family, one species deposits the eggs on the blade of a reed above water, and then folds and glues the blade to protect the eggs, while another species places the eggs in a folded and glued leaf underwater (Wager, 1965). *Leptopelis* of the same family buries the eggs in moist soil near water, and, after hatching, the larvae wriggle into the water (Wager, 1965).

One Australian hylid and the neotropical *Phyllomedusa and Agalychnis* and several species of *Hyla* also lay eggs on vegetation above water (see Martin, 1971). The independent evolution of this habit in these several arboreal families attests to the presumed advantages of escaping, during early life history stages, from the pressures of predation and competition in the aquatic medium.

Neotropical *Hyla* of the *H. faber* group build nest pans at the edge of the water (see Lutz, 1973). The males build these by pushing up walls about 5 to 7 cm high in a circle about 30 cm in diameter. They defend these against other males and eggs are laid in these small pools and the larvae develop there.

Direct Development

In addition to the terrestrial breeders with direct development which have evolved from foam nesters, there are other terrestrial direct-development types among the principal families. No foam nest is involved. This is true of the ascaphid genus *Liopelma* of New Zealand, but not of the North American genus *Ascaphus,* which practices internal fertilization, but only as a mechanism to ensure fertilization in the mountain torrents in which it lives. The African microhylid *Breviceps* lays about 30 eggs in a cavity about 30–45 cm below the surface. The female often stays with the eggs. The young dig their way to the surface (Wager, 1965). Several genera of leptodactylids show direct development. Among the several New World genera are three that occur today in the United States: *Eleutherodactylus, Hylactophryne,* and *Syrrhophus.* Among the Australian leptodactylids that probably have direct development are *Metacrinia* and *Myobatrachus;* the Australian genera *Crinia* and *Pseudophryne* show various stages of the evolution of terrestrialism among their several species (Martin, 1967). Among hylids, direct development occurs in some of the neotropical genera in which the female transports the young on her back, including *Cryptobatrachus, Hemiphractus,* and *Gastrotheca* (Martin, 1971). In the African ranids *Anhydrophryne* and *Arthroleptis,* up to 20 or 30 large-yolked eggs are laid in moist soil or decaying leaves, and there is direct development (Wager, 1965). The terrestrial larvae of another African ranid, *Arthroleptella* (as described by Wager, 1965), appear to fit on an intermediate step leading to this condition.

One remarkable variant in the trend toward terrestrialism is found in the African ranid *Hemisus.* Eggs are laid in underground nests, and the female remains with the eggs. After the larvae have hatched, the female tunnels to water followed by the wriggling tadpoles (Wager, 1965).

Care of Young

The simplest form of care for the progeny is seen in such terrestrial breeders as *Breviceps, Hemisus,* and some leptodactylids in which the female remains with the developing eggs. A microhylid, *Synaptanurus salseri,* of the Colombian Amazon lays about 4–6 terrestrial eggs in a burrow and the male remains with the embryos which show direct development (Pyburn, 1975). A step beyond this is seen in the practice of dendrobatids and of a few hylids of transporting the larvae on the back of one of the parents. This strategy is limited to anurans that inhabit consistently humid regions. In the dendrobatids, the larvae are carried on the back of the male and eventually released into the water. In hylids, the female carries the young on her back. Development may be direct (*Cryptobatrachus, Hemiphractus,* and some *Gastrotheca*) or the larvae may be deposited in water (*Flectonotus* and some *Gastrotheca*) (see Martin, 1971). In *Pipa,* which is completely aquatic, the larvae develop in pits on the back of the female. Rabb (1960) has described the remarkable maneuver by which the eggs reach the back of the female. An extreme specialization is that of *Rhinoderma* of the southern Chilean forest, in which the larvae are carried in the vocal sac of the male. In the Australian leptodactylid *Assa* (= *Criniu*) *darlingtoni,* the larvae enter and undergo development in bilateral brood pouches in the iguinal region of the male (Ingram *et al.,* 1975). The most remarkable specialization is that of the Australian leptodactylid *Rheobatrachus silus* which broods the larvae and juveniles in the stomach of the female (Corben, Ingram, and Tyler, 1974).

The mechanism of viviparity has been achieved in the bufonid genus *Nectophrynoides.* In these toads of east and west Africa, fertilization is internal, and up to 100 young may develop in the oviduct of the female. The embryos lack gills, adhesive organs, labial teeth, or horny beaks; the young are born as fully metamorphosed toads (see Goin and Goin, 1962).

REGIONAL ADAPTATION

The nature of each major ecological formation of the world determines to a large degree the kinds of anuran life form and of life history that have evolved there, or have been able to invade there. The tropical rain forests, on the one hand, and the world's deserts, on the other, provide extremely contrasting environments for anuran evolution. Some of the aspects of anuran adaptation to these very different environments will be discussed.

Tropical Forest Anurans

Major features of the tropical forest of significance for an anuran are (1) the general availability of moisture so that there is scant danger of desiccation, (2) the relatively minor variations in temperature on either a diel (24-hour) or an annual cycle, and (3) the great structural complexity of the ecosystem, especially that of the vegetational components. The relatively certain availability of moisture has major implications for anurans. It makes burrowing to escape desiccation essentially unnecessary. It makes possible the kinds of modifications of the life history toward terrestrialism that were discussed earlier. Transport of eggs and larvae on the back would seem feasible only in the constantly moist environment of the rain forest. The combination of dependable moisture and relatively low diel temperature variation under the shade of the forest canopy makes possible a degree of diurnalism that would be impossible in the desert. In the neotropical forest, such anurans as bufonids, dendrobatids, leptodactylids, and others may be found active on the forest floor in daytime.

The forest itself, with its high canopy and vertical stratification, provides a vertical dimension to the system that is almost lacking in the desert. The forest anurans fall broadly into two ecological groups, those that live on the forest floor such as bufonids, dendrobatids, and *Leptodactylus* and those that have become arboreal such as hylids, rhacophorids, or hyperoliids. The great structural complexity of the forest is presumably a major factor in permitting the evolution of a great many species of anurans, as well as of other kinds of animals. Lutz (1973) listed 70 species of the single genus *Hyla* from Brazil alone, and many of these are animals of the Amazon forest.

The existence of many sympatric species of the same genus within the complex structure of the rain forest implies much interspecific interaction, and both the opportunity and the necessity for fine subdivision of the ecological niche. In a study of three species of *Eleutherodactylus* in a Puerto Rican forest, Cintrón (1970) found one species mostly in bromeliads, another mostly inside palm petioles with a few under petioles, but not in bromeliads, and a third species primarily under petioles.

The relatively minor seasonality of the rain forest climate permits the forest anurans to remain active throughout the year, in contrast to the limitations imposed by seasonal lack of moisture and seasonally low temperatures in deserts. In general, then, the tropical rain forest has attributes that make it a seemingly optimal ecosystem for anuran amphibians.

Desert Anurans

If the rain forest is an optimal ecosystem for anuran evolution, then the desert is at an opposite extreme, being one of the most unfavorable. The xeric environment carries a continual threat of desiccation and death for the individual. There is unpredictability of the rains needed to provide temporary waters in which to breed. After eggs are deposited, there is danger of the pools drying up before the larvae can metamorphose. Water temperatures in the unshaded pools may become critically high.

Anurans that have been able to evolve into truly desert-adapted types are quite few, but evolutionarily interesting, because of the mechanisms they have employed. The Sonoran Desert of North America has only 12 species of anurans, some of which avoid the issue by remaining near permanent water; the Monte Desert of Argentina has 15 species, some of which are also restricted to the vicinity of permanent water (Blair, 1976).

The littoral habit provides a preadaptation that permits a species possessing it to enter a desert area without more than minimal adaptive change. In the Sonoran Desert, a member of the *Rana pipiens* complex does this and, in the Argentine desert, *Leptodactylus ocellatus* does so. Additionally, taxa which are nonaquatic and nonlittoral outside of the desert have desert species that exist there in the vicinity of permanent water in which they breed. Examples are *Bufo alvarius* and *B. microscaphus* in the Sonoran Desert and *B. arenarum* in the Argentine desert. The Australian *Hyla* (= *Litoria*) *rubella* and *H. caerulea* are other examples (Martin, 1967). The desert *Bufo* just mentioned have given up dependence on rainfall as a stimulus for reproduction. The same is true of some populations of other anurans that occur in the Sonoran Desert, including *Hyla arenicolor, Scaphiopus intermontanus, Bufo punctatus,* and *B. woodhousei* (Blair, 1976).

A few highly desert-adapted anurans have evolved in both North and South America. In North America, it is the pelobatid genus *Scaphiopus*. In South America, it is the ceratophrynid genera *Lepidobatrachus* and *Ceratophrys* and the leptodactylid genus *Odontophrynus*. The life-history strategies are quite similar in the two deserts. The adults are capable burrowers, although they may also use burrows of other animals. Much of the life is spent underground. There are adaptations to conserve water during this period of fossorial existence. Breeding assemblages are formed quickly in temporary pools after infrequent heavy rains in the desert. Larval development is rapid in *Scaphiopus*; the rates are unknown in the South American forms.

The most desert-adapted North American species seems to be *Scaphiopus couchi*, which has received extensive study. Populations that apparently did not emerge or breed for as long as 3 years have been reported (Mayhew, 1962). Buried individuals develop a body cover of dried, dead skin which reduces water loss through the skin (Mayhew, 1965). Physiological adaptations that make this behavior possible include (1) storage of urea in body fluids to the extent that the plasma osmotic concentration may double while underground, (2) high tolerance of the muscles of hypertonic urea solutions, (3) fat utilization while underground, (4) tolerance of water loss of 40–50% standard weight, and (5) storage of up to 30% of standard body weight as dilute urine to replace water lost from body fluids (McClanahan, 1964, 1967,

1972). Response to heavy rainfall is rapid, and breeding congresses can form within hours. Larval development is accelerated, and the larval stage can be passed in as few as 10 days (Wasserman, 1957). The larvae are tolerant of high temperatures, and have been observed in nature at temperatures of 39° to 40°C (Brown, 1969).

Lepidobatrachus is an apparent ecological equivalent of *Scaphiopus* in the Argentine desert, but it has been less thoroughly studied. These anurans bury themselves in the soil and emerge to breed after rains (Reig and Cei, 1963). While buried, they also develop a cocoon of compacted dead cells of the stratum corneum (McClanahan *et al.*, 1973).

One habit that has evolved in the desert frogs of both deserts is that of cannibalism. The larvae of some species of *Scaphiopus* are cannibalistic (Bragg, 1964). In the ceratophrynids, both larvae and adults may be cannibalistic (Cei, 1955; Reig and Cei, 1963; Blair, unpublished data); adults of the small *Ceratophrys pierotti* are extremely so.

The shortening of the larval stage just mentioned in *Scaphiopus couchi* is paralleled in other desert anurans. The Argentine leptodactylid *Pleurodema nebulosa* passes the larval stage in 7 days (A. Hulse, personal communication). There is evidence that the Australian desert hylid *Hyla* (= *Litoria*) *rubella* also has a larval life of as few as 7 days (Martin, 1967). Desert *Bufo* that have been investigated do not show this adaptation of shortened larval life (Blair, 1976).

A remarkable exception to the general rule that desert anurans must become either aquatic or semiaquatic or become fossorial is seen in the hylid *Phyllomedusa sauvagei* of the Argentine dry Chaco and the African rhacophorid *Chiromantis xerampelina* (Shoemaker *et al.*, 1972). These tree frogs secrete uric acid and develop a skin covering that reduces water loss. In the *Phyllomedusa*, the water loss through the skin was found to be comparable to that of a lizard.

A LOOK AHEAD

Hopefully, the preceding discussion has avoided any implication that all is known that there is to know about the history and the evolutionary relationships of the amphibians. Much has been added to our knowledge in these areas of amphibian biology in the past quarter of a century, as both vertebrate paleontologists and students of recent vertebrates have introduced new methods of study. The fine screening of sediments for recovery of small vertebrate fossils, pioneered by the late Claude Hibbard, was one significant advance. The emergence of the multidisciplinary approach in systematic studies (see Blair, 1973) and the introduction of the techniques of numerical taxonomy (Inger, 1967; Kluge and Farris, 1969) have opened an era that should see major advances in our knowledge of amphibian history and relationships. Recognition of the species as a dynamic system, rather than sole reliance on the morphological characters of preserved specimens as a basis for classification, has been another significant aspect of this new era (Blair, 1956). However, the advances of the past several years may be viewed as only a prelude to a major advance in understanding amphibian evolutionary biology that is possible in the years ahead.

The Fossil Record

The rich herpetofauna from the Paleocene of Brazil presently being studied by Estes (see Estes and Reig, 1973) has contributed importantly to the knowledge of amphibian history, and will contribute more so as this material is described and published. The significance of this material is evidenced by the fact that it pushes the known history of the family Bufonidae, and, in fact, that of the genus *Bufo*, back more than 30 million years beyond the previously known oldest date. More remarkably, it indicates the presence in the Brazilian Paleocene of a species group, *B. calamita* group, that is extant today in Eurasia.

In general, these new discoveries are showing that the evolutionary lines represented by living families and genera of amphibians were established earlier in geologic time than there was previous evidence to demonstrate.

Classification of Living Amphibians

Although there is already a great deal of information about the diversity of living species of anurans and about the relationships of the major evolutionary lines of anurans, much still remains to be learned. What is the number of living species? Additions to the lists of species are resulting from two kinds of activities. One is the exploration of remote and previously neglected regions, especially in the tropics, with the resultant discovery of previously unknown species. For example, 20 new species of *Hyla* were described from Brazil in the 6-year period of 1961–66 (see Bokermann, 1966). Additional species continue to be described from the neotropics, and there is little doubt that additional species remain to be discovered there and elsewhere. Recent discoveries are not limited to the tropics, nor to the species level.

A distinctive new leptodactylid genus, *Insuetophrynus*, was described from temperate southern Chile as recently as 1970 (Barrio, 1970b). A distinctive new genus of primitive leptodactylid (*Rheobatrachus*) was described from Queensland as recently as 1973 (Liem, 1973). Most future discoveries of this type will probably be made in the southern hemisphere, where large areas are still inadequately explored and where amphibian biologists are still scarce.

The second kind of activity that has revealed additional species has been the application of newer methods of analysis to populations of anurans. Demonstration that the physical characteristics of the mating call are an important attribute of anuran species (Blair, 1958, 1962, 1964; and many other authors) has led to the discovery of so-called cryptic, but biologically distinct, species among some of the most thoroughly studied anuran taxa in the world. The "leopard frog" is probably the most extensively utilized amphibian for research by biologists of many specialties. Yet it is now clear that what was once called *Rana pipiens* is really a complex of several good biological species that replace one another geographically with varying degrees of overlap at their borders (Post and Pettus, 1966; Littlejohn and Oldham, 1968; Platz and Platz, 1973; Mecham *et al.*, 1973; Pace, 1974). The gray tree frog, one of the commonest anurans of the eastern United States, was long considered a single species, *Hyla versicolor*. Studies of the mating call (Blair, 1958; Johnson, 1959) and of karyotypes (Wasserman, 1970) reveal that this is a complex of one or two diploid species with one type of mating call and presently called *Hyla chrysoscelis* that are separated geographically by a tetraploid species with a different mating call and now called *Hyla versicolor*. These are close-to-home examples of the increased knowledge of anuran species diversity that is being acquired by use of the mating call in taxonomy. Application of this technique to Australian anurans has been pioneered by Littlejohn (1968); application to South American anurans has been led by Barrio (1964). Application of biological criteria of genetic compatibility (Blair, 1969) and of characters of the mating call (Tandy and Keith, 1972) has made it possible to clarify relationships and species boundaries in the long-puzzling *Bufo regularis* group of African toads.

Examination of karyotypes has revealed a surprising incidence of polyploid populations among anurans, and more are to be expected as additional taxa are surveyed. The South American genus *Ceratophrys* has species which are normal diploids (e.g., *C. pierotti* with $2n = 26$) and others which have both diploid populations and octoploid populations (e.g., *C. ornata* with 26 and 104 chromosomes). Another South American anuran, *Odontophrynus americanus*, has diploid ($2n = 22$) and tetraploid populations (Saez and Brum, 1959, 1960; Bogart, 1967; Barrio and Rinaldi de Chieri, 1970b; Beçak *et al.*, 1970a; Barrio and

Pistol de Rubel, 1972). The South American hylid *Phyllomedusa burmeisteri* is a tetraploid species, with 52 chromosomes (Beçak *et al.*, 1970b). Two South American species of *Pleurodema* (*P. bibroni* and *P. kriegi*) have been shown to be tetraploids, with 44 chromosomes (Barrio and Rinaldi de Chieri, 1970a). Since only a fraction of the karyotypes of living anuran species has been examined, the results to date suggest that polyploidy will prove to be a fairly common form of chromosomal evolution in anurans.

Finally, with respect to the anurans in particular, marshaling of all of the available kinds of biological information in a worldwide analysis of anuran relationships seems to present the most significant challenge to the next generation of amphibian biologists. Evidence can now be marshaled with respect to genetic compatibility, karyotype, vocal apparatus and vocalizations, biochemical characters of skin venoms or proteins, etc., in addition to the conventional morphological characters (Blair, 1973). Such an effort would have to be a team effort, involving many kinds of specialists. It would have to be an internationally coordinated effort. The author's studies of the genus *Bufo* (Blair, 1972) represent an effort of this sort, but they involve only a single cosmopolitan genus.

A worldwide effort of this type would mark a revolutionary advance in the evolutionary biology of the anurans. Most previous studies have been continental, at most, in scope. A comparative study of the different continental faunas, especially of the diverse faunas on the southern continents, should give a much better understanding of the evolutionary history and of the phylogenetic relationships of the anurans. A comparable statement could be made about the urodeles or the apodans, but the anurans, because of their wide distribution and great ecological diversity, offer the most interesting challenge.

Captions for Color Plate

1. *Hyla leucophyllata* from Brazilian rain forest. (Photo by G. Lutz.)

2. *Dendrobates pumilio* from Costa Rican rain forest, showing aposematic coloration.

3. *Leptodactylus laticeps* from Argentine Chaco showing aposematic coloration.

4. *Bufo periglenes* (♂, ♀) from Costa Rica showing extreme of anuran sexual dichromatism.

5. *Proceratophrys boiei*, a forest-floor leptodactylid from Brazil.

6. *Bufo superciliaris* from west African rain forest showing "dead leaf" pattern. (Photo by W. Low.)

7. *Lepidobatrachus llanensis*, xeric-adapted ceratophrynid from Argentine Chaco. (Photo by J. Cei.)

8. *Ceratophrys pierotti*, cannibalistic ceratophrynid from Argentine Chaco. Note head size. (Photo by J. Cei.)

9. *Ceratophrys ornata*, octoploid ceratophrynid from Argentina.

10. *Bufo alvarius*, semiaquatic toad from Arizona.

11. *Rana palmipes* from Colombia, the only ranid in South America.

12. *Fritziana goeldi*, ♀ carrying eggs, from South American rain forest. (Photo by J. Bogart.)

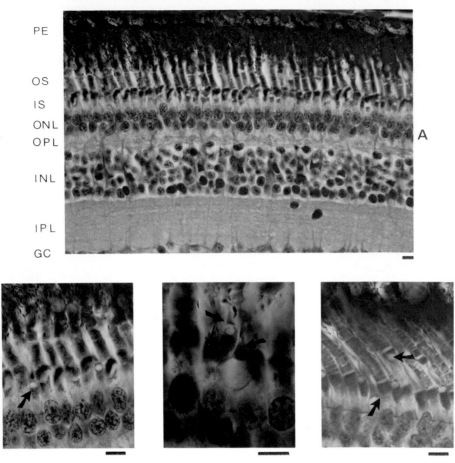

Fig. 1. Photomicrographs of sections of frog retinas that have been stained with Cason's Mallory Heidenhain. The horizontal bar under each photomicrograph represents 10 μm.

(A) The layers of the frog retina. PE, pigment epithelium; OS, receptor outer segments; IS, receptor inner segments; ONL, outer nuclear layer containing receptor nuclei; OPL, outer plexiform layer; INL, inner nuclear layer containing the nuclei of horizontal, bipolar, and amacrine cells; IPL, inner plexiform layer; GC, ganglion cells (*Rana pipiens*).

(B) Receptors. *Left panel:* The arrow points to a single cone (*Rana pipiens*).

Middle panel: Double cone, the left arrow points to the principal cone and the right arrow to the accessory cone (*Rana pipiens*).

Right panel: The lower arrow points to a 502 (red) rod and the upper arrow points to a 432 (green) rod. Note that the outer segment of the 432 rod starts up higher and is shorter than the 502 rod outer segment (*Rana clamitans*). See Fig. 3 for a schematic drawing of the receptors. (Courtesy of I. LaBossiere and K. Fite.)

Anatomy and Physiology of the Frog Retina

James Gordon and Donald C. Hood

INTRODUCTION

Studies of the frog retina have played a major role in the evolution of our knowledge of the vertebrate visual system. Observations of frog retinas led early photochemists to conclude that the action of light upon the visual pigment was like the action of light upon many other chemicals —a photochemical change of state (Müller, 1851; Boll, 1876). The frog retinal pigment, rhodopsin, became the most studied pigment (Kühne, 1878). In fact, much of what is presently known about visual pigments has also resulted from subsequent work on these animals. The names, rods and cones, which describe the major vertebrate receptor types originated from early anatomical studies of retinas like that of the frog where, unlike human receptors, the outer segments do, in fact, look like rods and cones (Müller, 1851). When electrophysiology came of age, research on the frog visual system was clearly at the forefront, and many early descriptions of the gross electrical responses of the eye came from frog research (see Granit, 1947). Furthermore, the first single-fiber recordings from a vertebrate visual system were obtained from frog ganglion-cell fibers (Hartline, 1938). Thus, many important aspects of the retinal anatomy and physiology of vertebrate visual systems have first been described in frogs. As will be discussed in this chapter, this has continued to occur. What follows is a selective review of current knowledge concerning the anatomy and physiology of the frog retina.

ANATOMY

The frog retina, like all other vertebrate retinas, is a thin, but complex, structure with three nuclear layers and two plexiform layers. The receptors are located toward the back of the eye and the more proximal layers of the retina are nearer to the front of the eye. Figure 1A* shows a light photomicrograph of a section of frog retina in which the basic layers of the retina are identified.

There are approximately 2 to 3 receptors and 5 to 7 bipolar and horizontal cells for each of the 450,000 ganglion cells (Maturana *et al.*, 1960). Figure 2 shows the number of each type of receptor and of ganglion cells as a function of retinal location for *Rana catesbeiana*. There is generally, an area centralis where there is an increased number of cells, but the frog has no foveal pit. This area is characterized by a thickening of the retina resulting from an increase in the number of receptors, inner nuclear layer (INL) cells, and ganglion cells, as well as an increase in the size of the inner plexiform layer (IPL). Table 1 shows the percentage of each receptor type in the retina of *Rana pipiens*.

Receptors

There are actually four types of receptor in the frog retina—two are rods and two are cones. Photomicrographs of these receptors are shown in Fig. 1B.* The rods will be considered first. The red and green rods were so named due to their colored appearance in a freshly excised retina and their cylindrical, rodlike outer segments. These rods are differentiated more appropriately according to the photopigment they contain, rather than their appearance; thus the red rod will be called the 502 rod and the green rod the 432 rod. These numbers refer to the wavelength of light that is absorbed maximally by each of these rods. The 502 rods can be further distinguished from the 432 rods since their outer segments are quite long and their myoids are short, while the 432 rod outer segments are short, and

---

* For Fig. 1, see color figure facing p. 29.

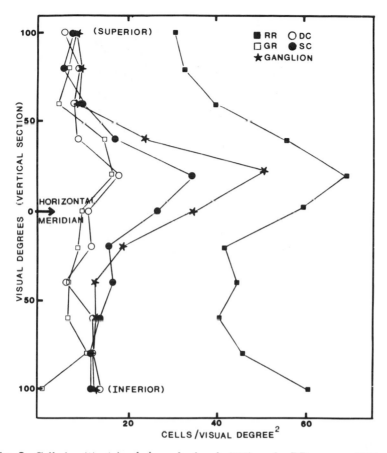

Fig. 2. Cell densities/visual degree^2 of red (502) rods, RR; green (432) rods, GR; double cones, DC; single cones, SC; and ganglion cells obtained from a vertical section, 25° temporal to the central vertical meridian in a right eye of *Rana catesbieana*. (From Carey, 1975.)

their myoids are long and thin. A diagram of receptors based on electron microscopy (Fig. 3) shows that the outer segments of rods are made up of a series of vertically stacked discs encapsulated by the plasma membrane. These discs begin as invaginations at the base of the outer segment, but are later pinched off and become separated from the plasma membrane (Nilsson, 1964b). The visual pigment in the outer segments actually forms part of the structure of the discs (see Dartnall, 1962).

The formation and movement of discs in the rod was first traced in the frog using autoradiographic electron microscopic techniques (Young, 1970). New discs are continuously formed at the base of the outer segment and move up the outer segment until they finally detach and are

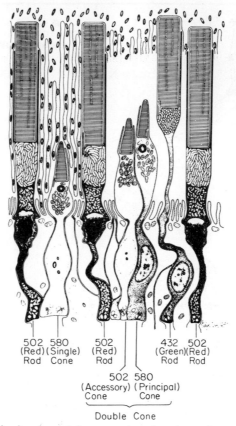

Fig. 3. Schematic drawing of frog receptors based on electron microscopy. (Redrawn from Nilsson, 1964a.)

absorbed by the pigment epithelium. Thus, the rods are constantly renewing themselves; the cones apparently do not renew themselves in this fashion (Young, 1970).

There are two types of cones in the frog—the single cone and the double cone. The cones were so named because of the conelike shape of their outer segments. The outer segments of all cones, whether a single cone, or the principal or accessory member of a double cone, are very similar (Fig. 3). Both the single and the principal cone contain a photopigment with a maximal absorption at 580 nm, while the accessory cone has a photopigment with maximal absorption at 502 nm (Liebman and Entine, 1968). The cone outer segments are made up of what appears to be a stack of discs of decreasing diameter. In the cones, these discs are actually a series of invaginations of the plasma membrane.

All receptor outer segments are attached to their inner segments by a very thin, eccentric connecting cilium. The inner and outer segments interdigitate with long strands from the pigment epithelial cells at the back of the eye. The inner segments of both the single cone and the principal member of a double cone are virtually the same. Both contain an oil droplet in their ellipsoids that is essentially transparent to visible light and so has no effect as colored filter (Liebman and Entine, 1968). (In some species such as pigeon, the oil droplet is colored, changing the spectral composition of the light reaching the visual pigments. This will affect the spectral sensitivity of the receptor.) The accessory member of the double cone has no oil droplet and its nucleus is separated from the principal cone by only the plasma membrane (Nilsson, 1964a). There is evidence that the accessory cone may in fact develop from a rod which, at some stage, fuses with a single cone (Saxén, 1954, 1956). The photopigments contained in each of these receptors will be described in detail in the next section. In contrast to most other vertebrate retinas, the nuclei of the rods lie next to the outer limiting membrane, while the nuclei of the cones are more proximal in the outer nuclear layer (ONL).

Outer Plexiform Layer

The structure and synaptic connections within the retina have been examined with the electron microscope and a summary diagram of these connections for the frog retina is shown in Fig. 4 (Dowling, 1968). In the outer plexiform layer (OPL), the receptor terminals contain invaginations into which three processes protrude. These terminals are basically the same for both rods and cones (Evans, 1966; see Dowling, 1968). The central element of the triad [so labeled because there are three postsynaptic elements (Dowling and Boycott, 1966)] is from a bipolar cell, while the two lateral elements are from horizontal cells. The receptor has a synaptic ribbon, surrounded by vesicles, that is located at the top of the invagination; the ribbon points toward the middle of the triad and the synapse is called a ribbon synapse.

In addition to the connections occurring at the invaginations, there are also a few connections between the surface of the receptor terminal and postsynaptic elements (most probably bipolar cells, but possibly from horizontal cells or from other receptors). Typically, there is a density increase in the pre- and postsynaptic membranes, but there are no clusters of vesicles at these connections.

A few conventional synapses are also found in the OPL. In these synapses, there is no ribbon, but rather a cluster of vesicles in the presynaptic membrane and increase in pre- and postsynaptic membrane

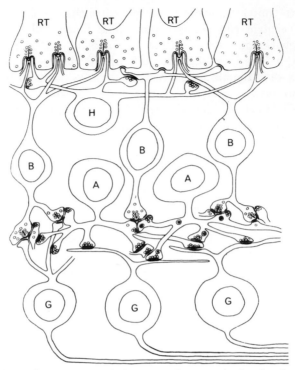

Fig. 4. Schematic summary of the synaptic contacts in the frog retina. RT, receptor terminals; H, horizontal cell; B, bipolar cells; A, amacrine cells; G, ganglion cells. (From Dowling, 1968.)

densities. The presynaptic element is probably a horizontal cell process, while the postsynaptic elements are sometimes horizontal cells and occasionally bipolar cells. The frog OPL appears quite similar to that of the primate, although the primate lacks the conventional synapses (Dowling, 1968).

Bipolar Cells

Several types and subtypes of each of the cells in the INL have been described (Ramón y Cajal, 1892). Figure 5A contains several examples of these cells. The processes of bipolar cells ramify in the outer plexiform layer and synapse with the receptors. The diameters of the bipolar dendritic arborizations vary from about 20 μm to 80 μm (Maturana et al., 1960). There may also be some bipolars with very small dendritic fields of from a few microns up to 10 μm in extent (Matsumoto and Naka, 1972). There is some suggestion of a layering of the OPL such that 502

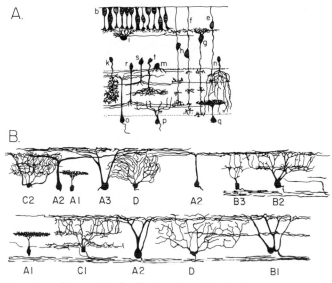

Fig. 5. Drawings of frog retinal cells based on Golgi staining.

(A) Examples of the various types of cells in the frog retina. b, receptors; i, horizontal cell; h, g, bipolar cells; e, displaced bipolar cell; f, bipolar with Landolt club; k, r, s, t, m, n, amacrine cells; o, p, q, ganglion cells. (From Dowling, 1968; slightly modified from Ramón y Cajal.)

(B) Frog ganglion cells labeled according to Cajal's classification. A's have single layered dendritic trees, B's double layered, C's triple layered, and D's diffuse dendritic trees. The numbers 1, 2, and 3 represent a subtype within a category and indicate differences, such as, what layers in the IPL a dendritic tree projects, or the amount of branching between layers of the IPL. (Redrawn from Ramón y Cajal, 1892.)

rods, 432 rods, and cones terminate at different levels which may correspond to different levels of clustering of the bipolar cell terminals (Ramón y Cajal, 1892). Some bipolar cells have a process (the Landolt club) that continues right up and through the OPL to terminate just on the distal side of the outer limiting membrane. The proximal ends of the bipolar cells ramify and terminate in the IPL. There is also a distinct layering in the IPL and different bipolar cells seem to terminate in one or more of these layers (Ramón y Cajal, 1892; Maturana *et al.*, 1960).

Horizontal Cells

The cell bodies of the horizontal cells lie most distally in the INL. The processes from these cells course laterally through the OPL and end in the vicinity of the receptor terminals. Ramón y Cajal has described two types of horizontal cell and an example of one is shown in Fig. 5A. The dendritic field of these cells has been estimated by Matsumoto and Naka (1972) to be 15–40 μm in diameter with one or two lateral processes extending from 100 to 200 μm, in agreement with Ramón y Cajal, who described many horizontal cells with a number of relatively short lateral processes and a single, very long, lateral process.

Amacrine Cells

The amacrine cells (so-called by Ramón y Cajal to indicate that they were without any true axon) lie most proximally in the INL, and their processes extend both into and laterally within the IPL. Ramón y Cajal described two basic types of amacrines—the diffuse and the stratified—examples of each are shown in Fig 5A. The diffuse cells have arborizations that end in all levels of the IPL, while the stratified cells have arborizations that, depending on the particular cell, end in one or more of the distinct layers of the IPL.

Inner Plexiform Layer

The IPL is somewhat more complex than the OPL. The IPL represents the region where bipolar cells, amacrine cells, and ganglion cells are connected by synapses (Fig. 4). The bipolar cells synapse onto postsynaptic elements through ribbon synapses, such that a synaptic ribbon in the bipolar cell (surrounded by vesicles) points between two postsynaptic elements (a dyad). In the frog, both of the postsynaptic elements in most dyads are amacrine cell processes; the other dyads have an amacrine cell as one postsynaptic element, and a ganglion cell as the other element. The reverse situation holds for the primate in which the latter type of synapse predominates. There are about the same number of ribbon synapses in the IPL of both frogs and primates (Dowling, 1968; Dubin, 1970).

There are also many conventional synapses in the frog IPL; in fact, there are about ten times more conventional synapses than ribbon synapses. In the primate, there are about the same number of ribbon synapses, but many fewer (about one-quarter as many) conventional synapses (Dowling, 1968; Dubin, 1970). In all of these conventional synapses, the presynaptic element is probably an amacrine cell. There are three types of conventional synapses depending upon the postsynaptic element. In one type, the postsynaptic elements are bipolar cells so that there is a strong possibility of a bipolar cell feeding forward onto an amacrine cell and also receiving feedback from that cell. In the second type, the postsynaptic elements are amacrine cells. In fact, serial synapses have been found in which one amacrine process synapses onto another, which, in turn, synapses onto yet another amacrine process. Such serial synapses are common in frogs, but occur only infrequently in primates. These synapses are an indication of the complex interactions among neurons which can occur in the frog IPL.

The third type of postsynaptic element in the IPL conventional synapse is a ganglion cell process. Very often, the dendrite of a ganglion cell has been found to be covered with these conventional synapses from amacrine cells, whereas conventional amacrine ganglion synapses appear to occur infrequently in primates. Thus, Dowling (1968) has suggested that since the bipolar cells synapse mostly onto amacrine cells and amacrine cells often synapse onto ganglion cells, the amacrine cell in the frog may be a true interneuron which, in most cases, drives the ganglion cell, while the direct driving of a ganglion cell by a bipolar cell presumably occurs much less often. This is the reverse of the situation for the primate retina in which direct, bipolar ganglion-cell synapses are more common. There is also some physiological evidence indicating that amacrine cells frequently drive ganglion cells in the frog retina (Burkhardt and Berntson, 1972; Burkhardt and Whittle, 1973).

Developmentally, there is a dramatic increase in the number of serial conventional synapses in the IPL as a tadpole metamorphoses into a mature frog (Fisher, 1972). This change has been related to an increase in the anatomic and physiological complexity of the mature frog retina in comparison with that of the tadpole (Pomeranz and Chung, 1970; Pomeranz, 1972).

Using electron microscopy, Dowling (1968) and Dubin (1970; see Boycott and Dowling, 1969) have looked for a layering of the types of synapses in the IPL of the frog without success, although Dubin (1970) did find some suggestion of layering of the IPL of the pigeon retina.

Ganglion Cells

The ganglion cells of the frog retina vary widely in their size, lateral spread, and stratification of their dendritic arborizations. Most cell bodies are between 7 μm and 10 μm, but a few cell perikarya are as large as 20 μm. The dendritic arborizations of the cells are typically between 100 μm and 300 μm, but they may be as small as 50 μm or as large as 600 μm; in general, larger cells have larger arborizations (Maturana et al., 1960). Since the ganglion cells are quite close together, their dendritic fields overlap to a large extent. A given ganglion cell may receive inputs from hundreds of bipolars and tens of thousands of receptors, and a given receptor may project to hundreds of ganglion cells (Maturana *et al.*, 1960). This convergence and divergence is only part of the complexity, however. As shown in Fig. 1A, there are many more cells in the INL than there are ganglion cells. The ways in which these cells are used for processing visual signals and abstracting and coding various kinds of information will be discussed in later sections.

Ramón y Cajal (1892) separated frog ganglion cells into ten classes based on the structure of their dendritic trees. Lettvin and co-workers (1961) later categorized ganglion cells into a somewhat more restricted system of five classes. There are some similarities and some differences between these two classifications. Both classifications have two categories of cells that branch into just a single layer of the IPL; one group has dendritic trees that spread out over a large area (Fig. 5B, cell A2, or Lettvin *et al.*'s "broad tree"). The other group has dendritic trees restricted to a fairly small area (Fig. 5B, cell A1 or Lettvin *et al.*'s "constricted tree"). Both Ramón y Cajal and Lettvin and associates also describe cells that have diffuse dendritic trees and send processes into all regions of the IPL with no distinct layering (Fig. 5B, cell D, or Lettvin *et al.*'s "diffuse tree").

The differences between these categorizations involve amount of layering and amount of branching. Cajal categorized cells that branched into more than one layer of the IPL with regard to whether they branched into two (B-types) or three (C-types) layers, the size of their dendritic spread, and the amount of branching that occurred between the layers of the IPL. Lettvin *et al.*, however, distinguished between these multilayered cells only on the basis of whether or not they had any branchings at all between layers of the IPL (type E-tree versus type H-tree—only two types). For example, cell B1 with no branching between layers is equivalent to the H-tree, while cell B2 with some branching between layers is equivalent to the E-tree (Fig. 5B).

Thus, the Lettvin *et al.* classification does *not* discriminate between those cells with very little branching between layers of the IPL and those with a great deal of branching as long as their is some branching. Both cell B2 (which has a little branching) and cell C2 (which has a great deal of branching) fit into the same category (the E-tree) in Lettvin *et al.*'s scheme. This possibility of an anatomic continuum (in this case with respect to amount of branching) rather than two distinct categories may account for some of the overlap found between cell types that have been categorized electrophysiologically.

Lettvin *et al.* (1961) have related their anatomic classes to their functional classification of ganglion cells based on electrophysiological recording. (We will consider this classificaton as well as the other functional classes into which frog retinal ganglion cells have been divided later in this chapter.) Also in support of the relationships drawn by Maturana *et al.* (1960) between anatomy and function are developmental experiments by Pomeranz and Chung (1970). In tadpoles, one of the anatomical classes of ganglion cell appears to be missing and electrophysiological recording has shown that its functional counterpart is similarly missing. No direct test of the relationships between anatomy and function has been made for frog ganglion cells. Such a test might involve intracellular ganglion cell recording to determine function and a dye, such as procion yellow, subsequently injected to determine anatomical configuration.

Finally, Ramón y Cajal looked very carefully for evidence of centrifugal input to the frog retina and found some suggestive evidence, but no strong evidence such as he observed in birds. Maturana (1959) also described indirect evidence for efferents in his study of the frog optic nerve. Although the effects are not particularly dramatic (Shortess, 1963; Branston and Fleming, 1968), there is some electrophysiological evidence for centrifugal input to the retina.

VISUAL PIGMENTS

The outer segments of the receptors contain a photochemical referred to as the visual pigment. Vision is initiated when a few visual pigment molecules each absorb a quantum of light—one quantum absorbed by one molecule suffices to change the output of a receptor (Hecht *et al.*, 1942). The only direct effect of light is to change the shape of, or isomerize, the chromophore of the visual pigment molecule from its 11-cis to an all-trans configuration. Following isomerization, the visual pigment molecule undergoes a series of conformational changes and passes through a number of stages referred to as photoproducts (for a review, see Wald, 1968; Dartnall, 1972). Some of these photoproducts last only microseconds, but some remain for relatively long periods of time and, while these longer-lasting photoproducts are not involved in the initial visual response, they may be important in long-term sensitivity changes that occur during adaptation.

The effect of quantal absorption on a visual pigment molecule—the isomerization from cis to trans—is thought to be the same regardless of the wavelength of the incident quanta. However, although a visual pigment molecule will absorb a quantum over a wide range of wavelengths, the probability of absorption is dependent on wavelength. The *absorption spectrum* of a visual pigment is a function that relates this probability of absorption to the wavelength of light. There are numerous visual pigments and the absorption spectrum can be used to distinguish among them.

There are various techniques now available for obtaining absorption spectra. One of the oldest is a method of extracting the visual pigment molecules from the outer segment and producing an *in vitro* sample of the visual pigment. This method depends upon having a high concentration of extractable pigment molecules of one type. The pigment of the frog's 502 or red rod comprises over 90% of all visual pigment molecules in the frog retina (Liebman and Entine, 1968) and is present in large amounts (over a million molecules per receptor). Dartnall (1957) observed that although different visual pigments had their maximal absorption at different wavelengths, the shape of the relative absorption spectrum* was invariant if plotted on a frequency rather than wavelength axis. And, in fact, he derived a nomogram for determining absorption spectra of pigments with different wavelengths of maximal absorption. This nomogram was based on the frog's rhodopsin pigment. Consequently, a visual pigment could be uniquely specified by its wavelength of maximal absorption. However, the absorption spectrum also depends upon the concentration or density of the pigment in the outer segment. Dartnall (1962) points out that the nomogram describes the absorption spectrum of a visual pigment if the optical density in the outer segment is less than 0.1. As pigment density is increased, the absorption spectrum becomes broader. Recently, pigments have been found that differ in shape from the Dartnall nomogram. This includes the pigments found in the frog's 432 rod and 580 cone (Liebman and Entine, 1968).

A more recently developed *in situ* technique, called microspectrophotometry, involves passing light through the outer segments of single receptors. An estimate of the absorption spectrum can be derived after various corrections have been made, including one for the absorption of light by photoproducts. Using this technique, Liebman and Entine (1968) have made various measurements of the frog's visual pigments. Table 1 is a summary of these findings. For the 502 rod, the absorption spectrum, uncorrected for pigment density, fits Darnall's nomogram. Liebman and Entine estimate that the 502 rod pigment density is 0.75 for an axial length of 50 μm. (The corrected absorption spectrum is plotted in Fig. 10A). For the 432 rods, Liebman and Entine's absorption spectrum is also in good agreement with early extraction work (Dartnall, 1967) and has a slightly broader absorption spectrum than does the nomogram. The Liebman and Entine study supplies the only direct measurement of the

---

* Unless the pigment has a density less than 0.1, the absorption spectrum technically should be called an absorbance (extinction coefficient) spectrum or a density spectrum, plotted relative to maximum (see Dartnall, 1957, pp. 13–20).

Table 1 Receptor Parameters[a]

Parameter	Rods		Cones		
	432 (Green)	502 (Red)	580[b] (Princ.)	502 (Acc.)	580 (Single)
% Population	8	50	12	12	18
λ_{max} (nm)	432	502	580	502	580
Axial length (μm)	40	50	15	15	15
Diameter (μm)	4	6	3	(Base) 3	3
Axial density	0.56	0.75	0.2	0.2	0.2
O.S. volume (μm)^3	500	1400	35	35	35
% Total pigment in retina	5.5	92.8	0.5	0.5	0.75

[a] Modified from Liebman and Entine (1968).

[b] The cone pigment has been called 580 rather than 575 since the microspectrophotometry (Liebman and Entine, 1968, Fig. 16), ERP (Goldstein, 1968), and receptor electrophysiology (Hood and Hock, 1973) all peak at 580 nm or slightly longer (see Fig. 10B).

absorption spectrum of the frog cone pigments. The principal and single cones contain a pigment whose absorption spectrum has a peak around 580 nm (see Fig. 10B) and is narrower than the nomogram. The accessory cone has a pigment with an absorption spectrum that peaks at 502 nm and fits the nomogram. This extensive information available on frog receptors and pigments is, in part, why the frog is such a valuable research subject.

The frog has been of pivotal importance in the study of visual pigments. Because of the large amount of visual pigment in its 502 rods, it was the first vertebrate pigment to be observed (Müller, 1851) by the naked eye, to be seen to be destroyed by light (Boll, 1876), to be shown to regenerate [making it likely that the initial stage of vision is photochemical (Kühne, 1878)], and, finally, to be extracted (Kühne, 1878). During the twentieth century, frog pigment research has continued to be of importance in furthering knowledge of the pigment molecule, its sensitivity and response to light, its role in visual excitation, and the process by which it regenerates following the absorption of a quantum of light [Chapters by Wald (1953, 1968) and Dartnall (1957, 1972) contain reviews of some of this important material.] A number of recent findings ensure the continued importance of frog pigment research in furthering understanding of the physiology of the retina. It has been known since Kühne (1878) that without the pigment epithelium found in back of the retina the *rod* pigment does not regenerate following exposure to light. Recently, however, Goldstein (1967) (discussed under *Adaptation*) has shown that the 580 *cone* pigment can regenerate without the pigment epithelium. Future research should help to determine whether this is a general rod-cone difference and, in fact, to what extent this may help explain functional differences between rods and cones. The future study of the frog's 502 cones, 502 rods, and 432 rods may also help to determine how much of the functional difference between rods and cones is due to different pigment molecules and how much is due to receptor morphology. In the case of the 502 cones and 502 rods, there are apparently identical visual pigments living in different receptor types. Although the physiologist has collected a fair amount of information about 502 rod function, virtually nothing is known about the functioning of the 502 cones. The important rod-cone comparisons must await this information. The 432 rod may also supply important clues toward understanding rod-cone differences. This receptor has the morphology of a rod, a pigment whose wavelength of maximum absorption is in the range of "blue" cone pigments and a physiology that appears in some ways to be between the frogs' 580 cone and 502 rod (Goldstein and Wolf, 1973; Donner and Reuter, 1962). Again, detailed conclusions await more physiological and photochemical information about both the frog's 580 cone and 432 rod.

BASIC ELECTROPHYSIOLOGY

Single Unit Responses

Intracellular Recording

Although there has been a very limited amount of intracellular recording from the frog retina (due mainly to the technical difficulties of this kind of experiment), some records have been obtained from most types of frog retinal neurons (Fig. 6). Intracellular records from frog rods (Fig. 6A) have been obtained by Toyoda *et al.* (1970) and, as in other vertebrate rod photoreceptors (Grabowski *et al.*, 1972; Fain and Dowling, 1973; Kleinschmidt, 1973), the response to light is a sustained, hyperpolarization with a slow onset and a slow decay at offset. The spectral sensitivity of the intracellular rod response (Fig. 10A) matches the rhodopsin absorption function corrected for an optical density of 0.35. Successful intracellular recording from frog cones has yet to be achieved.

The fact that vertebrate visual receptors hyperpolarize in response to light was first demonstrated in *Necturus* (Bortoff, 1964) and carp retinas (Tomita, 1965). Since the receptors and most horizontal cells show an increase in membrane resistance accompanying the light-elicited hyperpolarization, it was suggested by Tomita that receptors *decrease* their release of a depolarizing transmitter substance in response to light. That

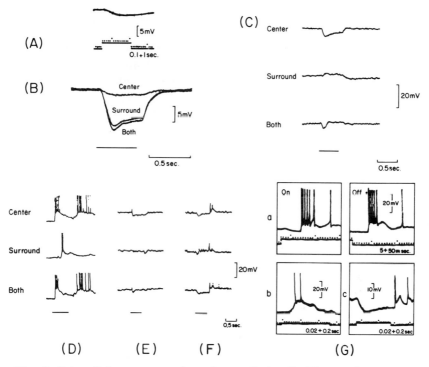

Fig. 6. Intracellular responses from frog retinal cells. Upward deflections are positive (depolarizing) potentials.

(A) Rod response to 500 nm light. The response to light of all wavelengths is a hyperpolarization. (From Toyoda et al., 1970.)

(B) Horizontal cell responses to a 0.4 mm diameter spot (center), an annulus with a 0.8 mm inner diameter and a 3 mm outer diameter (surround), and the spot and annulus together (both). The responses to both center and surround stimulation are hyperpolarizations and the response to both simultaneously is larger than either alone indicating spatial summation. (From Matsumoto and Naka, 1972.)

(C) Bipolar cell responses. Stimulating conditions are the same as in (B). The cell is hyperpolarized by the spot (center), and depolarized by the annulus (surround). It gives a smaller response to simultaneous annulus and spot stimulation (both) than to either alone indicating a spatially antagonistic receptive field. (From Matsumoto and Naka, 1972.)

(D, E, F) Responses of three different presumed amacrine cells to stimulation as in (B). The cell in (D) responds with transient depolarizations and some spikes to both the onset and offset of a spot. All of the cells show some spatial antagonism between center and surround stimulation, but the effects are more subtle than those shown in (C) for the bipolar cell. (From Matsumoto and Naka, 1972.)

(G) The responses of three ganglion cells of the (a) on-off, (b) on, and (c) off types. The on-off cell (a) responds with depolarizations and superimposed spikes at both onset and offset of light. The on cell (b) responds with a depolarization and superimposed spikes during light on. The off cell (c) responds with a hyperpolarization for the duration of the light and with a depolarization and superimposed spikes at light offset. (From Tomita et al., 1961.)

magnesium, known to decrease transmitter release in other preparations, also hyperpolarizes horizontal cells was taken as further evidence of a light-initiated decrease in synaptic activity (Dowling and Ripps, 1973). Recently, Schacher et al. (1974) have supplied direct evidence for this hypothesis by measuring synaptic activity with a cytochemical technique (the uptake of horseradish peroxidase into vesicles). The frog receptors show a high synaptic activity in the dark, and a substantial decrease in rod synaptic activity occurs with moderate light levels. Consequently, it appears that not only do the vertebrate visual receptors hyperpolarize to light, but this hyperpolarization is accompanied by a decrease in transmitter release.

The response (S-potentials) of almost all frog horizontal cells is a sustained hyperpolarization to all wavelengths of light (Naka et al., 1960; Tomita et al., 1961; Tomita, 1963; Toyoda et al., 1970). As in other species (for example, carp; Tomita, 1965; Necturus; Werblin and Dowling, 1969), the frog horizontal cells have large receptive fields and the responses to stimulation of all parts of their receptive fields are hyperpolarizations (Fig. 6B). Toyoda and associates (1970) found that the responses of horizontal cells were characterized by more rapid onsets and offsets than were those of rods and, furthermore, the spectral response functions for the horizontal cells were maximal around 570 nm, which suggests the possibility that frog horizontal cell responses were primarily controlled by cones even at relatively low intensities.

The bipolar cells of the frog retina show a clear spatial antagonism of excitation and inhibition (Matsumoto and Naka, 1972; Fig. 6C) as described for other vertebrates (Necturus: Werblin and Dowling, 1969; goldfish: Kaneko, 1970; carp: Toyoda, 1973). Two types of bipolar cells have been described, one with a hyperpolarizing response following stimulation of the cell's receptive field center and a depolarizing response following stimulation of the cell's receptive field surround (Fig. 6C). The other type responds in just the reverse manner—a depolarizing response to central stimulation and a hyperpolarizing response to surround stimulation. The response to simultaneous center and surround stimulation is smaller than the response to either area stimulated separately, because the hyperpolarizing and depolarizing responses cancel each other out.

The response pattern of frog amacrine cells (Matsumoto and Naka, 1972) is more complex than that of the more distal neurons just described. These cells respond with graded potentials, although some respond with spikelike potentials as well. One type of amacrine cell (similar to those found in Necturus: Werblin and Dowling, 1969; goldfish: Kaneko, 1970; and carp: Toyoda et al., 1973) responds with transient depolarization at both the onset and offset of light and shows little, if any, spatial antago-

nism between center and surround responses (Fig. 6D). Still other amacrine cells respond in a more sustained way, with some showing evidence
of an antagonism between center and surround responses (Fig. 6E,F).
This is similar to the response pattern of sustained amacrine cells found in
the carp retina (Toyoda et al., 1973).

Ganglion cells in the frog retina respond with action potentials only
to an "appropriate" pattern of light stimulation. The various functional
categories into which these cells have been placed are discussed in detail
in subsequent sections. The original classification of these cells was based
upon whether or not the cell responded to the onset, offset, or both onset
and offset of light (Hartline, 1938). Intracellular records (Tomita, 1963)
from these "on," "on-off," and "off" cells are shown in Fig. 6G. Some of
these cells have spatially antagonistic inputs as revealed by different
response patterns depending upon whether the center, surround, or both
parts of the receptive field are stimulated simultaneously (Matsumoto
and Naka, 1972).

Extracellular Recording

As previously mentioned, the first recording of single-unit activity
in the vertebrate visual system was accomplished by Hartline (1938,
1940a,b) in studies where the axons of frog retinal ganglion cells were
dissected away from the retinal surface of the opened eye and picked up
onto wick electrodes. Since then, a variety of techniques have been employed to study the extracellular responses of these neurons. These techniques have included the use of microelectrodes to record from the
retinal surface (e.g., Granit, 1947; Barlow, 1953), from the optic nerve,
or from the terminations of optic nerve fibers in the tectum (e.g., Maturana et al., 1960). The results from these experiments will be considered
in detail in later sections.

Before the single-unit, extracellular recording techniques were developed, other methods were used to study retinal function. Since it is
still not possible to record extracellularly from single retinal neurons other
than ganglion cells and since, with intracellular methods, it is very difficult to maintain stable long-term recording, the recording of gross potentials has been used to study the retinal functions of neurons other than
ganglion cells.

Gross Potentials

Over one hundred years ago, Holmgren (1870–1871) recorded an electrical response to light from vertebrate eyes. This response, called the

electroretinogram (ERG), is a complex, gross potential recorded between the front and back of the retina. The ERG has a number of waves that can be distinguished. Figure 7A shows a schematic drawing of an ERG response with its four prominent waves, the a, b, c, and d waves. Granit (1933) postulated that the ERG actually represented the summed activity of three major components which he designated PI, PII, and PIII. Reviews of the relevant experimentation and details of this component analysis can be found in Granit (1938, 1947). Figure 7A, from Granit and Riddell (1934), shows how these components presumably summed together to yield the light- and dark-adapted frog ERG. Although Granit's analysis has been modified often (e.g., Brown, 1968), it still appears to be largely correct and, at the very least, represents a good point of departure for any discussion of the origin and nature of the ERG.

The evidence is quite convincing that the PI component responsible for the c-wave is generated by the pigment epithelium, although PI is probably triggered by light absorbed by the receptors (Noell, 1954; Brown and Crawford, 1967; Liebman et al., 1967). (PI is not seen in the isolated retina since the pigment epithelium is not present.)

Although PII (which produces the b-wave) has been shown to consist of two components in the mammalian ERG, it appears that cold-blooded vertebrates have only one of these components (Brown, 1968). Tomita (1963) used depth recording to localize this PII component in the inner nuclear layer. Recent evidence (Miller and Dowling, 1970) strongly implicates the Müller cell as the generator of the portion of the mammalian PII that is common to cold-blooded animals. This cell is thought to act as a sink for potassium ions and thus produces a potential, PII, that represents a summed indication of INL activity.

Granit's (1947) suggestion that PIII (which is responsible for the a- and d-waves) might be subdivided further into two components is now widely accepted. These two components are the proximal PIII, localized in the INL (Tomita, 1963, 1965; Murakami and Kaneko, 1966), and the distal PIII, generated by the receptors (Murakami and Kaneko, 1966).

At the leading edge of the a-wave (Fig. 7B,C) is a very rapid (note the time scale), biphasic potential with zero latency to onset. This early receptor potential (ERP) is generated by the initial photochemical responses of the receptors (Cone, 1965). The frog's ERP is produced primarily by cones (in spite of the fact that 95% of the frog's photopigment is in the rods), although the rods also generate a small ERP (Goldstein, 1967, 1968; Goldstein and Wolf, 1973). Because the ERP is proportional to the number of pigment molecules that absorb light (Cone, 1964; Cone and Cobbs, 1969), it has proved to be a valuable response for the measurement of pigment bleaching and regeneration (cf. Goldstein, 1970).

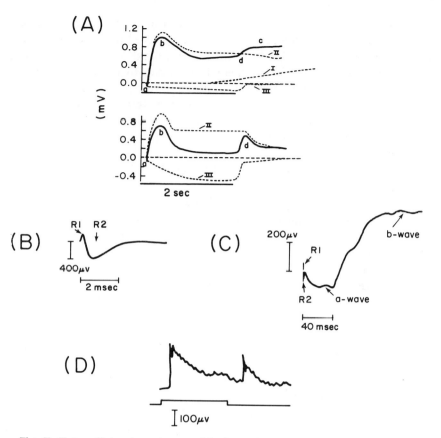

Fig. 7. Extracellular (gross) potentials from the frog retina. Upward deflections are corneal positive except for (D).

(A) Electroretinogram (ERG) of a light adapted (lower) and dark adapted (upper) frog eye. The solid lines represent the responses with the a, b, c, and d waves indicated. The dashed lines represent an analysis of the ERG into its component parts PI, PII, and PIII. (Modified from Granit and Riddell, 1934.)

(B) Early receptor potential (ERP) of the frog with the positive (R1) and negative (R2) phases of the response indicated. Note the fast time scale and brief latency of the response. (From Cone, 1965.)

(C) The ERP shown in relation to the a and b waves of the ERG. Note the slower time scale than in (B). (From Pak, 1965.)

(D) Proximal negative response (PNR) of a light-adapted frog. The stimulus is a 0.25 mm diameter spot and the duration of the record is one second. In this record, negative is up and the response consists of transient negative potentials at the onset and offset of the light. (From Burkhardt, 1970.)

A variety of techniques have been used to isolate the PIII component. Many of these procedures, such as ammonia (Laufer *et al.*, 1961; Murakami and Kaneko, 1966; Frank, 1971), make use of the fact that the receptors are relatively unaffected compared to other structures by toxic agents or oxygen withdrawal. The most recent technique has been the application of sodium aspartate to the retina (Furukawa and Hanawa, 1955; Sillman *et al.*, 1969; Witkovsky *et al.*, 1973). Aspartate is an amino acid that appears to block all synaptic activity by depolarizing postsynaptic membranes (Cervetto and MacNichol, 1972, Dowling and Ripps, 1972). Although all postsynaptic activity is blocked by aspartate, there is a slow potential (presumably generated by Müller cells) that is of nonreceptor origin (Witkovsky *et al.*, 1973); thus care must be taken in evaluating these gross potentials (see Hood and Hock, 1975, p. 546). Hood and Hock (1973) and Hood and Mansfield (1972) have successfully separated the cone and rod receptor potentials recorded from the aspartate-treated frog retina, and the spectral sensitivities of each receptor potential fits the appropriate photopigment absorption function quite well (see Fig. 10). The time course of the rod and the cone PIII responses are quite different, with the rod having a slow onset and a very slow decay at offset (which is like the intracellular rod response—see Fig. 6A), while the cone has a brisk response with both a fast onset and offset.

A recently described retinal potential (recorded with an intraretinal microelectrode) comes from the region of the amacrine cells and has been called the proximal negative response (PNR). There is good evidence that it is, in fact, generated by a small group of amacrine cells in the region of the retina near the recording electrode (Burkhardt, 1970). In light-adapted retinas, the PNR is a very transient response (Fig. 7D) with a negative wave at both the onset and the offset of a light which also looks very much like the intracellularly recorded graded potential of the transient amacrine cell response (compare with Fig. 6D). The PNR from dark-adapted retinas is sustained (Gordon and Graham, 1975) which suggests that (if this potential truly comes from amacrine cells) the intracellular amacrine cell response is sustained under dark-adapted conditions. Since stable PNR recording can be maintained for several hours in the frog eye, this appears to be a good method for the study of amacrine-cell function in this retina.

FUNCTIONAL ELECTROPHYSIOLOGY

Any well-developed visual system must abstract and encode various aspects of the visual world. Information concerning the size, shape, and other physical characteristics of objects is supplied to the eye in the form of spatial and temporal variations in light intensity. The first section here deals with the aspects of frog retinal physiology relevant to the neural coding of these changes in light intensity. Objects also have different spectral characteristics and some visual systems can detect these differences. A second section deals with the retinal coding of this chromatic information. Finally, the visual system must be able to respond to all of these aspects of the visual world in spite of enormous changes in ambient illumination. The final portion of this chapter is concerned with the problem of adaptation.

Coding of Spatiotemporal Variations in Intensity

Since an image of the visual world is focused upon the receptor mosaic and a topographical representation of this mosaic appears to be maintained throughout the visual system, early investigators were tempted to view each cellular layer as a mosaic of identical cells mirroring the point-to-point and moment-to-moment variations in intensity present in the image. This view has been shown to be incorrect in three ways. First, it was clear from the early, gross recording from the Conger eel optic nerve (Adrian and Matthews, 1927a,b, 1928) that individual ganglion cells must receive input from a large area of the retina. Hartline (1938, 1940a,b) in his pioneer recordings confirmed this in frogs at the level of single optic nerve fibers. Borrowing a Sherringtonian concept, Hartline called this region of the retina the fiber's *receptive field*. Second, and even more important, Hartline noted that these fibers responded to (or coded) only certain aspects of the light stimulus—that is, they did not simply mirror the variations of light intensity. Finally, and perhaps most surprisingly, he observed that all fibers did not perform identical abstractions, but could be classified into three types of fibers, (*on, off,* and *on-off*) according to whether the fiber responded at the onset, offset, or both onset and offset of a light stimulus. Thus, Hartline's research determined the course of subsequent work by defining the concept of receptive field, by pointing out the highly abstracted nature of the visual response, and by raising the question of physiologically distinct classes of cell types. This section selectively reviews subsequent recording from frog ganglion cells and ganglion cell fibers. Other reviews of this material include Varju (1969) and Grüsser and Grüsser-Cornehls (1970, 1973).

Considering first the question of classes of cell types, Hartline was able to categorize most of the ganglion cell fibers into three classes based on their responses to light. The *on*-cells gave a sustained response to the presence of light, the *on-off* cells gave a transient response to both the onset and the offset of light, and *off*-cells gave a transient or sustained response to light offset. Hartline (1938, p. 403) cautioned that, "These categories, however, are not absolutely rigid, and it would be a mistake to ignore the occasional fiber whose response is intermediate in character." Hartline's simple scheme was not really challenged until 1959 when Lettvin, Maturana, McCulloch, and Pitts published their now classic study of *Rana pipiens'* ganglion cells (Lettvin *et al.*, 1959; Maturana *et al.*, 1960). This work has substantially influenced the study of sensory systems by both physiologists and psychologists. Lettvin *et al.* argued that in order to discover those invariants in the visual environment that are being abstracted at the level of the ganglion cell a more "naturalistic approach" must be employed. This approach involved modifications of the earlier recording and stimulating techniques. These investigators developed a technique for recording from ganglion cell fibers either in the optic nerve or at the site of optic fiber terminations in the superficial layers of the optic tectum. Their frogs were alive, but curarized and had fully intact optical systems. Instead of having spots of light projected onto the retina, Lettvin's frogs viewed a screen upon which stationary or moving stimuli of various shapes, sizes, and contrasts (both "light" and "dark") could be presented. From these experiments, it was concluded that "The ganglion cells form five natural classes." A brief summary of the characteristics Lettvin *et al.* ascribed to these cell classes is as follows:

Class 1 (Sustained Edge Detection)—This class of cells responds to moving or stationary edges of light or dark objects that may be of any size or shape, but not to changes in diffuse illumination. However, there is an optimal size as well as optimal speed of movement. These cells are said to have responses that are not "erasable." That is, although the sustained response to a stationary edge is suppressed with complete darkness, it returns, after a brief delay, upon reillumination of the field. These cells have *responsive receptive fields* (RRF) of 1°–3° in diameter. Since the size of the receptive field of any cell depends on both the stimulus characteristics and the definition of a response, these authors operationally defined an RRF as that area of the visual field over which a moving, 1° dark spot would elicit a response.

Class 2 (Convex Edge Detection)—These cells also respond to moving or stationary dark objects, but not to diffuse changes in illumination. The response is mainly to small objects or to the convexity (e.g., corners) of large objects. These cells differ from class 1 cells in that they respond poorly or not at all to light objects, have sustained responses to stationary objects that tend to be less prolonged, show "erasability" (i.e., reillumination of a dark object after a transient change to darkness will not excite the cell), and do not respond to the straight edge of a large object. They have RRF of 2°–5°.

Class 3 (Changing Contrast Detection)—These cells respond to both local and diffuse increases or decreases in illumination. They do not respond to stationary objects and are very sensitive to object movement. They correspond to Hartline's *on-off* cells and have RRF of 7°–12°.

Class 4 (Dimming Detection)—These cells give a response, usually prolonged, to the offset of light. The response to object size, contrast, and shape depends on the decrease produced in illumination of the receptive field. They correspond to Hartline's *off* cells and have a large RRF of up to 15°.

Class 5 (Dark Detection)—These cells are continuously active and this activity increases as ambient illumination decreases.

The description just given in parentheses is the operation that Maturana and co-workers (1960) concluded these ganglion cell types performed on the visual image. Furthermore, the fiber terminals corresponding to these cell types were found to be arranged into four layers in the superficial neuropile of the tectum, with classes 1 through 4 in separate layers and with class 5 found among the class 3 fibers. Each of these layers contained a topographic map of the visual field. Therefore, Maturana *et al.* concluded that every point of the visual image was being analyzed ". . . in terms of four qualitative contexts (standing edges, curvatures, changing contrast, and local lessening of light intensity) and a measure of illumination . . ." and that this analysis was invariant with ambient light level.

There are a number of questions that should be asked with regard to this important study. First: Have cells that fit into these classes been found by other investigators with other techniques? Overall, the agreement in subsequent work has been impressively high. Ganglion cells having the characteristics of classes 1 through 4 have been described in numerous studies using both the intact frog (cf. Grüsser-Cornehls *et al.*, 1963) and the eyecup preparation (cf., Schipperheyn, 1965; Reuter, 1969; Reuter and Virtanen, 1972). Class 5 cells, said to be rare by Maturana and associates (1960), have been reported in only two studies (Reuter, 1969; Reuter and Virtanen, 1972) where they represented only 3 out of 239 cells studied. However, everyone seems to agree that an additional type of cell exists. This type, which we will call class 6, gives a sustained response to the presence of either a spot or full-field light. These cells probably represented at least a portion of Hartline's *on*-cells and were missed by Maturana *et al.* since these cells project to the diencephalon and not to the tectum (Muntz, 1962a).

A second question is: Do the cells reported in subsequent research have the detailed qualitative characteristics reported by Lettvin *et al.*? Again, in general, the answer is yes. There have, however, been some minor points of disagreement, such as that regarding the duration of the response to stationary stimuli by class 1 and class 2 cells (cf. Keating and Gaze, 1970a). And recently the simplicity of class 4 cells has been challenged. The response of these so-called "off" or "dimming" cells was originally explained as an *off*-response to the decrease in light intensity on some part of the receptive field. However, Grüsser *et al.* (1968a) found these cells capable of giving an *on*-and *off*-response to changes in diffuse illumination when a stationary dark edge is present in the field. Further, Keating and Gaze (1970a) have shown that these cells give a long-latency response to the onset of a 2° spot of light falling in parts of their receptive fields. Consistent with these findings is the observation of Reuter and Virtanen (1972) that 19 out of the 21 class 4 cells they studied had an *on*-response controlled by the 432 rods. The control of the *off*-response by cones and the *on*-response by the relatively slower 432 rods is a possible explanation for the latency differences observed by Keating and Gaze. Chung *et al.* (1970) report another interesting characteristic of these class 4 cells. They found that all class 4 cells are spontaneously active if left in the dark long enough. Low levels of light were found to modify the pattern of spontaneous activity without, in some cases, modifying the average rate of discharge. Interestingly, Donner and Reuter (1965) also reported that ganglion cells often increased their spontaneous activity with time in the dark. However, they found that this activity stopped after complete dark adaptation (over 2 hours).

In general, then, most of the basic qualitative characteristics of these cell types have been confirmed in subsequent work. This is not to say that additional properties have not been described. Some of this work, in particular, the description of inhibitory surrounds and the quantitative work of Grüsser and Grüsser-Cornehls and their colleagues will be discussed.

A number of investigators have reported cells that fit the Lettvin *et al.* classification and these cells have, more or less, the characteristics they described. But after reviewing these studies, we are still left with questions: Are these classes really mutually exclusive and exhaustive? Can *all* frog ganglion cells be categorized as belonging to one and only one class? Maturana *et al.* (1960) cautioned, in regard to class 1 and class 2 cells, that ". . . the two classes seem to correspond to the two sharp peaks of a bimodal population." Other investigators (Grüsser and Grüsser-Cornehls, 1970) have concluded that the distinction between class 1 and class 2 cells is less clear than that between other classes. Indeed, Reuter and Virtanen (1972) found that of 65 cells they could classify as belonging to class 1 or class 2, 21 could not be unequivocally assigned to one or the other. Interestingly, attempts to classify ganglion cells in two related species (*Bufo bufo* and *Hyla septentrionalis*) resulted in one grouping with properties of both class 1 and class 2 cells, rather than two separate classes (cf. Grüsser and Grüsser-Cornehls, 1970). The generally accepted differences between class 1 and class 2 have just been listed. Each of these differences has been challenged as an absolute criterion for differentiating cells into two classes (see especially Keating and Gaze, 1970a, pp. 138–139). One way to test a bimodal hypothesis is to see how the cells in a sample of the two classes fall along the various dimensions of the proposed response differences (e.g., duration of response and degree of response to light objects). If there exists a single bimodal population and if each criterion distinguishes between the modes, then the cells in this sample should order themselves in a bimodal fashion along each dimension, and these orderings should be positively correlated. The quantitative data needed to do this analysis have not been published. Consequently, for class 1 and class 2 cells, even the bimodal explanation offered by both Maturana *et al.*, and Keating and Gaze seems too strong for the existing data.

In contrast to the uncertainties of class 1 and class 2 assignment, there is general agreement that class 3 and class 4 are mutually exclusive, but some investigators have questioned whether they are exhaustive. That is, there are dimensions along which class 3 or class 4 cells separate into two or more classes. Keating and Gaze distinguished four types of class 4 cells. All of these types showed the standard RRF where responses are elicited by moving black discs. However, each also had receptive fields over which light spots elicited *on* or *off* responses. The four types are distinguished based on the extent of the receptive fields (i.e., full visual field, band across the diameter of the field, one quadrant of the field, or coextensive with the RRF). Chung and co-workers (1970) have also subdivided class 4 cells, but in their study the pattern of spontaneous activity was used as the distinguishing characteristic. Maturana and associates also speak of a variety of class 3 fibers found at the interface of classes 2 and 3 which is characterized by sustained activity under room illumination and more prolonged bursts to moving edges. The authors' unpublished data show that some *on-off* cells have only *on* responses at low background intensities. There is no obvious end to this game.

If one assumes for the moment that class 1 and class 2 cells belong to a single category and that class 5 cells are rare or nonexistent, a simpler question can be asked: Are classes 1 or 2, 3, 4, and 6 mutually exclusive? That is: Can all fibers now be placed in one and only one category? Unfortunately, even this simple question cannot be unequivocally answered.

Only two studies even attempt to classify all cells encountered, by supplying both total numbers of recorded cells and the breakdown into classes. Both those studies involved recordings from the excised eyecup preparation where sampling of cells, although far from unbiased (e.g., the size of the electrode tip probably influences cell type selection), does not have the problem inherent in recording from the tectum where cell types vary with recording depth. Reuter and Vertanen were able to categorize 129 cells into 7 categories: class 1 (20), class 2 (24), class 1 or 2 (21), class 3 (39), class 4 (21), class 5 (2), and class 6 (2). Interestingly, Reuter (1969) reported that he could not reliably classify all the cells he studied into the Lettvin *et al.* classes. He suggested a number of factors that could influence classification: species (*Rana temporaria*); preparation (he used the eyecup); and recording (he recorded from cell bodies). It is just as likely that a major problem lies in aspects of the classification scheme or aspects of the stimulation used. When an eyecup is used, it is usual to project onto the retina spots of light whose intensity relative to background lights is much greater than is the case with natural contrasts. It would be surprising if this factor did not influence categorization.

For fibers recorded at the tectum, it is generally believed that classes 1 or 2, 3 and 4 are mutually exclusive, although not enough data exists to support this conclusion. Maturana and co-workers (1960) note that ". . . the borderline cases, found only in borderline regions between adjacent layers, suggest some kind of continuity between groups." In the case of class 1 or 2 cells, this borderline region appears large enough for us to question the existence of two classes. Is this also true of the other classes? No one reports quantitative data for *all* classes and for a number of stimulus dimensions, such that intra- and interclass variability can be assessed. The early studies (e.g., Grüsser-Cornehls *et al.*, 1963; Schipperheyn, 1965) that are taken as replications of the work of Lettvin and associates do not supply this information, or for that matter very much data at all. Over the last ten years Grüsser, Grüsser-Cornehls, and their coworkers have systematically varied contrast, object velocity, etc., and have collected an impressive amount of quantitative data from the various classes of ganglion cells (see Grüsser and Grüsser-Cornehls, 1973, p. 359, for a summary table). However, these functions and statistics for each cell type are not enough to resolve the fundamental question regarding mutually exclusive classes. Figure 8 illustrates the type of data that are necessary to answer this question. In this study, Grüsser *et al.* (1968a) have shown that although class 2 and class 3 cells both respond to a moving, dark spot, their responses differ quantitatively. More important, the variability within classes is small compared to between-class variability. (The curves would have been further separated had the same-sized spot been used, see legend, Fig. 8.) We would feel confident that mutually exclusive classes exist if these same cells grouped themselves on several other important (but not necessarily all) dimensions.

To summarize, it is possible to classify most ganglion cell fibers projecting to the tectum into three classes (1 or 2, 3, and 4) with relatively few stimuli [e.g., Grüsser and Grüsser-Cornehls (1970) claim four]. These classes have the characteristics just discussed, as first described by Lettvin *et al.* and later quantified by others, especially Grüsser, Grüsser-Cornehls, and colleagues. Although these categories appear to a first approximation to be mutually exclusive, more data such as those of Fig. 8 are needed. However, the answer to the question of mutually exclusive and exhaustive categories clearly depends upon the choice of stimuli. If any manipulation of the stimulus is allowed, it is likely that any two cells could be shown to differ in their responses to some stimulus. Any conclusion about the existence of distinct classes must be based on the assumption that a set of stimulus dimensions has been chosen that is reasonable in some sense and a belief that intraclass response variability is considerably less than interclass response variability. But how does one choose a "reasonable" set of stimulus dimensions? There is no clear answer to this question, which we will encounter again in the following discussion of feature detectors.

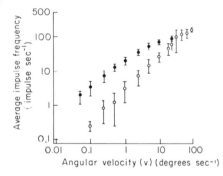

Angular velocity (v) (degrees sec⁻¹)

Fig. 8. Response (average impulse frequency) of 25 class 2 (filled in circles) and 30 class 3 (open circles) neurons to variations in one stimulus dimension (angular velocity of a moving, black spot). The black spot was 1.2° in diameter for class 2 neurons and 2.7° in diameter for class 3 neurons. Since the response of class 3 neurons is greater to a 2.7° spot than to a 1.2° spot, the separation between the data points for class 2 and class 3 would have been greater had a 1.2° spot been used for both. In addition, since all class 4 cells (as distinguished by their response to the offset of diffuse light or by their spontaneous rates) in this study do not respond at all to a dark 1.5° spot, then this class of cells is also distinguished by this stimulus dimension. (Modified from Grüsser *et al.*, 1968a.)

Feature Detectors

The work of Lettvin and co-workers on the frog together with that of Hubel and Wiesel (1959), who studied cat cortical neurons, has ushered in a "feature detector" era in the interpretation of both psychological and physiological studies of sensory processes. Basically, these experiments have been taken as evidence that neurons in the visual system are sensitive to very specific spatiotemporal patterns of light (the feature). For example, a cat cortical neuron may respond only to a line falling within a narrow range of widths, slanted within a particularly narrow range of orientations (a so-called orientation specific, line detector). Today, a feature detector is most commonly defined as a neuron, either real or hypothetical, that is *most* sensitive to a particular feature and is very insensitive (or does not respond) to all other features.

Although the Maturana *et al.* (1960) ganglion cell response classes are often referred to as one of the first evidences of detectors, labels given these classes do not fit comfortably within the definition of a feature just given.* Class 1 cells, or "edge detectors," do not respond best to edges, but to spots. In fact, only the labels of classes 3 and 4 come close to meeting the definition. Class 3 is said to be a "changing contrast detector" and class 4 a "dimming detector." These classes do indeed respond best to stimuli that have these features. But note that these are not very specific features. And, in fact, dimming is also a change in contrast. Furthermore, since class 1 and class 2 cells respond best to moving spots, all classes of cells respond *best* to changing contrast. Studies on the frog visual system, which have often been taken as evidence for the existence of feature detectors, can be used to illustrate some of the alternative definitions of a feature detector, as well as some of the more general problems with this approach.

Clearly, the "maximally excitable" definition of a feature detector just given cannot be applied to the classes of Maturana and associates. At times, these authors appear to imply this definition, such as when they say that the cells of each class ". . . respond maximally to one or another quality . . ." (Maturana *et al.*, 1960, p. 145). At other times, a somewhat different definition is implied. For example, they say these cells were described in terms of what ". . . common factors in a large variety of stimuli cause response and what common factors have no effect" (Lettvin *et al.*, 1959, p. 1951). However, this definition cannot be successfully applied to all the class names either. For example, why is a class 1 neuron an "edge detector" when it responds well, in fact best,

---

* The labels mentioned here are from Maturana *et al.* (1960). Those in the Lettvin *et al.* (1959) paper differ slightly.

to moving spots? It can be argued that more than one definition of a feature detector is implied in their class names. The "sustained edge detectors" do not respond "best" to a stationary edge, but they are the *only* cells that respond at all to such a stimulus. The implied definition is that an "X" detector is the only cell type among the various classes that responds to "X." In the case of class 2, there are cells that respond both to spots and changing contrast being called "convex edge detectors." From their discussion, it seems possible that the notion of feature detector used is one in which a cell must respond optimally to the feature and, in addition, have some special physiological mechanism for so responding. This is similar to the directionally sensitive movement detectors in the rabbit retina that are thought to have unidirectional inhibition (Barlow *et al.,* 1964). On the one hand, it is difficult to find one definition that will generate the Maturana *et al.* class names; on the other hand, alternative and reasonable definitions of a feature detector appear to be present.

So far, only one-half of what is usually meant by the term, feature detector has been discussed. This aspect can be considered as an answer to the question, "How do the various stimuli affect the cell's activity?" Giving feature names to cell types (even when names are generated with a single definition) is misleading since cells are never uniquely sensitive to one stimulus dimension (or feature) and, furthermore, a single feature is not likely to excite only one cell type. An even greater confusion results when the second half of what is usually meant by the term, feature detector, is considered. This second aspect can be considered as an answer to the question, "What does the feature detector's firing (activity) mean to the organism?" For example, a line detector neuron may be uniquely sensitive to a line of particular length and width (answer to the first question); and when this cell fires, the organism "perceives" a line of that particular length and width (answer to the second question). An example from a physiological model of color vision illustrates that the answers to these questions do not have to be the same. In a physiological version (De Valois *et al.,* 1966) of an opponent model of color vision (Hurvich and Jameson, 1957) the "Green +, Red —" cell is so named, not because a monochromatic light that appears pure green to a human observer maximally excites this cell (it doesn't; a yellowish-green appearing light gets a stronger response), but because the theory predicts that the sensation of green*ness* is related to this cell's firing rate. Consequently, this cell, based on the answer to the first question, could be called a 540 nm cell (since it is maximally sensitive to a 540 nm light), a short wavelength light cell (since it is excited by monochromatic lights of wavelengths less than about 600 nm), or based on the answer to the second question, a "green cell" (since the theory predicts its firing results in the sensation of green). It would certainly be less confusing if cells were not named. Instead their responses to various stimulus dimensions can be described, and the assumed or hypothesized answers to the second question stated.

Another general point to be made is that even if a feature-detector approach with distinct cell types is adopted, the code for any stimulus dimension will undoubtedly exist in the pattern of activity across cell types and not within any one cell type.* For the wavelength of light (the stimulus dimension), the physiological code appears to be represented in the pattern of firing across a number of distinct cell types. The wavelength of the light stimulus cannot be determined by knowing the firing of any one cell type. Likewise, the behavioral consequence, or sensation, will result from a pattern of activity. To predict the color sensation of a light stimulus, we must know this pattern of activity. To know whether a light that excites a Green +, Red — cell appears as pure green to the organism, or as green-yellow, or blue-green, the firing of the Blue +, Yellow — cell must be considered. That is, the pattern of activity across the several cell types must be known. However, one must be careful about adopting color vision as a general model. It is *not* a necessary consequence of a feature detector approach that an X detector when fired always adds a given sensation. In the case of color sensation, the model predicts that the firing of a Red +, Green — cell will always add a "red" sensation. This works for color vision presumably due to the "existence" of four basic hue sensations.

For the frog, when Lettvin and associates address the second question of what the fiber types measure, they say: "We have considered it to be how much there is in a stimulus of that quality which excites the fiber maximally, naming that quality." So, the dimming detector ". . . tells us how much dimming occurs in the largest area . . ." (Lettvin *et al.*, 1959, p. 1949). But, again, just considering class 1 cells, a problem with this definition becomes evident. A small dark, convex, moving spot *highly* excites a class 1, sustained edge detector. It this cell really telling of the presence of a stationary, sharp boundary? Probably not. But this is obviously a more difficult definition to test—usually necessitating a model and behavioral tests.

The question has been raised as to how one chooses a set of stimuli for cell classification. One argument that has been made for choosing some set of stimuli and, in fact, feature names is that they represent important features in the animal's natural environment. For example, the class 2 cells have been called "bug perceivers," since they respond so well to

---

* For a general discussion of pattern codes and their appearance in other sensory modalities, see Uttal (1973).

buglike stimuli. However, according to Barlow (1953) ". . . it is difficult to avoid the conclusion that the [frog] 'on-off' units . . . act as 'fly detectors'." That is, the class 3 cells were "bug detectors." From their physiological recordings, Grüsser and Grüsser-Cornehls (1970) conclude that none of the behaviorally important stimuli for the frog (e.g., worm, fly, dark hiding place) excite only a single cell type, but rather each natural stimulus excites a number of cell types with the result that the relative activity patterns across cells are different.

In conclusion, it appears that it is reasonable to ask how cells group themselves into classes based on their responses to a wide range of stimuli. However, assignment of feature names and the accompanying implicit assumptions about the cells' excitability on one hand, and what the activity of one cell means to the animal on the other, is, at best, misleading. Instead, a more reasonable approach involves a description of the code within and across cells for various stimulus dimensions, such as Grüsser, Grüsser-Cornehls and colleagues have done for both "biologically natural" stimuli and for moving stimuli, in general. This could then be followed with a testable model that makes explicit the relationship between the firing of the cell types and behavior.

Analysis of Receptive Fields

Adrian and Matthews (1927a,b) inferred that individual ganglion cells in the Conger eel must receive input from a large area of the retina. Hartline (1938, 1940a,b), who demonstrated this to be true also for single, frog ganglion cells, defined the receptive field as ". . . the region of the retina which must be illuminated in order to obtain a response in any given fiber" (Hartline, 1938, p. 410). Hartline later (1941–1942) anatomically defined the receptive field as "The retinal region occupied by visual sense cells whose connections converge upon a given retinal ganglion cell . . ." and included in his physiological definition, inhibitory as well as excitatory influences: "Not only do excitatory influences converge upon each ganglion cell from different parts of its receptive field, but . . . inhibitory influences converge as well." In addition, he described some of the characteristics of ganglion cell receptive fields. He noted that, although the receptive field was fixed in location, its size depended upon the state of adaptation of the eye as well as upon the intensity and size of the test stimulus (a point often missed by current researchers). Figure 9 shows his measurements of the receptive field of a single optic nerve fiber. The contours represent loci of equal sensitivity. Note that there is a region of highest sensitivity and that sensitivity decreases rapidly on all sides away from this area.

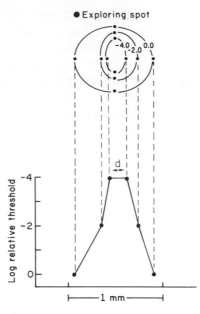

Fig. 9. Upper panel: Receptive field map of a single ganglion cell. The contours of equal sensitivity were determined by moving the exploring spot (50 μm diameter) which was set at one of the three log relative intensities shown. The data points indicate the places in the receptive field where this spot would just elicit a discharge of impulses. (From Hartline, 1940a.)

Lower panel: Receptive field profile. Hartline's data are replotted in terms of log threshold intensity as a function of distance across receptive field.

The nature of the receptive field of frog ganglion cells offered a possible mechanism for the psychophysical phenomenon of areal summation. Human psychophysical experiments (cf. Graham and Bartlett, 1939; Graham *et al.*, 1939) had shown that larger stimuli could be detected at lower intensities than could smaller stimuli and that, in fact, detection depended upon total energy (area $\times$ intensity) for all areas up to some critical size. Indeed, Hartline (1940b) demonstrated that areal summation did, in fact, take place at the level of the ganglion cell.

Interestingly, Barlow (1953) demonstrated that the connection between receptive field sensitivity and areal summation was not simple. He noted that complete areal summation took place over wider regions than the plateau of equal sensitivity in the receptive field. That is, even for spots greater than diameter d, in Fig. 9, equal energies produced a constant response of one action potential. Why should complete areal summation extend into regions of lower sensitivity? One explanation he offered assumed that ". . . the effects contributed to the ganglion cell are not strictly proportional to intensity of light but to the 0.83 power of intensity." In other words, areal summation extended beyond the plateau of equal sensitivity because local decreases in sensitivity with distance were offset by the relative gain due to decreased intensity. This assumption of a local nonlinearity of the response to light is consistent with recent retinal recordings (Easter, 1968; Burkhardt and Berntson, 1972; Graham and Ratliff, 1974; Lovino and Abramov, 1075).

In the early 1950s, the importance of opposing excitatory and inhibitory influences in an understanding of retinal receptive fields was demonstrated by Barlow (1953) in the frog and Kuffler (1953) in the cat. In particular, Barlow's arguments for an inhibitory region surrounding the excitatory receptive field of frog *on-off* cells were based on two experiments. First, stimulus spots larger than the measured receptive field elicited smaller responses at both stimulus on and stimulus off than did small spots. Second, when a spot placed outside the receptive field was flashed simultaneously with one placed inside, the total response produced was smaller than when the center spot was flashed alone. Unlike the cat ganglion cells studied by Kuffler, these cells did not respond to stimulation of their antagonistic surround. Stimulation of these surrounding regions only served to decrease activity simultaneously elicited by center stimulation.

Subsequent research has confirmed the inhibitory surround regions for cells of classes 1 and 2 in the frog. The presence of inhibitory surrounds in classes 1 and 2 cells can be inferred from the observation that large moving, black objects elicit a smaller response than do small moving, black objects. This is particularly marked in the class 2 cells for which a straight edge, wider than 2°, will not elicit a response. Since these cells responded to the corner of large objects, Maturana *et al.* (1960) argued that convexity or curvature was the important stimulus aspect that elicited the response. Gaze and Jacobson (1963b), however, showed that the absence of a response to large objects was due to stimulation of a strong, inhibitory surround and not necessarily to a lack of convexity. In fact, these cells responded to straight edges if the surround was shielded from stimulation. The presence of inhibitory surrounds in class 1 and 2 cells has been demonstrated directly by a decrease in activity due to dark objects presented to the surround region (Gaze and Jacobson, 1963b; Grüsser-Cornehls, *et al.*, 1963; Pickering and Varju, 1967; Keating and Gaze, 1970a). For example, Keating and Gaze (1970a) showed that a moving 25° edge in the surround strongly inhibited the class 1 and 2 responses to a standing edge. This peripheral stimulus (one that did not elicit a response of its own) could be as much as 45° away from the excitatory field.

Is the Frog That Different from Other Vertebrates?

In the early 1960s, following the work of Lettvin *et al.*, it was clear that the frog ganglion cell types were far more complex than mammalian ganglion cell types, and particularly in comparison with the most frequently studied mammal, the domestic cat. The cat appeared to have only two classes of ganglion cell (*on* center–*off* surround and *off* center–*on* surround) and the frog five or six. The demonstration (Dowling, 1968; Dubin, 1970) of greater anatomical complexity of frog amacrine-ganglion cell connections supplied a structural basis for this greater physiological complexity. However, while the cat described in 1960 was simple, the cat of the 1970s appears to be far more complex. The evidence is now overwhelming that each of the two classic ganglion cell types can be further divided into two categories called X and Y cells (cf. Enroth-Cugell and Robson, 1966). There is also growing evidence for the existence of an additional, large group of ganglion cells, referred to by Stone and Hoffman (1972) as W-cells. This group does not have the traditional center-surround organization and can be subdivided based on whether the cell's activity is suppressed or increased by light or dark objects in the visual field. Thus, even if one discounts the various reports of aberrant cell types and the recent report of a subdivision of all X and Y cells into "brisk" and "sluggish" (Cleland and Levick, 1974), by conservative estimate, there are 6 cell types. In addition, anatomic complexities have been seen in the cat inner plexiform layer that are similar to those seen in the frog (Kolb and Famiglietti, 1974). That differences exist between the responses of cat and frog ganglion cells is clear. The extent and nature of these differences and, for that matter, the comparative complexities, are far from clear.

Coding of Chromatic Information

There is good behavioral evidence that the frog can discriminate between lights that differ in wavelength regardless of intensity differences (Birukow, 1939; Muntz, 1962b; Chapman, 1966). For the visual system to discriminate between lights of different wavelength, it may either (1) have two or more photoreceptors with absorption maxima in different spectral locations, or (2) a single receptor must respond differently to quanta of different wavelengths. According to the principle of univariance, the latter mechanism is incorrect. This principle states that once a quantum is absorbed it produces the same effect on a photoreceptor regardless of wavelength (Naka and Rushton, 1966). There is ample support for the principle of univariance from intracellular and extra-cellular recordings from frog rods and cones (Toyoda *et al.*, 1970; Hood *et al.*, 1973), as well as from other photoreceptors. It has been demonstrated quite clearly that all changes in receptor response resulting from a change in the wavelength of the stimulus are due to a change in the probability of absorption and thus can be compensated for merely by changing the stimulus intensity. It is, if course, well-known that the scotopic or rod system in humans, with just one photopigment, cannot discriminate between different wavelengths. Thus, there must be photoreceptors in the frog with different spectral characteristics and, in fact, there is direct evidence that this is so.

As previously discussed, there are two types of rods, two types of cones, and at least three different photopigments in the frog retina. In recent years, a number of electrophysiological techniques have been developed which have allowed investigators to study the actual responses of the photoreceptors. As indicated in Fig. 10, there is excellent agreement between spectral sensitivities measured electrophysiologically and absorption spectra of the photopigments themselves. There are no direct measurements of the responses of the 432 (green) rods or the accessory cones. However, Donner and Reuter (1962) have used chromatic adaptation to isolate the 432 rod input to retinal ganglion cells, and the resulting spectral sensitivity agrees well with photopigment measurements (Fig. 10C).

Chromatic Coding at the Ganglion Cell

There is now substantial evidence which indicates that the ganglion cells in the frog retina receive inputs from at least two different receptor types (Granit, 1942; Donner, 1958, 1959; Donner and Rushton, 1959a,b; Chapman, 1961; Reuter, 1969). The input from a specific receptor type may be excitatory, inhibitory, or both (Reuter and Virtanen, 1972). There is also some evidence that a few cells of the inner nuclear layer—most probably horizontal cells—are connected to receptors which differ in their spectral sensitivities in such a way that short wavelength light changes the polarity of the cell's response in a direction opposite to that of long wavelength light (Naka *et al.*, 1960). This type of cell, called the C-type (chromatic) in other vertebrates, demonstrates the potential for wavelength discrimination within a single cell at a very early stage in the visual system. However, the majority of the horizontal cells of frogs respond with a hyperpolarization to all wavelengths of light and consequently cannot by themselves be used for wavelength discrimination (Naka *et al.*, 1960; Tomita *et al.*, 1961; Tomita, 1963).

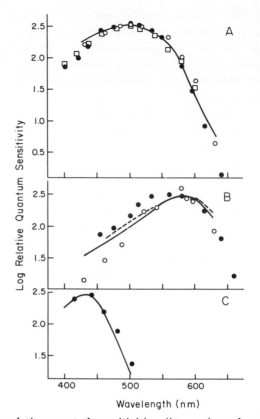

Fig. 10. Log relative spectral sensitivities (i.e., reciprocal number of quanta required to achieve a criterion response) of frog receptors and ganglion cells.

(A) Dark-adapted (scotopic) spectral sensitivities. Open circles, dark-adapted, aspartate-treated, isolated retina. (From Hood and Mansfield, 1972.) Filled circles; intracellularly recorded rod response. (From Toyoda et al., 1970.) Open squares; dark adapted ganglion cells. (From Reuter, 1969.) The continuous curve is an absorption spectrum for a Dartnall nomogram pigment with a λ max at 502 nm adjusted for an optical density of 0.75.

(B) Light-adapted (photopic) spectral sensitivities. Open circles; aspartate-treated, isolated retina. Sensitivity determined for 580 cone by finding the intensity of a steady monochromatic background required to decrease the response to a 630 nm test flash by a criterion amount. (From Hood and Hock, 1973.) Filled circles; average sensitivities of two light adapted on-off ganglion cells determined in the presence of a 577 nm or a 553 nm background. (From Reuter, 1969.) This function is virtually identical to Granit's photopic dominator. Dashed line; relative absorption of the frog's 580 cone pigment measured by microspectrophotometry. (Liebman and Entine, 1968.) Continuous line; estimate of the 580 cone's absorption function based on the ERP and determined by taking the difference between ERP spectral sensitivity functions obtained with and without an intense red background. (From Hood and Mansfield, 1972; data from Goldstein, 1968.)

DOMINATORS AND MODULATORS. Based on his studies of the frog and other vertebrate retinas, Granit divided ganglion cells into two categories based upon their spectral sensitivities (see Granit, 1947). The "dominators" have a broad-band spectral sensitivity function which is determined by cones in the light-adapted state and by rods in the dark-adapted state. The "modulators" have narrow-band, spectral sensitivity functions and thus respond well to only a restricted region of the spectrum. Granit categorized modulators into several groups depending upon whether their peak sensitivity occurred in the short, middle, or long wavelengths.

The model of the visual system which Granit suggested based on his electrophysiological recordings is one in which there are two channels, one for brightness and one for chromaticity. [This is a model that many psychophysicists (Hurvich and Jameson, 1957) and electrophysiologists (De Valois, 1965) consider correct at the present time.] Because dominator sensitivities resembled the photopic luminosity function, Granit theorized that the function of the cells which respond well over a wide range of wavelengths was to encode the intensity of a visual stimulus. Their activity was thus taken as a neural representation of brightness. The function of the modulators, cells which respond to a restricted band of wavelengths, was to encode the wavelength properties of a stimulus.

The modulators were taken as the first clear electrophysiological analogs to the specific nerve fibers of the Young-Helmholtz theory of color vision. The relative activity across modulators was believed to be the neural representation of the perception of hue. Granit, of course, noted that modulators (which comprised the chromaticity channel) also respond well to changes in intensity. Interestingly, there is psychophysical evidence that some brightness information is carried within the chromatic channels (Boynton, 1973).

DOMINATOR-RECEPTOR INPUTS. The dark-adapted or scotopic dominator has a peak sensitivity around 500 nm and its spectral sensitivity is similar to a rhodopsin photopigment absorption function (Fig. 10A). Thus, the receptor input to the scotopic dominator appears to be the 502 rods. Donner (1958) found that the fully dark-adapted scotopic dominator had a broader sensitivity function than did a somewhat less completely

---

(C) Spectral sensitivity of single ganglion cells determined in the presence of a 582 nm adapting field chosen to selectively adapt the 502 rods and the cones, but leave the 432 rods relatively unaffected. Filled circles; ganglion cell sensitivity. Continuous line; Dartnall nomogram for a pigment with a peak sensitivity at 435 nm. (From Donner and Reuter, 1962.)

dark-adapted scotopic dominator. More complete dark adaptation allowed more photopigment to regenerate so that the concentration of photopigment was increased. Since a more concentrated photopigment has a higher optical density and, therefore, a broader action spectrum, complete dark adaptation can serve to somewhat broaden a spectral sensitivity function (see Dartnall, 1962).

The spectral sensitivity of the photopic dominator is a broad, smooth function peaking at about 560 nm (Fig. 10B). Coincidentally, it is deceptively well fit by the photopigment, iodopsin (chicken-cone photopigment), although it may be slightly narrower (Donner, 1958; Wald, 1959; Chapman, 1961). The question is whether the dominator has one or more receptor inputs. Donner and Rushton (1959a) and Scheibner and Baumann (1970) found that the spectral sensitivity of the photopic dominator measured using the silent substitution method (adjusting the intensity of two alternating wavelengths of light so as to produce no response) was the same as that produced by single-flash techniques. This has been taken to imply, although not prove, the existence of a single spectral mechanism. Donner and Rushton (1959b) utilized the Stiles-Crawford directional sensitivity of the cones to demonstrate that the photopic dominator, in fact, receives only cone input. However, Granit (1947) often noticed a slight dip in the photopic dominator at about 570 nm and also noticed that strong light adaptation shifted the peak sensitivity to 570 nm (Granit, 1942). He suggested that the dominator might be made up of two inputs. Furthermore, the frog retina does not appear to have a photopigment with a 560 nm peak (Liebman and Entine, 1968; see previous photopigment section); the cone photopigments peak at 580 nm and 502 nm. Reuter (1969) attempted to sum the 502 cone and the 580 cone by using linear combinations, but was unable to produce a photopic dominator. Thus, he concluded that there must be some nonlinear transformation taking place before the two cone inputs summate to produce the photopic dominator. Donner (1959) used chromatic adaptation on the photopic dominator and found that intense, short wavelength adaptation selectively depressed the short wavelength side of the spectral sensitivity function and shifted the peak sensitivity to about 580 nm. He also found that long wavelength adaptation simply depressed the entire spectral sensitivity function no matter how intense the adapting light; and peak sensitivity was not shifted. He further concluded that there were two inputs to the photopic dominator—one that peaked at 580 nm (the long wavelength cone λ_{max}) and a second that peaked at a shorter wavelength.

It is interesting to note that long wavelength adaptation does *not* isolate the short wavelength cone input. Perhaps the short wavelength cone (accessory member of double cone) may simply be more susceptible to adaptation than is the long wavelength cone. Alternatively, it is possible that adaptation of the long wavelength cone also adapts the short wavelength cone, but this adaptation may not work, or at least not as strongly, in the reverse direction.

In primates and goldfish, spectrally different receptors may sum to produce a mechanism that cannot be easily adapted chromatically and, thus, may give the appearance of a single element as does the frog photopic dominator. The receptors in this case, may have summed their inputs distal to the mechanism producing the adaptation and are, therefore, equally affected by adaptation regardless of wavelength (Abramov, 1972; Sirovich et al., 1973). After the receptors have summed to produce a spectral mechanism, different spectral mechanisms may sum to produce, for example, opponent cells (see following section). In this case, adaptation of one mechanism has relatively little effect on the other mechanisms, and they can be easily separated by chromatic adaptation.

MODULATORS-RECEPTOR INPUT. Granit (1942) described three modulators, each with a different spectral locus of peak sensitivity. The short wavelength (or blue) modulator with a peak occurring around 460 nm has been confirmed in many subsequent studies (Donner and Rushton, 1959b; Chapman, 1961; Muntz, 1962a; Reuter, 1969). The frog retina contains no photopigment with a peak at 460 nm (the short wavelength rods peak at 432 nm), but since the short wavelength modulator does not show a directional sensitivity (Stiles-Crawford effect) the short wavelength modulator probably represents a purely rod effect (Donner and Rushton, 1959b) consisting of predominant input from the 432 rods and a small contribution from the 502 rods. Reuter (1969), however, suggests that the secondary, long wavelength peak sometimes seen in the short wavelength modulator (Granit, 1942; Muntz, 1962a) indicates that an excitatory cone input may partially account for a peak at 460 nm rather than at 432 nm. Selective chromatic adaptation can isolate the 432 rod input to these cells (Fig. 10C).

The other two modulators (peak sensitivities at 520–540 nm and 580–600 nm) described by Granit (1942) have not been found consistently by subsequent investigators (Donner and Rushton, 1959a,b; Chapman, 1961; Reuter, 1969), although such studies have reported ganglion cells with several peaks in their spectral sensitivity functions in which one or more of the peaks occurred in the region of Granit's modulator peaks. Donner and Rushton (1959b) showed such results for partially dark-adapted ganglion cells in which a peak sensitivity at 520–540 nm resulted from a summation of the 502 rods and the cones (by using the Stiles-Crawford directional sensitivity of the cones to demonstrate the presence of both inputs).

The 580 modulator may be the result of an input from the 580 cones in which the photopigment has a narrower absorption spectrum than that predicted by the Dartnall (1962) nomogram. Finally, Granit occasionally observed a long wavelength modulator with a peak sensitivity at 600 nm. Chapman (1961) also observed a secondary peak at 600 nm or beyond in some of his units. It is possible that this 600 nm modulator resulted from an interaction between the 580 cones and the 502 rods, or the accessory cones. Another interesting possibility is suggested by the experiments of Reuter and co-workers (1971) in which parts of the adult bullfrog (*Rana catesbeiana*) retina have been shown to contain the vitamin A2 rod pigment porphyropsin (λ_{max} = 532 nm) rather than the A1 pigment rhodopsin (λ_{max} = 502 nm). Since these experiments also demonstrated that the pigment epithelium behind the retina ultimately determines whether the rod photopigments will be A1- or A2-based, it is likely that the cone pigments in porphyropsin areas will also be A2-based and thus be shifted to longer wavelengths. Reuter (1969) has shown that tadpole retinas (which in early stages are A2) have retinal ganglion cells with spectral sensitivities at 600 nm. Thus, the long wavelength sensitivities reported by Granit (1942) and by Chapman (1961) may be due to the fact that they were obtained from the retinas of *Rana esculenta* (European water frog) and *Rana catesbeiana* (American bullfrog) and may thus constitute species differences.

To summarize, it is likely that the middle wavelength modulators are, in fact, dominators in an intermediate state of adaptation in which the 502 rods are also contributing to the response. The long wavelength modulator reflects a primary input from the 580 cone and the short wavelength modulator is based primarily on an input from the 432 rods. Results will now be considered which indicate that these 432 rods are, in fact, extremely important for color vision in frogs.

BLUE SENSITIVITY. Muntz (1962a) recorded from the optic nerve terminals in the frog thalamus and found that almost all of these fibers responded like the retinal *on* units of Hartline (1938). He measured the spectral sensitivity of these *on* fibers and found them to be most sensitive to short wavelengths. Previous studies which involved recording from the optic nerve terminals in the tectum (which receives the majority of optic nerve fibers) had failed to find these "on" cells (Maturana et al., 1960). Thus, it appears that different types of optic nerve fibers project to different regions of the brain—a finding that has now been extended to the ground squirrel (Michael, 1970) and cat (Hoffman, 1973). Evidence will be presented later which implicates these cells in the preference that frogs have for blue light.

Subsequent studies have revealed that the primary receptor input to these *on* units is the 432 rods, but there is also an input from 502 rods (Donner and Rushton, 1959b), and probably cones as well (Reuter, 1969). The interaction of these inputs is *not* simple. There is an excitatory long wavelength input as indicated by both a peak sensitivity at 460 nm, rather than 432 nm (where the 432 rods are maximally sensitive), and a secondary peak sometimes seen at long wavelengths (Muntz, 1962a). There is an inhibitory, long wavelength input indicated by the decrease in response produced by the addition of long wavelength light. The responses to short and long wavelength light in these units are also qualitatively different. Short wavelengths elicit long sustained responses, while long wavelengths elicit very short, transient responses. These differences could be used by the frog for wavelength discrimination (Donner, 1950; Liberman, 1957; Reuter, 1969).

Muntz (1962b) and Chapman (1966) have done some behavioral experiments with *Rana pipiens* and *Rana catesbeiana* which relate very nicely to the electrophysiological findings. If a frog is forced to jump, it will "prefer" to jump toward blue rather than green, or other long wavelength light. This response is *not* based upon an intensity preference, but upon a wavelength preference. Frogs will choose a more intense blue light over a less intense blue light. Yet, when green light is added to a blue field (which makes it more intense), the frog will still choose the field containing only blue light, even though it is less intense. These results are quite similar to the responses of the blue-sensitive ganglion cells and demonstrate that the frog can actually discriminate between wavelengths.

Kicliter (1973a) surgically removed the frog's anterior thalamus and demonstrated behaviorally that the blue preference was lost. Thus, the projection of the short wavelength *on* cells to the thalamus appears to play a major role in the frogs' preference for blue light (see Chapter 3).

OPPONENT COLOR CELLS. The blue sensitive *on* cells previously described are not the only cells which give qualitatively different responses to different wavelengths. In fact, 80% or more of the frog retinal ganglion cells may have antagonistic, or opponent, spectral inputs (Reuter, 1969; Reuter and Virtanen, 1972) with qualitatively different responses to different wavelengths. In some species, such as monkey (De Valois, 1965) and goldfish (Wagner *et al.*, 1960), the cells have a spontaneous or maintained discharge in the absence of stimulation which makes the opponent nature of these cells immediately apparent; they are inhibited by light from one spectral region and excited by lights from another. In most frog retinal ganglion cells, there is no spontaneous activity and opponent characteristics are thus more difficult to demonstrate.

Reuter (1969) has divided the frog *on-off* cells into two types—chromatic and nonchromatic. In the nonchromatic type, both the *on-* and *off*-responses are controlled by the cones; these are the dominator cells. In the chromatic cells, the 432 rods constitute the major input which produces the *on* responses, while cones produce the *off* response. Thus, in these cells, short wavelength lights are primarily excitatory and long wavelength lights are primarily inhibitory in their effects. Note that in these experiments either a yellow or red background was used to suppress the 502 rod input by means of selective adaptation. A second type of chromatic cell has an excitatory or *on* component resulting from inputs from both the 432 rods and the 580 cones, but an *off* component originating only from the 580 cones. In the nonchromatic cells, selective chromatic adaptation has little effect on the shape of the spectral sensitivity function, but, in the chromatic cells, the two inputs are easily separated by this kind of adaptation. The *on* and *off* responses of the chromatic cells are mutually inhibitory, which makes it difficult to measure the sensitivity of one component in the spectral regions where the other is more sensitive. This kind of mutual antagonism has been observed in many species (e.g., in the goldfish spectrally opponent cells and in cat spatially opponent cells). The total spatial extent of the 432 rod and the 580 cone inputs is *not* the same—the input from the 432 rods originates from a larger area than does the 580 cone input so that the 432 rod input predominates in the outer edges of the receptive field and the 580 cone input (when there is no yellow adaptation to suppress them) predominates in the center of the field (Reuter and Virtanen, 1972). Furthermore, the receptive fields of the *on-off* cells in the frog are surrounded by a "silent" inhibitory surround which may also be spectrally opponent (Reuter and Virtanen, 1972).

These spectrally opponent cells, which are excitatory to short wavelengths, inhibitory to long wavelengths, and basically neutral at some point in the middle of the spectrum, provide a possible physiological basis for discriminating one part of the spectrum from the other, and there is at least one behavioral experiment that supports this idea. Birukow (1939) placed frogs in a rotating drum of alternating gray and colored stripes. When the colored stripes were green, a gray could be found which would match them sufficiently so that the frog did not display any optomotor response. However, for all of the intensities of gray used, there was always an optomotor response for the blue or red stripes. Reuter (1969) has suggested that the chromatic *on-off* cells would respond in just this way if the green Birukow used fell near the neutral point for these cells, and therefore they might provide the physiological basis for Birukow's finding.

Light Adaptation

Light adaptation refers to adjustments in absolute sensitivity occurring in the visual system as ambient intensities are varied. These adjustments enable the organism to detect naturally occurring contrasts (which rarely produce intensity differences of more than a factor of about 20) over a range of naturally occurring ambient intensities that exceed 10^8.

Increment-Threshold Functions

Vertebrates have evolved two physiological systems to cover this enormous range of ambient intensities: the rod system, which operates at lower light levels, and the cone system, which operates at higher light levels. Thus, one aspect of light adaptation relates to the presence of two systems with different receptor types. A second aspect concerns the decrease in absolute sensitivity seen for both systems as ambient light level is increased. The increment-threshold function provides a quantitative description of both these aspects of light adaptation and relates the test-light intensity required to elicit a constant response to the intensity of the ambient (or background) light upon which the test light is superimposed. The constant (or criterion) response can be defined psychophysically as a constant probability of detection or electrophysiologically as a given value of some aspect of the response such as its latency or magnitude.

Figure 11 (righthand panel) shows increment-threshold functions measured by Donner (1959) for a frog ganglion cell. Threshold for the ganglion cell is defined here as the test light intensity necessary to produce one spike.

Rod and cone portions of these functions are clearly visible. For low ambient light intensities (adapting field), the rod system controls the ganglion cell response, as can be seen by the agreement between the cell's relative sensitivity to monochromatic lights and the relative probability of absorption of the rod pigment (Fig. 11, left panel). At high ambient intensities, the relative sensitivity to monochromatic light has changed and now the cone system has taken control. Note that for both rod and cone systems, as the background intensity is increased above some level, the increment-flash intensity required to elicit a single ganglion cell action potential also increases. This is a feature common to all increment-threshold functions, including those that have been determined for human observers, as well as for single cells and gross potentials recorded from verte-

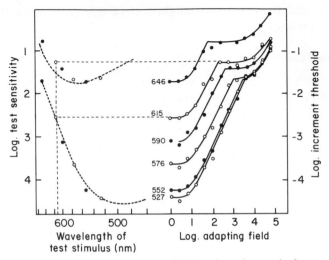

Fig. 11. Right panel: Increment-threshold functions for a single ganglion cell. The background was 464 nm light and the test flash wavelength was varied.

Left panel: Spectral sensitivities are shown for dark-adapted condition and for the plateau seen at higher background intensities. The lower interrupted curve is Dartnall's nomogram curve for rhodopsin, the upper interrupted curve is Granit's photopic dominator for the frog. (Modified from Donner, 1959.)

brate and invertebrate visual systems. Thus, the two aspects of light adaptation just mentioned can be seen in this figure and will be dealt with separately below.

Mechanisms of Sensitivity Loss

The mechanism(s) responsible for the sensitivity changes of rod and cone systems (which are seen at the level of the frog ganglion cell) are not yet completely understood. One approach has been to investigate the retinal locus of these changes. For example, changes similar to those seen in Fig. 1 have been recently observed for several species at the receptor level. For the frog, Frank (1971) and Hood and Hock (1972, 1975) have supplied evidence of sensitivity changes in the frog's rod and cone receptors. Figure 12a from Hook and Hock shows receptor data obtained under one set of conditions. To obtain complete functions for each receptor type separately, special procedures must be employed. Using background lights of different wavelengths and a procedure analogous to Stiles' (1959), increment-threshold functions for the frog's 502 rods and 580 cones were obtained and these functions are presented in Fig. 12b. It is clear that the location and shape of these functions depend upon both receptor type and exposure duration, and these receptor increment-threshold functions show many of the same general characteristics as do other increment-

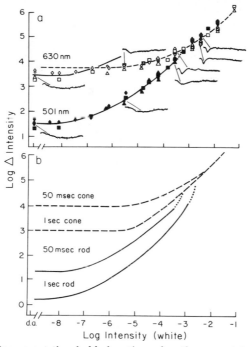

Fig. 12 (a). Increment-threshold functions for the aspartate-isolated receptor potential. The test flash was 50 msec and either 501 or 630 nm light. The sample records are of threshold responses (10 μV) and the entire trace represents 2 sec. The smooth curves are rod and cone increment-threshold functions for 50 msec test flashes (see Fig. 12b). The rod curve (solid) is drawn through both 630 and 501 nm data points. The cone curve (dashed) is drawn through the 630 nm data points. (From Hood and Hock, 1975.)

(b) Increment-threshold curves for 502 rod and 580 cone receptors and for two test flash durations. The curves are positioned vertically for a test light of 501 nm. (From Hood and Hock, 1975.)

threshold functions. The effect of exposure duration is most marked on the cone functions, where a change in the cone receptor's ability to sum the effects of light (see also Hood and Grover, 1974) results in curves that coincide at high background intensities, but not at low background intensities.

Of course, simply because receptors show characteristics similar to those of some more proximal stage in the visual system does not necessarily mean the receptor is the site of all, or even most, of the sensitivity changes. One way to assess receptor involvement is to compare receptor data quantitatively to data obtained from higher-order cells. A direct comparison between receptor and ganglion cell sensitivity losses in the frog retina was made by Fusco and Hood (1974, 1976). They measured increment-threshold functions under identical conditions with test and

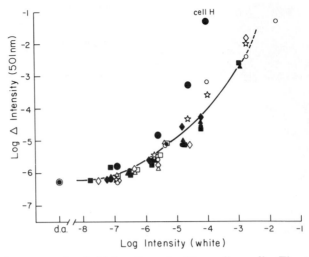

Fig. 13. Increment-threshold functions for 10 ganglion cells. The test flash was a 1 sec, 501 nm light. To adjust for differences in sensitivity, the data from individual cells were shifted vertically to coincide at the dark-adapted condition. The solid curve is the rod receptor increment-threshold function (see Fig. 12b). (From Fusco and Hood, 1974, 1976.)

background lights both covering the entire retina. The data from ganglion cells are shown in Fig. 13, along with the increment-threshold curve for the rod receptors. Although different ganglion cells had different absolute sensitivities, the data from all but one cell (cell H) fall along the receptor increment-threshold curve. Note that the PNR (Gordon and Graham, 1975) and b-wave (D. C. Hood and P. A. Hock, unpublished) increment-threshold curves are also virtually identical to the rod receptor curve.* The ganglion cell data are consistent with a model of steady-state adaptation in which the receptor sets the sensitivity observed in most of the cells. It should be carefully noted that this conclusion holds only (1) for most ganglion cells (cell H suggests that further sensitivity losses do occur between the receptors and some ganglion cells), (2) for cells of classes 3, 4, and 6 (i.e., those cells that respond to full-field test lights used in this study), and (3), for the conditions of this study, stimulation with full-field test and adapting lights. Even with such qualifications, these data appear to contradict some specific frog retinal studies, as well as some more generally held conclusions about vertebrate rod systems. The contradiction to the frog work is more apparent than real, however, since

* Recent evidence indicates that the increment-threshold curves for the cone controlled ganglion response do not agree with the cone receptor curve (Hock, 1975; Hock et al., 1975).

the previous frog studies were not done under steady-state light conditions (Burkhardt and Berntson, 1972), or involved spatially nonoverlapping test and adapting lights (Lipetz, 1961). However, these data are more seriously at odds with evidence from human psychophysics (cf. Barlow, 1957; Rushton, 1965), cat ganglion cell recordings (Enroth-Cugell and Shapley, 1973), and skate receptor and ganglion cell recordings (Green et al., 1975) which indicate that losses in sensitivity occur at background intensities lower than those that desensitize the receptors.

Enroth-Cugell and Shapley (1973) proposed a model based on cat ganglion cell data that places sensitivity losses beyond the receptor. In fact, this model predicts an increment-threshold function for each cell that is similar in form, but is displaced horizontally, based on the cell's sensitivity. Fusco and Hood (1974, 1976) have shown that this model clearly does not describe their frog ganglion cell data. A model that may be consistant with all the data puts the sensitivity losses at the receptor level for relatively insensitive ganglion cells and more proximally for all ganglion cells more sensitive than some given level. This level may depend upon species being studied. In favor of this view are the observations that cell H was the most sensitive studied and, furthermore, that the least sensitive cells in the Enroth-Cuggell and Shapley study all showed similar increment-threshold functions, possibly that of the receptors.

A number of other explanations have been offered to account for the loss in sensitivity occurring in the presence of background lights. One model places this loss at the receptors and has been made explicit by Boynton and Whitten (1970). Such a model makes two assumptions. First, it is assumed that the receptor response reaches a maximum soon after any light is turned on and stays at that maximum as long as the light remains on (i.e., there is no "accommodation adaptation"), except at high light levels when substantial pigment bleaching occurs. At these higher light levels, the decrement in the background response is due solely to the change in the probability of quantal absorption. Second, the nonlinear function that described the response to test lights in the dark can now be used to account for the response to a test light superimposed on a background, simply by assuming only that the response to the test light is equal to the response to the background intensity plus the test light intensity, minus the response to the background. This model described the data Boynton and Whitten (1970) recorded from monkey cones using extracellular gross recording and K. T. Brown's (1968) clamping technique. For the frog, P. A. Hock and D. C. Hood (unpublished) have shown that the model does not fit the 580 cone response. In particular, a background intensity that produces a dark adapted cone response that is 74% of maximum only reduces the maximum response to incremental stimuli by 33% instead of the 74% predicted by the model. One problem with this model appears to be the assumption of no accommodation adaptation (Dowling and Ripps, 1972; Kleinschmidt, 1973; Norman and Werblin, 1974). In the rod and cone retina of *Necturus* (Norman and Werblin, 1974), where cone accommodation adaptation is extensive and rod accommodation adaptation is small, this model comes close to fitting the rod increment-threshold function, but not that of the cones.

Recently, Schacher *et al.* (1975) have found a possible synaptic consequence of this proposed difference between rod and cone accommodation-adaptation. Using a cytochemical procedure to measure synaptic activity, they found that rod synaptic activity decreased with increasing background light intensity up to the light level which saturates rod activity (−3.0 log background intensity in Fig. 12b). The cone synaptic activity, on the other hand, changed little over a wide range of background intensities.

Although the Boynton and Whitten (1970) model has not been substantiated in the experiments just mentioned, it has supplied a quantitative framework within which receptor data can be compared. It also speaks to the important problem of changes in sensitivity to suprathreshold stimuli. In particular, at any given ambient intensity, the organism must be able to respond to a range of stimulus intensities. This information is not given in the increment-threshold function; one procedure for obtaining this relevant information involves measuring some aspect of the size of the response as a function of stimulus intensity. Little is known about the frog's response-intensity function and how it is affected by background lights, but this important problem is beginning to be investigated. Burkhardt and Whittle (1973) have recently investigated response-intensity functions and, in particular, how this information is transmitted between the level of the proximal negative response, PNR (presumably generated by amacrine cells), and the ganglion cell.

The Switch from Rod to Cone Systems

Returning to the increment threshold functions of Fig. 11, it is clear that the rod system is more sensitive in the dark, but that at some background intensity the cone system becomes the more sensitive system. This raises two questions: (1) What are the differences between systems that allow rod responding at low, ambient light levels and cone responding at high levels? (2) How does the visual system switch from rod to cone control? A partial answer to the first question starts with the fact that the rod system is much more sensitive in the dark. This rod-cone difference is, at least, due in part to a difference in rod and cone receptor sensitivities (Fain and Dowling, 1973; Norman and Werblin, 1974; Hood and Hock, 1975), but possibly may also be due to neural summation. With increased background intensity, the sensitive rod system loses sensitivity as described by its increment-threshold function and the cone system, perhaps due to its lower sensitivity in the dark, has yet to lose sensitivity. (The case of rod saturation becomes a special case of the loss of sensitivity of the rod system). Finally, the rod system becomes less sensitive than the cone system and the latter system gains control. Thus, the cone system's relative insensitivity combined with the factors of bleaching and accommodation-adaptation just discussed allows the cones to operate at high light levels. This is a relatively simple "passive" explanation for the switch from the rod to the cone system. A second class of explanations ("active") does not deny these relative changes in sensitivity, but adds that either the rod system inhibits the cone system in the dark and releases this inhibition in the light and/or that the cone system inhibits the rod system at higher background lights when the cone system is excited. This inhibition can be due to a specific, inhibitory connection of cone-controlled onto rod-controlled cells or to a decreased response due to a refractory or inhibitory period left by the system that "gets to the ganglion cell first" (e.g., Gouras, 1965). [More generally, there is evidence for an inhibitory period following both the *on*-response (Nye and Naka, 1971; Gordon and Graham, 1973) and the *off*-response (Gordon and Graham, 1973) of the frog *on-off* ganglion cells.]

The physiological and psychophysical literature concerned with this problem is quite large, and one can find some evidence for all of the various types of explanations given before. For example, Rushton's (1959) "excitation pool" is an example of a passive explanation for the results of frog ganglion cell recordings. On the other hand, frog ERG and ganglion cell experiments have provided evidence for both rod-cone (Therman, 1939; Dodt and Jessen, 1961; Kuznetsova, 1963; Hood, 1972a,b) and cone-rod (Crescitelli and Sickel, 1968) inhibition. In addition, Reuter and Virtanen (1972) suggest a mechanism similar to that described for the monkey ganglion cell (Gouras, 1965) to describe the "inhibition" at the frog ganglion cell of 432 rod activity by the 580 cone system.

It is uncertain whether anything more complicated than a passive explanation is needed to explain most, if not all, of the steady-state switch in systems seen in the increment threshold function. Evidence for the active mechanisms does not come from, or relate directly to, the switch in control of steady-state sensitivity as seen in the increment-threshold functions. The experiments viewed as evidence for rod-cone inhibition are indirectly relevant, since they suggest that dark-adapted cone sensitivity is lower, in part, due to an active inhibition by the rods.

Dark Adaptation

When a steady background light is turned off, sensitivity does not instantaneously return to its steady-state, or maximum, level. The process by which sensitivity returns is called dark adaptation. In our everyday experiences, this is perceived as an increase in brightness and an appreciation of low-intensity details with prolonged time in the dark. In the laboratory, dark adaptation is usually measured by determining the amount of light required to produce a constant response at various times after the ambient light is turned off. Again, the constant response can be psychophysically defined as a constant detectability or constant brightness, or physiologically defined as a constant number of spikes, amplitude of response, etc. For example, Fig. 14 shows a dark-adaptation curve for the frog measured with a constant ganglion cell response of a single action potential. The intensity of the test flash needed to elicit the criterion response is plotted against time in the dark. This curve was measured following exposure to an intense light and is typical of dark-adaptation curves recorded from vertebrate visual systems which have both rods and cones. Similar results for the b-wave of the frog's ERG were first shown by Riggs in 1937. The phenomena of dark adaptation

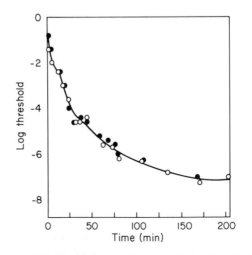

Fig. 14. Dark adaptation curve for the *on*-response of a single *on-off* cell. The thresholds were measured with a 5 sec, 503 nm light. (Modified from Donner and Reuter, 1965.)

have provided visual scientists with a powerful tool for probing various physiological mechanisms.

Theories of Dark Adaptation

When a pigment molecule absorbs a quantum of light, it ultimately breaks down into a chromophore (retinal) and a protein constituent (opsin); the pigment molecule is said to have been bleached. Since a molecule that has absorbed a quantum of light can not again initiate vision until it is returned or *regenerated* to its original state, it was natural for early theories of dark adaptation to focus on pigment regeneration as the causal factor for the return of sensitivity during dark adaptation. When actual pigment content was measured, however, it became clear that this relationship was not a simple one, since lights that bleached very little pigment, say less than 1% of the pigment molecules, substantially increased the response threshold (Lythgoe, 1940; Rushton and Cohen, 1954). Dowling, in a series of important experiments (Dowling and Wald, 1958; Dowling, 1960, 1963), was the first to demonstrate that it is the log of the relative sensitivity loss that is linearly related to the relative number of pigment molecules in the unregenerated state; he called these sensitivity changes *photochemical dark adaptation*. Since various investigators argue that some of these changes are not due to pigment regeneration, although they may be due to photochemicals (e.g., photoproducts), the term *regeneration-dependent adaptation* will be used to refer to sensitivity changes directly dependent upon the regeneration of pigment molecules. However, for years, there has been evidence (cf. Lythgoe, 1940; Rushton and Cohen, 1954; Dowling, 1963) that there are sensitivity changes in the dark that cannot be attributed to pigment regeneration; these changes have often been called *neural*. Although the site of some of these neural changes have been shown to be proximal to the receptors, some changes have indeed been seen at the receptors (cf. Dowling and Ripps, 1972; Grabowski et al., 1972; Hood et al., 1973). Consequently, the term *regeneration-independent adaptation* will be used to refer to changes in sensitivity that are not dependent on the regeneration of pigment, per se.

REGENERATION-INDEPENDENT ADAPTATION. One way of examining sensitivity changes uninfluenced by pigment regeneration is to use the isolated retina preparation. Under appropriate conditions (in the isolated retina) (Frank, 1969; Baumann, 1970), the frog's rhodopsin rods do not regenerate their bleached pigment molecules and, consequently, rod-controlled retinal sensitivity changes measured after light exposure *cannot* be attrib-

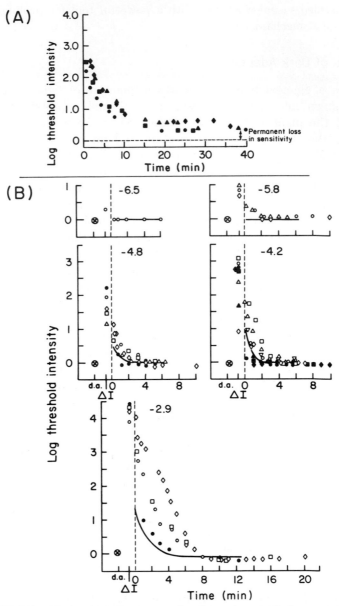

Fig. 15 (A). Dark adaptation curves for the rod controlled, aspartate-isolated receptor potential. The thresholds were measured with a 50 msec, 501 nm test light following a 5 min adapting light that bleached 19% of the rod pigment, rhodopsin. The preadaptation threshold intensity is shown by the dotted line. (From Hood *et al.,* 1973.)

(B) Dark adaptation curves for the rod controlled, aspartate-isolated receptor uted to pigment regeneration. Baumann (1967) first showed that the frog b-wave recorded from an isolated retina recovered large amounts of sensitivity following exposure to intense lights. Since these observations were made, rod dark-adaptation curves have been measured for frog receptors (Frank, 1971; Hood et al., 1973), b-wave (Frank, 1971), and ganglion cells (Baumann and Scheibner, 1968; Fusco and Hood, 1976) of the isolated retina. Several important aspects of regeneration-independent adaptation have been seen in these various studies. Figure 15 illustrates these aspects for the frog's receptors. First, as seen in Fig. 15A, large amounts of sensitivity recover without pigment regeneration, although there is a small permanent loss (about 0.3 log unit) in sensitivity, presumably due to the unregenerated pigment—in this case about 19% of the total pigment. Second, low background intensities that bleach little pigment (see solid receptor curves in Fig. 15B) substantially raise the threshold in the dark. Note also, that although the recovery following exposure to low background intensities is rapid, the recovery can be very slow following backgrounds that bleach more pigment. For example, recovery takes 20 min in Fig. 15A and can be as long as 60 min following extensive bleaches.

What are these regeneration-independent sensitivity changes attributable to? After a visual pigment molecule has absorbed a quantum of light, it undergoes a series of conformational changes resulting in molecules called photoproducts. Some of these changes take place quickly, but some of the photoproducts remain for minutes. In a number of species, photoproducts have been implicated as a threshold-elevating factor, although this remains a source of controversy. For the frog, Donner and Reuter (1965, 1967, 1968) attributed much of the sensitivity changes in the dark to the decay of meta II. Meta II is a photoproduct that develops quickly upon exposure to light, but passes to subsequent stages slowly (half-time of about 9 min at 14°C). For a number of conditions (various temperatures and amounts of pigment bleached), Donner and Reuter found that the decay of a photoproduct absorbing maximally at 380 nm

---

potential (solid curves) and for single ganglion cells (data points). Different symbols denote different ganglion cells. Each figure shows the preadaptation dark-adapted threshold (d.a.), the incremental threshold (ΔI) in the presence of the adapting field, and the log threshold intensity as a function of time after adapting field offset. The open symbols are for the *on*-response; the closed for the *off*-response. To adjust for differences of sensitivity, the data from individual cells were shifted vertically to coincide at preadaptation, dark-adapted threshold (d.a.). The number in the upper right hand corner of each figure is the relative log intensity of the 5-min, white-adapting light. The value 0.0 log intensity corresponds to an illuminance of 130 ft. cd. (From Fusco and Hood, 1976.)

(presumably meta II, but see Donner, 1973) paralleled the return of log sensitivity at the ganglion cell. Frank (1971) argued against a photo-product explanation, since the rate of recovery of frog b-wave and iso-lated PIII sensitivity did not change much with changes in temperature. (The decay of photoproducts is highly temperature dependent.) Since Donner and Reuter (1967; see also Donner, 1973) show large temperature-dependent differences in meta II recovery (that parallel temperature dependent changes in ganglion cell sensitivity), the frog research has yet to offer the final answer to this more general controversy.

There are also clearly nonreceptor factors that contribute to regenera-tion-independent adaptation in the frog. Lipetz (1961) showed that sensitivity losses could be more drastic and dark adaptation could take longer if the test and adapting fields did not overlap and if the adapting field was placed on the most sensitive part of the receptive field. Others have shown changes during dark adaptation that are hard to attribute to receptors, such as differently shaped dark-adaptation curves for different spot sizes and for *on* versus *off* responses (Donner and Reuter, 1965).

To summarize, large regeneration-independent sensitivity changes are seen at the rod receptors, but some regeneration-independent sensitivity changes can also be shown to be proximal to the receptors. How much of the sensitivity changes seen during dark adaptation can thus be attributed to changes in the receptors? A study by Fusco and Hood (1976) provides a starting point for answering this question. Dark adaptation was mea-sured at the ganglion cell under the same stimulating conditions as were used in obtaining the receptor data of Fig. 15B. Figure 15B shows these ganglion cell data along with the receptor curves for comparison. For the *on* response of *on-off* cells, there are large sensitivity changes that can not be attributed to the receptors. Although ganglion cell and receptor sensitivities start at about the same distance above dark-adapted thresh-old, the ganglion cell sensitivity returns more slowly to this level. Green and co-workers (1975) have reported similar results in their comparisons of skate receptor and ganglion cell data. It is also clear from Fig. 15B that the *off* response sensitivity returns much more quickly than does that of the *on* response and its curve might possibly be described by the receptor curve.

REGENERATION-DEPENDENT ADAPTATION. Although during dark adapta-tion there are large recoveries of sensitivity in the isolated retina, there are also permanent sensitivity losses when pigment molecules are un-regenerated. For now, assume that the steady-state permanent loss (see Fig. 15A) due to bleaching can be taken as a measure of regeneration-dependent adaptation. Figure 16A shows a plot of this permanent loss as a function of percent pigment bleached by a 5-min light. Nearly identical

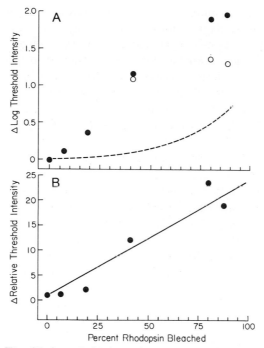

Fig. 16 (A). The filled symbols show the permanent loss in sensitivity (change in log threshold intensity measured as shown in Fig. 15A) as a function of the percent of rod pigment bleached by a 5-min adapting light. Bleaching pigment molecules decreases the number of molecules available to catch quanta. The dashed curve represents the change in log threshold intensity needed to maintain a constant quantum catch. The open symbols show the data corrected for this "trivial" effect of pigment bleaching. Lower points were not plotted since they are identical to the filled symbols. (Modified from Hood *et al.*, 1973.)

(B) Relative sensitivity loss, corrected for changes in the probability of quantal absorption, as a function of the percent of rod pigment bleached. These points are the antilogs of the open symbols in Fig. 16A.

functions have been found for intracellular rod recordings from *Axolotol* (Grabowski *et al.*, 1972) and for extracellular recordings of isolated PIII from the rat (Ernst and Kemp, 1972). There are a few interesting implications in these studies for theories of dark adaptation. First, it is striking how small the loss in sensitivity due to the unregenerated pigment is, compared to the overall changes in sensitivity during dark adaptation (see Figs. 14 and 15). However, these changes, although relatively small, are still larger than would be predicted if loss of sensitivity due to unregenerated pigment were caused entirely by the decreased number of pigment molecules available for light absorption (see dashed line in Fig. 16A).

If the basic findings in Figs. 15 and 16A do hold for intact mammals, then there are serious implications for the often found log-linear relationship between sensitivity and unregenerated pigment. In particular, if the large, slow regeneration-independent sensitivity changes are responsible for most of the changes during dark adaptation, then the functional significance of the correlation between sensitivity and bleached pigment is questionable. Of course, there is also the possibility that a combination of species and preparations produces a result that is in conflict with the functional relationship between pigment and sensitivity. Or, alternatively, it is possible that when regeneration is allowed to take place, sensitivity might then be linked to the unregenerated pigment. It is probably worth pointing out here again, that the log-linear relationship between sensitivity and amount of pigment has been found to hold for human psychophysical thresholds (Rushton, 1961; Rushton and Powell, 1972), frog b-wave thresholds (Baumann, 1967) rat b-wave thresholds (Dowling, 1960, 1963; Weinstein et al., 1967), and skate b-wave and ganglion cell thresholds (Dowling and Ripps, 1970). However, the slope has ranged from 3.6 to 37 in these experiments. Thus, the form of the function is the same, but the predicted sensitivity loss per 10% of the pigment bleached ranges from 0.36 to 3.7 log units, a 2000-fold difference! For the receptors in Fig. 16A, a log-linear relation with a slope of about 2 is seen. Here, the total loss is small, and much of it is consequently due to the decreased number of molecules available for quantal absorption. For example, when 90% of the pigment is unregenerated, then only one-tenth as many quanta will be absorbed. Thus, this simple factor accounts for 1.0 log unit of the 1.8 log units of sensitivity loss. To assess the connection between unregenerated pigment and sensitivity, the open symbols in Fig. 16A are corrected for the changes in probability of quantal absorption and show intensity expressed as the relative number of quanta absorbed at threshold. Here, for these receptor data, log sensitivity is not linearly related to percent of unregenerated pigment.

Donner and Reuter argued in 1965 that there was no simple connection between percent of unregenerated pigment and sensitivity of frog ganglion cells. Their model (Donner and Reuter, 1965, 1968) attributes sensitivity changes following extensive bleaches to photoproduct decay and rate of pigment regeneration. Most of the sensitivity changes are attributable to the decay of photoproducts. However, the last 1.5 log units or so of sensitivity recovery occurs after the decay of photoproducts, but while rhodopsin is regenerating from 40 to 100%. Since they found little change in log threshold occurring while pigment regenerated from 40 to 70%, they concluded that no simple connection existed between percent of unregenerated pigment and sensitivity. Instead, they argued that sensitivity is depressed by about 1.5 log units when the rate of regeneration is high and constant and increased as the rate of regeneration decreased. The data of Figs. 15 and 16A agree with this model, including the observation (see open symbols of Fig. 16A) that relatively small threshold changes are attributable to the regeneration of rhodopsin and that log threshold is not linearly related to percent of unregenerated pigment. However, since the rate of regeneration in the experiments of Fig. 16 is zero, their model should predict *no* threshold increase due to the loss of pigment. In addition, the plot of Fig. 16B suggests that there may, in fact, be a simple connection between receptor threshold and percent of unregenerated pigment. In Fig. 16B, relative threshold increase (not log relative threshold increase—in fact, the antilogs of the open circles in Fig. 16A) is plotted against percent of unregenerated pigment. A straight line provides a good fit to these data, although, admittedly, more data are needed. It is as if each unregenerated molecule raised threshold by a constant amount.

CONES. Unlike the rods, the 580 cones are capable of regenerating their pigment in the isolated retina. By recording early receptor potentials from the 580 cones, Goldstein (1967, 1970) showed that 80 to 90% of this cone pigment is regenerated in the isolated retina. The cone controlled b-wave (Baumann, 1967), ganglion cell response (Baumann and Scheibner, 1968), and aspartate-isolated receptor response (Hood and Hock, 1973) recover most of their sensitivity following bleaching lights. In fact, the cone's receptor sensitivity following a 90% bleach was found to parallel the pigment regeneration as measured by Goldstein (Hood and Hock, 1973).

Since the cone's pigment regenerates in the isolated retina, it cannot be used to study cone regeneration-independent adaptation in the same way it can for the rods. Sillman (1974) has shown that the aspartate-isolated cone response undergoes a transient loss in sensitivity following a flash of light. This loss is more transient than that observed for the rods (Sillman *et al.*, 1973). Although not much more can be said about re-generation-independent sensitivity changes in the cones, inferences can be made from the recovery following bleaching lights. One minute after exposure to a light that bleaches 90% of the cone pigment, the receptor sensitivity is 2.0 log units below its dark-adapted level. Consequently, regeneration-independent adaptation cannot be very extensive and must be far less extensive than in the rods where sensitivity is so low it could not be measured (see Fig. 15A for a 30% rod bleach). Interestingly, the unrecovered sensitivity during dark adaptation, when considered as a function of unregenerated cone pigment (regeneration-dependent adaptation), appears to be similar to the function relating rod sensitivity to unregenerated rod pigment in Fig. 16. Perhaps, there is no regeneration-independent adaptation in the cones, with the exception of the first few seconds, and this rod-cone difference may be attributable to the quicker decay of some photoproducts.

CONCLUSION

In this chapter, we have selectively reviewed the current knowledge of frog retinal anatomy and physiology. It should be clear that, at present, there is an enormous quantity of knowledge concerning the anatomy, photochemistry, and physiology of the frog retina, which underscores why the frog has been, and will continue to be, a valuable research subject. The frog has often been the source of basic facts in vertebrate vision; since its visual system is relatively well understood, it should continue to provide an important testing ground for general theories of vision, as well as in the study of such basic visual problems as transduction, receptor function, synaptic mechanisms, adaptational mechanisms, and the important problems of sensory coding, in general.

While the frog visual system has often been used as a model for other vertebrates, there are clear and important differences between frog and mammalian visual systems; consequently, such comparisons should be made with caution. Some of these real differences between frogs and mammals have been pointed out. (Substantial differences also exist among mammals as well, for example, between cat and monkey). On the other hand, it appears that the frog retina is often regarded as being more complex, partly because of a more extensive knowledge of the frog retina when compared with other vertebrate retinas. Perhaps, other presumed differences require additional and comparable information on other species in order to be established as genuine.

ACKNOWLEDGMENTS

The preparation of this chapter was supported by the following grants: National Science Foundation Grant BMS 73-02435, National Eye Institute Grant EY188, and National Institute of General Medicine Grant GM 01789.

We thank A. Campbell, N. Graham, E. B. Goldstein, and R. M. Shapley for their critical reading of this manuscript and their many helpful suggestions. They are not to be held responsible for any errors or omissions in this chapter. We are particularly grateful to our editor, K. V. Fite, for the improvements she made to the text and for the great patience she showed us.

3

Central Visual Pathways In The Frog

Katherine V. Fite and Frank Scalia

INTRODUCTION

The ranid or true frogs have been among the half dozen or so vertebrates most frequently chosen in recent years for neuroanatomic and neurophysiological studies on the vertebrate visual system. Several factors, including their abundance and ease of maintenance, have contributed to their relative popularity. Perhaps the most significant of these has been their longstanding focus of research in experimental biology and embryology and the extent to which they rely upon vision for survival. Indeed, several useful concepts currently employed in sensory neurophysiology have derived from microelectrode investigations of the frog retina; e.g., the concepts of receptive field (Hartline, 1938, 1940a) and feature detection (Barlow, 1953; Lettvin et al., 1959; Maturana et al., 1960). Both of these concepts have been extensively employed in subsequent research on sensory mechanisms and information processing in vertebrate and nonvertebrate nervous systems (see also Chapter 2).

In behavioral studies, frogs have not been particularly satisfactory subjects for the more traditional animal behavioral and psychophysical techniques; nevertheless, their relatively stereotyped, species-typical behaviors are highly predictable and appear to show little modification as the result of experience. Thus, the effects of learning are largely eliminated in studies where the major emphasis has been upon the neural basis of visually guided behavior. Recent investigations have focused increasingly upon the natural behavior of anurans and on those stimuli, both internal and external, that control them. As a result, there is now

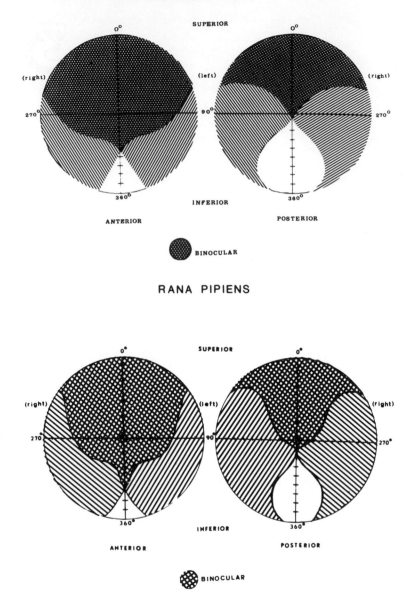

Fig. 1. Perimetric maps of anterior and posterior fields of view as measured for *Rana pipiens* and *Rana catesbieana* showing right and left eye's visual field and region of binocular overlap. (From Fite, 1973.)

a substantial body of knowledge which promises to be a source of new insights into the general principles of stimulus-bound behavior in vertebrates (see also Chapters 4, 5, and 8).

It must be noted, however, that frogs are clearly unique and highly specialized animals whose specific adaptations must be recognized apart from the more fundamental patterns of vertebrate neural and behavioral organization (see Chapter 1). For example, anurans possess the most extensive visual fields found among vertebrates, fields which, in some species of frog, subtend nearly 360° of visual angle (Schneider, 1954a,b; Fite, 1973). The large size of the field of view is due to the periscopic position of the eyes and to the large angle of divergence between the visual axes of the two eyes. Perimetric mapping studies have revealed that anurans have a large binocular field of view, which, in frogs, may extend some 40–55° below the horizontal meridian and expand upward to include an area 160–170° directly over the head. Family and species differences are observed primarily in the shape and extent of the binocular visual field (Fig. 1). The frog retina itself is not topographically homogeneous, but contains regions differing in thickness and in ganglion cell and receptor density (Walls, 1942; Jacobson, 1962; Fite and Carey, 1973). Retinal topography maps (Fig. 2) have indicated that the shape and location of such retinal areas vary across species and that in some frogs two regions of increased cellular density may be found within a larger area of greater retinal thickness and ganglion cell density (Carey, 1975). Since there are no significant, visually guided eye movements in frogs, a relatively invariant relationship exists between retinal locus and that portion of the visual field, relative to the body axis, from which visual stimulation arises. Major changes in fixation occur only as a result of changes in the orientation of the entire body relative to the visual stimulus, since dis-

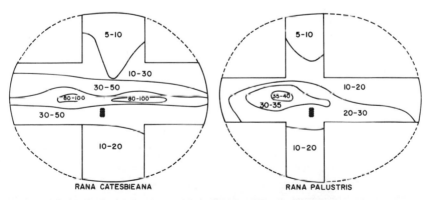

Fig. 2. Retinal topography maps showing ganglion cell densities (isodensity contours) for *Rana catesbieana* and *Rana palustris*. (From Carey, 1975.)

crete head movements are also relatively infrequent in frogs. The retinal locus of the stimulus may, therefore, carry relatively specific information concerning the spatial locus of the physical object relative to the body axis. These facts suggest, further, that functional differences in visual information processing from different retinal areas may be important, perhaps also in relation to different central projection areas.

The remainder of this chapter will be devoted to both anatomic and physiological data which bear upon the roles that the major retinofugal projections play in anuran vision, with particular reference to ranid frogs.

OPTIC NERVE

Bruesch and Arey (1942) estimated the number of myelinated axons in the optic nerve of *Rana pipiens* to be 15,300. Their estimate of 29,000 unmyelinated fibers, however, has been shown to be several times too low in more recent electron microscopic observations (Maturana, 1959). According to Maturana, the unmyelinated fibers in anurans outnumber the myelinated fibers by 31 to 1, as estimated in samples of small areas of the optic nerve examined in transverse section. This ratio brings the number of unmyelinated fibers to a reported 470,000 and the total number of optic nerve fibers to over 485,000. The unmyelinated fibers are grouped closely together in fascicles and have small diameters averaging 0.2–0.3 μm. This undoubtedly accounts for much of the difficulty involved in accurately counting them in transverse sections by light microscopy. The myelinated fibers have diameters of 0.8–4.0 μm.

The total number of fibers in the optic nerve of *R. pipiens* appears to be clearly comparable to the number of retinal ganglion cells in that species, which has been estimated to be about 452,000 (Maturana, 1959). Of these, some 12,000 have large diameters (14–20 μm); the remainder fall into a separate class of smaller diameter (7–10 μm) neurons. Since the ratio of small to large ganglion cells is comparable to the ratio of unmyelinated to myelinated optic nerve fibers, it may be reasonable to assume that the smaller cells give rise to the unmyelinated axons.

According to these figures, there is a small disparity between the estimated numbers of optic nerve fibers and retinal ganglion cells, the fibers outnumbering the cells by some 33,000. The extent to which this numerical difference may be accounted for by a systematic error involved in comparing quantities estimated by two different methods (cell counting and fiber counting) is not clear. However, since Maturana (1959) counted only those ganglion cells located within the ganglion cell layer, it is not surprising that the cell count was at least some magnitude less than the fiber count. The numerical difference ought to be at least as large as the number of displaced ganglion cells of the inner nuclear layer. Displaced ganglion cells (cells of Dogiel) were identified in *R. pipiens* by Ramón y Cajal (1892), using the Golgi technique, and they have been observed (F. Scalia and D. R. Colman, unpublished data) in that species in experiments using modification (Scalia and Colman, 1974) of the horseradish peroxidase (HRP) tracing method for retrograde transport (LaVail and LaVail, 1972). At present, however, the number of displaced ganglion cells in *R. pipiens* is not known, but a rough estimate from the HRP-stained sections suggests there may be as many as 5 displaced ganglion cells for every 100 in the ganglion cell layer proper.

According to Ramón y Cajal (1892), the displaced ganglion cells in *R. pipiens* are large and few in number. The displaced ganglion cells observed by means of the HRP technique (F. Scalia and D. R. Colman, unpublished) could be characterized as both small and large in relation to the size classification (previously mentioned) for the cells in the ganglion cell layer proper, and the smaller displaced cells were the more numerous. Since it is only the larger of the displaced ganglion cells that can be readily identified in normal histological sections of the frog's retina, the total number of displaced cells has undoubtedly been underestimated in previous studies not utilizing a specific marking technique.

Although omission of displaced ganglion cells may account for some part of the numerical disparity between Maturana's (1959) estimates of the ganglion cell and optic nerve fiber populations, it is also obvious that any efferents to the retina would add a differential to the optic nerve fiber population. The existence of efferent fibers in the optic nerve of the toad (*Bufo americanus*) and several species of frog is certainly suggested (Maturana, 1958a,b) by the observation of surviving myelinated fibers in the central stump of the optic nerve several months after optic nerve transection. And these observations form the basis for the estimate (Maturana, 1958a) that efferents to the retina account for the differential between the number of myelinated fibers (15,300) in the optic nerve and the number of large ganglion cells (12,000) in the ganglion cell layer. Since no surviving unmyelinated fibers were observed in the central stump of the optic nerve in these experiments, the larger part of the optic nerve fiber excess—an excess on the order of 30,000 fibers—could not be accounted for in these terms. The presence of efferent axons in the optic nerve of the toad has also been assumed to explain certain electrophysiologically recordable events (Ewert, 1974), and Branston and Fleming (1968) have observed changes in receptive field size and organization in *R. pipiens*, which they ascribe to the action of efferents. Byzov and Utina (1971) further suggest that such centrifugal effects in the frog retina are mediated through amacrine cells as has been described in the avian retina (Maturana and Frenk, 1965; Dowling and Cowan, 1966; Cowan, 1970b).

The central origin of the efferent axons in the optic nerve of the bird is known (Cowan et al., 1961; Cowan and Powell, 1963; McGill et al., 1966a,b) to be the isthmo-optic nucleus, and recent studies on the retrograde transport of intraocularly injected (HRP) have further confirmed this fact (LaVail and LaVail, 1972). In the various species of frogs and toads, however, no neurons have yet been identified as a possible source of optic efferents. The only cells in the brain of R. pipiens found to be labeled by retrograde transport of HRP (Scalia and Colman, 1974) following intraocular injection were neurons in the extraocular motor nuclei, and it seems unlikely that these cells are involved in efferent innervation of the retina. Such cells were labeled only occasionally, when there was reason to suspect that some of the peroxidase has leaked out of the eye and into the extraocular spaces. The possibility that central efferent neurons were not observed because all of the injected volumes had leaked out of the eye is not a serious consideration because anterograde transport of the peroxidase to the terminal neuropil within the brain was observed in every case, some of which survived as long as 7 days postinjection. Even when the HRP was applied directly to the surgically severed ends of the optic nerve in the orbit in another series of experiments (Scalia and Colman, 1974), there was no evidence of either retrograde transport or back-filling to central neurons that might be the source of efferent fibers. It is by now widely known by personal experience that direct application of HRP to severed axons may lead to both an active retrograde transport, which labels cytoplasmic vacuoles, and a diffusive retrograde flow (back-filling) that stains the axon, the cell body, and the dendrites homogeneously. Both effects have been reported in the literature (Adams and Warr, 1974; de Vito et al., 1974). The HRP-tracing methods are new, however, and the failure to identify any centrifugal neurons in the optic pathway of the frog by these procedures may be the result of presently unknown technical or physiological factors. The optic pathway of the toad has not yet been studied by these methods.

CENTRAL VISUAL PATHWAYS

A number of studies have described the retinofugal projections of the retina in adult ranid frogs using silver-staining techniques for axonal (Knapp et al., 1965) and terminal degeneration (Scalia et al., 1968; Lázár and Székely, 1969; Lázár, 1971; Scalia and Fite, 1974). Certain aspects of the optic pathway have been reexamined, using the autoradiographic tracing technique in the adult (Scalia, 1973) and developing frog (Currie and Cowan, 1974b). In addition, the techniques of horseradish peroxidase histochemistry have been recently applied to the visualization of the optic pathway following the bidirectional, intraaxonal migration of HRP experimentally delivered to the cut ends of the optic nerve (Scalia and Colman, 1974). Electron microscopic data (Székely *et al.*, 1973) and recent study of Golgi impregnations (Potter, 1969, 1972) have further supplemented the morphological analysis of the frog's optic pathway.

The following general description of the overall distribution of the optic tract has been consistently observed in these studies: After incomplete decussation in the optic chiasma, the optic nerve fibers proceed across the lateral aspect of the diencephalon in a dorsocaudal direction, as the principal part of the optic tract. Upon reaching the anterior border of the tectum, each optic tract divides into medial and lateral components, which continue, respectively, along the medial and lateral margins of each tectal hemisphere. The medial and lateral tracts gradually reduce in size, as fibers enter the superficial layers of the tectal plate to terminate there in a series of laminae. In addition to terminating in the optic tectum, the principal optic tract fibers innervate the lateral geniculate and pretectal complexes of the diencephalon. Whereas the optic fibers ending in the tectum arise in the contralateral eye, the diencephalic targets are reached both by crossed and uncrossed fibers. Quantitative information on the relative numbers of contralaterally and ipsilaterally directed fibers is not available, but it is certain that the ipsilateral component is the smaller.

A slender fascicle of optic nerve fibers leaves the region of the optic chiasma separately from the principal optic tract and may be termed the accessory optic tract, or basal optic root. This courses directly posteriorly along the dorsal border of the hypothalamus, just within the lateral surface of the brain, and terminates in the basal optic nucleus in the midbrain. The optic nerve fibers in this tract originate from the contralateral eye.

Optic Chiasma

As they approach the ventral surface of the diencephalon, the optic nerves are directed ventrally, medially, and slightly posteriorly. The X formed at the optic chiasma is, therefore, rather short in an anteroposterior direction, but is broad in the transverse direction (see Fig. 3). As a result, the initial part of the optic tract (i.e., the posterior limb of the

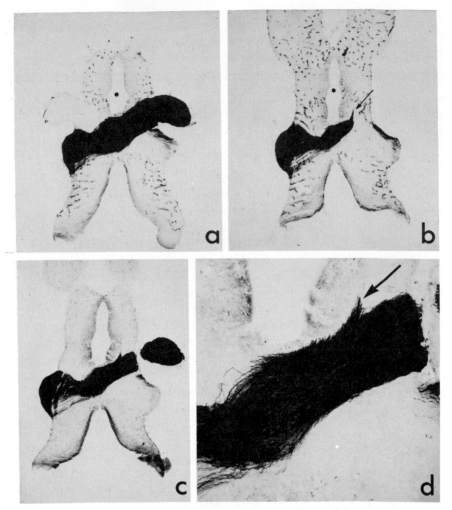

Fig. 3. Photomicrographs of the optic chiasma of *Rana pipiens*, as observed in horizontal sections following intraaxonal migration of horseradish peroxidase applied to the severed ends of the right optic nerve. Anterior is toward the top of the photographs. The upper pair of sections were taken from the same brain; (a) is ventral to (b); the two sections may be superimposed, approximately, by aligning the *dots* within the preoptic ventricle. The late-crossing fascicle (arrow) is seen entering the dorsal part of the optic chiasma in (b). Section (c) was taken from a different brain and occurs at a level intermediate between (a) and (b). The late-crossing fascicle is labeled (arrow) in (d), a higher power detail from (c).

optic chiasma) begins its ascent across the lateral surface of the diencephalon immediately posterior to the entering root of the optic nerve. In fact, the leading edge of the optic tract is curved anteriorly above the area of implantation of the optic nerve and, in a transverse series of sections, the anterior edge of the optic tract is encountered several sections before the anterior side of the optic nerve has joined the brain wall. In their further course, the fibers in the anterior edge of the optic tract turn progressively more posteriorly in order to become oriented toward the optic tectum. By contrast, the fibers in the posterior edge of the optic tract cross the surface of the diencephalon more directly, and are always aimed posterodorsally, i.e., toward the optic tectum.

The optic nerve is circular in cross section and the optic tract is flat or ribbonlike. However, the transition from nerve to tract through the optic chiasma is not a simple matter of the gradual flattening of the nerve to conform to the surface of the diencephalon. There appears also to occur a significant rearrangement of topography during the transition across the midline. This is well illustrated by the course of the late-crossing component of the chiasma. These fibers, as the term implies, are among the last to cross, and they form the posterodorsal edge of the optic chiasma. They enter the chiasmatic complex, however, from the anterior side of the optic nerve, and, remaining ipsilateral to the midline, they arch along the dorsal (dorsalanterior) surface of the chiasma, virtually parallel to the sagittal plane, while other fibers cross the midline. These late-crossing fibers do not turn toward the opposite side until they reach the dorsal, posterior margin of the optic chiasma. Since the cross-sectional outline of the optic chiasma (i.e., its appearance in a midsagittal plane) is such that its posterior edge is dorsal to its anterior edge, these late-crossing fibers are directed dorsoposteriorly. They course in an arc and are somewhat separated from the main part of the chiasma. Anteriorly, they are directed straight up, alongside the periventricular preoptic cell mass. Some fibers in some individual frogs are even angled anteriorly. Posteriorly, before turning across the midline, they are directed straight back.

These relationships have led some observers (Knapp et al., 1965; Vullings and Kers, 1973), who were apparently unsuccessful in properly reconstructing the course of the late-crossing fibers, to the erroneous conclusion that they constitute a so-called preoptic bundle, directed upward (and forward?) from the optic chiasma to a termination in the lateral margin of the periventricular preoptic cell mass. The actual course of the late-crossing fibers is difficult to appreciate in material in which the fibers are degenerating (Knapp et al., 1965; Vullings and Kers, 1973). However, when optic nerve axons are filled with a dye, such as the HRP reaction product (Scalia and Colman, 1974), it is a simple matter to follow the movements of the late-crossing fibers from section to section. In such material, the course of the late-crossing fibers has been reconstructed in several specimens and it has been consistently observed that no optic fiber directed dorsally alongside the preoptic gray failed to turn posteriorly, either to join the late-crossing component of the optic chiasma directly, or to make a hairpin loop and return to the main body of the chiasma.

Diencephalon

The Optic Neuropil

The areas of termination of optic nerve fibers in the diencephalon are (1) the "nucleus" of Bellonci, (2) the corpus geniculatum thalamicum, (3) the posterior thalamic "nucleus" (of Bellonci), (4) the large-celled pretectal nucleus, and (5) a small, hooklike neuropil in the caudal diencephalon, the uncinate pretectal "nucleus." In anurans, the perikarya of most of the diencephalic neurons receiving optic innervation do not occur within the laterally placed terminal fields of the optic tract fibers, but are located more medially in cell masses displaced toward the third ventricle. The cell bodies extend long dendrites laterally into the relatively cell-free, terminal neuropil to mingle with the terminal branches of optic fibers, where axo-dendritic synaptic contacts are presumed to occur. The shape and location (Fig. 4) of these synaptic zones appear to be remarkably constant from one frog to another and are identifiable after enucleation and silver-staining as well-defined areas containing dense concentrations of silver grains. Hence, the terms "nucleus" of Bellonci, corpus geniculatum thalamicum, and posterior thalamic "nucleus" refer to areas of neuropil. The uncinate "nucleus" is similarly organized, but is located quite deep within the wall of the brain on the diencephalo-mesencephalic boundary. The large-celled pretectal nucleus, however, is a cell mass. Two anatomical studies (Lázár, 1971; Scalia and Fite, 1974) have described the topographic organization of the retino-diencephalic projections, the main findings of which are incorporated in the following summary.

The "nucleus" of Bellonci and corpus geniculatum are virtually contiguous areas of neuropil, that are distinguishable, in part, by their configuration. They resemble, respectively, an inverted, elongated cone and a lens- or ovoid-shaped area. Both of these regions begin near the rostral end of the thalamus and extend posteriorly a little beyond the posterior edge of the optic chiasma. In *R. pipiens*, the principal input to both the "nucleus" of Bellonci and corpus geniculatum comes from the contralateral eye, although both receive a substantial ipsilateral projection. In retinotopic terms (see Fig. 5), the temporal and dorsal quadrants of the retina project contralaterally to the posterior half of "nucleus" of

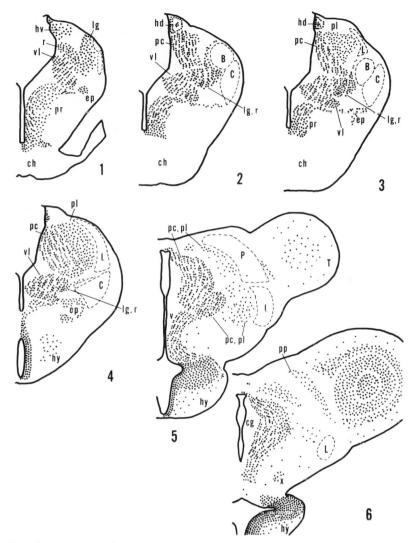

Fig. 4. Drawings of sections (1–6) of frog brain (*Rana pipiens*) showing the cell masses of the thalamus in relation to the major areas of neuropil. B, "nucleus" of Bellonci; C, corpus geniculatum thalamicum; L, lateral neuropil; P, posterior thalamic "nucleus"; cg, central gray; ch, optic chiasma; ep, posterior entopeduncular nucleus; hd, dorsal habenular nucleus; hv, ventral habenular nucleus; hy, hypothalamus; lg, lateral geniculate nucleus; pc, posterocentral nucleus; pl, posterolateral nucleus; pp, large-celled pretectal nucleus; pr, preoptic area; r, nucleus rotundus; v, posterior ventral thalamus; vl, ventrolateral nucleus; x, basal optic nucleus. (Courtesy of Springer-Verlag.)

Bellonci and corpus geniculatum, while the anterior halves of these areas receive projections from the ventral and nasal quadrants. Further, the ventral and temporal quadrants of the retina project onto the superior halves of each neuropil, and the inferior parts receive input from the nasal and dorsal quadrants. The ipsilateral projection originates almost entirely from the temporal quadrant of the retina, although a small portion of the ventral quadrant is also involved.

A third diencephalic area associated with the primary optic pathway, the posterior thalamic "nucleus," is separated from the more rostral areas of the optic neuropil by a midthalamic zone (the lateral neuropil), which receives tectal, instead of, optic afferents (see following discussion). The posterior thalamic "nucleus" (neuropil) is situated in the pretectal region and has the appearance of a vertically oriented cylindrical body, the dorsal end of which is curved somewhat medially. The temporal and dorsal retinal quadrants project contralaterally to the caudal end of the posterior thalamic "nucleus," while the ventral and nasal quadrants project to the rostral portion of this structure; the ventral and temporal quadrants project superiorly, and the nasal and dorsal quadrants project inferiorly. Ipsilateral input to this region again comes primarly from the temporal retina. The uncinate pretectal "nucleus" is found along the medial side of the posterior thalamic nucleus. Although it might appear to be an extension of the latter, it contains an independent map of the retina. It receives its retinal input predominantly from the contralateral eye, but a significant contribution from the ipsilateral eye is also seen.

In an experimental study on the development of the optic pathway in *R. pipiens,* Currie and Cowan (1974b) have shown that the crossed components of the retino-diencephalic projection are formed during the earliest larval stages, but the uncrossed or ipsilateral retino-diencephalic projection first begins to develop near the onset of the metamorphic climax (stage XX). This projection assumes the adult configuration (but not density) by Stage XXV, when the tail has disappeared. An ipsilateral retino-diencephalic projection quantitatively comparable to that in the adult is found in the 5-week postmetamorphic juvenile frog. It is significant that the eyes begin to migrate from a lateral position to a superior, frontally directed one in the later larval stages (stages XIX–XV), which is accompanied by a dramatic increase in the size of the binocular visual field and also coincides with the formation of the polysynaptic ipsilateral visuo-tectal projection (Jacobson, 1971). All of these facts, taken together, strongly suggest that ipsilateral projections are related to binocular vision in anurans. What specific role(s) binocular vision plays in their behavior and visual capabilities is a question that bears generally upon the phylogenetic origins and functions of binocular vision in vertebrates.

It should be noted that the polarity of the naso-temporal axis of the retina in each of the retino-diencephalic maps is reversed with respect to that of the retino-tectal map, although the polarity of representation of the dorso-ventral axis of the retina is the same (Fig. 5). These differences may provide information concerning the developmental processes underlying the polarization of cell proliferation and differentiation gradients at the diencephalo-mesencephalic interface.

As previously noted, the optic tectum projects to the diencephalon. Its diencephalic projections are part of a larger system of efferent connections (Rubinson, 1968; Lázár, 1969), which includes descending projections to the nucleus isthmi, nucleus lateralis profundus, superior olive, interpeduncular nucleus, bulbar reticular formation, and cervical spinal cord. The tectal projections to the nucleus isthmi and superior olive are ipsilateral; the projections to the reticular formation and spinal cord are

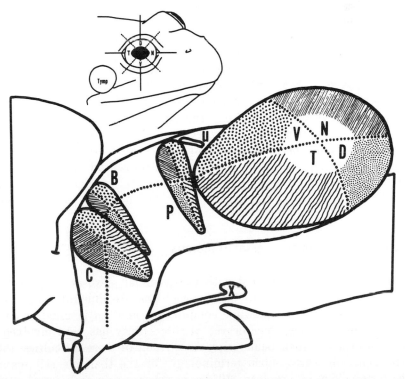

Fig. 5. Schematic representation of the retinal maps projecting to the contralateral diencephalon and tectum. Inset: Frog's head as seen along left optic axis. N, nasal; D, dorsal; T, temporal; V, ventral. (From Scalia and Fite, 1974.)

crossed; and the projections to the other regions, including the diencephalon, are bilateral, although the ipsilateral component is predominant. The crossed fibers traverse bulbar, tegmental, tectal, and postoptic commissures. In the diencephalon, the tectal efferent fibers end in the posterior thalamic nucleus, lateral neuropil (Fig. 4), corpus geniculatum thalamicum, and the supra-chiasmatic region of the hypothalamus.

The lateral neuropil is quite extensive. It occupies virtually all of the superficial neuropil of the thalamus not taken up by the "nucleus" of Bellonci, corpus geniculatum, and posterior thalamic "nucleus." It extends obliquely caudalward from a position dorsal to the "nucleus" of Bellonci (Fig. 4, section 3) to a position ventral and caudal to the posterior thalamic "nucleus" (Fig. 4, section 6). Its broadest vertical extent occurs at a midthalamic level, where it intervenes between the posterodorsal aspect of the corpus geniculatum and the anteroventral aspect of the posterior thalamic "nucleus."

It is apparent that in the thalamus each of the major segments of the superficial neuropil is innervated either by the retina (n. Bellonci) or the tectum (lateral neuropil), or they are innervated by both the retina and the tectum (c. geniculatum, posterior thalamic n.). These relations are interesting because they demonstrate that the afferent terminal fields of the frog's thalamus are organized in a highly specific way and suggest that further experimental analysis may be rewarded with new insights into the special roles of the diencephalic cell masses in processing visual information. Indeed, there is now evidence that some parts of the diencephalon project to the tectum (Trachtenberg and Ingle, 1974) and that two ascending tracts exist, which are directed toward different parts of the cerebral hemisphere and arise in separate dorsal thalamic cell masses. Before describing this evidence, however, it may be useful to survey the nuclear organization of the dorsal thalamus.

The Cell Masses of the Dorsal Thalamus

The cell masses associated with the terminal plexuses of the retinal and the tectal projections to the diencephalon are illustrated in Fig. 4. Their organization is somewhat complicated and, as is usual in cytoarchitectonic analysis, some degree of subjectivity has been involved in the delineation of their boundaries. As a result of these difficulties, there is no generally agreed-upon terminology for the thalamic cell masses. The terminology of Frontera (1952), however, seems to be coming into wider usage, although some variability in the application of his terms is apparent. In the following, the thalamic cell masses will be described in terms of their relationship to the retinal afferent and tectal afferent neuropil, in lieu of a detailed cytoarchitectonic treatment.

The cell masses immediately medial to and spatially coextensive with the "nucleus" of Bellonci (B) and corpus geniculatum thalamicum (C) have been termed the lateral geniculate nucleus (lg), nucleus rotundus (r), and ventrolateral area (vl). The remainder of the dorsal thalamus has been assigned to a large group of cells termed the postcrocentral-posterolateral complex (pc, pl). This complex is found immediately internal to the lateral neuropil (L) and posterior thalamic "nucleus" (P). It is certainly not a uniformly organized aggregate, however. In the first place, the compounding of the terms posterocentral and postero-lateral speaks to the tendency for this complex to show mediolateral subdivision, although the cytoarchitectonic characteristics of this sub-division vary with position within the complex. Second, close inspection of transverse and horizontal series allows one to distinguish regions in the complex topographically associated with the lateral neuropil from the region associated with the posterior thalamic nucleus. That is to say, the whole of the complex is divisible into two parts by an oblique line corresponding to the boundary between the posterior thalamic nucleus and the lateral neuropil. Third, that part of the complex abreast of the lateral neuropil itself shows subdivision into an anterodorsal and a posteroventral part. In general terms, these two subdivisions are found, respectively, rostral and ventral to the cells associated with the posterior thalamic "nucleus." The anterodorsal part of the complex has the form of a round, compact mass of closely aggregated cells when observed at midthalamic levels (Fig. 4, section 4). In this part of the complex, the posterocentral and posterolateral components are somewhat difficult to distinguish. In the posteroventral region (Fig. 4, section 5), the posterocentral and posterolateral components are clearly distinguish-able, and the posterolateral cells are large and loosely aggregated. Finally, there is a group of large neurons located along the ventral edge of the anterodorsal part of the posterocentral nucleus. These cells arc closely associated with the lateral geniculate nucleus and nucleus ro-tundus and appear to form a special subunit related to the "nucleus" of Bellonci (see the following discussion).

Golgi studies (Ramon, 1894; Herrick, 1925; Scalia and Gregory, 1970) have shown that, in general, the dendrites of the thalamic neurons extend laterally into the neighboring neuropil. However, in some areas, the adjacent margins of the cell masses overlap one another, and careful analysis is necessary to determine the specific innervation of the neuro-pil. Such an analysis (Scalia and Gregory, 1970) has shown that a number of cell groups are involved in the formation of the "nucleus" of

Bellonci and corpus geniculatum thalamicum. The "nucleus" of Bellonci is formed primarily by the dendrites of cells in the lateral geniculate nucleus, which is immediately adjacent to it, but also receives the dendrites of cells in the nucleus rotundus and in the ventral limb of the anterodorsal division of the posterocentral nucleus. The corpus geniculatum is formed also by lateral geniculate dendrites and dendrites from the nucleus rotundus and ventrolateral area.

The observation that the dendritic supply for the "nucleus" of Bellonci and corpus geniculatum thalamicum arises from a number of different cell masses certainly introduces a complication in the experimental analysis of the further distribution of visual information from the thalamus. Moreover, it may imply to some observers that the finer details of the morphology of the thalamic cell masses, although regulated by morphogenetic processes, are without functional significance. However, recent findings on the organization of the *thalamofrontal tract* of Herrick (1925) have begun to substantiate the cytoarchitectonic analysis just summarized and to provide a basis for reconstruction of the functional significance of the thalamic nuclei.

The Thalamofrontal Tract

Lesions inflicted in the anterodorsal part of the pc, pl complex in the bullfrog (F. Scalia and K. Gregory, unpublished) caused the degeneration of a strong fascicle of axons which, as determined in Fink-Heimer stained sections, descended from the nuclear complex in a posteroventral direction and turned anteriorly into the lateral and medial forebrain bundles, to terminate densely throughout the ipsilateral striatum, and lightly in the medial cortex (primordium hippocampi) of both sides. These observations are consistent, in part, with the results of two recent degeneration studies (Kicliter, 1973b; Gruberg and Ambros, 1974) showing a projection to the striatum from some unidentified nuclear masses in the thalamus, a projection carried by the lateral forebrain bundle. In one of these studies Gruberg and Ambros, 1974), electrical recordings were obtained from the striatum following visual stimulation. Evoked potentials, furthermore, have been recorded from the medial cortex (Karamian *et al.*, 1966; Vesselkin *et al.*, 1971), following optic nerve stimulation, and the latter investigators also found evidence of terminal degeneration in the medial cortex, following lesions of the dorsal thalamus.

To confirm the earlier observations and to identify the nuclei of origin of these projections in *R. pipiens*, the striatum and medial cortex were injected (F. Scalia and D. R. Colman, 1975) with horseradish peroxidase (HRP), and the retrograde movement of the enzyme was traced. In these preparations, the telencephalic afferent axons are filled with HRP reaction product and can be traced back through the lateral and medial forebrain bundles to their cells of origin. These axons begin to turn dorsally, immediately caudal to the corpus geniculatum thalamicum, and can be followed directly to cell bodies in the dorsal thalamus. The cells are either marked with intracytoplasmic grains of HRP reaction product, or they are filled and densely colored by the product. The cell bodies are located along a continuous column running through both the anterodorsal and posteroventral parts of the *posterolateral nucleus* when the injection involves the *striatum*. None of the cells in the posterocentral nucleus nor in the posterodorsal part of the posterolateral nucleus (i.e., the cells adjacent to the posterior thalamic "nucleus") are labeled by retrograde flow from the striatum. When the injection is given to the *medial cortex*, the marked cells are found in the ventral limb of the anterodorsal division of the *posterocentral nucleus* (i.e., the cells closely associated with the "nucleus" of Bellonci). The initial course of the fiber systems noted here, i.e., the segment that descends from the dorsal thalamus to the forebrain bundles, is most certainly identifiable with Herrick's (1925) *tractus thalamo-frontalis*.

This new information on the organization of the thalamo-frontal tract provides a firm morphological background for further investigation of possible tecto-thalamo-telencephalic and geniculo-telencephalic components in the amphibian visual system because the cell masses from which the two parts of the thalamo-frontal tract arise are themselves closely associated with the terminal fields of the tecto-thalamic and retino-thalamic projections. A critical component of the argument will consist of evidence that the terminals of the retinofugal and tectofugal fibers ending in the diencephalic neuropil do in fact contact the dendrites of the cells of origin of the thalamo-frontal pathways. As noted previously, Golgi studies have shown that, in general, the dendrites of the thalamic neurons extend laterally into the superficial neuropil. By virtue of this relationship, it is quite certain that neurons in that part of the posterolateral nucleus which projects to the striatum are postsynaptic to the tecto-thalamic outflow. In fact, when the dendrites of these cells are back-filled with horseradish peroxidase administered in the striatum, they are observed to extend into the lateral neuropil. However, adequate back-filling of the dendrites of those cells of the posterocentral nucleus which project to the medial cortex has not yet been achieved, and it has not been possible to specifically demonstrate that these cells send their dendrites into the "nucleus" of Bellonci. Golgi impregnations may show that certain neurons in the relevant part of the posterocentral nucleus do provide a dendritic supply for the "nucleus" of Bellonci, but it remains to be shown that the particular cells marked by the retrograde label are among those that innervate the "nucleus."

Physiological Studies

Relatively few single-unit studies have explored the response properties of neurons in the frog diencephalon. Muntz (1962a), recording from some 20 units in the dorsal thalamus, reported two major groups of neural elements responding to visual stimuli: (1) tectal efferents similar to the "newness" and "sameness" neurons of the tectum, and (2) *on* fibers which lay ventral to and separate from the tectal efferents. These units had small receptive fields and were all exceptionally sensitive to "blue" light, but did not respond well to moving contours or spots of light. Muntz also described a rough degree of retinotopic mapping in the dorsal thalamus in the sense that the horizontal axis of the retina projected onto the anteropostero axis of the thalamus. This description is in good agreement with recent anatomic studies (Lázár, 1971; Scalia and Fite, 1974). Muntz did not attempt to localize his recording sites; however, it is likely (judging from his diagrams) that the majority of his recordings were obtained from the corpus geniculatum. Although Muntz reported finding only contralateral units, M. J. Keating (personal communication, 1974) has recently recorded from ipsilateral units in the anterior thalamus of *Rana temporaria*, which appear to be the endings of optic nerve fibers. Several binocular units with relatively small receptive fields and *on* responses have also been recorded in *R. pipiens* by K. V. Fite (unpublished data). Such units were localized primarily in the anterior thalamus in the region of the lateral geniculate nucleus, nucleus rotundus, and ventrolateral area (terminology of Frontera, 1952). According to Scalia and Gregory (1970), neurons in these areas are postsynaptic to the retinal projections. Liege and Galand (1972) have also reported *on* binocular units in the diencephalon (exact recording sites unspecified), some of which showed *on-off* responses to transient changes in illumination and responsiveness to cutaneous stimulation. Brown and Ingle (1973) have recently described binocularly driven units in the posterolateral nucleus (of Frontera) having very large (180°) receptive fields.

Behaviorally, the "blue preference" of frogs, a positive phototaxis toward short wavelength light, is now well documented as a true wavelength discrimination independent of luminosity (Muntz, 1962b; Boycott *et al.*, 1964; Chapman, 1966; Jaeger and Hailman, 1971; Kicliter,

1973b; Hailman and Jaeger, 1974). Muntz (1962a) has suggested that this positive phototaxis is mediated by the "blue-sensitive" fibers projecting to the diencephalon. Recently, bilateral lesions of the dorsal thalamus—lateral geniculate nucleus, nucleus rotundus, and ventrolateral area—have been correlated with a loss of wavelength discrimination in *R. pipiens* (Kicliter, 1973a) and, in some cases, with a loss of flux discrimination as well. Exact differences in lesion placement could not be distinguished in these two cases, however, which leaves unresolved the question of which specific fiber terminations, nuclear groups, or fibers of passage are necessary for the deficits. Since color-coded units have also been described in the optic nerve as a whole (Reuter and Virtanen, 1972; see Chapter 2) wavelength discrimination in the frog very likely involves both tectal and diencephalic components.

Although similar studies have not yet been reported in frogs, Ewert (1971) has recorded from the toad caudal thalamus and has found visually driven units with the following characteristics: sensitivity to either moving or stationary visual objects; units with receptive fields of 15–30° responding optimally to dark, moving targets 10° or larger; large-field contralateral units 90–180°, sometimes with an ipsilateral region and showing either rapid or little adaptation to repeated stimulus motion; units with changeable receptive field sizes; units sensitive to movement along the x-axis toward the animal; units responding with a tonic discharge to a change of room illumination; spontaneously active units whose activity was either increased or inhibited by moving objects; units activated by moving objects that continued to discharge for 10 sec or more after the object had disappeared and, finally, units that showed a prolonged response to stationary objects. The majority of such units were found in the caudal part of the posterocentral nucleus and ventral thalamus (of Frontera). Whether or not similar types of units exist in the posterior thalamus of the frog remains to be established.

Other evidence (Ewert, 1968b; 1970a) indicates that, at least in toads, the posterior thalamus is associated with avoidance behavior and the ability to discriminate "predator" objects (see Chapter 5). There does appear to be considerable interaction with the optic tectum, however; and Ewert (1970a) has suggested that the excitability of tectal neurons is modulated via inhibitory connections from the caudal thalamus, which might affect both habituation and size-selectivity characteristics of tectal neurons. Ingle (1973c) has recently demonstrated a similar disinhibition of tectal "newness" neurons in the frog tectum following lesions of the pretectal region, which includes an increase in receptive field size and a decrease in habituation or adaptation of response to a repeated stimulus.

Optic Tectum

Although there have been numerous descriptions of the cytoarchitecture of the anuran tectum (Ramon, 1894; Gaupp, 1899; Larsell, 1929, 1931; Ariens Kappers *et al.*, 1936; Lázár and Székely, 1967; Potter, 1969, 1972), a brief description of this structure will be given here as an introduction to the material presented in this section: The paired optic tecta appear as hollow, hemispheric elevations of the dorsolateral surface of the midbrain. Each hemisphere consists of a relatively thin (500–700 μm) curved plate covering the roof of the midbrain ventricle. By a combination of myelin- and cell-staining procedures, a distinctive laminar architecture is readily observed in the tectal plate (Fig. 6). The laminae were described by Ramon (1894) as consisting of 15 layers, numbered consecutively from the innermost (ependymal) layer outward. For our present purpose, however, we shall use a system that combines the named-layers scheme of Ariens Kappers and coworkers (1936) and the lettered-layers of Potter (1969), both of which contain elements of Ramon's discription. *Stratum periventriculare* is a thick multilaminar region, containing most of the tectal neurons. It is located on the ventricular side of the tectal plate. Moving outward, one encounters in succession: st. album central, layer G, st. griseum centrale, layer F, and then layers E through A. The last layer (layer A) is found just below the pia mater, but only in the anterior half of the tectum. *Stratum album centrale* contains a heavy band of myelinated, tectal efferent fibers. *Stratum griseum centrale* is a moderately dense

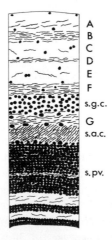

Fig. 6. Laminar arrangement of myelinated fibers and cell bodies in the anterior part of the optic tectum of *Rana pipiens*. Unmyelinated fibers are not drawn.

layer of cell bodies, although it is not nearly as thick as the periventricular gray. *Layers A through F* and *layer G* contain retinal afferent axons and terminals. Separate layers are morphologically identified in this superficial region by virtue of a differential stratification of myelinated and unmyelinated axons. Layers B, D, and F (and G) are heavily myelinated; layers A, C, and E contain predominantly thin, unmyelinated axons.

Golgi studies on the optic tectum (Ramon, 1894; Lázár and Székely, 1967; Potter, 1969, 1972) have shown that the major cell types have long ascending dendrites directed toward the retinal afferent layers. Among these neurons are three of the types of cells described by Potter (1972). Two classes of neurons situated in the deep layers are the *pyramidal* cells, with narrowly defined dendritic arborizations in the superficial zone, and the *candelabra* cells, whose large apical dendrite divides to form two horizontal branches in lamina 7. These branches may run for considerable distances before giving off other branches which terminate after directing themselves toward the pia. *Multipolar* cells found in laminae 6 and 7 of Ramon send dendrites toward the pia, and their axons enter the intermediate fiber system of lamina 7. These neurons, along with the candelabra cells, probably constitute the major efferent neurons of the tectum. In addition, superficial granule cells are found near the pia and give rise to single processes that ramify and branch repeatedly in the superficial zone.

Some information on the morphology of the optic nerve endings in the tectum has also been reported from observations on Golgi-impregnated material. As a result of one of the earlier Golgi studies (Lázár and Székely, 1967), it was suggested that the retinal axons pass along the outer surface of the tectum and turn inward at retinotopically appropriate loci to form vertically oriented, bell-shaped, terminal arbors in the superficial neuropil. According to this proposition, it would appear that the various parallel layers of myelinated and unmyelinated fibers in the superficial neuropil, as enumerated by letters in Potter's (1969) description of the tectum, have little to do with the organization of the retinotectal projection. However, clear evidence had been obtained in an early Nauta study (Knapp et al., 1965) that at least the myelinated fibers of layers B, D, F, and G, which degenerate following eye removal, enter their own strata directly at the margin of the tectal plate.

In other studies using silver-staining methods (Scalia et al., 1968; Lázár and Székely, 1969; Potter, 1972), terminal degeneration was observed virtually throughout the superficial tectal neuropil following eye removal, and several strata of axonal degeneration were noted. Little evidence of axonal or terminal degeneration was observed, however, at the surface of the tectum (i.e., in layer A), except near its posterior end, where layer A is absent. This data prompted a reinterpretation of the course and distribution of the retinotectal axons (Székely *et al.*, 1973), as seen in Golgi material, in which several parallel strata of retinal axons are now recognized. From a combined study of Golgi-stained material and electron microscopic analysis of normal and experimentally enucleated frogs, Székely and associates (1973) indicate that neither axonal nor terminal degeneration occurs at the tectal surface, but that the vertically oriented, bell-shaped terminal arbors are the endings of retinal axons which turn down (inward) from certain of the various parallel fibrous layers.

However, it has been recently shown (Scalia, 1973), using the autoradiographic tracing technique, that some component of the retinal afferent supply does exist in the most superficial tectal layer (layer A, st. zonale), and retinal terminals as well as retinal axons have been visualized in layer A (Scalia and Colman, 1974) by means of the anterograde intra-axonal movement of horseradish peroxidase. The terminals observed in layer A were more or less horizontally oriented and resembled the type DB terminal described by Potter (1972). Examples of other terminals were observed in the deeper parts of the superficial neuropil, and they also were horizontally oriented and conformed to the images described in Potter's (1972) Golgi study as type DB or WB.

The terminal arbors observed by Potter (1969, 1972) and attributed to retinal afferent axons (Potter, 1972) are quite different in appearance from the bell-shaped arbors described by Székely and colleagues (1973). They appear to be only associated with large diameter (myelinated) fibers, and they form horizontally oriented, tortuous complexes, elongate in the direction of the parent fiber. The types DB and WB refer to more compact or more loosely arranged terminals associated, respectively, with the fibers in layers B and D or F and G. The observed spreading of these terminals into layers C and E and the upper region of st. griseum centrale appears fully consistent with the occurrence of terminal degeneration in these layers following eye removal (Scalia *et al.*, 1968; Potter, 1972). Potter observed no evidence either for the sharp vertical descent of any axons in the superficial neuropil or for the existence of the vertically oriented bell-shaped terminals.

According to Potter (1972), only the axons in layers B, D, F, and G are retinal afferents. These axons clearly degenerate following eye removal. The fine, unmyelinated axons in layers A, C, and E (Potter, 1969) did not show the typical evidences of axonal degeneration (Potter, 1972) when observed in enucleate frogs in silver-stained sections. However, at least some of the fibers in layers C and E, as well as fibers in layer A, have been filled by an anterograde movement of horseradish peroxidase (Scalia and Colman, 1974), and evidence has been presented of their relative resistance to axonal degeneration during a time scale in which the fibers and terminals of layers B, D, F, and G degenerate and lose the peroxidase stain. However, no data on the form of the terminals of the layer C and E axons have yet been obtained.

The importance of reliable morphological information on the laminar and synaptic organization of the tectum is underscored by the well-known electrophysiological evidence (Maturana et al., 1960) that optic nerve axons having various feature-detecting functions terminate in spatially segregated sublayers within the retinal afferent neuropil in the tectum. Four or five such functions were identified (see Chapter 2), and the terminals specifically associated with them were localized in three sublayers separated from each other by layers in which retinal afferent discharges did not occur. At the present time, however, morphological studies have not succeeded in clearly identifying the elements correlated with these and other electrophysiological data. The existing interpretations of Golgi material are discordant. Reliance on anterograde degeneration alone to mark the retinal terminals for electron microscopy has been shown to be insufficient. And, the more reliable marking techniques (including electron microscopic autoradiography) have not yet been utilized in the electron microscopic analysis of the synaptic morphology of the optic tectum. Even the apparently simple problem of morphologically identifying the layers containing the electrophysiologically defined terminals has resisted easy solution. A significant element complicating this problem is the fact that histological data on electrode tip positions were not reported in the original studies. The absence of such information has allowed for considerable variation in the interpretations offered in subsequent anatomical studies.

According to Maturana and co-workers (1960), the first class of optic terminals in R. pipiens (type 1) is encountered immediately as the electrode penetrates the pia mater. In further penetration, the type 1 terminals persist through some depth and are gradually replaced by type 2 terminals. The population of type 2 terminals, however, abruptly ends at a deeper level, where an electrophysiologically silent zone is encountered. After passing through the silent layer, the type 3 terminals begin to appear, and these persist down to the level of a second electrophysiologically silent layer. Associated with the type 3 terminal is a minor population of type 5 terminals. The type 4 terminals are encountered below the second silent layer and form a narrow lamina immediately above what is presumed to be layer 7.

In terms of this account, anatomical techniques that mark optic terminals *in situ,* ought to reveal the presence of three layers of terminals (call them R_1, R_2, R_3) separated by two layers in which optic terminals are absent or few in number (N_1 and N_2). The lamination pattern produced by these layers should appear as follows: Layer R_1 begins at the tectal surface (it contains the types 1 and 2 terminals); it is followed by (the electrophysiologically silent) layer N_1; layer R_2 (containing the type 3 terminal) is found below N_1 and above N_2 (the second silent layer); layer R_3, finally, is found below N_2 and immediately above layer 7 of P. Ramon. Layer R_3 contains the type 4 terminal. In such a lamination pattern, the clarity of separation of the layers R_1, R_2, and R_3 would depend upon the size of layers N_1 and N_2 in relation to the population density of any optic terminals they may contain. Also, the appearance of layer R_1 would depend upon the population distribution in the region of interspersal of type 1 and type 2 terminals.

At a particular survival time following eye enucleation, a laminar distribution of terminal and/or fiber degeneration may be observed in the tectum in Fink-Heimer stained sections, which is similar in many respects to the hypothetical pattern just described (see Scalia and Gregory, 1970, Fig. 10). The first layer of degeneration, which might suggest the hypothetical layer R_1, consisted almost entirely of the kind of granular silver deposit usually considered to represent degenerating terminals. This degeneration approximated laminae B and C of Potter. The second layer of degeneration (R_2?) was separated from the first by a narrow zone (N_1?) relatively free of degeneration. This layer of degeneration approximated laminae E and F of Potter and extended down through the upper half of stratum griseum centrale. It also consisted predominantly of discrete silver grains, although some large diameter degenerating fibers were present in the position of lamina F. Below this, there was another degeneration-free zone (N_2?), followed by a narrow layer (R_3?) of degenerating axons accompanied by silver grains. This last layer, being lamina G, was located along the upper aspect of the stratum album centrale (layer 7).

The pattern of degeneration just described is not stable in time. At somewhat earlier survival times, one sees two layers of "terminal" degeneration in the place of the first layer described, so that four instead of three layers of degeneration are apparent. It is not obvious why this happens, but it is probably the reason for the report (Lázár and Székely, 1969) that four layers of terminal degeneration, which were considered to be comparable to the 4 types of electrophysiologically identified terminals, occur in the tectum following enucleation. At longer survival times, more degeneration characteristic of axonal fragmentation appears in the tectal plate and tends to fill up the space (lamina D of

Potter) attributed before to the hypothetical layer N_1. Axonal degeneration also appears in lamina B, and more of the fibers in lamina F degenerate. Ultimately, the terminal degeneration disappears, and one may observe four distinct and widely separated layers of degenerating axons in laminae B, D, F, and G. This last pattern corresponds to what was observed originally by Knapp and co-workers (1965), using the Nauta stain.

An obvious problem generated by these anatomic data concerns the fact that the patterns of terminal degeneration described in the various laboratories (Scalia et al., 1968; Lázár and Székely, 1969; Scalia and Gregory, 1970; Potter, 1972) consistently failed to extend all the way to the pial surface; i.e., little or no degeneration was observed in the stratum zonale (layer A). However, stratum zonale is thin on the dorsal surface of the tectum, where electrode penetration is usually centered, and it might be argued that in the process of dimpling through the pia mater, electrodes probably frequently explode through stratum zonale before coming to rest at a somewhat deeper level. Of course, the auto-radiographic demonstration of retinal afferents in layer A (Scalia, 1973) and the subsequent visualization of optic terminal arbors in that layer (Scalia and Colman, 1974) show that the constructs obtained by the techniques of anterograde degeneration were simply not complete.

The presence of optic terminals in layer A must also be taken into consideration in any discussion of the numerical correlation between the electrically recorded and anatomically observed layers of terminals. Despite the fact that the initial electrophysiological model required the presence of only three morphologically or spatially distinct layers of terminals, the existence of four types of terminal was apparently the focus of many investigators interested in the correlation of anatomic and physiological data. Thus, Knapp and associates (1965) and Gaze (1970) emphasized the significance of the *four* layers of myelinated *fibers* (B, D, F, and G) observed to degenerate following eye removal, and Lázár and Székely (1969) called attention to the *four* layers of *terminal* degeneration they observed in Fink-Heimer stained sections. Even studies portraying only *three* layers of *terminal* degeneration (Scalia et al., 1968; Scalia and Gregory, 1970) have been misquoted to support this numerical correlation. Whether three or four layers of terminal degeneration are taken to be representative of the results of anatomic studies, it would appear necessary to increase the number by one to accommodate the new information on retinal afferents in layer A. Quantitative estimates (Fig. 7) of the spatial distribution of retinal afferent elements in the optic tectum, as determined by the autoradiographic technique, generally show the presence of four major peaks of

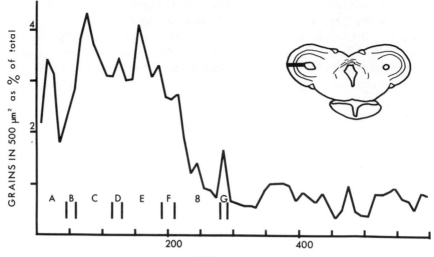

Fig. 7. Graph of grain counts in an autoradiograph as a function of depth through the tectal laminae. Grains were counted in a sector (column) 50 μm across and 600 μm deep, oriented perpendicular to the tectal surface. (See inset for orientation and rostrocaudal level.) Counts are plotted at 10 μm depth intervals and graphed as percent of total counts in the entire sector. Depths of major tectal laminae are indicated by vertical bars and labeled according to Potter (1969). Lamina A is stratum zonale. Taken from frog surviving 24 hours postinjection with 20 μCi of tritiated leucine. (Courtesy of Elsevier Publishing Co.)

radioactivity (including the peak corresponding to layer G) in regions in which layer A is well developed.

Indirect Ipsilateral Projection

While the optic tectum is the largest central nervous system target of optic tract fibers, it receives *direct* input only from the contralateral eye. However, a substantial *indirect*, polysynaptic projection from the ipsilateral eye does exist (Fig. 8), which appears to arise from the contralateral tectum. The indirect ipsilateral projection was carefully mapped for the first time by Gaze and Jacobson (1962) using multiunit evoked responses from the dorsal aspect of the tectal surface. Briefly, the left half of the anterior-superior binocular field projects through both eyes to the anterior part of the right tectum, while homologous points in the right half of the anterior-superior binocular field project to the tectum. The central portion of the binocular field, i.e., points in the anterior part of the midsaggital plane of the animal, are represented at symmetrical locations of the two tectal lobes.

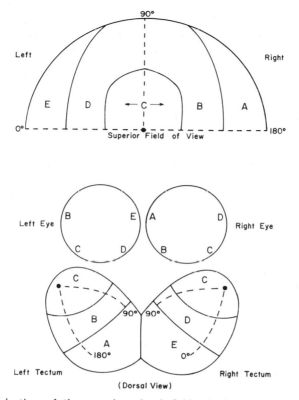

Fig. 8. Projection of the superior visual field of view onto each retina and to the optic tecta in *Rana temporaria*. Area C represents the center of the binocular field and projects through both eyes (direct contralateral, indirect ipsilateral) to the rostral third of each tectal lobe. Area D projects through both eyes to the left tectum; area B through both eyes to the right tectum. Areas A and E represent the monocular fields of view and project only through a single eye to a single tectal lobe. Area DCB, therefore, represents the superior, binocular visual field. (Modified from Gaze and Jacobson, 1962.)

The specific pathways responsible for mediating the ipsilateral response component are still the focus of some controversy, although evidence is accumulating that at least two such pathways may exist—one projecting via the postoptic commissure, another via the tegmental commissures. Gaze and Jacobson (1962) initially reported that the latency of the response to stimulation of the ipsilateral eye was on the order of 20–30 msec longer than the response obtained from the contralateral eye. When the homologous region of the contralateral tectum was destroyed, the ipsilateral response component vanished. Degenerating fibers from such a focal lesion were observed primarily in the ventral tegmental commissures.

Fite (1969), recording from single units in the deep tectal layers, eliminated the ipsilateral response component from binocularly driven neurons under two conditions: (1) lesions of the contralateral tectum and (2) section of the deep tegmental commissures. Such lesions were confined exclusively to the tectal-pretectal region and did not include the postoptic commissure. These findings were in agreement with the earlier report of Gaze and Jacobson concerning the loss of ipsilateral response in the superficial tectal layers following section of the deep tegmental commissures.

However, degenerating fibers from tectal lesions have also been described as crossing in the postoptic commissures to terminate in the diencephalon (Rubinson, 1968; Lázár, 1969; Keating and Gaze, 1970b). Some portion of the indirect ipsilateral tectal pathway may thus involve two, and perhaps three, stages—the projections from the eye to the contralateral tectum; from the contralateral tectum to the diencephalon, by way of the postoptic commissure; then to the ipsilateral tectum. Although Rubinson (1968) did not report any direct tecto-tectal fibers traveling in the postoptic commissure, he did report tectofugal fibers terminating in the opposite diencephalon, particularly in the lateral neuropil, the corpus geniculatum, pretectal region, and mesencephalic tegmentum of the contralateral side. Degenerating fibers from tectal lesions were also seen entering the deep tegmental commissure, but they did not enter the contralateral tectum.

In a recent study, Trachtenberg and Ingle (1974) report that focal lesions of the dorsal anterior thalamus and corpus geniculatum, in particular, yield terminal degeneration in the superficial and deep layers of the ipsilateral tectum. The degeneration was primarily confined to the rostral one-third of the tectum, which subserves the anterior, binocular field of view. Some portion of these thalamo-tectal projections may very well represent ipsilateral visual information originating from the contralateral tectal lobe.

Additional information concerning the physiological properties of indirect ipsilateral fibers comes from single and multiunit action potentials recorded from the superficial tectal layers (Gaze and Keating, 1970; Keating and Gaze, 1970a; Raybourn, 1975). Raybourn (1975) has recorded rather large differences in ipsilateral response latencies of units from the uppermost 200 μm of the tectum, as compared with ipsilateral units recorded below a depth of 200 μm. The deeper units have shorter latencies by some 40–50 msec.

The apparent discrepancies between studies with respect to the specific pathway(s) mediating the indirect ipsilateral projections to the tectum is, perhaps, best resolved by a consideration of evidence in favor of at least two such pathways, both of which may project to the superficial layers of the tectum. For example, an unreconciled controversy currently exists between developmental laboratories with respect to whether or not early binocular visual experience is necessary for the development of functional correspondence between direct contralateral and indirect ipsilateral tectal projections. It is possible that individual investigators may be recording from different populations of ipsilateral afferents that may have different developmental properties. Alternatively, genuine species differences may exist among anurans in the configuration of the indirect ipsilateral projection itself.

The role of indirect ipsilateral projections in visually guided behavior also remains unresolved, although it seems likely that such pathways are involved in prey catching and orienting responses to stimuli appearing primarily within the frontal, binocular field of view. These pathways are not present in anurans until metamorphosis (as is also the case for the direct ipsilateral retino-thalamic projection), at which time the eyes migrate from an extreme lateral position to a more frontal-superior position with an accompanying increase in the frontal-superior binocular field (Jacobson, 1971; Beazley et al., 1972). Direct ipsilateral retinal afferents to the superior colliculus are found in some mammals, and the proportion of such uncrossed retino-collicular fibers appears to be related to the degree of binocular overlap. Whether the indirect ipsilateral projection of anurans bears any functional relation to the direct ipsilateral collicular projection in mammals is yet to be established.

At the present time, there is no direct evidence that stereoscopic vision either exists or constitutes a major factor in the accurate judgment of depth and distance in anurans. Liege and associates (1973) and Gaillard and co-workers (in preparation) have recently provided electrophysiological evidence recorded from the tectal surface in *R. esculenta* which suggests the existence of a horoptor, represented in the horizontal plane through the anterior binocular field by a circumference 10 cm in diameter, and which passes through both eyes of the animal. Although a fixation point does not appear to exist, the location of the horoptor zone appears to correspond with the region surrounding the midline where most prey-catching and accurate depth localization occurs. Other evidence indicates that monocular enucleation in *R. pipiens* produces a marked increase both in the number of prestrike orientations and in prey-catching error rates in the visual field contralateral to the enucleated eye which would normally fall within the field of view of both eyes (Fig. 9). Contrary to previous reports (Ingle, 1972; Fite, 1973), extensive quantitative behavioral observations (Fite and Rego, 1974) have

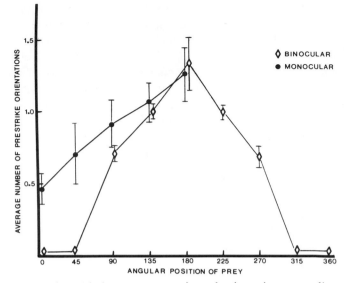

Fig. 9. Comparison of the average number of orientations preceding prey capture at eight different locations around the body of *Rana pipiens* before and after monocular blinding. Zero and 360° correspond to a point directly in front of the frog, 180° is directly behind the frog. Prey (live mealworms) were presented at a distance of 6–9 cm. Vertical lines represent standard error of the mean for each point.

revealed that these changes in prey-catching behavior do not show a transient recovery to normal patterns, but appear to be a permanent alteration in the animal's behavior. Thus, where prey-catching is concerned, it seems that two eyes are indeed better than one. Further studies are required to clarify what role, if any, the direct and indirect ipsilateral visual projections play in prey-catching accuracy and depth localization.

Postsynaptic Neurons

To date, relatively little information exists concerning the physiological response properties of intrinsic tectal neurons. In a brief, but intriguing report, Lettvin and co-workers (1961) reported single-unit recordings from the deep zone of the tectum and described two classes of neurons which they named "newness" and "sameness" neurons. These neurons showed response properties that were remarkably different from those of optic tract terminals recorded in the superficial tectal layers. Newness neurons had receptive fields of some 30°, showed little response to marked changes in illumination, but responded well to moving objects depending upon the parameters of object size, velocity, direction, and "jerkiness" of movement, but never with a sustained discharge. Repeated presentation of an object across the same path in the receptive field markedly reduced the neural response (adaptation or habituation). These cells have been interpreted by subsequent authors as "novelty detectors."

Sameness neurons showed complex response properties, including a type of "selective attention" to movement of small targets within their receptive fields. When presented with two small, moving targets, sameness neurons seemed to "attend" to one or the other, but not to both simultaneously. These neurons showed a sustained response lasting about 2 min to an object whose movement in the receptive field had recently ceased. Lettvin and colleagues (1961) reported after examining over a hundred cells, that there were ". . . several types of which the two mentioned are extremes"—a qualification that has been frequently overlooked. Fite (1969) also recorded from neurons in the deep tectal layers and suggested that, instead of "sameness" versus "newness" (Lettvin *et al.* 1961), a more useful characterization of neuron response properties would relate to the degree of adaptation (or habituation) shown by the neuron to a repeated stimulus event across the same path through its receptive field. The majority of tectal neurons appear to fall between the two extremes of rapid versus little adaptation to a repeated stimulus.

Other response properties described by Fite (1969) indicated that tectal neurons in the periventricular layers of the rostral tectum could be classified as either monocular or binocular, and as monosensory (exclusively visual) or multisensory (some combination of visual, vibratory, tactile, or auditory input). These tectal neurons showed either off or on-off responses to rapid change in illumination, and thus appear to receive their visual input from class 3 and class 4 afferents, as described by Maturana and co-workers (1960). Similar findings have been reported by subsequent investigators (Liege and Galand, 1972; Skarf, 1973; Grüsser and Grüsser-Cornehls, 1973; Skarf and Jacobson, 1974).

Midbrain Tegmentum

The posterior accessory optic tract projects to an area of neuropil and cell bodies located at the ventrolateral edge of the rostral tegmentum immediately behind the hypothalamus, which has previously been described by several names, including nucleus opticus tegmenti (Herrick, 1925), nucleus ectomammalaris (Gaupp, 1899), and basal optic nucleus (Wlassak, 1893). This projection emerges from the caudal aspect of the optic chiasma and travels in the most ventral part of the thalamus toward the basal optic nucleus and carries fibers only from the contralateral eye (Knapp *et al.*, 1965; Scalia *et al.*, 1968; Lázár and Székely, 1969). The existence of a retinotopic organization within the basal optic nucleus has not yet been established, although the functional significance of this projection has been recently described by Lázár (1973). Destruction either of the accessory optic tract or the basal optic nucleus completely abolished the frog's ability to respond to a moving striped pattern that induces optokinetic nystagmus in normal animals. Destruction or ablation of other visual areas did not eliminate optokinesis, although some changes in the characteristics of the response (amplitude and frequency) were observed following ablation of the tectum or pretectal area. Transection of the accessory optic tract also produced extreme pupillary dilation in the ipsilateral eye.

CONCLUSION

Amphibians are among the oldest classes of vertebrates that possess the major visual projections found in mammals (Riss and Jakway, 1970; Ebbesson *et al.*, 1970), with the possible exception of the retino-hypothalamic projection. Frogs, in particular, possess not only the major contralateral neural substrates of vision, but bilateral retino-thalamic projections as well. The degree of homology in these primary visual pathways across vertebrates is not entirely clear and their functional correlates in behavior are also, at present, incompletely understood. Delineating the structural and functional correlates of multiple maps of the visual world in the central nervous system of vertebrates continues to represent, in general, one of the most significant problem areas in the neurosciences. Future research on the anatomic, physiological, and behavioral substrates of vision in frogs as a "model" vertebrate may yield an increasingly comprehensive and integrative framework from which new insights may emerge concerning the existence of a fundamental organizational "bauplan" upon which vertebrate visual systems are constructed.

4

Spatial Vision in Anurans

David Ingle*

INTRODUCTION

In the last decade, there has been a renaissance of comparative neuroanatomy that draws attention to the striking parallels in the visual organization of all vertebrates (Ebbesson *et al.*, 1970; Riss and Jakway, 1970). Studies of fishes and amphibians, now as well as earlier in this century, have usually been undertaken with an evolutionary aim—to shed light upon the still mysterious emergence of neocortex from rudimentary telencephalic structures. From this perspective, the frog can be studied with an eye open for homologies: identification of a "geniculate" within rostral thalamus and possibly a geniculotelencephalic projection (Kicliter and Northcutt, 1975; Gruberg and Ambros, 1974; Scalia and Coleman, 1975) as well. A second major emphasis upon frog vision has arisen from the unique ability of amphibians (along with fish) to rapidly regenerate central visual connections (see Chapter 7). However, frogs and toads are discussed here, not in terms of their evident uniqueness,

*The author was supported by a NIMH Career Scientist Award (KO-2-13,175) during preparation of this chapter.

119

but as valuable "models" for analysis of common vertebrate visual behaviors. The convenience of such experiments is based upon behavioral traits, peculiar to the frog, but also upon the assumption that comparable functional systems exist from fish to primate, in response to a common set of challenges from nature.

One example of a successful model visual system—the *Necturus* retina—is discussed elsewhere in this volume (see Chapter 6). Although variations of retinal morphology are easily observed within and between phyla, these studies of *Necturus*, in particular, have given us a fundamental "bauplan" for discussing visual information flow from receptor to ganglion cell. The beginning of an attempt to extend the bauplan notion from retina to the pattern of retinofugal projections has been reviewed by Riss and Jakway (1970), who emphasize the consistent tendency among all vertebrate classes for these projections to include four target regions of thalamus and midbrain: anterior thalamus, posterior thalamus, optic tectum, and accessory optic tract (see Chapter 3). An attempt has been made to sort out homologies among retinothalamic targets of various vertebrate groups by Ebbesson (1972), while comparative reviews of structure and function of the optic tectum have also appeared (Ingle, 1973b; Ingle and Sprague, 1975). The present essay ventures beyond these somewhat cautious, anatomically rooted comparisons in asking what the visual system must do for the organism. My aim is to set the frog squarely within a broader biological framework, without which comparative psychology may continue to languish. Other attempts along this line appear elsewhere and contain material that may supplement the present review (Ingle, 1970, 1971a,b, 1975).

PROBLEMS IN STUDYING SPATIAL VISION

In this chapter, some problems of spatial vision that probably confront most members of all vertebrate classes are raised. During locomotion through a realm of various surfaces and objects, animals continually decide where they may step, when to duck under barriers, how to sidestep to obtain a better view around an edge, whether to hide within a hole, or how far to leap onto another surface, etc. Obviously, the visual system plays a major role in many species in updating the brain on the location, distance, and velocities of countless points and edges as their locations are transformed during locomotion. Perhaps because these visual functions are usually "unconscious" in man and provide the framework within which our attention focuses upon and evaluates particular objects, they have largely been ignored by psychologists (preoccupied with studies of object recognition) and by zoologists (concerned with stimuli that elicit consummatory responses). The oversight is easily understood, given our explicit concern for epistemological and ethological issues in behavior, but the omission constitutes a serious deficit in the deveolpment of a comparative neuropsychology. Therefore one primary aim of this chapter is to show that spatial vision can be studied in the frog by methods familiar to psychologists and ethologists and that such is necessary to compare visual functions among the vertebrates. A second, more subtle, aim is to explore possible relationships between the somewhat rigid visuo-motor patterns observed in fish and amphibians and the more flexible and "abstract" visual abilities (e.g., visual constancies) attributed to man and the higher mammals.

In an attempt to analyze the "foundations" of vertebrate visual behavior, the frog is a convenient organism, not only because it possesses a relatively primitive brain pattern (without neocortex), but also because it normally sits quite still before responding to the experimenter's pro-vocations. This situation vastly simplifies calculations of the relationship between stimulus and response; each type of response can be linked to variations in stimulus *size, distance, directions,* or *velocity* relative to the frog's eye. By contrast, discrimination studies with fish, birds, or mammals typically involve unpredictable shifts of head or eye position, such that the critical retinal image undergoes complex displacements, expansions, or rotations during the time that behavioral decisions occur. This situation creates a practical difficulty in controlling the attributes of a stimulus that determine its detectability or its recognition. It is difficult to perform an animal psychophysics of movement-perception that can be directly compared with single-unit response variations measured in the paralyzed animal. It is likewise difficult to explore higher-level abilities such as size-invariant shape recognition when using a typical discrimination test that requires an animal to approach stimuli for food reward, since large variations in retinal image size necessarily occur during training. While it is possible to train animals to perform tests under conditions of re-stricted movement, such methods are not usually suitable for rapid and flexible collection of data. Artificial restraint also precludes the examina-tion of stimuli controlling many "natural" behaviors.

Gibson (1966) has offered a major theoretical perspective concerning types of visual information available for spatial perception during loco-motion. Trevarthen (1968b) has extended this approach to a considera-tion of visual behavior in fish, as well as man. Elsewhere, the author has taken hints from Gibson in considering the behavioral uses which many animals make of the directionally sensitive units found within retina and optic tectum (Ingle, 1968b, 1973b, 1975). Except for studies of man, there are few efforts to demonstrate how animals do use information inherent in self-produced motion patterns. If active motion of the organism is critical for certain classes of spatial vision (e.g., depth discriminations that rely upon motion parallax), the frog might be deficient in these types of behavior. On the other hand, the frog may have evolved ways of using stationary visual images to the same end. If that is true, then the critical visual cues should be much easier to analyze for the frog than for other vertebrates.

LOCALIZATION OF PREY OBJECTS

As the geometrician begins his postulates with statements about the relative location of points, it may prove logically satisfying to consider how a frog localizes a small moving bug—the nearest equivalent of a perceptual point. Of course, frogs do attend to features of prey objects other than their location (as Ewert describes for the toad elsewhere in this volume), but once a response is triggered, it appears as a fixed motor sequence varying only with location of the prey. At present, we shall ignore the fact that a toad may behave differently toward a large prey than to a small moving stimulus and treat the ideal case. First, though, a fundamental distinction will be made between two forms of localizing behavior: the *reorientation* of the frog's body directly toward the interesting stimulus and the consummatory *snapping* response in which the prey is withdrawn via the sticky tongue or seized with the jaws. Although body turning and tongue extension need not occur simultaneously, either response can be elicited by the same prey object, depending upon the distance and radial orientation of the object (Ingle, 1970, 1972; Fite, 1973). The orienting response is directed toward an object and can be defined in terms of radial orientation and elevation of the final head position, while the snapping response can be defined within 3 dimensions by location of the tip of the frog's tongue at its furthest extension.

Some authors have casually remarked that frogs snap at frontal stimuli and only reorient to lateral stimuli, but this is somewhat misleading. In fact, the common American frogs (e.g., *Rana pipiens, Rana clamitans*) will snap at nearby objects as far caudally as their hindlegs, but will orient toward frontal stimuli that are too far to reach by a single strike. For most regions of the frog's visual field, a stimulus viewed along any given line of sight will elicit either a snap or a reorientation, depending upon its distance (Ingle, 1970, 1972). When describing behavior

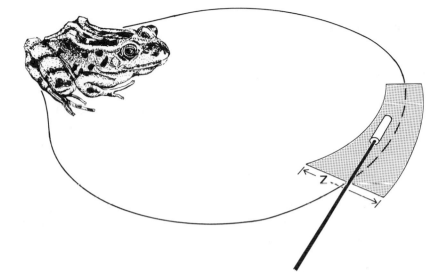

Fig. 1. The snapping zone of a typical frog (*Rana pipiens*) as derived from film records of feeding toward a dummy wormlike stimulus. When the prey-object moves to-and-fro at least 1 inch within the zone, only snapping responses are elicited. There is a 1-inch wide "ambiguous zone" (z) at the boundary where both snaps and orienting movements are observed. Beyond that zone, only orienting or hopping behavior is elicited by a prey object. For normal binocular frogs, the ambiguous zone was measured for prey placed in the stippled area near the midline (Ingle, 1972). For each of 10 frogs, a 1-inch wide zone was found, such that the nearest stimuli elicited nearly all snaps and the farther stimuli elicited nearly all orientations. A similar depth resolution is obtained for objects placed at 90° from the midline, within the monocular visual field (Ingle, unpublished data). A similar plot of the snap zone for the toad, *Bufo marinus*, was illustrated in Ingle (1971a).

toward objects moving along the ground (bugs or worms), one can describe a "snapping zone" (Fig. 1) that extends furthest along the rostral midline—roughly two to three times the body length of the frog. The zone illustrated in Fig. 1 is an abstraction based upon detailed ciné records of 12 frogs. The essential shape and stability of this zone is very similar from frogs of a given species, when body sizes are comparable. Actually the snap zone is a "shell" around the frog's head, expanding near the dorsal midline, but the exact shape is still undetermined. It should be mentioned that the snap zone of the toad (*Bufo americanus, Bufo cognatus, Bufo torrestris, Bufo bufo,* and *Bufo marinus*) is narrower than that of the *Ranidae* thus far mentioned (Schneider, 1954b; Ingle, 1971a; Fite, 1973).

DEPTH ESTIMATION

Measurements of the "sharpness" of the snap-zone boundary would provide useful data for analysis of the frog's depth-discrimination abilities. Preliminary measurements of this kind have been made by the author by placing dummy wormlike stimuli along the frog's midline in order to define the transitional region between snapping and orienting responses (Ingle, 1972). Figure 1 shows the essentials of this method. The width of the ambiguous zone was less than 1 inch for all frogs tested, such that they might reliably discriminate a worm at 6 inches (but not at 7 inches) as reachable by a direct lunge and snap. These stimuli were intentionally varied somewhat in height above the floor, so that differences in angle of elevation could not serve as depth cues. Upon what cues might this type of depth discrimination be based? It seems very unlikely that the small ($\frac{1}{2}°$) ocular tremor produced by the frog's respiration (Schipperheyn, 1963) would provide sufficient parallax for discrimination of object distance (especially a single object against an untextured floor). It is the more surprising therefore to discover that monocular blinding did not reduce the accuracy with which frogs estimated the limits of the snap zone. These observations eliminate binocular stereopsis as a necessary mechanism for this particular discrimination, but they do not rule out a possible advantage of binocular integration for other types of depth discriminations.

Although monocularly enucleated frogs did continue to snap discriminately at worms, depending upon their distance, they were unusually poor in actually hitting worms that fell within the contralateral rostral field more than 15° from the midline. However, when film records of strike accuracy of monocular frogs were analyzed, as shown in Fig. 2, it was clear that the distribution of snap distances to contralateral stimuli was no more varied than that of snaps made to ipsilateral worms actually hit (Ingle, 1976c). Nor was the average lateral snap error greater for contralateral than for ipsilateral stimuli. Although the frog's behavior toward contralateral stimuli was certainly maladaptive, it did not appear to be sloppy. Thus, there remains the puzzling result that frogs undershoot their prey on the enucleated side of the visual field, but not on the side ipsilateral to the remaining eye. Presumably, in the binocular frog, the ipsilateral eye would dominate, since it has been found that monocular frogs always choose an ipsilateral prey dummy over a symmetrical alternative (Ingle, 1973a).

In an earlier paper (Ingle, 1968a), the author suggested, for lack of a good alternative, that depth estimation in the frog might be based upon

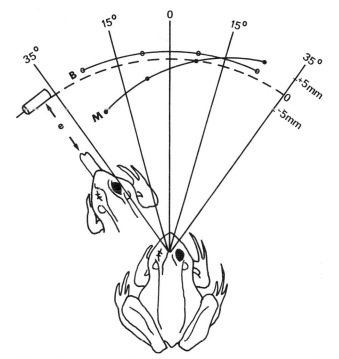

Fig. 2. Schematic representation of frog's snapping errors after monocular binding (left eye). The depth error (e) was measured from single-frame projections of 16 mm film, and represented the difference in mm between the near edge of the wormlike target just prior to the snap and the tip of the wet tongue mark on the slate floor. The mean tongue extention of normal binocular frogs (B) slightly overlapped the stimulus at any location within the rostral binocular field. However, monocular frogs fell short (M) on the average for locations 15–35° from the midline, within the contralateral visual field. Since snap errors are not significantly greater than normal within the ipsilateral visual field, it is concluded that monocular information is sufficient for depth perception in frogs.

some implicit "knowledge" of the accommodative state of the eye that was required to produce a standard, sharp retinal image. That hypothesis —although unsupported by any direct evidence—might account for the peculiar data obtained with monocular frogs. If we imagine a frog in optimal accommodative state for an object along the optic axis, then an equidistant stimulus viewed in the opposite visual field is presumably located beyond the focal plane, and further accommodative effort is required to bring it into focus. But, according to the hypothesis in question, the extra-accomodative effort required for contralateral versus ipsilateral stimuli would be taken as an indication that the former stimulus was nearer to the frog and the frog would snap short of the contralateral worm. Although it will be difficult to measure accommodation shifts in the freely behaving frog, the use of appropriate contact lenses should produce predictable snapping errors.

SELECTION AMONG TWO PREY STIMULI

Although the frog presented with a single, wiggling worm often resembles a spring-loaded toy in his automatisms, some elements of "deliberation" may be seen when a frog is confronted by two simultaneous prey objects within the frontal field. In a recent study (Ingle, 1973a), it was found that presentation of two synchronously moving, dummy prey stimuli, located 30° on opposite sides of the frontal midline (see Fig. 3), would delay the usually sudden snapping response elicited by a single stimulus. However, this striking inhibition effect was not observed in two other situations: when the two objects appeared 60° apart on the same side of the toad, or when presented at 90° loci within opposite monocular fields. An interhemispheric, crossed-inhibitory mechanism

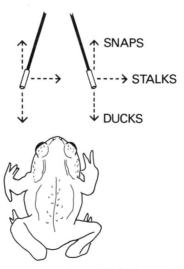

Fig. 3. A qualitative summary of unpublished experiments with *Bufo marinus* (shown here) and *Bufo americanus* viewing synchronous motion of a stimulus pair. A hungry toad will immediately snap at one of the retreating stimuli, yet will either hesitate or duck to a rapid approach of the pair. When the stimuli move sideways, toads usually walk sideways with the nose directed ahead at the leading object as if "stalking" prey. This movement resembles that of a toad cautiously following the head of a long earthworm. The "head-preference" has been objectively confirmed by reconstruction of film records. (Ingle and McKinley, unpublished study).

was invoked as an explanation of the "caution" induced by this particular stimulus configuration. Inhibition resulting from two objects moving horizontally (one behind the other) was also observed by Ewert and coworkers (1970). Could this also result from an interhemispheric inhibitory mechanism? Of course, two simultaneous foci of motion might simulate separation, up to 32°, is compatible with that hypothesis. Therefore, frogs were also tested with rotating double stimuli separated by 30° (Ingle, 1973a), in an attempt to replicate the results of Ewert and associates (1970) with toads. With binocular frogs, the double stimuli did reduce feeding activity to about half the rate seen toward the single object, but monocular frogs showed no difference in feeding toward single versus double stimuli. What would be the ecological significance of such a mechanism? Of course, two simultaneous foci of motion might simulate a larger (and potentially dangerous) object. However, synchronized movements of small stimuli would be rare in nature, and this configuration was not "threatening" when presented on one side of the frog. Rather, this might be viewed as an "interhemispheric rivalry" phenomenon, which prevents both optic tecta from initiating responses at the same moment. Ingle and Sprague (1975) have recently discussed such rivalry mechanisms as common to midbrain centers in various veterbrate species. One specific suggestion made by these authors is that crossed inhibition aids in "shifting attention" from one hemisphere to the other, as an animal moves through a structured visual world.

The exact patterns of double-stimulus motion contribute to the type of elicited behavior, as much as does their exact location. A summary of qualitative observations given by Ingle (1971a) is given in Fig. 3. Here, the marine toad (*Bufo marinus*) is depticted, with three response alternatives (snapping, ducking, or stalking) as stimuli either recede, approach, or move laterally. These toads never avoid a single small stimulus moving toward the head, so that it may be assumed that a summation of two objects is necessary to simulate a "threatening" object. Double-stimulus summation was, in fact, observed by Ewert (1971) within the receptive fields of many wide-field neurons of the toad's caudal thalamus, and the behavioral implications of this finding are discussed in greater detail in Chapter 5 of this volume. On the other hand, the toad's stalking behavior has not received comparable attention, although the side-stepping response does resemble that elicited by barriers (Ingle, 1970), which is illustrated in Fig. 8. It may be that stalking is a compromise movement between direct approach and backing away—i.e., a cautious but interested attitude by the toad. Stalking behavior is less apparent in the common frogs, *Rana pipiens* or *Rana clamitans* and a comparative study of *Rana* and *Bufo* would be well worthwhile.

DIRECTIONALITY OF AVOIDANCE BEHAVIORS

While it is obvious that animals orient accurately toward objects which they wish to investigate or to grasp, the spatial organization of avoidance behaviors has been generally overlooked. One might imagine that animals always do the best they can to maximize the distance between themselves and a threatening stimulus, but the matter is certainly not so simple. When approached by a large, dark object (a "predator" stimulus), frogs can take alternative courses of action: freezing, ducking, shuffling backward, reorienting the body, or leaping forward. Jumping away is the most common response of a healthy frog (*Rana pipiens*), but the ducking and shuffling movements are the more common in some toads (*Bufo*). Details of these behaviors probably vary somewhat among anuran species. Nonetheless, when frogs are selected as "good avoiders," their jumping directions are highly predictable from the location of the threatening stimulus. As Fig. 4 shows, frogs "map out" their avoidance directions as a compromise between the preferred forward direction and that directly away from the stimulus. The monocular frog shows the same pattern of contralateral jumping and does not seem to mind leaping into his blind visual field.

Although the frogs in the author's experiments seem to behave according to simple rules in an empty test arena, the visual decisions of a frog in the real world are more complicated. Yet it is because the unimpeded frog is so stereotyped that the effects of adding visual structure to the test situation can be observed step by step. Figure 4 shows one simple manipulation: a black stationary barrier is set within the frog's preferred jump path. Not surprisingly, the frog leaps further to one or the other side to escape the approaching disc. The author's unpublished data show that even when a barrier is placed near the lateral limits of the normal jump distribution (45° from the midline) the jumps are significantly shifted to the opposite side. This simple method of inducing detours could certainly be used to study threshold detection of barriers by frogs. The method is also adaptable to study of depth-discrimination abilities, which would bear comparison with prey-catching abilities just described.

A recent study (Ingle, 1973d) indicated that frogs will turn more than 90° to the side to avoid a hemicylindrical barrier covering the frontal field. As Fig. 5 illustrates, frogs usually avoid the lateral edge of this grid barrier by 10–20°, just enough to assure head clearance. On the basis of this observation, a double-barrier test situation (Fig. 6) was recently designed to measure the frog's ability to judge the clearance space *between* two frontal vertical barriers (Ingle and Cook, 1976). When frogs were

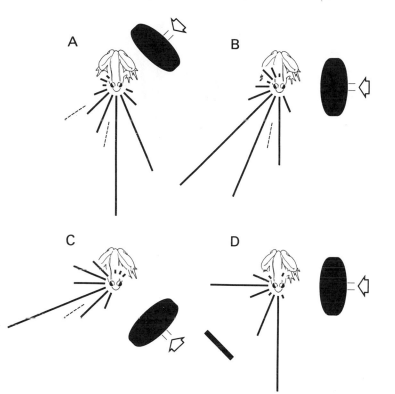

Fig. 4. Avoidance-jump directions summed for 10 frogs (*Rana pipiens*), in response to a looming black disc. The motor-driven disc stopped 1 inch from the frogs to ensure that visual information alone provided the directional cue. The distribution of jumps (total = 100 for each figure) shifts systematically with angle of stimulus approach (A, B, C). In D, a black barrier was placed near the preferred jump direction, but frogs hit the barrier on only one occasion.

pinched on the tail, they tended to jump straight forward. But as the interbarrier distance is reduced toward a critical value (not much wider than actual head width) the frogs turn more often toward the side. This judgment is sharply tuned for barriers 3 inches away from the frog's eye since a change of separation from 26° to 23° decreases the jump-through score from 75% to 25%.

Given this accurate adjustment, it was interesting to find that frogs lack "size-distance constancy" in this test. When barriers were placed at distances of 3, 4½, 6, and 7½ inches, the critical visual angle between the posts that inhibited jumping was always the same. It seems that evolution has designed this visual inhibitory mechanism for measuring the width of nearby apertures; it may be ecologically unimportant that the frog is

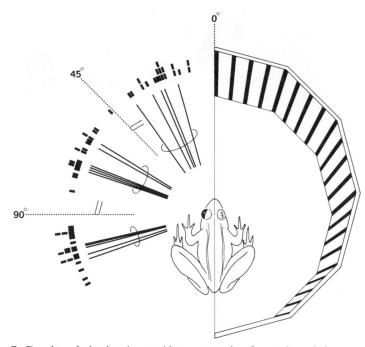

Fig. 5. Results of the barrier avoidance tests for five unitectal frogs using the eye projecting to the lesioned half of the brain. The visible edge of the 15-cm-high barrier was set at either 0°, 45°, or 90°, and the avoidance jump directions were measured from stopped ciné projections. The angle by which the frog cleared the barrier is represented here for each trial by a vertical black rectangle to the left of the barrier edge. Group data are presented as radial histograms, and the responses of one individual are shown by three sets of radial lines, corresponding to the three barrier locations. Reproduced from Ingle (1973d).

also afraid to jump toward more distant apertures that he could easily negotiate.

The failure of frogs to show size-distance constancy in measuring aperture width contrasts with the frog's ability to shift his "optimal prey-size" preference as a function of distance (Ingle and Cook, 1976). The method in the latter experiment was to measure the frog's relative preference for various size objects as against a standard 3° stimulus (set within the opposite monocular field). Figure 7 shows that a 2.3° stimulus was preferred when rival objects appeared 6 inches from the frog's eyes, but a 6° stimulus was optimal in eliciting feeding when set only 3 inches away. These data closely match those obtained for toads by Ewert and Gebauer (1973). This change in size preference was probably not an effect produced by retinal image blur, since recording of class 2 ("bug-detector") retinal axons showed that the 3° stimulus elicited more spikes than did the 6° object at either 3-inch or 6-inch distances.

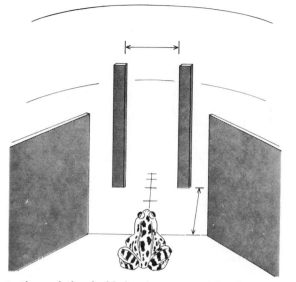

Fig. 6. Illustrations of the double-barrier test used by Ingle and Cook (1975). The frog views two black vertical strips from the open end of a black enclosure. When pinched, the frog either jumps straight forward or veers off to one side. Frogs readily jump between such barriers with a 30° angular separation, but with reduction to 25° or less they consistently turn toward the side. When the distance from frog to barriers is systematically varied, frogs did not show evidence of "size-distance constancy"—i.e., their choice of jump direction was based upon interbarrier visual angle, rather than upon actual distance between the inner edges (Ingle and Cook, 1976).

The size-constancy experiment implies that certain central neurons within the frog's feeding system (perhaps in the optic tectum), must alter their size-selection properties as a function of viewing distance. In line with an earlier suggestion (Ingle, 1968a) is the hypothesis that such shifts in central thresholds could be linked with the visual accommodation mechanism. Shifts of excitability and receptive field size have already been demonstrated in frog tectal neurons (Ingle, 1973c) in association with the excessive feeding tendencies that follow thalamic lesions. Since frogs show increased feeding activity toward nearby stimuli, the size-constancy mechanism (for feeding) may be a special case of the general rule that larger stimuli are relatively more potent during increases in "response readiness" (Ingle, 1973e). This suggestion fits closely with the hypotheses, reviewed in Chapter 6 by Ewert, that thalamic visual mechanisms modulate functions of the optic tectum.

The compensations for object distance shown by the frog toward prey stimuli is a limited constancy—perhaps more "motivational" than "perceptual." For example, our data show that no further constancy is observed when prey stimuli are moved from 6 inches to 9 inches away

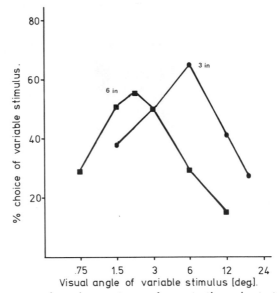

Fig. 7. Summary of a size-constancy demonstration via tests of prey size-preference in normal frogs. Pairs of wormlike stimuli (see Fig. 2) were presented such that each moved 90° from the rostral midline, on opposite sides of the body within monocular fields. Stimuli were placed at the same distance on a given trial, either 6 or 3 inches from the nearest eye. However, one object always subtended 3° in height while the opposite stimulus varied from trial to trial. Ten frogs were tested 10 times each on each size-variation, so that the points of the two curves depicted above each represent 100 forced-choice trials. The preferred size of prey viewed at 3 inches is about twice the visual angle preferred at a 6 inch distance.

from the frog's eye. The idea that prey-catching judgments are related to motivational state contrasts with the rigid behavior required by strictly "spatial" structures in the frog's world. On a moment-to-moment basis, prey catching is optional—the object is to get the largest prey available without running too much risk of approaching a dangerous organism. But avoiding barriers is not optional, and the frog must have a fixed set of rules for describing sizes and distances of stationary objects around or through which he moves. Whether or not a frog (e.g., *Hyla*, the tree climber) could *learn* more adjustable "rules" about spatial relationships is an important question for further study.

ORIENTATION AND SHAPE IN DISCRIMINATION OF BARRIERS

The observation that frogs notice the exact distances between objects seems to be related to their tendency to jump through horizontal rather than through vertical apertures (Ingle, 1973f). Since the frog's body cross section is horizontally elongated, this discrimination ability is adapted to selection of the smallest negotiable escape apertures. Vertical edges might have more salience in inhibiting jumps, or summation of inhibition from two edges might operate effectively along the horizontal axis. Elsewhere, the author has reviewed (Ingle, 1971b) behavioral and physiological evidence that some teleost fish may also "scan" visual shapes more effectively along the horizontal axis (the usual axis of their own motion).

In addition to evidence that frogs measure interedge distances accurately, there is some indication (Ingle, 1971c) that they detect vertical barriers more effectively than horizontal barriers. The rate of detour responses elicited by prey stimuli seen behind a wide vertical grid was 78% as compared to only 10% success using a horizontal grid. Since the ends of this grid were too far away for the frogs to circumvent, it seems that edge orientation per se was important in elicitation of the sidestep response and some neural elements in the barrier-detection mechanism were better tuned to vertical edges. When facing the horizontal grid, frogs sometimes made a creeping movement, with head lowered, as if trying to duck under the interposed fence. Toads will make similar movement while sitting on a ledge and observing mealworms crawling on the floor below. As the worm moves underneath the toad, the latter steps back and thrusts his nose into the floor as if trying to look under the horizontal edge. In short, the presence of an edge may have more perceptual salience than the "solidity" of the floor on which the toad rests.

STEPPING ONTO SURFACES

In addition to detecting barriers that impede progress in escape or in pursuit of prey, (such as that in Fig. 8) frogs and toads notice stationary edges or surfaces as places to step upon or jump toward. It is perhaps surprising that "visual cliff" studies have been lacking for amphibians, although birds and some reptiles avoid the deep side of such a cliff quite consistently. Frogs have been tested on a simple visual cliff test (Ingle 1976c) in which *Rana pipiens* tend to reorient away from the deep side and jump instead to the shallow side. This simple test would probably be a good starting point for quantitative studies of visual cues for depth and for "solidity" of the visual substrate.

Stepping onto surfaces is a response similar to the visual placing response found with many mammalian species, as they are lowered toward a surface or table edge. A well-directed foreleg "placing" response is often seen in the toad (Fig. 8) when moving to observe a worm over a low barrier: either foreleg can be placed neatly upon the top of the fence.

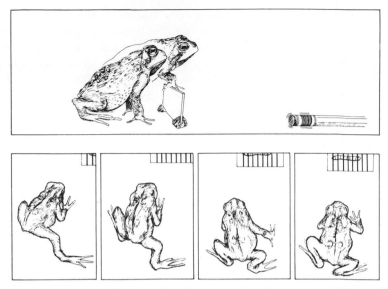

Fig. 8. Toad confronted with a low barrier (top) orients toward "dummy" prey object by placing one or both forelegs on the barrier. When confronted with a transparent grid barrier (bottom), a toad makes a sidestep sequence in preparation for a direct strike. This single-frame film sequence proceeds from right to left.

This observation raises the question as to whether *horizontal* edges might be prepotent in releasing the placing response, or in guiding a jump to another surface, just as *vertical* edges seem to be prepotent in releasing a sidestep detour. In fact, frogs do jump preferentially toward a surface covered with horizontal rather than vertical stripes, even when the two surfaces are equated for visual angle of stripes (Ingle 1976c).

ORIENTATION TO THE BANK OF PONDS

In a test arena the avoidance behavior of frogs is dependent upon the spatial location of the threatening stimulus. However, in nature, other determinants of spatial orientation appear to be more important. Grüsser and Grüsser-Cornhels (1968a) reported field observations on *Rana esculenta*, who would typically flee toward their home site near a stream or water ditch when frightened. Comparable observations have been made on over 20 *Rana clamitans* living in a mountain pond (D. Ingle, unpublished data) by using a long-handed threat stimulus similar to that used in the lab (but manually controlled). It was difficult to induce flight away from the pond, even when frogs were placed some 5 to 6 feet away on the grassy bank. Frogs would typically jump directly toward the pond, despite near collision with the approaching threat object. Interestingly, this pond reflected only green trees, while an open sky appeared on the side *away* from which the frogs leaped. Therefore, the pond-seeking behavior could not be simply explained as a blue-positive photoaxis (Muntz, 1962b). Somewhat surprising was the additional finding that (for each of 50 observations) frogs would follow up a leap into the water by an immediate reorientation toward the pond's edge. If the frog entered the water tangentially to the edge, the reorientation was not through 180°, but only far enough to face the bank squarely. Whether the sequence was preprogrammed at the start of the escape jump or depended upon a second visual orientation after entering the water is not known. It is clear that orientation to the land-water interface is an important natural behavior for which the critical sensory cues remain unknown.

The strong attachment to the pond bank was also seen in premetamorphic tadpoles during the authors observations of the pond. When disturbed, they would swim to deep water, but would soon—sometimes immediately—return toward the weedy bank. Two recent studies by Wiens (1970, 1972) have made important analyses of developmental factors that may influence the tendency of Ranid tadpoles to orient toward the pond bank. By exposing early larval stages to either striped or square patterns in the laboratory, Wiens was able to demonstrate an "imprinting" effect of particular patterns upon the later orienting preferences of tadpoles. When testing the mountain frog, *Rana cascade*, Wiens found that they could only be imprinted upon a square covered substrate (not upon stripes) which roughly resembled the splotchy bottom of their barren ponds. On the other hand, the valley frog, *Rana aurora*, could be imprinted upon stripes, but not on squares, in accord with his normal view of vertical plant stems. It appears that some familiarity with the "natural" stimulus is required for a reliable orienting preference, but species-specific factors determine *which* pattern can be effective for imprinting. This type of experiment may become a prototype for genetic-environmental interaction studies involving visual mechanisms. Although it has been widely assumed that amphibian visual systems are unmodifiable by visual experience (however, see Chapter 7), Wien's studies should open a new experimental chapter for electrophysiologists, as well as for behaviorists.

DIFFERENTIATION OF LOCALIZING BEHAVIORS AND THEIR ANATOMIC BASIS

Thus far, localizing behaviors have been discussed as individual actions, without regard to broad functional classifications. Since the frog's retina projects to at least four distinct target areas, it seems likely that each of these pathways is associated with particular modes of visual behavior. Some evidence now exists to confirm this suspicion. For example, Muntz (1962a) has associated the function of blue-sensitive retinal on fibers (which project to rostral thalamus) with the frog's well-known phototactic preference for jumping toward the blue light. Kicliter (1973b) has supported this hypothesis by observing that large lesions of rostral thalamus abolished normal blue preference of frogs, while deafferentation of optic tectum did not. The tectum has been associated with prey catching since the pioneering studies of Bechterev (1884). The tectum is not required for good optokinetic responses to rotating stripes, but transection of the basal optic tract abolishes this response entirely (Lázár, 1973). Finally, studies of Ewert (see Chapter 6) have localized caudal thalamus as a region critical to visual avoidance behavior in anurans.

Some recent studies in the author's laboratory have shed new light upon the relationships between optic tectum and visual thalamus in avoidance behaviors. First, the finding of Bechterev—that frogs with tectal ablation totally fail to avoid or duck in response to large, black, looming objects—were confirmed. This fact is in good agreement with an observation that the wide-field neurons of caudal thalamus [which Ewert (1971) first suggested as good candidates for meditation of avoidance behavior] receive most of their input from optic tectum (Brown and Ingle, 1973). Not only do tectum and thalamus collaborate in guidance of feeding behavior (see Ewert, Chapter 6), but it appears that they must work together for elicitation of avoidance behaviors as well. The recording studies (Ingle, 1973c; Brown and Ingle, 1973) and anatomic studies (see Chapter 4) support the conclusion that these reciprocal connections constitute a "functional loop" (see also Ingle, 1973b). However, it is still not possible to decide whether a burst of neuronal activity in thalamus, tectum, or in both together is the final event eliciting an avoidance response.

A further line of research (Ingle, 1973d) indicates that visual thalamus functions quite independently of optic tectum in guiding behaviors toward or away from *stationary* objects. Frogs with unilateral tectal ablation performed detour jumps past the grid barrier (Fig. 5) using the eye contralateral to the damaged brain half. When the optic fibers from this eye later regenerated to the ipsilateral tectum, mirror-image responses were elicited by prey, but barrier avoidance jumps were still realistically directed. Recently, by reconstructing the visual avoidance directions elicited by looming objects in such wrong-way regenerated frogs, it was found that *all* jumps are directed ipsilaterally by contrast to normal contralateral jumps. The rewired retinotectal pathway thus misdirects jumps elicited by visual threat while orientations guided by barriers remain realistically directed.

RETINOTOPIC SPECIFICITY IN LOCALIZING BEHAVIORS

In relating specific modes of visual behavior to particular anatomic subdivisions of the frog brain, it may be useful to remember that behaviors differ significantly toward stimuli viewed in different regions of the visual field. An obvious example concerns the failure of frogs to avoid looming objects that approach below the horizon (D. Ingle, unpublished data). If it is assumed that input from tectum to thalamus is required for avoidance behaviors, one class of thalamic neurons may be found not to receive input from the lower visual field. Furthermore, dorsal and ventral regions of the tectum could be compared for differences in at least one morphological class of neuron. Although frogs may use the upper field for avoiding predators, surfaces upon which frogs jump would normally be located within the lower field. A frog planning to leap out of a walled enclosure first tilts his head upward so that the object to be cleared now falls within the lower visual field. These facts may provide useful hints to physiologists and anatomists who compare neuron response properties or morphologies in different regions of a given retinofugal target area.

Some differences may also be found among central visual neurons receiving from rostral versus caudal regions of the visual field. The author's unpublished studies of the frog's ability to orient toward apertures within dark enclosures indicates that most frogs fail to turn toward a window more than 120° laterally, and 90° is usually the limit of efficient escape behavior. Yet the same frogs easily orient to objects 180° to the rear as prey stimuli. As yet, nothing is known of the relative density of retinal projections to rostral versus caudal zones of each thalamic target zone. However, single-unit studies (D. Ingle, unpublished) in frogs with optic tectum ablated indicate so far that most visually activated thalmic units have rostral or lateral rather than caudal receptive fields. Furthermore, Trachtenberg and Ingle (1974) reported that thalamotectal projections (from either geniculate or posterior thalmus) did not extend into the posterior one-third of the optic tectum. Reports of tectothalamic projections did not mention whether lesions confined to caudal tectum resulted in the complete pattern of thalamic degeneration. It should be recalled, in this respect, that the frog's ipsilateral tectal projection [which derives from crossed tectal efferents via the postoptic commissure, according to Keating and Gaze (1970b)] represents only the upper and rostrolateral visual field. There are, in summary, enough examples of physiological and behavioral nonhomogeneity in the relationships between visual function and visual field location to encourage anatomists and physiologists to explore each visual station with a sharp eye for regional specialization.

FROG VISION IN PHYLOGENETIC PERSPECTIVE

Most of the experiments reviewed in this chapter were prompted by general questions which might be applied to other vertebrate species as well. There are two basic uses to be made of this data, when attempting phylogenetic comparisons: (1) identification of *common* visual mechanisms and (2) suggestions as to what evolution has *added* to behavior during the development of an elaborate telencephalic system (reptiles, birds, and mammals). Since very little is known of detailed operations of any visual structures beyond retina in nonmammals rather recent knowledge of frog tectal and thalamic mechanisms may be a useful beachhead for new comparative forays. Three specific areas in which comparative work is likely to prove fruitful are discussed in the following sections.

Variations of the Orientation Reflex

Most vertebrates make rapid and reflexive orienting movements of head, eyes, or body toward food objects or toward "startling" visual events. In frogs and toads, approach movements are made in a particularly stereotyped fashion, by turning the body directly toward the target. Unlike some fish and reptiles, the anurans do not seem to be able to make partial body turns, except occasionally as a result of prolonged habituation to a food object. Fish can either turn their bodies parallel to a neighbor or orient head-on toward prey or conspecific. Reptiles and birds often turn the head so as to bring an object in alignment with the central retinal region of high acuity (which may involve turning the nose away from the object to be "fixated"). It seems likely that separate visuomotor mechanisms are required to elicit or guide these various modes of spatial localization. At present, quantitative studies of visual orienting are limited to the frog's prey-catching and avoidance responses and the monkey's eye saccades. Studies using innate feeding and avoidance and locomotion skills could provide truly comparative data that might reveal the visuomotor subleties which telencephalic development have provided to the "higher" vertebrate groups.

Depth Discrimination Abilities

Frogs accurately discriminate the distances of prey objects or stationary barriers, perhaps without using information derived from either motion parallax or stereopsis. It has already been suggested that frogs may correlate the sharpness of focus of a retinal image with the state of lens accommodation in order to discriminate distances of nearby objects. Some data on accommodative power of fish are relevant to my hypothesis. Sivak (1973) has shown that bottom-feeders, which move slowly and carefully fixate their food from short distances, have a large accommodative range, while fast-moving predators have much less accommodative power. Presumably the latter group depend more upon motion feedback to judge distances between themselves and prey. It is worth noting that fish and birds thus far investigated have many directionally sensitive units in the retina, while frog ganglion cells appear to show little directional bias. There are few comparative studies of tectal and thalamic neurons which indicate *how* visual centers make use of directional specificity. Thus, neurophysiological comparisons between certain teleost fish and frogs should prove instructive when combined with analytical studies of depth estimation. The question should also be raised as to whether mammals that remain still for many seconds at a time (e.g., a "freezing" rabbit) might use accommodation–based cues for depth estimation.

Size-Distance Constancy

The ability to realistically estimate object size at various distances is taken for granted for man and the higher mammals. However, no parametric studies are reported for subprimates other than for frogs and toads. Herter (1930) suggested that fish have size-distance constancy but this conclusion was supported by minimal data and needs to be replicated. The data reviewed before suggest that *Rana pipiens* has a limited size constancy, perhaps useful only for distances of 6 inches and less when prey catching. Whether this ability should be termed cognitive—i.e., sizes objectively recognized as such—or motivational is not yet clear. A careful series of stimulus-generalization tests in fish and in (teachable) anurans would be well worth the effort. The failure of *Rana* to show size constancy during barrier-avoidance tests suggests that an "abstract" correlate of size variability may not exist in this species. Ewert (see Chapter 6) has reviewed data showing a remarkably sharp size optimum for threat avoidance behavior in *Bufo,* and it would be interesting to use this behavior in size-constancy experiments.

The existence of limited size-constancy behavior in frogs is also interesting in light of psychophysical experiments of Richards (1968) which show a distance-dependent "rescaling" of size-dependent visual functions in tests not based upon actual size-constancy judgments. Richards' limited constancy mechanism is believed to be an automatic (perhaps unlearned) adjustment of firing patterns within the human afferent visual pathway. This hypothesis receives some support from recordings of human neurons in visual cortex (Marg and Adams, 1970) during shifts of accommodation. The idea that an innate accommodation-induced modulation of size-perception exists in man fits with my hypothesis that frog tectal neurons are also modulated during accommodative changes, although critical experiments remain to be done in both species. Possibly a limited automatic mechanism of size-constancy might be available to the human infant as a "foundation" upon which to build more flexible constancy rules through experience. Perhaps the frog has no ability to correlate feedbacks concerning size and perspective changes in relation to his own movements, and he may never "progress" beyond the limited constancy that both Ewert and Ingle have shown. Thus, as a first hypothesis, evolution of visual cortex may relate in an important way to the advantages of evolving more flexible visual constancies.

CONCLUDING REMARKS

From the viewpoint of this author, the frog is most useful as a vertebrate specialized for stereotyped behavioral patterns. The frog provides enough "rigidity" in his behavior to tempt a physiologist to make correlations between stimuli which activate single units and those which provoke the whole frog into sudden action. Yet there is enough complexity in the frog's vision to interest a psychologist weaned on problems of spatial constancy, gestalt perception, and selective attention.

5

The Visual System of the Toad: Behavioral and Physiological Studies on a Pattern Recognition System

J.-P. Ewert

INTRODUCTION

The recognition of visual signals is the precondition for sensory control of visually guided behavior for man and animal alike. Misinterpretations—of warning or information signs in road and highway traffic, to cite an obvious example—can have unpleasant consequences for us. The question of which mechanisms form the basis of these cognitive processes is one of a whole complex of problems that occupies neurophysiologists, ethologists, communications engineers, and systems theorists (for examples, on pattern recognition in biological and technical systems, see Grüsser and Klinke, 1971). Basic experimental research in this area has made especially good progress in the case of mammals. Moreover, ideas have been developed about a number of neuronal circuits as a result of neurophysiological experiments which allow various parameters of a stimulus to be analyzed (Hubel and Wiesel, 1962; for reviews, see Grüsser and Grüsser-Cornehls, 1969, 1973). However, relatively little is known about processes that serve to link the analyzed features of an object together again, so to speak, in nervous code, and how this code is read.

The analysis of such operations for the higher vertebrates is, in fact, problematical, since it is often unclear as to which signals are significant, and therefore ought to be isolated for experimental analysis. Furthermore, higher vertebrates sometimes derive the meaning of a stimulus from individual experience. The experimenter, however, has almost no point of reference for dealing with these important components. Thus, new directions for progress—including the posing of new questions—in the analysis of pattern-recognition processes should be expected to arise from the field of ethology. In comparative ethology, those stimuli are called key stimuli that activate fixed patterns of behavioral responses—as a key is related to its lock (Uexküll, 1909; Lorenz, 1939; Marler and Hamilton, 1966; Eibl-Eibesfeldt, 1967; Tinbergen, 1972). That central nervous filtering system, which comprehends whether "the key fits the lock," is the so-called innate releasing mechanism (IRM). The neurophysiological study of its functions proceeds from the following preliminary conditions (Ewert, 1973, 1974; Scheich and Bullock, 1974): (1) the key stimulus can be represented by means of appropriate dummies; (2) the related behavior reaction of the animal can be repeatedly elicited with this stimulus; (3) the effectiveness and, along with it, the significance of the key stimulus to the behavior can be measured. Such quantitative description of sensory-motor transformations may then guide the study of particular parts of the sensory system to determine their individual input-output functions.

Fixed behavioral patterns and appropriate key stimuli can be reliably studied, especially in the case of lower vertebrates. In this context, amphibians offer several advantages (Ewert, 1974). This chapter analyzes the neurobiological bases of a visual pattern-recognition system—the IRM—which aids the toad, *Bufo bufo* (L.), to identify prey, ignore irrelevant objects, and avoid enemies.

QUANTITATIVE ANALYSIS OF THE KEY STIMULI "PREY" AND "ENEMY"

The Key Stimulus "Prey"

Prey-Catching Behavior

In toads, prey-catching behavior involves a fixed sequence of motor patterns (Schneider, 1954a): (1) orienting movement toward prey by means of head and body turning; (2) following the prey; (3) fixating it and snapping, (4) gulping, and (5) cleaning the snout with the forefeet. This behavioral sequence consists of a stimulus-response chain in which each reaction provides a trigger stimulus for the following response (Ewert, 1967b). For example, binocular fixation stimulates snapping; mechanical stimulation triggers swallowing and wiping. All these behavioral patterns, however, are somehow "connected" via the central nervous system. When, for example, the prey object is quickly eliminated during the moment of fixating, then the next motor patterns of the sequence—snapping, gulping, and wiping—follow in spite of the situation vacuum (Hinsche, 1935). These and other observations first suggested ideas for the analysis of the prey-recognition system. Toads express their initial interest for a prey object by an orienting, turning movement. Should a stimulus pattern have no prey features, then this orienting movement usually ceases. Furthermore, experiments with one-eyed toads showed that binocular prey fixation was not a precondition for recognition. Thus, it was possible to measure the relative effectiveness of prey dummies simply by the occurrence of orienting movements.

Discriminative Value of a Stimulus

Schneider (1954a) and Eibl-Eibesfeldt (1951) first noted during dummy experiments that prey and enemy key stimuli have two common features: (1) movement and (2) contrast. The discrimination between prey and enemy, however, is guided by "size." Small, moving objects, mainly at ground level, are potential prey, while large objects, mainly in the air, are enemy. One must first determine which form parameters are linked to a prey object and which are linked to an enemy object.

During the quantitative behavior experiments (Fig. 1A), the toad sat in a cylindrical glass vessel and could turn either toward or away from a continually circling black (on a white background) or white (on a black background) visual object (piece of cardboard), held at a constant distance of 7–10 cm, which moved in a horizontal direction with a standard angular velocity of 20°/sec (Ewert, 1969b). When the dummy fitted the category "prey," the toad followed it with successive turning movements. With increasing releasing value of a dummy for prey catching, both its effective displacement in the visual field (Fig. 1A) and the corresponding average angle of turn was decreased. Under these conditions, the number of responses within a fixed interval of 1 min increased. When the toad followed the dummy continuously, the product of the turning frequency (orienting activity, R) and the average turning angle ($\bar{W}$) was constant:

$$R \times \bar{W} = c \qquad \text{(degrees per min)}$$

or

$$R = c/\bar{W} \qquad \text{(turning movements per min)}$$

where the constant c is the angular velocity of the stimulus related to its center of rotation. Thus, for constant angular velocity, it was possible to measure the releasing value of a visual object by using the orienting activity R, which can also be used as an index for the discriminate value of the stimulus. In other words, R is an index for the probability that the stimulus fits the category prey. To avoid possible habituation effects, successive trials with the same toad were separated by a 1-min recovery period.

Form Parameters

Since toads (*Bufo bufo* L.) respond only to moving objects with prey-catching responses, it seemed necessary for the analysis of the key-stimulus prey to investigate those form parameters linked to the horizontal direction or plane of object movement (Ewert, 1968b, 1969b). Figure 1B shows the result of those experiments. Elongation of a small stripe in the direction of movement, during successive experiments, increased the prey-catching activity (Fig. 1Ba, a). In the reverse type of experiment, however, prey-catching activity decreased (Fig. 1Ba, b). With square objects of different sizes, the course of prey-catching activity (Fig. 1Ba, c) showed some kind of summation of the horizontal-stimulat-

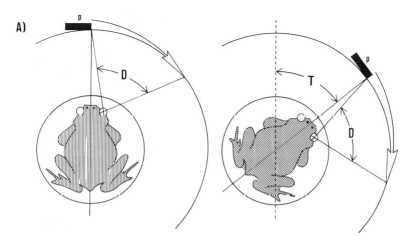

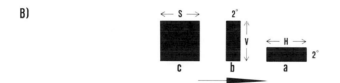

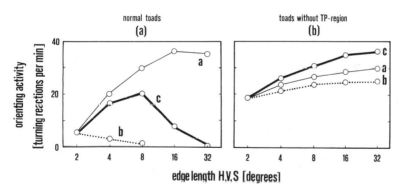

Fig. 1. Key stimulus for prey catching. (A) Procedure for measurements of the prey-catching orienting activity; prey dummy (p) moved with 20°/sec around the toad at a constant distance of about 7 cm; (D) effective displacement of the dummy in the visual field; (T) angle of a turning movement by the toad. (B) Influence of size parameters of a visual pattern on the prey-catching activity (average responses) in normal and thalamic/pretectal (TP)-lesioned toads. Stimuli were rectangular pieces of black cardboard each moved (see arrow) against white background. (S) Square edge, (V) vertical, and (H) horizontal length of a stripe are each elongated by logarithmic steps. Each point represents averages from 20 individuals. (From Ewert, 1972.)

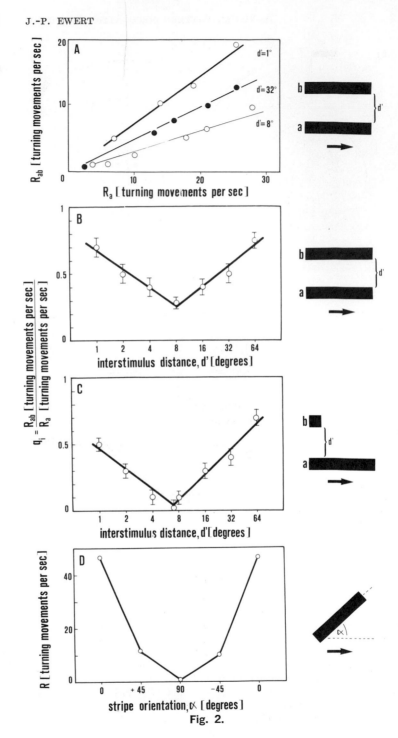

Fig. 2.

ing and the vertical-inhibiting edge. Squares of 30° size were ineffective; larger ones released avoidance. From these results, we can conclude that object expansion in the direction of movement signifies prey, while object expansion perpendicular to the direction of movement decreases this releasing value. In other words, wormlike objects are particularly attractive to toads, but when the same object is rotated in a vertical position, it loses its efficiency for the release of prey-catching behavior (Fig. 2D). There are no worms "walking on their heads" for toads.

The present kinds of experiments gave no indication, for instance, that toads analyze the angle that a stripe subtends within the horizontal plane. Toads showed the same prey-catching activity to a *disc* of 8° diameter, a *square* with an 8° edge, and a 2° × 10° *stripe* oriented from the horizontal plane by 45°, all when moved in horizontal direction (Ewert, 1968b). These patterns have the same maximal expansion component *with*, and *perpendicular* to, the direction of movement. Such form parameters seem to play an important role in the first stage of prey recognition. They also explain the releasing value of other stimulus patterns (Ewert *et al.*, 1970). But this does not imply that toads are unable to discriminate more complex forms (Eibl-Eibesfeldt, 1951; Birukow and Meng, 1955).

Double Stimulation Effects

Another manner of demonstrating inhibitory area effects of vertical size components results from behavioral observations (Schneider, 1954a). The prey-catching behavior of the toad is generally inhibited by simultaneously moving stimuli caused by a "group" or a "swarm" of prey animals (for instance, mealworms). This phenomenon can be investigated in dummy experiments (Ewert *et al.*, 1970). If two horizontal stripes *a* and *b* were simultaneously moved—one above the other (Fig. 2B)—with the same angular velocity, the orienting activity to the double stimulus,

Fig. 2. Inhibiting effects of vertical size components, perpendicular to the direction of horizontal movement (see arrow), on the average prey-catching orienting activity. (A) Two horizontal bars. Rate of orienting, R, as a second moving stimulus is added. Relation between orienting activity to the single moved stimulus, R_a, and the double stimulus, R_{ab}, by changing the stimulus intensity (stimulus background contrast), measured for different interstimulus distances (d'). (B) The inhibition quotient $q_i = R_{ab}/R_a$ varies in relation to the interstimulus distance, d', between a and b. (C) Using a small 2° × 2° square as a second stimulus, the inhibition effect is even stronger. (D) Releasing value of 2° × 16° stripes with different orientation to the direction of movement. Each point represents averages from 20 individuals. (From Ewert *et al.*, 1970.)

R_{ab}, always averaged less than the activity, R_a, to the singly moved object, a:

$$R_{ab} < R_a \quad \text{(turning movements per min)}$$

By changing the stimulus intensity (variation of the stimulus background contrast), there was a linear relationship between R_{ab} and R_a (Fig. 2A):

$$R_{ab} = q_i R_a \text{ (turning movements per min)}$$

That means the "inhibition quotient," q_i, is independent of the stimulus background contrast. However, q_i varied depending upon the inter-stimulus distance (d') between a and b (Fig. 2B):

$$q_i = \lambda |\log d'/d^*| + k$$

In this equation λ, d^*, and k are constant values; d^* ($\approx 8°$) is the distance for maximal inhibition.

Figure 2C demonstrates that with a small $2° \times 2°$ square as a second stimulus the inhibitory effect was even stronger. Corresponding double stimulation experiments with a $0.5° \times 0.5°$ second stimulus—which when singly moved had no releasing value for prey catching—showed similar inhibition. From these observations, it can be concluded that the inhibitory effects were not necessarily the result of too many visual "releasers" (conflict) but, the consequence of *intra*hemispherical (pretectum-tectum) inhibitory interactions of the visual system.

Inhibitory effects by double stimulation were also found if two prey dummies were moved, one behind the other, in the same horizontal plane. During these experiments, inhibition of prey-catching activity generally increased with increasing interstimulus distance. It seems likely that this effect was also linked to interhemispherical (intertectal) influences (for evidence in frogs; see Ingle, Chapter 4).

Angular Velocity

When the form and background contrast parameters of a prey dummy were held constant and the stimulus visual angular velocity was varied, then the correlation between the orienting activity R and the average turning angle $\bar{W}$ changed depending on the velocity. In these experiments, therefore, R could not be used any longer as an index for the dummies releasing value. By means of another procedure, the prey dummy rotated around a given point in space and the prey-catching activity R' (orienting movements toward the dummy) was measured (for procedure see Ewert and Härter, 1969; J.-P. Ewert, unpublished results). Within the range of $2 \leq v \leq 50°/\text{sec}$, the stimulus-response relation can be described by the power function:

$$R' = k_1 v^\alpha \quad \text{(orienting movements per min)}$$

where k_1 and α (≈ 0.6) are constants; k_1 depending upon the other stimulus parameters and the toad's motivation level. Stationary prey objects were ineffective for prey-catching.

Stroboscopic Vision

Toads show the so-called phi phenomenon during prey-catching behavior, which means they are not able to discriminate real stimulus movements from "apparent" movements (Ewert, 1968a). To investigate this particular problem, prey-catching activity toward a moving dummy exposed to stroboscopic illumination was measured as a function of light-flash frequency. For optimum angular velocity, the prey-catching activity was very low at 5 cps, reached a maximum between 10 and 20 cps, and was independent of the light-flash frequency above 20 cps. These results agree well with corresponding electrophysiological findings on class II ganglion cells of the frog's retina (Grüsser-Cornehls, 1968). They demonstrate that the variable of significance is not the continuity of movement of the stimulus, but the change of its position.

Stimulus Background Contrast

If the angular velocity and form parameters of a prey dummy were held constant, the orienting activity increased with increasing amount of stimulus background contrast, C:

$$C = (l_s - l_b)(l_s + l_b)^{-1}$$

where l, luminance (asb*), s, stimulus, b, background. Within the range $0.02 \leq |C| \leq 0.95$, the stimulus-response relation can be described by the power function:

$$R = k_2 |C|^\beta \quad \text{(turning movements per min)}$$

where k_2 and β (≈ 1) are constants; k_2 depending on other stimulus parameters and the toad's motivation for prey catching.

For evaluation of the direction of contrast upon the releasing value of a prey dummy, experiments with square objects gave the clearest

* asb = apostilb.

results, although a square is not as effective as a horizontal stripe (cf. Fig. 1Ba, a and c). With a "wormlike" dummy form, the toad's prey-catching behavior was only slightly influenced by changes in the direction of contrast of the stimulus. However, if the shape of a dummy did not fit well the category "prey" (squares), then the direction of contrast did become an important parameter for the evaluation of prey. Prey-catching activity was much higher for white objects moved against a black background than for black objects of the same size moved on white, if the amount of the stimulus background contrast was constant. Some toads did not show any response to black squares or vertical stripes moved on a white background (Ewert, 1968b). Since black objects moved on white did not fit optimally the natural "picture of prey," then the animals, in these cases, payed more attention to the form. However, the *general* size-dependent relationships of Fig. 1Ba were scarcely influenced by the contrast direction. Since toads are active during twilight and nighttime, the following investigations were focused on black-white moving patterns. (Color vision has been described by Meng, 1958.)

Seasonal Dependencies

As described before, during summertime, white, square dummies moved on a black background were much more attractive as effective releasers than were black on white. Surprisingly, during the winter months, this relation undergoes a reversal (Fig. 3). The response to black objects remained constant, but the response to white ones sank below black objects. These experiments indicate that the evaluation of the visual world throughout the year by the toad is not at a constant value.

Motivational Components

The releasing value of a stimulus also depends upon the animal's motivation (time of the day or night, saturation level etc.; for details, see Ewert, 1965). But such differences in response were usually specific to the general level of activity, with the details of stimulus-response relationships remaining relatively constant. It was possible to manipulate the prey-catching motivation level by presenting the "familiar" odor of mealworm excrements (Ewert, 1968b). Toads had been previously exposed to the odor during feeding ("self-training"). When stimulated by this odor, subjects exhibited a heightened feeding tendency to the extent that they would even orient and snap at those objects whose forms did not fit optimally the category "prey" (Fig. 4), which indicates that the discriminatory ability of the visual recognition system was altered.

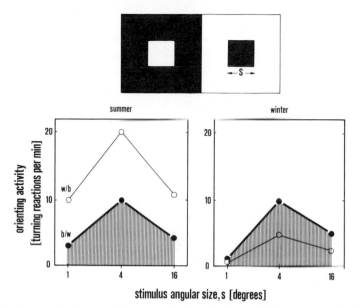

Fig. 3. Seasonal changes. Influence of the direction of the stimulus background contrast on the releasing value of a square object for prey catching during summer- and wintertime. w-b, white object moved with $20°$/sec against black background; b-w, vice versa. The amount of the stimulus background contrast was held constant with $|C| = 0.95$; the stimulus distance from the toad was about 7 cm. Each point represents averages from 20 individuals. (From Ewert and Siefert, 1974b.)

Habituation Effects

If a toad was stimulated within a *long*-term stimulus series with the same prey dummy, the prey-catching activity decreased (Fig. 5A), which indicated that the toad becomes habituated to this stimulus object (Eikmanns, 1955). The reason for this decrease could be stimulus-specific aftereffects, which accumulated during successive stimulation (Ewert, 1967d). Stimulus specificity means that following habituation for a dummy form A another form B immediately will be effective (Birukow and Meng, 1955; Meng, 1958). During other experiments, it was interesting to note that toads also habituated selectively for the specific area on the retina being stimulated. This phenomenon is called locus specificity (Eikmanns, 1955; Ewert, 1967a,d). The biological relevance of stimulus- and locus-specific habituation phenomena may be to keep the IRM for prey catching alert toward "new" stimuli. Furthermore, these experiments indicated (Meng, 1958; Ewert and Kehl, 1976) that the toad's visual system is able to store information (aftereffects) on different and also

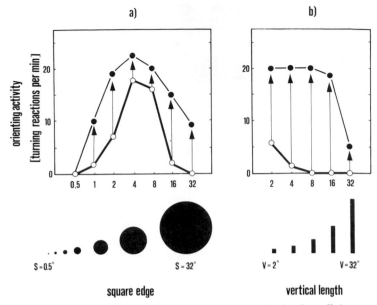

Fig. 4. Motivational effects. Increase (see arrows) of stimulus efficiency for prey catching with simultaneous presentation of prey odor. Experiments with discs (a) and vertical bars (b). Each point represents averages from 15 individuals. (From Ewert, 1968b.)

complex pattern forms selectively via particular retinal projection paths as a result of habituation processes. Indices of the decrease of those after-effects could be measured by the temporal "recovery" curve to the same stimulus presented at the same retinal locus (Fig. 5B). From such data, it is evident that two (or more) storage processes are involved—a short-term (first 10 min) and a long-term process (6 to 24 hr). During successive stimulus series, each separated by a constant recovery interval, the number of prey-catching responses decreased (Fig. 5C). The amount of decrease depended upon the length of the recovery pauses.

Other Orienting Responses

During springtime, prey catching or avoidance responses toward appropriate dummies are less frequently obtained. A behaviorally relevant visual stimulus during this time of year is the sexual partner. The female releases an orienting movement from the male as a result of her relatively large size, which signals the onset of courtship (clasping) behavior (H. Heusser, unpublished). This phenomenon has not yet been analyzed in more detail. During future experiments, it would be important to

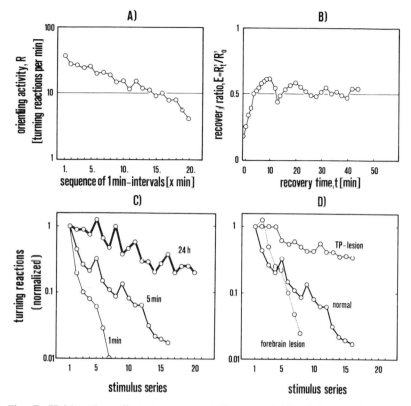

Fig. 5. Habituation effects to a repeatedly moved 2° × 16° prey dummy. (A) Decrease of the dummy's effectiveness as a result of long-term presentation. (B) Increase of the dummy's effectiveness following habituation as a function of inter-stimulus interval. Recovery is measured by the ratio $E = R_t'/R_0'$. (R_0' is the number of orienting movements within a stimulus series occurring until habituation; R''_t gives the number of responses until habituation which follows a recovery pause, t.) (C) Habituation effects summate in successive stimulus series separated by constant recovery pauses (1 min, 5 min, or 24 hr). The length of the pause influences the course of habituation. (D) Effect of brain lesions on the course of habituation (recovery pauses 5 min). Each point represents averages from 10 individuals, except D, which (each curve) is for one animal. (From Ewert, 1967d and 1970a.)

investigate whether the "switching off" of prey catching or avoidance is a precondition for triggering courtship responses. It would also be of interest to know whether central nervous mechanisms for prey and enemy detection are involved (or "occupied") in this particular detection problem.

Some kind of orienting responses can also be released by a moving patterned surround. From the investigations of Birukow (1938) on *Rana temporaria,* these optomotor reactions are known to differ from prey-catching orienting movements in many aspects. (1) The optomotor response that functions to hold the patterned environment stationary relative to the retina consists of two kinds of head movements: the slow following or pursuit movement in the direction of a moving surround and a fast return movement in the reverse direction that brings the head again to a midline position. Both phases alternate successively. (2) The optimal key stimulus usually is a repetitive pattern of vertical stripes that moves in a horizontal direction. (3) There is something like a direct "coupling" between pattern movement and the slow pursuit head movement. During the time that the stimulus moves, the head moves also. (4) For patterns moved horizontally, only the pattern dislocations at the retina in a nasotemporal direction are effective. This phenomenon was studied in more detail by Birukow (1938) using monocular frogs. If, for example, a frog *Rana temporaria* (L.) is blinded in the left eye and the surround moves from right to left, then the animal does show optomotor reactions, which demonstrates that the response can be monocularly driven. However, if the stimulus moves around the same animal from left to right, optomotor responses are extremely weak or they fail to occur, due to the pattern dislocations at the retina in temporal-nasal direction. (5) In optomotor experiments, toads show no color discrimination, even when brightness differences are properly equated or randomized (Birukow and Meng, 1955).

Corresponding characteristics of the prey-catching orienting response that have the function of localizing a prey object in the environment are as follows: (1) the orienting movement consists of a head and/or body turn; (2) optimal key stimulus is a horizontal stripe moved with the long axis in the direction of movement; (3) there is a delay between stimulus and object movement, called effective dislocation; (4) nasotemporal as well as temporal-nasal pattern dislocations at the retina are effective, particularly the latter; (5) during prey-catching, frogs and toads show evidence of color vision (Birukow and Meng, 1955). Summarizing, it is evident that optomotor and prey-catching orienting responses have different behavioral functions and are each activated by different visual releasers. Lázár (1973) recently reported that optomotor nystagmus in frogs is mediated via the accessory optic pathway and the basal optic nucleus of the tegmentum.

The Key Stimulus "Enemy"

Depending on the shape of enemy or predator and its location in the visual field, the following types of responses could be observed: (a) ducking, jumping (enemy coming from the air); (b) turning away, running ("ground enemy").

Form Parameters

Key stimuli for avoidance (escape) behavior were objects with expansion components *in* and *perpendicular* to the direction of movement (Ewert and Rehn, 1969). When black discs of different sizes were moved through the dorsal visual field of the toad, a distance of 10 cm, those of about 50° diameter released maximal escape activity. Smaller and bigger ones were less effective. By gradually reducing the surface area of a 50° disc (Fig. 6B,a), identical, maximal releasing values were obtained with the following patterns: (1) a circular ring with a 10° width and 50° diameter (Fig. 6B,b); (2) a four-point pattern with a point diameter of 10° and distance between adjacent points of 30° (Fig. 6B,e). The escape activity could not be increased by changing the surface dimensions of these patterns, but could only be decreased (Fig. 6B,c and d). Disc (a), ring (b), and four-point pattern (e), have one common stimulus component which characterizes the "size" of the enemy key stimulus: "visual incidents" occurring on the retina with an optimal dimension of about 50° in and across the direction in which the stimulus is moved.

Another manner of demonstrating that the pattern expansion in this context did not necessarily need to be continuous results from the following observations. A $2° \times 16°$ horizontal stripe moved at a distance of 7 cm with the long axis in the horizontal plane was an optimal prey object. After adding a small 2° square dorsally over the edge of the stripe with an interstimulus distance of about 10° (Fig. 2C), the prey-catching response ceased and avoidance movements were induced in some animals. During recent behavioral studies on the natural enemies of the toad (Ewert and Traud, 1976), it appeared that such patterns may stimulate the configuration of a snake. The square corresponds to the head of the snake, the stripe to its body. Furthermore, it was interesting to note that the same "enemy picture" also fits the leech moving on land when it lifts the frontal sucker. However, when the sucker has a position *in* the direction of movement, the leech releases prey catching from toads.

Velocity and Contrast Parameters

When the parameters for size and contrast of an enemy dummy were held constant in their optimal ranges, the avoidance activity, R was increased with increasing angular velocity, v

$$R = k_3 v^\gamma \text{ (avoidance responses)}$$

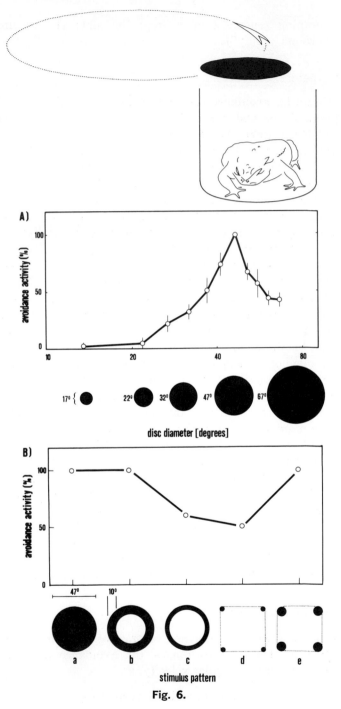

Fig. 6.

(valid for $1 \leqq v \leqq 50°/\text{sec}$). Comparing the exponents of the velocity power functions for orienting responses, $\alpha \approx 0.6$, and for avoidance responses $\gamma \approx 0.9$ (Ewert and Rehn, 1969), it is evident that $\gamma > \alpha$. Furthermore, it was found that $k_1 > k_3$. Consequently an enemy "should move" with more speed in order to elicit an avoidance movement from the toad than the prey object "would" in order to be caught. Prey as well as enemy objects that move faster than $100°/\text{sec}$ release almost no responses. This gives certain prey objects an increased chance to survive; i.e., a cockroach, for example, only seldom attracts the toad's attention, for it moves too fast. A slug, on the other hand, moves too slowly. The effectiveness of an enemy in prey catching should be increased by moving either quite slowly, ($v < 1°/\text{sec}$) or quite fast ($v > 100°/\text{sec}$).

Another parameter that may be important for the release of avoidance movements is object movement toward the toad's eye in the z-axis. Within limits, this effect appears to be relatively independent of the size of the moving object. Toads show similar avoidance responses to a hedgehog or a giant ant (*Componotus herculeanus* L.) when they move in a direction toward the toad's eye. However, if the giant ant crosses the toad's visual field, it signals prey.

For constant optimal values of size and velocity, the avoidance activity increases as the contrast between stimulus and background increases. In contrast to the prey-catching behavior, black objects moved against white background were much more effective than were white ones on black.

With repeated stimulation by an enemy object, the toad's avoidance activity was also decreased. Comparing this with the corresponding effects during prey catching, "recovery" after habituation took not more than 30 to 60 min.

Conclusions

Toads show two kinds of antagonistic visually guided behaviors: *approach* or orienting (to a prey object) and *avoidance* (from an "enemy" or predator object). Prey and enemy key stimuli which release these innate behavior patterns have two common features: movement and contrast. Prey and enemy are discriminated basically on their size dimensions, but other parameters, such as the direction of stimulus movement and direction of contrast, are also taken into account.

Fig. 6. Key stimuli, A and B, producing avoidance responses: The relevance of size dimensions. Each point represents averages from 15 individuals. (From Ewert, 1970b; Ewert and Rehn, 1969.)

In the first stages of prey recognition, two stimulus surface components seem to play an important role. Object expansion *in* the horizontal direction of object movement signals prey, while object expansion *perpendicular* to the horizontal direction of movement decreases this releasing value and signals enemy features. Recent experiments demonstrate that these figurational relations are independent upon the *orientation*—horizontal or vertical direction—in that the stimulus moves (Ewert and Becker, 1976). Large surface expansions in and perpendicular to the direction of stimulus movement are linked to an optimal enemy object. The prey-enemy recognition system can be altered by motivational and seasonal components.

Toads are able to store, selectively, information on different and complex patterns via particular retinal projection paths as the result of locus and stimulus specific habituation processes.

Orienting or approaching movements also can be involved in other kinds of behaviors such as optomotor responses; however, they are released by visual stimulus parameters that differ from those associated with prey-catching behaviors.

It should be emphasized that the present results on form discrimination have been obtained exclusively in common toads (*Bufo bufo* L.). We should be alert in future to learn also of possible species differences as well as ontogenetic aspects in this context. First comparative studies on prey "gestalt" recognition in different anuran species (*Hyla*, *Alytes*, *Bombina*) showed only slight differences from the results described for *Bufo* (Ewert and Burghagen, 1976a). Himstedt *et al.* (1976) obtained in the *larvae* of *Salamandra salamandra* (L.) that the shape of a stimulus is not an essential factor for prey-catching. After *metamorphosis*, however, the releasing mechanism of these animals becomes more selective: Following 8–10 months later prey-catching behavior can be released only with "wormlike" patterns that extend in the direction of movement by at least 32° and that extend perpendicularly to the direction of movement by no more than 16°. This "narrowing down" of the releasing mechanism is not caused by a learning process.

PREY CATCHING AND AVOIDANCE "ZONES" IN THE BRAIN

The information coming from one eye is transmitted mainly via contralateral fibers of the optic nerve to two brain areas: The optic tectum and the thalamus-pretectal region (on other terminations, see Knapp *et al.*, 1965; see also Chapter 3). During the following experiments, these structures were stimulated by implanted electrodes in freely moving animals. These kinds of elicited motor responses—in relation to results obtained from lesion experiments—give some information on the behavioral relevance of these brain areas.

Electrical Point Stimulation

Prey Catching

During electrical point stimulation of different tectal regions with a train of square-wave pulses (50–100 cps and 20–100μA), toads responded with motor patterns of the prey-catching sequence (1)–(5) as described previously (Fig. 7). In general, the average trigger threshold was increased from responses (1) to (5) (Ewert, 1967b,c, 1968b). In accordance with the retinotectal topography map (Gaze, 1958a; Ewert and Borchers, 1971), orienting responses were directed to appropriate parts of the visual field (Fig. 7A), when the corresponding brain area was stimulated. The actual response area for snapping (Fig. 7B) was relatively small, representing the natural "snapping zone" of the animal (see also Ingle, 1970). Gulping and wiping movements were elicited mainly by stimulating areas below the optic ventricle (subtectum). During certain experiments, it was also possible to combine electrical and visual stimuli. In one-eyed toads, the time between the initial prey fixation and the subsequent snapping response, was nearly twice that seen in normal animals. However, when the snapping area in the "blind" tectum of the monocularly blind animal was stimulated electrically below threshold when a visual prey object was present, the toad behaved normally and snapped frequently (Ewert, 1967b). It was possible to elicit snapping movements with electrical stimulation of the forebrain in the region of the basal ganglia. Orienting responses, however, did not occur.

Avoidance Behavior

The different avoidance patterns could be elicited mainly by stimulating the posterior thalamic (T) and pretectal (P) regions (Fig. 7C). From these areas, it was also possible to release body tilting which normally occurs during vestibular stimulation. With stimulation of points in the region between the TP-region and the rostral tectum, it was possible to trigger both avoidance and prey-catching responses (Ewert, 1968b).

Habituation Effects

Toads also showed habituation of prey-catching and avoidance responses with repeated electrical stimulation of the brain (Ewert and

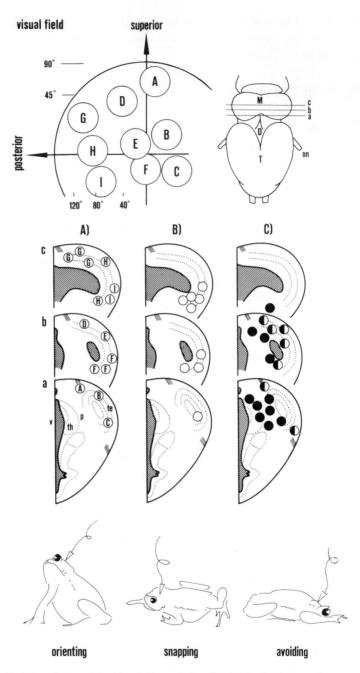

Fig. 7. Electrical point stimulation of the brain in freely moving toads, a–c: three brain half sections; on, optic nerve, T, telencephalon; D, diencephalon; M,

Rehn, 1976). During studies of avoidance behaviors, it was interesting to note that both the degree of habituation and recovery showed almost the same time course as in corresponding visual stimulation experiments with an enemy dummy. With combined electrical and visual stimulation, it could be demonstrated that the response threshold for the electrical stimulation of an avoidance area was increased following long-term habituation to a visual enemy dummy.

Interactions between Optic Tectum and Thalamus-Pretectum (TP)

The results just mentioned indicate that the brain centers relevant for prey catching are located in the optic tectum, while those for avoidance responses reside mainly in the TP-region. To obtain more information on possible interactions between these brain regions, a stimulating electrode was implanted in each area (Ewert and Rehn, 1976). Following habituation of the avoidance response by long-term stimulation of the TP-region, the response threshold for the elicitation of prey-catching movements by tectal stimulation was remarkably decreased (Ewert, 1968b). This gave the first indication that the optic tectum may receive inhibitory influences from the TP-region. In the reverse type of experiment, however, there was no comparable effect; i.e., long-term stimulation of the tectum did not seem to facilitate or inhibit thalamus-pretectum related behaviors.

Lesion Experiments

Thalamic-Pretectal Lesions

The results obtained from brain stimulation experiments on prey catching and avoidance "zones" were further supported by lesion studies (Ewert, 1967d, 1968b). Following unilateral ablation of the thalamic-pretectal region with high frequency coagulation (Fig. 8A) or by separating this region from the tectum with discrete knife cuts (Fig. 8B), prey-catching behavior directed toward objects moved in the contralateral

---

mesencephalon, v, ventriculum; th, dorsal posterior thalamus, p, pretectal region, te, optic tectum. (A) Orienting movements. Stimulation of a point in the optic tectum (letters) leads to an orienting response toward a particular part of the visual field that corresponds with the retinal topography. (B) The more "focused" area for snapping. (C) Stimulation points (filled in circle) for avoidance responses. From other points (half filled half opened circle) between "prey catching" and "avoidance zones," it was possible to release prey catching and avoidance patterns. (From Ewert, 1968b and 1970a.)

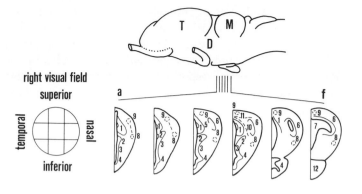

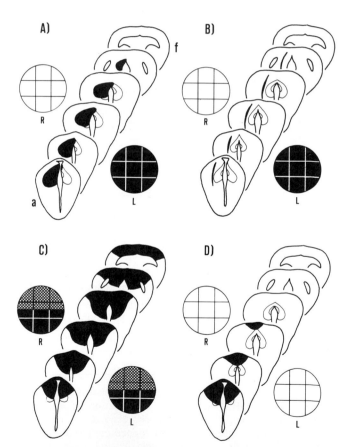

Fig. 8. Reconstruction of lesions in thalamic-pretectal areas. The blacked out regions indicate areas of tissue destruction. The blacked positions of the visual field indicate that disinhibited prey-catching responses occurred to stimuli in these

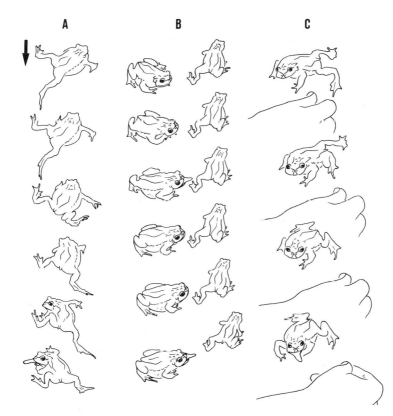

Fig. 9. Behavioral patterns of toads with thalamic-pretectal lesions (frame-by-frame analysis). The animals orient and snap at their own limbs (A), at another toad (B), the experimenter's hand (C). (From Ewert, 1967d.)

visual field appeared to be enhanced. Furthermore, avoidance behavior failed to occur. These animals also oriented and snapped toward behaviorally irrelevant objects (Fig. 9A–C), even toward those normally associ-

---

areas; no responses occurred to stimuli within regions that are cross-hatched; normal prey-catching response was obtained in white regions of the visual field. (A) Disinhibition of entire left visual field produced by caudal thalamic and pretectal lesions on right side. (B) Disinhibition produced by a knife cut. (C) A lesion that extended back through dorsal tectum and TP-areas producing "blindness" in the upper field, while responses were disinhibited toward stimuli in the lower field. (D) Lesions of rostral dorsal thalamus did not seem to influence the prey-catching behavior. 1, dorsal; 2, medial; 3, ventral thalamic area; 4, hypothalamus; 5, pretectal region; 6, optic tectum; 7, third ventriculum; 8, ventrolateral; 9, dorsomedial optic tract; 10, commissura posterior; 11, commissura tecti mesencephali. (From Ewert, 1968b and 1970a.)

ated with avoidance. After certain small lesions, the disinhibition effect seemed to be specific only to restricted areas of the visual field. When the lesion was completely bilateral, this effect occurred in all parts of the visual field. Quantitative experiments with these lesioned toads (Fig. 1B,b) further demonstrated that they were not able to discriminate the behaviorally relevant form parameters of a moving stimulus. Such experiments indicate that the TP-region must be involved in the prey-enemy recognition process as the result of inhibitory influences.

Tectal Lesions

Following ablation of the optic tectum, both visual prey-catching behavior and avoidance behavior failed to occur. Apparently, the toad cannot guide avoidance responses with the retinothalamic projection alone, which suggest that excitatory influences from tectum to thalamus-pretectum do exist.

Forebrain Ablation

After unilateral forebrain removal, prey-catching behavior failed to occur to objects moved through the visual field of the contralateral eye (Ewert, 1967d). Stimulation of the ipsilateral eye did release prey-catching responses, but activity was not as high as in normal toads. Toads with unilateral ablations of the telencephalon recovered feeding for objects presented to the contralateral eye after 1–2 weeks (D. Ingle, unpublished data). However, this was not the case following total bilateral removal of both hemispheres. Then, prey-catching behavior failed to occur for the whole visual field; whereas, the threshold for avoidance behavior was lowered. If these operated animals received TP-lesions, the prey-catching behavior again returned and was even hyperexcited, while avoidance behavior was entirely eliminated (Ewert, 1967d). The TP-region and forebrain also play a role in stimulus-specific habituation processes (Fig. 5D). Following TP-lesions, habituation to a visual prey dummy was decreased. After partial forebrain removal, however, it was increased. Presumably, these brain regions are involved in some kind of "transfer processes" that guide response activity in relation to the amount of stimulus-specific "aftereffects" that may exist (Ewert, 1967d).

Pharmacological Effects on the Optic Tectum

Behavioral tests after application of different drugs onto the surface of the optic tectum have provided evidence concerning neurotransmitters that may be relevant to the described inhibitory effects (for experiments with frogs, see Stevens, 1973; with toads, Ewert *et al.*, 1974). Application of curare or atropine to the optic tectum produced similar "disinhibition" effects on prey-catching behavior, as were observed following TP-lesions. After application onto particular regions of the tectal surface, the behavioral response was disinhibited toward objects moved through corresponding parts of the visual field, in relation to the tectal retinotopic map. Following applications of acetylcholine (ACh), prey-catching behavior to visual objects failed to occur, whereas avoidance behavior seemed to be normal. Interestingly enough, Stevens (1973), during recording experiments from single tectal cells, observed that response activity to visual stimulation increased after electrophoretic application of curare. This drug also caused spontaneous bursts to occur within the normal quiescent period of these cells. Furthermore, ACh appeared to reduce normal responses to visual stimulation and eliminated the electrophysiological effects induced by curare.

There are a number of mechanisms by which ACh may be acting to produce inhibition. For example, these results may be interpreted in the following way. Certain thalamic pretectal neurons project their axons to the optic tectum and have inhibitory synapses with those tectal neurons involved in triggering prey-catching behavior. In the case of cholinergic *presynaptic* inhibition, this inhibitory process could be reinforced by application of ACh and reduced by ACh-blocking agents. Shen and co-workers (1955) showed that the dorsal half of the optic tectum contains one of the highest concentrations of cholinesterase of any region in the frog brain. Anatomic evidence for axoaxonal synapses in the frog optic tectum has been obtained from electron microscopic studies by Székely and colleagues (1973). Similar results have been obtained in toads (Ewert and Schuchardt, 1976).

Conclusions

From brain stimulation and corresponding lesion experiments, it can be concluded that the optic tectum is involved mainly in triggering prey-catching behavior, whereas more rostral structures in the thalamic-pretectal (TP) region trigger avoidance responses.

Lesion experiments reveal new insights into the central interaction mechanisms that may control prey-catching and avoidance behaviors. Conceivably, the tectal prey-catching trigger mechanism may receive inhibitory influences from the TP-region, which in itself contains (or is part of) the trigger system for avoidance behaviors. The forebrain presumably modulates the activity of both systems via inhibitory pathways to the TP-region. One natural function of the forebrain is the demon-strated facilitation of prey catching by prey odor. After forebrain removal, the inhibitory influence from the TP-region appears to dominate the tectal prey-catching trigger system. Following additional TP-lesions, the prey-catching trigger system is then "disinhibited."

Pharmacological experiments indicate that the hypothetical inhibitory pathways from the TP-region to the optic tectum may be mediated by cholinergic transmission.

Similarities in the course of habituation to visual as well as to elec-trical stimulation lead one to suppose that the stimulated brain areas are parts of the "senso-motor system." Thus, it is possible to store up and to summate information related to visual *and* to electrical stimuli, which occur in close temporal proximity.

NEURAL CODING OF BEHAVIORALLY RELEVANT FORM FEATURES ALONG THE VISUAL PATHWAY

Based upon single-unit recording studies, the question has been answered as to whether or not there are neuronal "form-filters" in the brain which analyze the behaviorally relevant stimulus form parameters, such as expansion *in* and *perpendicular* to the direction of movement. By means of a perimeter device (Grüsser and Dannenberg, 1965; Ewert and Borchers, 1971), the same stimulus patterns used in the behavioral experi-ments were moved in front of a paralyzed toad through the receptive fields of neurons recorded from different levels of the visual system: (1) retina, (2) optic tectum, and (3) thalamus-pretectum.

Retinal Ganglion Cells

Classification

Three different types of ganglion cells were identified in the retinotectal projection (Grüsser and Grüsser-Cornehls, 1970; Ewert and Hock, 1972) which correspond to classes II, III, and IV in the frog (Lettvin *et al.*, 1959; Grüsser *et al.*, 1967). The ganglion cell axons terminate in specific layers of the superficial optic tectum: class II just below the surface, followed by class III, while class IV terminals are deeper (see Ewert and von Wietersheim, 1974a). The receptive field of all ganglion cells consists of an approximately circular excitatory receptive field (ERF) surrounded by an inhibitory receptive field (IRF). The following classification is based upon receptive field size and *on-off* response criteria (Scheme 1)

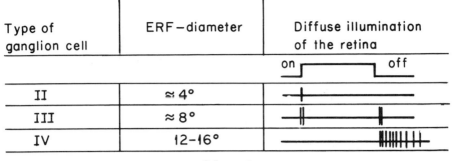

Type of ganglion cell	ERF–diameter	Diffuse illumination of the retina
		on ⎍ off
II	≈ 4°	
III	≈ 8°	
IV	12–16°	

Scheme 1

Coding of Form Parameters

The response of the neuronal types (Ewert and Hock, 1972) to those stimuli used in the behavioral experiments can be summarized as follows (Fig. 10). The values for the parameters angular velocity ($v = 7.6°/\text{sec}$) and stimulus background contrast were held constant ($C = -0.95$).

HORIZONTAL STRIPES. Stripe expansion by more than 2° in the direction of movement did not cause the discharge rate of any ganglion cells to change. Only the overall discharge rate reached different levels in the three types (Fig. 10A,a; 10B,a; 10C,a).

VERTICAL STRIPES. As long as the stimuli were smaller than the ERF, there was an increase in the discharge frequency as stripe length increased perpendicular to the direction of movement. The frequency reached a maximum when the length of the stripe equaled the diameter of the ERF and then decreased with further increases in stripe length due to encroachment upon the inhibitory surround. Maximal neuronal activation occurred for each class in the appropriate range of visual angular-size corresponding to the different ERF sizes; i.e., ≈4° (class II, Fig. 10A,b), ≈8° (class III, Fig. 10B,b,) ≈16°(class IV, Fig. 10C,b).

SQUARES. Increasing the edge length of a square had an effect on the discharge frequency similar to a corresponding extension of a vertical stripe (Fig. 10A–C; cf. b and c; for similar results in frogs, see Butenandt and Grüsser, 1968). From these results, it can be concluded that a single retinal ganglion cell is sensitive to the stimulus surface and mainly to its expansion perpendicular to the direction of movement. Therefore, the ganglion cell classes II and III "confuse" a square and a small vertical stripe having the same height, which is in contrast with the results of the

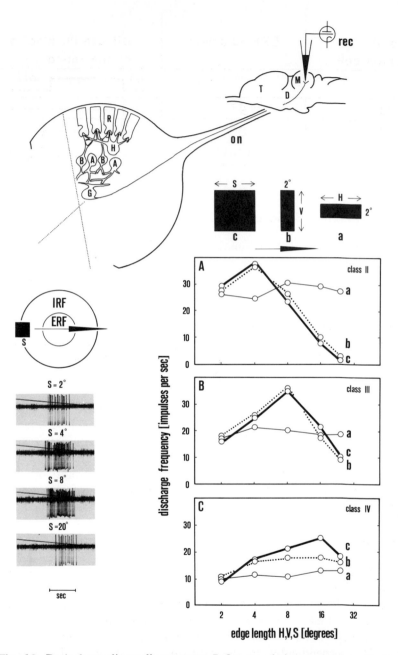

Fig. 10. Retinal ganglion cell responses. Influence of size parameters (S, V, H) of rectangular stimulus objects (horizontal stripe a, vertical stripe b, square c) on the average discharge rate of single class II, III, and IV neurons. Each stimulus

behavioral experiments. Undoubtedly, the neural information regarding object expansion by more than 2° in the direction of movement is transmitted to the brain via converging and sequential outputs of many ganglion cells. Thus, there are no specific "worm" or "enemy detectors" at the retinal level. The toad brain is not able to discriminate between prey and enemy objects based upon the neural stimulus transformation from the retinal ganglion cells alone.

Velocity and Contrast

For constant values of form and background contrast, the discharge rate of all neurons increased, within limits, with increasing velocity of a stimulus object moved through the receptive field. The relation between neuronal discharge rate, R_n, and velocity of motion can be described by the power function

$$R_n = k_4 v^\delta \text{ (impulses/sec)}$$

where k_4 and δ are constants; k_4 depending upon other stimulus parameters and the metabolic state of the neuron. The exponent δ was different for each of the three neuron classes: $\delta_{II} < \delta_{III} < \delta_{IV}$ (Grüsser and Grüsser-Cornehls, 1970; Grüsser-Cornehls, 1973a; Ewert and Hock, 1972). In class II and III neurons, the value of δ depended upon the direction of the stimulus background contrast, and in class II, upon the season (J.-P. Ewert and F. J. Hock, unpublished). The velocity function was investigated in all neuronal classes for $2 \leqq v \leqq 15°/\text{sec}$. Object movements faster than 100°/sec elicited weak activity in class III and IV neurons and were almost ineffective for class II. A stationary object without previous movements was not responded to by any neuron type, although class II neurons showed a short-term sustained response after an object was moved into the ERF and stopped in the field center. (For comparisons in velocity function between frogs and toads, as well as interspecies differences in frogs, see Grüsser-Cornehls, 1973a.)

With constant values for the parameters, form and velocity, the dis-

object was moved at 7.6°/sec through the center of the receptive field. ERF, excitatory; IRF, inhibitory receptive field; R, receptor cells; B, bipolars; H, horizontal cells; A, amacrines; G, ganglion cell; on, optic nerve; T, telencephalon; D, diencephalon; M, mesencephalon; rec, recording electrode. Examples of records from a class III ganglion cell during traverse of squares with different sizes. The unit is maximally activated when the stimulus size fits the diameter of the ERF. Each point represents average responses from 10 single neurons. (From Ewert and Hock, 1972.)

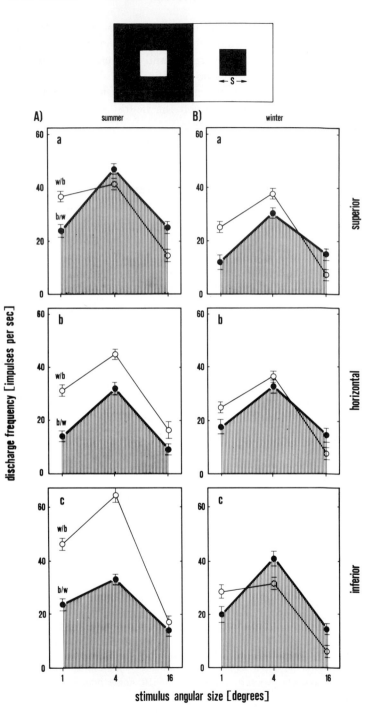

charge rate increased with increasing stimulus background contrast (for details, see Grüsser-Cornehls, 1973a). Class III and IV neurons were activated more by black objects moved against a white background than by white objects moved on black. For class II neurons, the response dependency upon the contrast direction of an object varied with both the localization of the ERF in the field of vision and with the time of the year (see following section). When the behavioral and neurophysiological results are compared, the angular velocity and contrast functions are in good agreement (see Ewert and Hock, 1972).

Seasonal Dependency upon Contrast Direction

Recently, it was noted (Ewert and Siefert, 1974a,b) that the activity of class II retinal ganglion cells showed a more complex variability in response to the contrast direction of a moving object as did behavioral prey-catching activity (Fig. 11). The black-white neuronal preference depended upon (1) the location of the receptive field, (2) the stimulus angular size, and (3) the season. During summer months, neurons with ERFs in the inferior half of the visual field were much more activated by white squares moved against a black background (w-b) than by black squares moved on a white background (b-w). These differences were greatest for objects between 1° and 4° degrees. However, neurons with ERFs in the superior half of the visual field were more activated by objects, between 4° and 16°, when they were black on white than vice versa. During autumn and winter, this relation undergoes a reversal (compare the summer and winter responses in Fig. 11).

Neuronal Adaptation

Immediately after a traverse of a visual pattern through the receptive field, the discharge rate for a second identical stimulus was greatly decreased for class II neurons, but was only weakly affected for class III and IV. One minute or less after stimulation, all neuron types had recovered (Grüsser et al., 1967; Ewert and Borchers, 1971). Comparing these results with those from the behavioral studies (Fig. 5), one can conclude that retinal neuronal adaptation is not the mechanism producing *stimulus-specific habituation* of prey-catching and avoidance behaviors.

Fig. 11. Seasonal change of retinal class II ganglion cell's sensitivity (average discharge frequency) for the direction of the stimulus background contrast of moving, square objects. Neurons with ERFs in different parts of the visual field (superior and inferior); w-b white stimulus moved with 7.6°/sec on black background through the receptive field center; b-w, vice versa. Each point represents average responses of 20 single neurons. From Ewert and Siefert, 1974b.

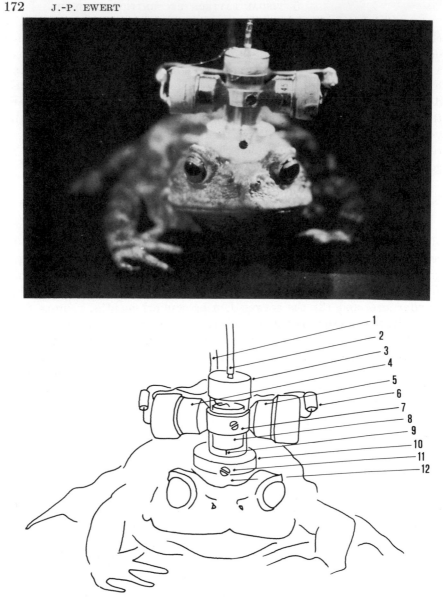

Fig. 12. Procedure for recording experiments in freely moving toads. The animal (*Bufo bufo L.*) carries a headpiece consisting amplifiers and a hydraulic system for positioning the recording microelectrode. (1) Wires for signal recording and power supplies; (2) tube with oil connecting the microdrive; (3) cylindrical device for the hydraulic system. (4–6) Two IC operational amplifiers with FET input and low impedance output; by means of differential recording technique, it was possible to avoid muscle potentials during movements of the animal. Direct connections between electrode and amplifier together with the low impedance output made it possible to record without Faraday cage. (7) Mounting ring; (8) piston which

Recording Experiments from Freely Moving Animals

Our previous knowledge of the response characteristics of retinal ganglion cells in amphibians was obtained from investigations performed with paralyzed animals. In freely moving toads (for methodological details, see Fig. 12; Ewert and Borchers, 1974b), the following questions should be answered: (1) How do retinal *"on-off"* (class III) and *"off"* (class IV) ganglion cells behave when the toad itself produced a shadow on the retina during eye closure? (2) Since toads have no involuntary eye movements (for details in frogs, see Autrum, 1959) are there respiratory eye movements (caused by respiratory pressure changes in the buccal cavity) by which a stationary stimulus pattern can be transformed into moving patterns (Schipperheyn, 1965)?

With regard to the first question, it was observed that during eye closure the expected off response of class III and IV ganglion cells did not occur. However, artificial stimuli, which corresponded to the eyelid shadow (ramp stimulus), presented to an open eye, activated both ganglion cell types. It is possible that with eye closure, an "efference copy" (von Holst and Mittelstaedt, 1950; Johnstone and Mark, 1971) may be transmitted to the retina to inhibit the *on-off* and *off* ganglion cells. The result is that the brain is informed mainly of those brightness changes that occur in the visual environment.

With regard to the second question, a $2° \times 2°$ black square object was moved in front of an unrestrained, motionless toad into the ERF center of a recorded class II neuron and was stopped in the field center. As long as the pattern was moving, the neuron discharged and showed a sustained response for some seconds after the stimulus was stopped. Class II neurons also showed this sustained response in paralyzed toads (Ewert and Hock, 1972). Important, however, was the fact that in freely moving animals no neuronal discharge occurred during a respiration movement. Class III and IV neurons showed neither a sustained response nor a discharge to the stationary stimulus during respiration movements. These experiments demonstrate that the brain of a motionless toad in the *present* stimulus situation does not receive information on the patterned stationary environment via the retinotectal projection (for corresponding findings for frogs, see Pigarev *et al.*, 1971). However, since toads move frequently, it seems likely that those movements will supply information for detection of stationary edges via classes II, III or IV; this information is "stored" for a few seconds.

---

serves as electrode carrier; (9) electrode; (10) plastic ring mounted on the cranial bone with two types of dental cement; (11) positioner, (12) dental cement. (From Ewert and Borchers, 1974b.)

Neurons of the Optic Tectum

Types of Neurons

After identification of a particular unit, small lesions were produced by passing an anodal DC current of 5 μA through the recording electrode. The resulting iron deposit was localized by means of the Prussian blue reaction in Paraplast-embedded brain sections after fixation in formalin. Adjacent 12-μm sections were stained with the Klüver-Barrera method to identify the cellular and fiber architecture surrounding lesion sites.

A variety of neuron types could be distinquished in the toad optic tectum (Ewert and Borchers, 1971): (a) Movement-specific neurons with an ERF diameter of about 27° located in the stratum griseum and album centrale (see layers d and e in Fig. 13B). Immediately after a traverse of a visual pattern through the receptive field, the discharge rate for a identical stimulus was greatly decreased, more than was found for retinal class II neurons. These neurons showed almost no response to diffuse light changes. (b) Movement-sensitive neurons with large receptive fields (layer f in Fig. 13B); one type (T_I) covering the entire frontal field, another (T_{II}) the inferior field, and a third type (T_{III}) covering the total contralateral visual field (Fig. 13A, a). These units were recorded from the periventricular layers of the optic tectum. (c) Subtectal or tegmental neurons recorded below the third ventricle. Neurons with the same large visual ERFs as just described were identified; however, they had additional inputs from other sense organs, such as the skin or ear. Figure 13C concerns this multisensory integration. (For similar results in frogs, see Lettvin et al., 1961; Fite, 1969; Grüsser and Grüsser-Cornehls, 1970; Liege and Galand, 1972.)

It is thought (Ewert and Borchers, 1971) that the tectal, large-field units type b serve to localize large visual objects relative to the degree of excitation in each neuron type. In an instance where all type b neurons are activated simultaneously, then the object is moving across the fixation point. By means of the additional inputs from other sense organs via the subtectum, the visual response threshold of these unit types and the animal's alertness may be influenced (Ewert, 1967a).

Grüsser and Grüsser-Cornehls recorded from the frog optic tectum the following types of neurons.

CLASS T_1. Binocularly driven units with frontal ERFs of about 15–30° (see also Fite, 1969).

CLASS T_2. Monocularly driven large-field units with frontal ERFs of about 90° diameter. Those units could show directional sensitivity for

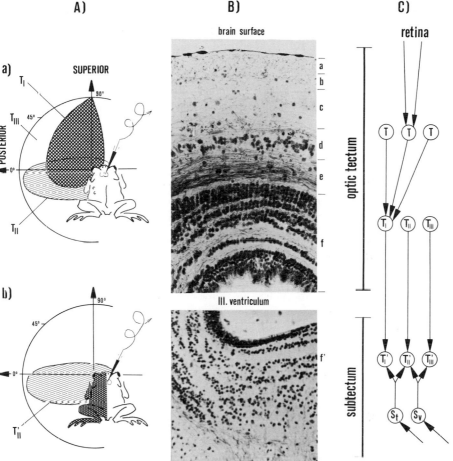

Fig. 13. Some examples of sensory integration in the optic tectum and subtectum. (Aa) "Large field units," types T_I–T_{III}, recorded from the periventricular layers of the optic tectum. (b) Bimodal unit of the subtectal region receiving visual input of type T_{II} and somatosensory inputs from the whole contralateral body skin. (B) Section (Klüver-Barrera stain) of the optic tectum. Terminals of retinal class II fibers were found in layers a and b, class III in c, and class IV in layer d. From layers d and e tectal "small-field units," types 1 and 2, were recorded. The tectal large-field units were obtained from layer f, subtectal units from f'. (C) Examples of "multisensory" integration: T tectal visual small-field units (not necessarily type 1 and 2); T_I, T_{II}, T_{III} tectal visual large-field units; S_t and S_v subtectal units receiving tactile or vibratory input; T_I', T_{II}', T_{III}' bi- and tri-modal units. (From Ewert, 1973.)

object movements from temporal to nasal positions. Stimulation in nasal positions were most effective. These units correspond to the toad's T_I neurons. (At present the numbering of unit types in frogs and toads is a bit confusing. In the future, it should be necessary to get a more uniform numbering system for classifications.)

CLASS T_3. Monocularly driven units with ERFs of about 20–30° diameter located in nasal field positions. They were optimally activated when an object more than 3° moved in a direction toward the frog's eye. (Neurons with similar response characteristics were found in the toad's thalamic-pretectal regions).

CLASS T_4. Large-field units with ERFs almost covering the whole visual field; several of these units had "multisensory" inputs (see also Fite, 1969). (These units correspond to the toads tectal neurons T_{III} and subtectal T'_{III}).

CLASS T_5. Units with relatively small ERFs of 8–20° diameter distributed in all parts of the visual field; several of them showed alternating excitatory and inhibitory zones in their receptive fields (some of those units may correspond to the toad tectal "small-field" units described previously.)

CLASS T_6. Units with large ERFs (greater than 126° diameter) located mainly in the dorsal part of the visual field. They could be activated by moving stimuli of more than 8° diameter. Following repeated stimulation, these units showed adaptation specific for the locus in the receptive field stimulated. (Similar units have been identified in the toad's TP-region.)

Coding of Behaviorally Relevant Form Parameters

Since toads are able to recognize prey objects with one eye, only units with monocular inputs were quantitatively investigated. (For details on binocularly driven units in frogs, see Fite, 1969; Raybourn, 1975.) Furthermore, it seemed unlikely that the large-field unit types are involved in the preliminary analysis of the form of a visual stimulus. Quantitative experiments with toads were therefore performed with the tectal small-field units. As previously described, these units have an approximately circular excitatory receptive field of about 27° diameter. Also, in these tectal layers (cells of d and e in Fig. 13B) the receptive fields show a topographical arrangement (Fig. 14A) that corresponds roughly to that of the more superficial retinal ganglion cell axon endings (Ewert *et al.*, 1974).

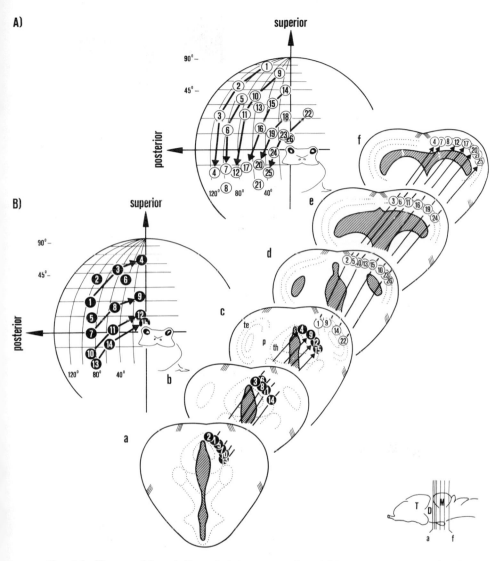

Fig. 14. Topographic relations between receptive field positions (centers) of tectal (A) and thalamus-pretectal (B) so-called small-field units and the localization of their cell bodies. (Recording positions of the stainless steel electrode tips—after passing anodal DC current—were identified in histological brain sections, a–f, by staining the iron deposit.) p, pretectum; th, dorsal posterior thalamus; te, optic tectum. (From Ewert *et al.*, 1974.)

Figure 15 (B and C) shows the result of experiments in which stimulus patterns used in the behavioral studies were moved through the receptive field of tectal small-field units. The values of the parameters for contrast

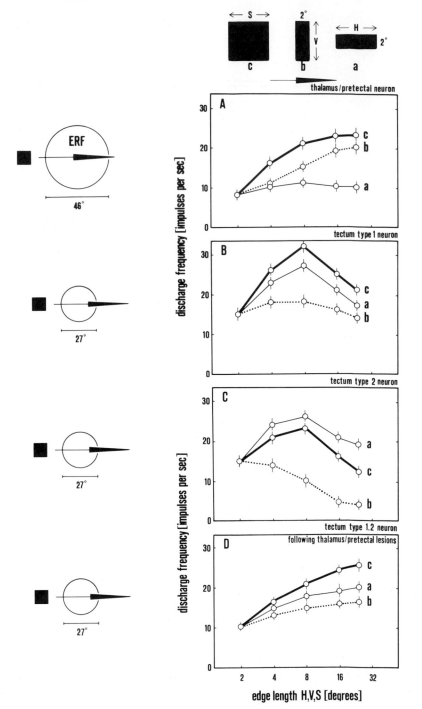

and velocity were held constant. Based upon their response characteristics, two types of neurons were identified. Most frequently recorded was the *tectal type-1 neuron* (Fig. 15B).

HORIZONTAL STRIPES. The discharge frequency of these tectal neurons increased as the stripe expansion in the direction of movement was increased up to 8°.

VERTICAL STRIPES. Elongation perpendicular to the direction of movement produced only a slight change in the neuronal activity.

SQUARES. Squares of increasing size produced a change in the unit's activity similar to that evoked by horizontal stripes with corresponding horizontal extension. The response characteristic of *tectal-type* 2 neurons differed only in that their activity was decreased by object extensions perpendicular to the direction of movement (Fig. 15C). By means of statistical methods (McNemar-Test, variance analysis, correlation analysis and t-Test) it was found (for $p < 0.01$) that both, tectal type-1 and -2 neurons are heterogeneous in their response characteristics and belong to two different neuron populations.

These experiments indicate that tectal type-1 neurons are sensitive mainly to object expansion in the direction of movement. With these stimulus transformations alone, the brain should not be able to recognize or discriminate prey and enemies. Interestingly enough, the tectal type-2 neurons are sensitive both to the object expansions in and perpendicular to the direction of movement.

Neurons of the Posterior Thalamus and Pretectal Region

Types of Neurons

The present report lists only those neuronal characteristics that could be determined with reasonable certainty. The system used for the follow-

---

Fig. 15. Responses of single neurons from the thalamus/pretectal region (mainly posterior thalamus) and the optic tectum (Stratum griseum et album centrale). Influence of the behaviorally relevant size parameters (S,V,H) of rectangular objects moved through the center of the receptive fields at 7.6°/sec on the average discharge frequency. (A) So-called small-field-units of the TP-region. (B) So-called small-field units of the optic tectum, type 1 neurons. (C) Other tectal small-field units, type 2 neurons. (D) Change of the response properties of tectum 1 and 2 neurons following thalamic/pretectal lesions. Each point represents average responses from 20 single neurons. (From Ewert and von Wietersheim, 1974b,c.)

ing classification of units (a–g) proceeds from more general characteristics to some special properties, but does not necessarily indicate a hierarchical ordering of receptive field "complexity," nor is it meant to imply an interpretation of the derivation of these properties from other visual system neurons (for details, see Ewert, 1971; for results on frogs, see Liege and Galand, 1972).

(a) *Darkness-sensitive units* included those with a tonic discharge following the dimming of room lights, and others that gave a tonic discharge to light-*on* and were inhibited during darkness.

(b) *Units sensitive to stationary objects* gave prolonged responses to large objects that were stationary in the receptive field (ERF 30–90°). Some of these neurons could also be activated by tactile stimulation. In this case, a tactile stimulus facilitated the response to a subsequent visual stimulus. Furthermore, units were obtained that responded specifically to stationary but not to moving objects.

(c) *Movement sensitive small-field units* were driven monocularly and had approximately circular receptive ERFs of about 46° diameter. These units were best activated by relatively large, dark objects moved against a bright background. They showed brief *off* responses to diffuse light changes.

(d) *Large-field units* had ERFs which included the entire contralateral or the whole visual field as seen via both eyes. Some of these units gave a long burst to each object movement throughout the entire ERF with little adaptation. Others were typically responsive to each new kind of object motion, but they quickly adapted to a repeated movement within a particular region of the field. These units were also described by Lettvin and co-workers (1961) in the frog optic tectum as "newness" and "sameness" cells.

(e) *"Memory units."* Object motion anywhere within the contralateral visual field (ERF > 90°) elicited repetitive bursts from these neurons, but even after an object disappeared, the unit continued with a strong afterdischarge, lasting up to 10 seconds. Following repeated object movement through the same ERF regions, the afterdischarge usually ceased, but such habituation was specific only to that region of the field. Units of this type were also obtained by Grüsser and Grüsser-Cornehls (1968b, 1970) in the frog optic tectum.

(f) *Units sensitive to object movement in the "z-axis"* showed relatively weak activity to an object moved around the toad. However, when it was moved toward the toad's eye, the unit response was suddenly increased. Approach from the upper field was more effective than from the front, and lateral field approach was even less effective. Similar units were also recorded from the pretectal region of the cat (Hoffmann, 1970) and from the optic tectum of the frog (z^+-neurons; Grüsser and Grüsser-Cornehls, 1968b; 1970).

(g) *Units with changeable ERF sizes* seemed to be variants of types (c) and (d). They could change their ERF size according to circumstances that are not yet known. (1) Small-field units that doubled their size along either the horizontal or vertical axis; (2) large-field units that had a distinct "blind area" centered about the rostral midline; the width of this area could change between 10 and 60° diameter; (3) large-field units that were continuously sensitive to the ipsilateral eye, but following tactile stimulation of the contralateral body side would respond to contralateral visual movement as well.

(h) *Units with selective response to tactile stimulation of the body skin.* The receptive fields included the entire body skin. Ipsilateral stimuli were less effective than contralateral ones. Some units were best activated by tactile stimuli *moved* upon the body skin.

(i) *Units with selective response to body tilting.* Four types of units were found which responded specifically to the direction of body tilting (J.-P. Ewert, unpublished data).

Although all the afferents to the caudal thalamus are still unknown, two things can be said by way of comparison with the well-known retinotectal pathway in frogs and toads: the thalamic neurons receive inputs similar to that of retinal class I neurons (sensitivity to stationary objects), but do not respond well to small objects that are optimal for class II retinal neurons. The first point is most interesting, since class I neurons have not yet been found within the toad's retinotectal projection (Grüsser and Grüsser-Cornehls, 1970; Ewert and Borchers, 1971; J. Y. Lettvin, unpublished). These results would lead one to suppose that retinal units sensitive to stationary objects send axons directly to the caudal thalamus in the toad. The sensitivity of caudal thalamic neurons to large objects and to dimming of room lights could be attributed to convergence of retinal class III and IV neurons; but it is not yet known whether such information derives directly from the retina or indirectly by way of tectal neurons. Furthermore, at present, it is not known whether some similarities or complexities of the response characteristics from tectal and thalamic neurons arise from parallel types of integration or interconnections between midbrain and diencephalic regions. Although these data offer only a cursory knowledge of the complexity of thalamic function, they demonstrate clearly that the thalamus, as well as the optic tectum, plays a central role in visual information processing.

In general, many of the neurons recorded from the TP-region were activated mainly by those stimuli which release behavioral "avoidance movements"; turning away from a threatening object (c, i) detour movements (b), and compensatory movements for body posture (i). These findings are in good agreement with brain stimulation experiments reported previously.

The following quantitative neurophysiological investigations were performed with the neuron type (c) that was derived monocularly and had an ERF diameter of about 46° (which was relatively small for this brain area). Small-field units were located lateral to the dorsal posterior thalamus and nearer to the pretectal region (Fig. 14B). Dorsal posterior thalamus and pretectal region are anatomically distinct areas (Knapp et al., 1965; Lázár, 1969). As a result of their close proximity, however, it was not possible to discriminate between these areas during physiological experiments; therefore, it is named TP-region. The receptive fields of small-field neurons located in this region show a topographical mapping such that the retina is also represented in this brain area (Ewert, et al., 1974). In relation to the sagittal axis, the retinal projection diagram in the TP-region is like a mirror image of the projection diagram in the optic tectum (cf. Figs. 14A and 14B; see also Chapter 3). Displacement of the recording electrode from rostral to caudal in the optic tectum produced a shift of receptive field positions from dorsal, anterior to ventral, posterior and in the thalamus from ventral, posterior to dorsal, anterior. Similar results have been previously described for the pretectum of the frog (Lázár, 1971; Scalia and Fite, 1974) and of mammals (Siminoff et al., 1966; Hoffmann, 1970).

Coding of Behaviorally Relevant Form Parameters

The values of the contrast and velocity parameters were held constant.

HORIZONTAL STRIPES. A $2° \times 2°$ moving object evoked only slight activity. In contrast to tectal neurons (Fig. 15B,C), discharge frequency in these TP small-field neurons (Fig. 15A) did not cause a marked change as the stripe expansion was increased in the horizontal direction of movement.

VERTICAL STRIPES. In contrast to tectal neurons, the discharge frequency increased with increasing stripe length perpendicular to the direction of movement.

SQUARES. The response was even stronger for an increasing edge.

From these results, it can be concluded that the investigated TP small-field units—similar to the retinal class IV neurons—provide information about two aspects of a moving stimulus: The object surface, mainly the expansion perpendicular to the direction of movement, and the relative darkness caused by an object entering the ERF. With these stimulus transformations alone, however, the brain is not able to discriminate between prey and enemy objects.

Conclusions

The toad's retinotectal projection is mediated by three types of retinal ganglion cells, which have approximately circular receptive fields of different sizes ($\approx 4°$, $\approx 8°$ and 12–16° diameter). They respond specifically (class II) or sensitively (class III and IV) to objects *moved* through their ERF. Furthermore, class III and IV neurons are activated by transient changes of room illumination. By shadowing the retina during active eye closure, the expected *off* response of these neurons failed to occur. Whereas the velocity and contrast relationships governing neuronal responses seem to be in good accordance with behavioral findings; area effects are not simply derived by retinal ganglion cell outputs. Class II and III neurons are sensitive mainly to object expansions perpendicular to the horizontal direction of movement, and class IV neurons to the degree of darkness entering the ERF.

The main projection areas of optic nerve terminals—optic tectum and thalamus-pretectum—consist of a variety of different neuron types. The quantitatively investigated small-field units have approximately circular ERFs, and they show topographical mapping. Whereas tectal type 1 neurons (ERF $\approx 27°$ diameter) are sensitive mainly to object expansion in the horizontal direction of movement, the TP-neurons (ERF $\approx$ 46° diameter) show sensitivity to the whole stimulus surface, mainly to the surface expansion perpendicular to the direction in which the stimulus moves. The response of tectal type 2 neurons (ERF $\approx 27°$ diameter) depends upon both expansion components.

Retinal ganglion cells, tectal- and TP small-field units have the following common general characteristics. They respond sensitively or specifically to object movement (M-neurons; Grüsser and Grüsser-Cornehls, 1973). The ERFs have an approximately circular shape. The apparent orientation-sensitivity differs from "classical" orientation detectors. Furthermore, they show no specificity for the direction in which the stimulus traverses the ERF (no directional sensitivity). In these neurons the reported figurational stimulus response relations are largely independent upon the orientation—horizontal or vertical direction—in that the stimulus moves.

It is interesting to note that W. Himstedt (unpublished results) recently recorded from the optic tectum of the salamander neurons show-ing response characteristics similar to those of the toad's tectal type 2 neurons.

HYPOTHESIS: THE FIRST BASIC STEPS IN PREY-ENEMY RECOGNITION

Some Neurobiological Evidence

In the toad's visual system, there exist something like neuronal "fil-ters" that are more sensitive either to the expansion of a visual object perpendicular to (retinal ganglion cells, TP-neurons) or in the horizontal direction of movement (tectal type 1 neurons). After comparing the neurophysiological and behavioral results for each visual pattern form tested, it is evident that prey-enemy recognition cannot be the result of the stimulus transformation by one kind of neuronal form filter alone. Since the activity of tectal type 2 neurons depends upon *both* expansion components of a moving object, it seems likely that their response char-acteristics result from excitatory inputs from tectal type 1 neurons and inhibitory inputs from the TP small-field neurons. Presumably, the tectal type 2 neurons may be involved in a trigger system for prey-catching orienting movements.

The prey-enemy recognition system for the toad would consist of three basic steps in visual information processing (Fig. 20A): (1) a first transformation of different stimulus parameters such as size, velocity, and contrast at the retinal level; (2) a particular amount of form anal-ysis by means of neuronal "form filters" (TP-neurons and tectal type 1 neurons); (3) the recognition process resulting from interactions between TP and tectal form filters. That means if the expansion of a visual ob-ject perpendicular to the direction of movement exceeds a certain amount, it is "categorized" as unsuitable for food, in which case the prey-catch-ing trigger system in the optic tectum is inhibited by TP-neurons. In case of an enemy object, presumably additional neuronal populations in the TP-region may be stimulated via excitatory pathways from the tectum as a function of the stimulus-expansion and triggers avoidance move-ments. This hypothesis originally formulated by Ewert (1968b) is sup-ported by results from the following experiments.

A stimulating electrode was implanted in the TP-region and a record-ing electrode was positioned in the central layers of the optic tectum (Fig. 16A,a–c) from which a unit responding to a moving visual object was recorded. The response to the same stimulus, however, was decreased

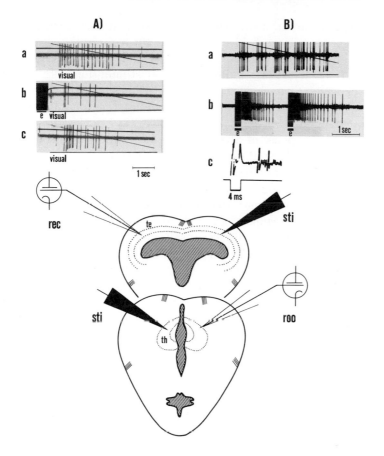

Fig. 16. Evidence for physiological connections between optic tectum and thalamus-pretectum. (Aa) Response of a tectal "small-field unit" to a black 4° square moved at 7.6°/sec against white background. (b) Three min later: Weak response to the same visual stimulus after previous electrical (e) point stimulation in the TP-region with a train of negative square-wave pulses of 50 cps, 5 msec pulse duration and intensity of 30 μA. (c) Recovery of the visual response 30 sec later. (Ba) Response of a thalamic-pretectal "large-field unit" (ERF ≈ 90°) to a 8° moving visual stimulus. (b) Activation of the same unit by electrical point stimulation of the optic tectum with a pulse train. (c) Response to a single electrical square-wave pulse (latency ≈4 msec). (From Ewert *et al.*, 1974.)

following electrical point stimulation of the thalamic-pretectal region. A couple of seconds later, the neuron showed a response to the visual stimulus that had been obtained prior to TP stimulation. Under physiological conditions, no neurons were found in this tectal region which could be activated by electrical stimulation of the TP-region. In the reverse type of experiment, when stimulation and recording positions were interchanged, large-field units of the TP-region (Fig. 16,B,a) were activated by electrical stimulation (16B,b) of the optic tectum (Ewert, 1973; Ewert et al., 1974). Following tectal stimulation with a train of pulses, TP-units then showed a relatively long-lasting afterdischarge, maybe as the result of positive feedback via interneurons. When the tectum was stimulated with a single pulse (Fig. 16, see c) a latency for the TP-unit response of about 4 msec was found (evidence for orthodromic stimulation). Excitatory inputs from tectum to thalamic wide-field units in frogs were also obtained by Brown and Ingle (1973).

As mentioned previously, after TP-lesions or curare application to the optic tectum, toads were not able to discriminate visual objects in a behaviorally relevant manner (Fig. 1B,b). A comparable "disinhibition effect" was also reflected in the response from tectal neurons of the central layers, which had their ERFs in the "disinhibited" areas of the visual field (cf. Figs. 1B,b and 15D; Ewert and von Wiersheim, 1974b). During those experiments, it was not possible to decide whether these were tectal type 1 or 2 neurons. Therefore, it seems likely that not only tectal type 2 but also tectal type 1 neurons receive inhibitory inputs from the TP-region. Anatomic evidence for projection from thalamus to the optic tectum has been described for the frog by Székely and co-workers (1973) and by Trachtenberg and Ingle (1974) on the basis of Fink-Heimer degeneration studies. Ingle (1973a) recently reported for frogs that Lettvin's (Lettvin et al., 1961) "newness cells" in the optic tectum are inhibited by TP-units. Following TP-lesions, those cells show remarkable changes in their receptive field sizes.

COMPUTER ANALYSIS OF THE HYPOTHETICAL PREY-ENEMY PATTERN RECOGNITION SYSTEM BY MEANS OF MODEL NERVE NETS*

The following investigation is concerned with the recognition of rectangular moving patterns in the toad's visual system. The data used are taken from the experiments described earlier in the chapter. In the present context, pattern recognition is defined as the classification of two-dimensional, time-dependent retinal distributions of brightness from the environment into innate or learned classes of functional significance. This operation proceeds in two steps: (1) the extraction of significant features, x_i, from the patterns to be perceived, and (2) the separation of the feature vectors, x, acquired by means of discriminating functions, D,

*By W. von Seelen, University of Mainz, Federal Republic of Germany.

in such a way that upon presentation of a pattern of the νth class of significance:

$$D_\nu(x) \geq D_\mu(x) \; \nu, \mu = 1, 2, \ldots M; \nu \neq \mu, \tag{1}$$

where M is the number of possible classes to be discriminated. This separation procedure, which can be effected by weighted neuronal threshold-value operations, will be called classification.

In this framework, the two classes of significance—prey and enemy—were to be distinguished by the toad ($M = 2$). The input signals used were rectangular patterns with sides of variable length as in Fig. 1B, which were moved at velocity, v. The response of the toads in the behavioral experiments is shown in Figure 1B,a. In addition to these behavioral experiments, single-cell recordings in the retina, the tectum and the thalamus-pretectum which originated from the same input signals were used to determine the parameters of the system. The proposed descriptive procedure can be extended to include any desired type of input signal.

Descriptive Procedure

It will be assumed on the basis of Ewert's experiments that the system consists of a sequence of two-dimensional neuronal networks (similarly in the frog) which are coupled by the mechanisms of inhibition and facilitation (Ewert, 1968b; Ewert, et al., 1970; Grüsser-Cornehls, 1968; von Seelen, 1970). The proposed model is designed to interpret the experiments just outlined functionally and also in part, structurally; the following assumptions are made: (1) the system is linear; (2) the system is homogeneous in the area considered, i .e., the coupling of the neurons depends exclusively on the distance of the elements from each other and not on their position; (3) the patterns are large with respect to the spacing of the receptors; and (4) the temporal influence of the system upon the signals varies for inhibtory and facilitatory couplings.

In the real system, these conditions are only valid for certain ranges (linearity range covers 10^2; Ewert et al., 1970). The validity range of the assumption of homogeneity has not yet been experimentally determined; however, the extension of this description to inhomogeneous systems is possible without much difficulty. The third condition makes it possible to treat the system as continuum. Deviations which may thereby arise from the transformations of the real system are slight and can be estimated. The fourth condition seems necessary, since a change of sign in a neuron's operation always requires an additional cell and so involves a further delay. The time relationships of the lateral neuronal connections are especially essential for the interpretation of the findings. An absolute latency, which may be seen when the patterns move very rapidly, must be taken into consideration due to the transmission time of the signals onto the dendrites; the signal delay at the synapses is even more pronounced and therefore operates at lower velocities also. This will be approximated below by a low-pass filter of the first order. Neuron networks coupled on the principle of inhibition can be interpreted as space filters, which, depending on the type of lateral coupling, attenuate certain space-frequency areas (von Seelen, 1970).

If $y(r,s,t)$ is the space- (r,s) and time-dependent input signal, $z(r,s,t)$ the output signal, and $H(r,s,t)$ the coupling function of the neurons, then, because of the previous assumptions of this section (von Seelen, 1970):

$$z(r,s,t) = \int_0^t \int_{-\infty}^{+\infty} \int_{-\infty}^{+\infty} H(r - r', s - s', t - \tau) y(r',s',\tau) \, dr' \, ds' \, d\tau \quad (2)$$

The impulse reaction function results in

$$g(r,s,t) = H(r,s,t) \quad (3)$$

which is a characteristic system value that completely describes the system. Thus, the analysis of such a system requires the determination of the time-dependent, spatial two-dimensional coupling functions, or alternatively its Fourier-transformations $F[g(r,s,t)]$ according to space and time, which is subsequently referred to as the frequency characteristic. The coupling function $H(r,s,t)$ was not directly determined experimentally. It can be derived from experiments carried out to determine characteristics of the space-dependent coupling function in the first processing stages (ganglion cell receptive field) is nearly radially symmetrical, has a positive maximum in the center and a negative surround, and converges toward zero for $r,s \to \infty$ (Ewert and Hock, 1972). The basic characteristics of such systems are—insofar as no discontinuity arises—dependent only to a slight degree on the exact nature of the coupling function (von Seelen, 1970). Therefore, in the present case, the coupling function will, for mathematical reasons, be approximated by the difference of two exponential functions of different width. The parameters are determinable in each case with the aid of the responses of the partial systems to one of the input patterns as in Fig. 1B. In the following, if no further measurements are available, the procedure for all the system parameters required will be that they will be determined with the reaction to one pattern and tested with the reactions to the other two patterns.

If the horizontal length of the patterns is $l_1 = 2a$ and the vertical length $l_2 = 2an$, then with the aid of step functions the result for the input signal moving at velocity $\bar{v}$ is

$$y(r,s,t) - [v(r + a + \bar{v}t) - v(r - a + \bar{v}t)][v(s + un) - o(s - un)] \quad (4)$$

The three patterns as in Fig. 1B can be fixed by variation of a and n. With the aid of Fourier-transformation the convolution integral according to Eq. (2) becomes

$$F[z(r,s,t)] = F[H(r,s,t)]\{F[y(r,s,t)]\} \qquad F = F_{r,s,t} \quad (5)$$

with

$$A_1(i\omega) = \frac{1}{1 + T_1 i\omega} \quad (6)$$

or alternatively

$$A_2(i\omega) = \frac{1}{1 + T_2 i\omega} \quad (7)$$

as time frequency characteristic for excitation (Eq. 6) or for inhibition (Eq. 7)—where T_1 and T_2 are the time constants for excitation and inhibition—then

$$F[H(r,s,t)] = F[H_e(r,s)]A_1(i\omega) - F[H_i(r,s)][A_2(i\omega)] \quad (8)$$

Here $H_e(r,s)$ and $H_i(r,s)$ characterize the space-dependent coupling function for excitation and inhibition. The coupling function

$$H(r,s) = m_1 e^{-(|r|+|s|)/B_1} - m_2 e^{-(|r|+|s|)/B_2} \quad (9)$$

allows the derivation of the excitation distribution at the system's output from Eqs. (4–8). Within the pattern, the resulting output signal is

$$z_i(r,s,t) = E_1\left[1 + \frac{e^{-\alpha}}{2(p-1)} - \frac{e^{\beta}}{2(p+1)} - \frac{p^2 e^{-(\alpha/p)}}{(p^2-1)}\right]$$
$$- G_1\left[1 + \frac{ke^{-(\alpha/k)}}{(\xi p - k)} - \frac{ke^{(\beta/k)}}{2(\xi p + k)} - \frac{(\xi p)^2 e^{-(\alpha/\xi)p}}{(\xi p)^2 - k^2}\right] \quad (10)$$

with

$$T_1\bar{v} = pB_1 \tag{11}$$
$$B_2 = kB_1 \tag{12}$$
$$T_2 = \xi T_1 \tag{13}$$
$$\alpha = (r + \bar{v}t + a) \tag{14}$$
$$\beta = (r + \bar{v}t - a) \tag{15}$$
$$E_1 = [1 - \tfrac{1}{2}e^{-(1/B_1)(s+an)} - \tfrac{1}{2}e^{+(1/B_1)(s-an)}] \tag{16}$$

The parameter G_1 corresponds to E_1, whereby B_1 is to be replaced by B_2.

This determines the output values of the system for all rectangular input signals which move uniformly at velocity, $\bar{v}$. Various *on* or *off* systems of any desired coupling width, coupling height, and time characteristic can be determined by determination of the parameters m_1, m_2, B_1, B_2, T_1, and T_2. If another coupling function is chosen, then, although the numerical values of the results change, the basic system characteristics remain the same (von Seelen, 1970). If k and $\xi > 1$, an *on* system is present; if both values are smaller than 1, an *off* system is defined. If the input signal consists of dark bars, then the pattern fixed by Eq. (4) is to be replaced by

$$y_{\text{off}}(r,s,t) = 1 - y(r,s,t) \tag{17}$$

When the movements are very rapid, the transmission time of the dendritic signals must be taken into consideration in Eqs. (6) and (7).

In the following sections, the model will be tested and specified in stages on the basis of actual experiments. Here, it is established that the basic structure is the same in the various stages of the system. Simple variation of neuronal coupling parameters is sufficient to determine the specific characteristics of the parts and thus the differentiated performances of the whole system.

Retina

The four-layer neuron network of the toad's retina is interpreted as a space filter in accordance with Eq. (2). The networks of the various classes of ganglion cells are to be treated separately. The investigations below will be primarily concerned with the class II neurons; the transformation of the other cell types can easily be derived from these. The determination of the coupling function and the time constants T_1 and T_2 would be necessary for quantitative treatment. These values could not be directly measured; the response of the system to the three moving patterns of variable side length as in Fig. 1B can be obtained to determine properties of the system. In accordance with the results from the frog's retina, a coupling function as in Eq. (9) will be assumed (Grüsser and Grüsser-Cornehls, 1968a,b). To determine the parameters B_1, B_2, T_1, and T_2, approximate values were used from the measurements of the receptive fields in the frog retina, which were then approximated iteratively to circumstances in the toad with the aid of the first four points of the responses of class II neurons (Fig. 10A, curve c). The response of the model in a system of coordinates moving at v is obtained from Eq. (10) with $m_1 = 1$. This function, which depends on r, is identical with the time characteristic of the reaction at a neuron, the position of which can be varied on the s-axis. There are a number of possibilities of establishing what is to count as a reaction; e.g., the maximum value, the total integral, the integral within a defined period of time or above a threshold. What defines a reaction is identical with an hypothesis as to what is regarded as information by the system; thus, the consequences of this must always be checked. For stimuli with a small surface area or moved with high velocity, the mean value of the reaction is approximately linear to the maximum value. In the present case, analogous to the experimental case, the mean value of the reaction above zero was determined. Figure 17A shows the result of the system output. A good approximation, even for the curves a and b, which are to be taken as test cases, are obtained from the values $B_1 = 0.8°$; $k = 2$; $\xi = 2.2$; $p = 1.1$; $\bar{v} = 7.6°$/sec. Apart from the coupling function, the different values of the three stimuli depend on the time relationships which, due to the directional movement property, generate an apparent anisotropy. The maximum value of the curves in Fig. 17A mainly depend on the coupling widths B_1 and B_2. Since the receptive fields of the class III and IV neurons are larger than those of the cell types treated here, their response characteristics are intelligible without further calculation.

Tectum

The tectum consists of several layers of two-dimensional networks of neurons, which have a number of other functions in addition to feature extraction. Data from this network have been obtained only in part from neurophysiological experiments. The use of behavioral experiments is problematical, since it is not known how decisions are formed in subsequent neural networks. However, it can be shown (Fig. 15A) that the TP-region plays scarcely any role in "decision-making" when the signals have a very small surface. Therefore, in the case of such signals, the remaining tectum parameters were determined by the same method as in the retina, which also takes into consideration several decision possibilities (mean value, maximum amplitude). Each of the curves a in Figure 18A–C show the outputs of the model system according to Eq. (10), if

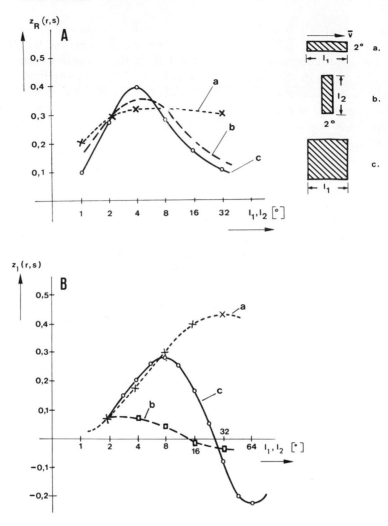

Fig. 17. (A) Responses of a neural net, simulating the retina (class II ganglion cell), to three moving patterns; $\bar{v} = 7.6°/\text{sec}$. (B) Responses of the neuronal "interaction model" (retina, thalamus/pretectum, and tectum) shown in Fig. 20B to the same stimulus patterns. l_1 corresponds to H and l_2 to V of Fig. 1B. (From Ewert and von Seelen, 1974.)

$B_1 = 1.8°$; $k = 2$; $\xi = 2.1$; $p = 1.5$; $\bar{v} = 7.6°/\text{sec}$. A reaction was taken to be the spatial mean value of the positive output amplitude which is associated with the time mean value of the neurons via $\bar{v}$. The outputs of the model system correspond essentially to the neurophysiological results. However, the output values for certain neuron populations of the tectum still show differences from the observed *behavior* of the animal (Fig. 1B,a), which indicates that further transformations must be re-

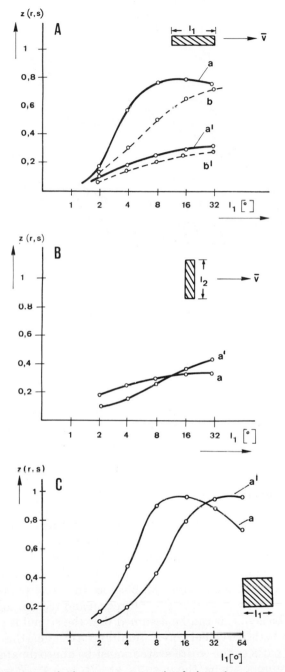

Fig. 18. Responses of the nerve nets simulating the tectum (a) and the thalamus/pretectum (a') to horizontal (A), vertical (B) stripes, and squares (C), all moved in horizontal direction with $\bar{v} = 7.6°$/sec. In part (A) the curves b and b' show the system responses for $\bar{v}_k = 5\ \bar{v}$. (From Ewert and von Seelen, 1974.)

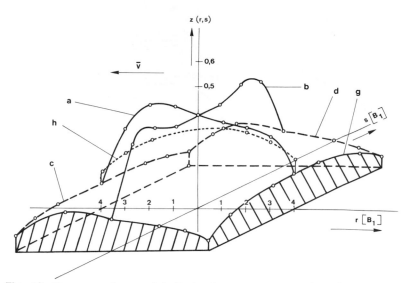

Fig. 19. Response of a model (tectum) to a square projected on the retina, $p = 0.6$, $a = 4B_1 = an$, $\xi = 3$, $k = 2.5$. Curve a: output for $s = 0$; curve b: $r = 0$; curves c,g: $r = -4B_1, 4B_1$; curve d: $s = 4B_1$; curve h: output of the thalamus/pretectum for $s = 0$. (From Ewert and von Seelen, 1974.)

quired. Owing to the network parameter(s), there appears, especially in the tectum, the apparent, movement-specific asymmetry of the system due to the fact that higher spatial frequencies of the patterns are attenuated to a greater extent in the direction of movement than perpendicular to it (cf. Eq. 17; Korn and von Seelen, 1972). To illustrate this operation, the space-dependent output signal of the tectum for a square stimulus input is plotted in Fig. 19.

Thalamus-Pretectum

The TP-region which is innervated from the retina in parallel with the tectum is also to be regarded as a two-dimensional nerve network (Ewert, 1971). The geometrical coupling data of the system can be determined from the sizes established for the receptive fields. However, no direct measurements are available for establishing the time parameters. Proceeding on the assumption that the TP-region and tectum together direct the animal's behavior, it can be assumed that the stimulus pattern must be present in both nerve networks simultaneously; i.e., the time parameters of both parts of the entire system must be approximately the same. On these presuppositions the results are $B_1 = 5.4°$; $k = 2$; $\xi = 2.1$; $p = 0.5$; $\bar{v} = 7.6°/\text{sec}$.

The curves a' in Fig. 18(A–C) are obtained for black patterns with the aid of Eq. (17). The output was defined in the same way as in the optic tectum. When the maximum amplitude is considered to be the reaction, the curves are only slightly altered especially for $l_1, l_2 < 8°$. In the course of a simulation program, the time parameters ξ and p (see Eqs. 10 and 17) were systematically varied on the computer to exclude a mistaken determination. As a consequence of the large coupling range, it is mainly the surface size of the pattern that is most relevant in the TP-region. The TP-region alone is not able to completely control either of the two behavior responses.

Interaction Models

To establish the quantitative relationships of the tectum/TP-transformations with the observed behavior, it must be determined whether or not further preprocessing steps are carried out as two-dimensional interactions of the two portions of the system and in what way decision formation takes place. The experiments with the TP-region removed suggest a subtractive interaction, which may take place two dimensionally. Two possible models, which interpret the behavioral experiments qualitatively, are sketched in Fig. 20 (B and C). Since recent experiments have found a cell type (tectal type 2 neuron) whose output volume corresponds to the animal's behavior, it appears that special neurons seem to be present for difference determination, and function model B is then the most appropriate (Ewert and von Seelen, 1974). If the prey-catching response above the decision threshold is considered, then

$$F[z_1(r,s,t)] = F[y(r,s,t)]\{F[H_1(r,s,t)]F[H_5(r,s,t)] \\ - F[H_2(r,s,t)]F[H_3(r,s,t)]\} \quad (18)$$

holds for the first model. If H_2 is destroyed by lesion, then in keeping with the experiments, prey-catching responses are the only ones that can be possibly occur. The coupling parameters H_3, H_4, H_5, H_6 have not yet been measured quantitatively; they were ascertained with the aid of the points on the curve a in Fig. 1B. In so doing, H_3 and H_4 were assumed to be identical, as were H_5 and H_6. The result for the combination H_3, H_5 is $B_1 = 0.3°$; $k = 1.4$; $\xi = 1.15$; $p = 8$. Owing to the low coupling widths, the difference determination is very broad banded, so that only a minor error occurs in the case of the specific patterns used, even when the Fourier transformations of H_3 and H_5 are replaced by constant values in Eq. (18). If the spatial mean of the amplitudes of the output signal above the experimentally ascertained threshold is retransformed

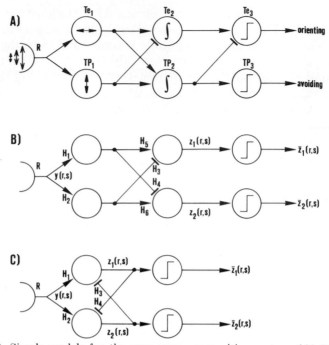

Fig. 20. Simple models for the prey-enemy recognition system. (A) Model constructed on the basis of the experimental results. The first steps of prey-enemy recognition may be a result of inhibitory (dashed lines) and excitatory (arrows) interactions between neuronal "form filters"; one in the TP-region (TP_1) sensitive to the surface of a stimulus object, mainly to object expansion perpendicular (perpendicular arrow) to the horizontal direction of movement, and the other in the optic tectum (Te_1) sensitive mainly to the object expansion in (horizontal arrow) the direction of movement (tectum 1 neurons). The three vertical double arrows in R symbolize the main stimulus area transformations of the three retinal ganglion cell classes on the basis of their different excitatory receptive field sizes. TP_2 (thalamus-pretectal neurons) and Te_2 (tectal type-2 neurons) receive converging inputs from Te_1 and TP_1 and trigger the prey-catching or escape response via other neurons (Te_3, TP_3). The inhibitory pathway from TP_2 to Te_3 avoids ambivalent responses. (B,C) Two possible system theoretical models. (All models do not take into consideration any size-constancy mechanisms that may exist.) (From Ewert and von Seelen, 1974.)

according to Eq. (18) and this value is taken as a reaction, then the relationships in Fig. 17B are the result for the responses to prey. The negative position of the curve, c, is to be taken as an avoidance response. In this case, the output volume of the TP-region is positive. Thus, the model approximates very closely not only curve, a, which was used to determine the parameters, but also the curves b and c, which are to be taken as tests. If a two-dimensional subtraction is assumed, then Fig. 19 illustrates the interaction operation. For $s = 0$, the difference of the curves a and h can be determined. This subtraction is to be carried out over the whole surface of the pattern. If the operations are assigned to feature extraction by means of H_1 and H_2, then the space-dependent course of H_3 and H_5 reproduces the function D in Eq. (1). The strength of the output, i.e., the number of prey-catching or avoidance responses depends on the number of times the threshold is crossed and also on the distance (effective dislocation) ·a certain shape has traversed across the retina until this occurs.

Conclusions

In this theoretical description, a neuronal structure is associated with the experimentally determined function of the system. It was shown that it is possible for simple parameter variations to produce discriminatory classification, although the coupling principle of the neurons remains the same.

The central point of the conceived model is the combined space-time filtering in neuronal networks and the weighted, two-dimensional subtraction of stimulus distributions. The different evaluations of the extension of the pattern in the direction of its movement and perpendicular to it occurs despite symmetrical coupling and is derived by an asymmetry in the time domain.

The features characterizing patterns emerge quantitatively as the difference of the two filter operations (space and time domain). The principle of two-dimensional subtraction of patterns is simple and efficient and may also exist as a basic principle in other nervous systems.

Provided that this functional description corresponds to the real physiological system, all experiments on pattern recognition concerning toad approach-avoidance behaviors should be predictable. It seems likely that the fundamental problems of feature extraction and decision formation can be solved in the present, relatively simple system. Other pattern classifications undoubtedly exist in addition to the prey-enemy one, and other behavioral responses should be investigated to understand the entire pattern recognition system.

In establishing the model, it has not yet been possible to determine exact values for the interaction between tectum and TP-region experimentally; thus, further investigations are required at this point. Moreover, how decision formation is accomplished by neurons and how such decisions are transformed into complex efferent commands remain significant questions for future research.

GENERAL DISCUSSION

Basic Mechanisms Concerning Form Evaluation

Toads are able to distinguish between a horizontal and a vertical stripe. But the underlying filter system that appears to exist evaluates those patterns in a manner fundamentally different from that of simple orientation detectors. The "simple cells" of the visual cortex respond to the orientation of a stripe pattern with respect to the main axial orientation of the enlongated receptive fields, depending upon the arrangement of excitatory and inhibitory receptive field subdivisions. The toad, in contrast, utilizes neuronal "form filters," which evaluate the size dimensions of a pattern together with the pattern's direction (plane) of movement independently of the shape of the receptive fields, which are approximately radially symmetrical.

To assess the role of these neuronal form-filters in information processing, it is first necessary to note which stimulus factors change with expansion of the object, either in or perpendicular to the direction of movement. By stepwise extension of the visual stimulus in the direction of movement, both spatial and temporal parameters are changed; i.e., at constant angular velocity, a longer horizontal black stripe darkens a larger receptor area (spatial component) and the shadowing remains for a longer time (temporal component). Surface extension perpendicular to the direction of movement, on the other hand, changes only the spatial components of the stimulus. From the system theoretical analysis (Ewert and von Seelen, 1974), it appears that the neuronal evaluation of the extension of the stimulus vertical to the direction of movement is achieved by means of (1) summation of spatial excitation in the receptive field. Evaluation of the pattern's extension in the direction of movement, however, occurs through spatial summation in connection with (2) a relatively long time delay between the excitatory and inhibitory processes in the receptive field. By different "emphasis" of operations (1) and (2) and as a consequence of the asymmetry of the time domain ("apparent anisotropy"), units appear that are more sensitive to either the expansion perpendicular to (retinal ganglion cells, thalamic/pretectal neurons) or expansion in direction of movement (tectal type 1 neurons).

Complexity of Sensory Detection Processes and Motor Functions

The findings just described have shown that for pattern recognition in prey-catching and escape behavior it is not only visual stimulus parameters, such as velocity of motion, size and contrast, that play a role. Learning and habituation processes, associated in part with motivation factors as well as seasonal effects, also have an influence. From these observations, it is to be assumed that additional neuronal populations, which have not come under individual investigation here, also take part in the total complex of information processing. At any rate, the described interaction system between two neuronal form-filters appears to underlie the basic wiring for the first steps in prey-enemy-recognition. That system can be approached for experimental analysis when all other parameters (except the primary form factors) are held constant within their optimal ranges. This account, of course, represents only an initial, crude simplification of what actually occurs in neuronal networks. For example, it does not explain "object size-constancy" phenomena that may exist (Ingle, 1968a; Ewert and Gebauer, 1973). Furthermore, the type 1 tectal neurons probably also receive inhibitory influences from the TP-region, for after TP-lesions, only neurons with "disinhibited" reaction characteristics are recorded from the stratum griseum and album centrale. Perhaps this is the "original" response characteristic of such tectal neurons. It should also be noted that the model concerns only the primary prey-enemy-recognition process that is responsible for the orienting movement. But this does not mean that the visual system is not able to discriminate more complex patterns as tested during the present experiments.

There are other neuronal systems involved in the control of the *total* behavioral sequence. Grüsser and Grüsser-Cornehls (1970) suggest for the frog that the activation of different tectal neuron classes (T_1–T_6) correspond to motor commands. Thus, the function of the optic tectum would include sensory mechanisms (pattern analysis) as well as motor control systems for the behavioral responses. The frog tectal class T_5 units may receive the resulting information of prey-detection processes. These units (similar as the toad tectal type 2 neurons) may be involved in a trigger system for the orienting movement toward prey. The total motor sequence during prey catching could result by means of sequential activation of tectal unit types in the following succession: *class* T_5 (orienting toward prey); *class* T_2 (enhancement of the turning movement); *class* T_1 (frog measures its own distance from the prey and judges the absolute object size; on the basis of those measurements, the jumping movement is triggered); *class* T_3 (neurons sensitive to object approaching trigger the tongue flip). Grüsser's hypothesis for the neuronal basis of such sequential activation of motor patterns seems to be supported by the electrical brain stimulation experiments in freely moving toads (See Fig. 7A, B).

The functions of the optic tectum and the TP-region are not exclusively limited to the tasks investigated here (McIlwain, 1972; Riss *et al.*, 1972). These regions presumably function for other sensory data processing as well, such as optomotor reactions and recognition of partners during courtship, to name but two examples. To determine to what extent the neuronal form filters described are involved in these behavioral processes requires further analysis.

Localization and Identification in Visual Systems of Vertebrates

For higher and lower vertebrates alike, stimulus localization and stimulus identification are based upon two distinct processes in the visual system that are physiologically distinct, in part, but very closely connected to each other functionally (Trevarthen, 1968a; Schneider, 1969; Ewert, 1973). In this context, the neuronal substrate for stimulus localization appears to have developed very early in evolutionary history, if one judges from its location at the subcortical level (optic tectum). Phylogenetically older visual identification systems (thalamus, pretectum, tectum) are still functional in some mammalian species. In tree shrews, for instance, with neocortical (striate cortex) ablations, they are necessary substrata for the relearning of certain visual pattern discrimination tasks (Snyder and Diamond, 1968). In split-brain cats, it has been found that behavioral responses to visual patterns depend on the brain half with lesions in the pretectum-superior colliculus regions. Marked deficits were found even when the visual cortex was intact. Sprague and co-workers (1970) concluded from these results that subcortical areas actively participate in visually guided behavior and pattern discrimination.

Phylogenetically older identification systems seem to operate predominantly in some neonates (for details on hamsters, see Schneider, 1970). In adult mammals, however, pattern recognition is performed mainly by nerve nets of the visual cortex. This pattern-recognition system can function in some species largely independently of the collicular localization system. Following ablation of the superior colliculus, the golden hamster (Schneider, 1969) is not capable of localizing patterns in space, although it can still distinguish them. In the reverse type of experiment following cortical lesions, pattern recognition is eliminated, but localization is possible (for experiments in monkeys, see Humphrey, 1970).

In the toad, evaluation and recognition of a visual stimulus occurs through the *interaction* of nerve nets for localization—retina and tectum— with a third network in the thalamic-pretectal region. For these animals, localization and identification are still relatively closely bound up with one another. Since the receptive fields of the neuronal form-filters are retinotopically ordered (Fig. 14), the toad's recognition process can be accomplished for each position of a stimulus in the visual field.

As the findings show in the case of toads, there seem to be two localization principles in the visual system: One is based on fixed motor programs that originate in the retinal projection fields of the optic tectum and that can be triggered according to the peripheral differences between stimulus and fixation positions; i.e., for a pattern w pictured on the retina outside the fixation area x, there is a corresponding projection point w' in the optic tectum. If the recognition process has identified the object to be prey, then an "address" corresponding to the localization differential $x - w$ will be "dialed." For all possible differences in stimulus and fixation positions there are predetermined programs at the central projection points. These programs can be called into play "by address" namely $x - w$, either by visual or electrical triggering and transferred to the motor system. The resulting turning reaction is then adjusted to bring the prey (w) into the binocular fixation area (x), so that $x - w = 0$, and thereby to activate the representation x'. The snapping response can be logically triggered at an optimal distance. Orienting to the object position happens "blindly," without any peripheral controls, in a "free chain of timing." Subsequent adjustment occurs by means of a feedback process.

The basis of the second localization principle are neurons with large receptive fields that have different size, form, and spatial arrangements. The location of a stimulus may be thus determined according to the degree of excitation produced in neurons belonging to the various classes.

It is of interest to consider whether or not formal evaluation principles such as the following may possibly be developed to serve the function of stimulus identification in the visual system. (1) Analysis and identification of key stimuli (releasers of instinctive action) may be accomplished on the basis of "preprogrammed" neuron circuiting. The key stimuli may be represented by means of response characteristics of so-called master units. They would be located at the end of the chain of information processing; above threshold they would trigger the appropriate motor response (the prey-catching movement or avoidance movement). Supposedly, such fixed (or innate) recognition systems (IRMs) are located mainly in the subcortical region and play a major role among the lower vertebrates. (2) In contrast, the analysis and recognition of learned patterns must be accomplished according to another set of principles, for it is unlikely innate anatomic principles can account for all patterns stored up and repeatedly recognizable in the course of an individual's life. Eysel and Grüsser (1971) thus argue for (2) a neuronal system made up of various classes, with each class including a subfeature of the pattern. The complete pattern is then represented by means of the total neuronal pattern of impulses. Millions of nerve cells represent, for instance, the letter "A" in the human's brain; the same millions of nerve cells with a different spatial and temporal distribution of excitation can represent other visual symbols. However, this assumption does not answer the question of how and by what means such a code is read in the central nervous system.

This unknown principle may also be part of the present equipment of the lower vertebrate, although it can be assumed that its greatest development became possible through the development and plasticity of the neocortex. The fact that toads are able to store up various patterns subcortically via locus- and stimulus-specific habituation processes may make it possible to also study these complex problems in neural recognition systems, at their lowest level of integration and occurrence.

ACKNOWLEDGMENTS

Supported by grants of the Deutsche Forschungsgemeinschaft (DFG) Ew 7/1-6, SFB 45, Forsch.-Gr. AZ.: 741, 29-EW, and a fellowship of the Foundation's Fund for Research in Psychiatry, Ew No. 669-461.

The experiments were performed in cooperation with Dr. H. W. Borchers, Dr. F. J. Hock, B. Rehn, G. Siefert and Dr. A. von Wietersheim. The computer analysis was elaborated by Professor Dr. W. von Seelen (University of Mainz, FRG).

6

The Urodele Visual System[*]

Ursula Grüsser-Cornehls and Werner Himstedt

COMMONLY STUDIED FAMILIES

Taxonomic and Ecological Considerations

Urodeles (the order Caudata), with few exceptions, are found only in the temperate zone of the northern hemisphere. Systematists distinguish eight families, ordinarily distributed among five suborders. This chapter is based on the descriptions by Noble (1931), Bishop (1943), and Mertens and Wermuth (1960).

With respect to habitat, urodeles are more restricted to water than most anurans. Since the salamander skin is incapable of preventing water

[*] Dedicated to Prof. R. Jung, Freiburg im Breisgau, on the occasion of his 65th birthday.

loss, the animals must remain in regions of high humidity when on land. They stay secluded among damp foliage and are active at twilight and in the dark. The degree of such dependence varies among the different families. Some species are aquatic throughout their lives, often as neotenic forms—that is, they reach sexual maturity in the larval stage. Others lead a terrestrial life, at least for certain periods. The manner in which most urodeles reproduce makes them dependent on an aquatic milieu. The gill-breathing larvae develop in water and proceed to the land after metamorphosis. Among these forms, the adult animals usually return to the water to mate and lay eggs. However, a few urodeles are entirely terrestrial. For example, the European alpine salamander *Salamandra atra* undergoes larval development and metamorphosis in the oviduct of the mother, and is born as a fully formed terrestrial salamander.

The best-known and best-investigated urodele groups will now be described.

Cryptobranchidae

To this family belong the largest living amphibians. The eastern Asian giant salamander *Megalobatrachus*, of Japan and China, grows to a length of over 1.5 m. The North American hellbender (genus *Cryptobranchus*) can be 30–55 cm long. Both genera display many primitive characteristics; these include, for example, external fertilization, which is also found in their close relatives, the primitive *Hynobiidae*. The Cryptobranchidae are purely aquatic forms which, even as adults, retain many larval characteristics. Among these are certain skeletal elements, the absence of eyelids, and the persistance in *Cryptobranchus* of an open gill slit. Lungs, however, are developed in both genera. The hellbender and giant salamander live on the beds of flowing streams, hidden among stones and the like. They are nocturnal in habit.

Ambystomidae

The three American genera *Ambystoma, Dicamptodon,* and *Rhyacotriton* constitute the family Ambystomidae. Ambystoma comprises eleven species, distributed from Alaska to Mexico. *Ambystoma tigrinum*, the tiger salamander, is the most common and widespread salamander in North America. Ambystomidae in general are terrestrial animals; during the mating season, in the spring, they return to the water. Like all the urodele families to be mentioned below, they have evolved internal fertilization. The male deposits on the ground a gelatinous spermatophore with a mass of sperm at its tip. The female takes up the sperm into her cloaca, where the eggs are fertilized shortly before they are laid. The larvae develop in the water. *Ambystoma opacum*, the marbled salamander, mates on land in the fall; there, too, the eggs are laid and watched over by the female until they are flooded by a heavy rain and the larvae hatch.

A purely aquatic member of the genus is the neotenic axolotl, *Ambystoma mexicanum*. Its natural habit is limited to the lake of Xochimilco, near Mexico City. As a laboratory animal, however, it has achieved worldwide distribution.

Salamandridae

Representatives of this family are to be found in Eurasia and North America. The best-known species belong to the European genus *Salamandra* and to the genus *Triturus*, which is distributed in both Europe and America.

Salamanders of the genus *Triturus* show the typical seasonal alternation of habitat. In the spring they move to the water, but for the rest of the year they lead a terrestrial life. Usually it is in small ponds that they mate and lay their eggs. During the mating season, males of the European *Triturus* species assume a nuptial dress of strikingly colored patterns as well as finlike structures and dorsal crests. A complicated courtship behavior induces the female to take up the spermatophore deposited by the male. The *Triturus* larvae develop in the water; after 2 to 3 months, as a rule, they metamorphose and emerge onto the land.

The *Salamandra* species are more independent of water. In the fire salamander, *S. salamandra*, mating occurs on land. The embryos develop in the female's oviducts; in the following year, she makes her way to a brook where she deposits 20 to 70 larvae, about 30 mm long. After metamorphosis, *S. salamandra* never reenters the water—even to give birth to the young. Rather, the females lie with only the posterior part of the body in the water. *Salamandra atra*, which lives in the Alps at altitudes above about 700 meters, gives birth to one or two already metamorphosed salamanders, and is thus quite independent of water for reproduction.

The families Amphiumidae and Plethodontidae are closely related to the Salamandridae. The former contains only one species, *Amphiuma means*, the Congo eel; this is a semilarval aquatic form. The Plethodontidae are lungless salamanders represented in America by numerous species. In fact, most of the American urodele species belong to this family.

Proteidae

This family, the systematic position of which is uncertain, consists of two species, the American mudpuppy (*Necturus*) and a blind cave dweller (*Proteus*) native to Europe. Both of these are purely aquatic and neotenic. Their larval character is especially apparent in the persistence of external gills throughout their lives. *Proteus* is restricted to a few subterranean bodies of water in the karst region of Yugoslavia; the several subspecies of *Necturus* are distributed in quite diverse habitats in the eastern United States. The mudpuppy lives in the clear water of lakes and rivers, as well as in muddy ponds, canals, and ditches.

VISUALLY GUIDED BEHAVIOR

Diurnal Activity and Phototaxis

Vision does not play as critical a role in the orientation of urodeles as it does with most anurans. For salamanders, the olfactory sense is always of great importance. The aquatic forms—larvae and adults in the case of newts—have an additional system of mechanoreceptors in the lateral line organ. This enables them to detect movements of the water caused by a prey animal or a predator. That urodeles can orient themselves without the assistance of their eyes is demonstrated by the blind cave forms found in the families Proteidae and Plethodontidae. In general, though, salamanders and newts have thoroughly functional eyes, so that a number of behavioral patterns can be visually controlled. Differences in habits, of course, make necessary certain adaptations of the structure and function of the eyes. For those urodeles with a life cycle involving a regular alternation between aquatic and terrestrial periods, it is important to be equipped for amphibious vision. Such an animal must be able to recognize its prey by sight, both in the water and on land.

Since the urodeles as terrestrial animals are defenseless and under continual threat of desiccation, it is to their advantage to be active at times of dusk and darkness, when they are not exposed to sunlight and are less obvious to their enemies. Among urodeles, then, an increased tendency to nocturnal activity can be viewed as an adaptation to terrestrial life. The European Salamandridae provide a good example of this tendency. The retinas contain a variable percentage of rods. In *Triturus vulgaris*, 13% of the receptors are rods, whereas the corresponding figure in *T. alpestris* is 21%, in *T. cristatus* 40%, and in *Salamandra salamandra* 56% (Möller, 1951). Measurements of locomotor activity (Himstedt, 1971) have shown that the degree of nocturnal activity varies among these four species; in fact, it increases in the order *Triturus vulgaris*, *T. alpestris*, *T. cristatus*, and *S. salamandra*. The eye of *S. sala-*

mandra, an animal which after metamorphosis leads a purely terrestrial life, is much better suited for twilight vision than, for example, the eye of *Triturus vulgaris.* Cones predominate in the retina of the latter.

Urodeles with predominantly cone retinas can evidently be active, during the terrestrial portion of their lives, only at the times of day when there is not enough sunshine to dry them out—but when it is not so dark that they cannot see. They are thus limited to brief periods at dawn and in the evening. In spring, on the other hand, while they are in the water, they can be active by both day and night. The bright sunlight presents no threat; on the contrary, they make good use of it for visual orientation with their predominantly cone eyes. At night, these aquatic animals can employ both their sense of smell and the sense organs of the lateral-line system. The level of activity of *T. vulgaris* is about ten times greater in the spring, when it lives in water, than on land in the summer (Himstedt, 1971). Fire salamanders were found to maintain a relatively low level of activity; they moved about less frequently than the aquatic forms. *Salamandra* was more active at night than during the day. During the hours of darkness, the illumination was less than 0.01 lux. One may suppose that the salamanders relied on visual orientation in this very dim light.

In conducting experiments on phototaxis in urodeles, one must take into account these differences in times of activity. An organism preferring a certain light intensity can show either positive or negative phototactic behavior, depending on the intensity of the imposed light stimulus (Kühn, 1929). The reaction of amphibia to stationary visual stimuli is, in general, a telotactic orientation to a particular location. When a crepuscular salamander is placed in bright surroundings, it will exhibit negative phototaxis and move toward a dark stimulus. This effect has been shown, for example, by Czeloth (1931) for *Triturus* and by Himstedt (1967) for *Salamandra* and *Triturus.* Ray (1970), in experimental training of *Ambystoma,* found that strong light could be used for negative reinforcement. Schneider (1968), on the other hand, found that *Ambystoma* larvae did not show negative phototactic behavior. Measurements of activity (Himstedt, 1971) showed that urodele larvae have a much greater tendency to be active during the day than do the adult animals. Accordingly, in dark surroundings they oriented toward the light. Muntz (1963) found different phototactic reactions in *Salamandra* and *Triturus.* Unfortunately, he gives no indication whether he was working with water or land animals. His conclusion that the retina of *Salamandra* contains no green rods is questionable. For experiments on the sensory physiology of urodeles, there are more suitable methods than the measurement of the quite variable phototactic reaction.

SPATIAL ORIENTATION

Urodeles, like other amphibians, have home ranges in which they ordinarily remain. Within this range, there is a sheltered place to which they return from their excursions each day. This homing behavior requires that the animals have a suitable orientation mechanism; it is possible that they orient by visual landmarks. According to Joly's (1963, 1968) observations, one can assume that *Salamandra salamandra* orients itself within its territory by trees, stones, and the like, which stand out as dark signs against the background. In other urodeles, the sense of smell appears to play a central role. Czeloth (1931) showed that *Triturus* can find its shelter by means of olfactory stimuli, and Madison (1969) demonstrated olfactory orientation in *Plethodon jordani*.

It is more difficult to comment on the mechanism of long-distance orientation, whereby the animals find the breeding pond, return to their summer quarters, or locate places to hibernate. In training experiments, newts are able to keep a constant angle to a light source (Landreth and Ferguson, 1967). The animals thus could use a sun compass. Urodeles also are able to orient by the plane (*e*-vector) of linearly polarized light (Adler and Taylor, 1973). Eyeless salamanders reacted as well as sighted animals; this ability therefore does not depend on vision. However, it must be considered that migrations of amphibia tend to occur in the twilight and darkness, when the weather is humid—usually rainy— and the sky is overcast. Under these meteorological conditions, the animals cannot make use of a compass based upon optical clues in the sky (Shoop, 1965). In *Taricha rivularis*, Grant and associates (1968) demonstrated olfactory orientation. Endler (1970) assumes that *Taricha torosa* uses kinesthetic orientation to maintain the direction of migration. It is probable that migrating urodeles find their way with the aid of several mechanisms, operating together. In general, it can be said that the visual system probably plays only a very subordinate role in the long-distance orientation of urodeles.

Prey-Catching Behavior

Behavior with Respect to Natural Prey

Urodeles are exclusively carnivorous animals. In contrast to the anurans, which in the tadpole stage also eat plants, salamanders and newts eat animal food both before and after metamorphosis. No urodele species is specialized for a specific food. For example, newts of the genus *Triturus* eat worms, snails, small crustaceans, and a great variety of insect larvae (Kühlhorn, 1959). Fire salamanders feed on worms, snails, wood lice, centipedes, spiders, and insects (Szabó, 1962). Practically any animal is accepted as prey if it is not too large, too small, or too fast. In all the larger urodele species, even cannibalism can occur (Noble, 1931). Stimuli releasing a prey-capture reaction can be of optical, chemical, or mechanical nature—that is, detected by eye, olfactory organ, or lateral-line organ. Matthes (1924) showed that *Triturus* could find its prey using only one sense, when the other two had been put out of operation. By using the olfactory sense in hunting, urodeles are able to detect motionless prey. It can readily be observed that newts in an aquarium eat their own eggs; they can find these only by smell, since they are stuck to the leaves of water plants and of course do not move.

In the case of European salamandrids, the behavior of which has been studied extensively, we know that vision plays the most important role in prey-capture, in water as well as on land (Matthes, 1924; Himstedt, 1967). In all species and developmental stages of the Central European *Salamandra* and *Triturus* species, the entire prey-capture behavior can be released with dummies incorporating only visual stimuli. The essential findings concerning the significance of visual stimuli in the release of prey-capture behavior are the following (Himstedt, 1967):

1. *Orienting movement*—As in other amphibians (see Chapter 5), the first reaction to a prey object is a turning movement, which permits the newt or salamander to fixate the object binocularly. In contrast to most anurans, urodeles perform the initial orientation with their heads alone.

2. *Approaching*—Since urodeles cannot jump like frogs, they must approach the prey by walking toward the stimulus. The second action, then, is the approach. As in toads, this is usually a cautious creeping forward until the prey is within range of the tongue.

3. *Olfactory test*—When the prey is within reach, an olfactory test is often made. This reaction can be recognized by a characteristic posture of the body. The animal extends its forelegs so that the front part of the body is raised, and then points its head down to a steep angle until the tip of the snout is directly above the prey. In this position, it makes more pronounced movements of the throat, sucking the odor substances into the olfactory organ. This testing procedure can be observed much more frequently in *Triturus* than in *Salamandra*, and appears more often during the aquatic period than when the animal is living on land.

4. *Snapping*—The reaction in which the prey is finally seized is called snapping. In the water, this is primarily a brief sucking of water into the mouth, which sweeps the prey in as well. On land, the tongue is stuck out to catch small objects, while larger ones are grasped in the jaws.

5. *Swallowing*—Swallowing is the final action in the prey-capture behavior sequence.

Behavioral Experiments

In experiments with dummies, the frequency of turning movements, approaching, and snapping reactions have been recorded (Himstedt, 1967, and unpublished results). The experimental animals were kept in a glass tank filled with water or lined with damp blotting paper. The front of the tank was made of frosted glass, and onto this were projected spots of light with variable shape, size, and brightness. The projector could be moved horizontally by a motor, in a range of chosen velocities. At the beginning of the experiment, the animal was coaxed to a position where the distance between the eye and the light spot was 3 cm.

Significance of Visual "Prey" Stimuli in the Water and on Land

Positive reaction to a spot of light can be elicited only if the spot is moved. However, urodeles show prey-capture movements in response even to stationary light spots if they are flashed on and off rhythmically. The optimal frequency of alternation is 2–10 Hz (Himstedt, 1969). In the following discussion, only reactions to moving stimuli are described.

Figure 1 shows the reaction of adult *Triturus vulgaris*, during its aquatic life in the spring and during its terrestrial period in the fall, to the same visual stimulus representing prey. This was a circular spot of light, with luminance five times that of the background. At the initial position of the animals, the spot subtended 4° in visual angle and its angular velocity was 10 deg sec^{-1}. Distinct differences in the reactions are apparent in Fig. 1. The first response—the turning reaction—appears with about the same frequency in the two groups. But the subsequent reactions are much more rarely recorded in the aquatic than in the terrestrial animals. Terrestrial newts snap at the moving light spot in 60% of the experiments, aquatic newts in only about 2%. This result demonstrates the greater significance of visual prey stimuli for terrestrial urodeles. In *S. salamandra*, the full prey-capture behavior was released by these light spots as frequently as in the terrestrial newts.

Size of the Stimulus

It is important for a carnivorous animal to be able to judge the size of its prey. Urodeles have in their visual system a stimulus-filtering mechanism which passes certain optimal image sizes more readily than

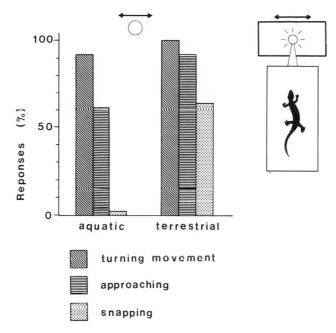

Fig. 1. Prey-capture reaction of newts (*Triturus vulgaris*) during aquatic and terrestrial life. Stimulus: a spot of light 5 mm in diameter, five times brighter than the background, moving at a velocity of 10 deg sec^{-1}.

either smaller or larger ones. Figure 2 shows the dependence of the reaction upon the size of circular prey dummies for *S. salamandra*, in terms of the number of turning movements elicited per minute. The optimal object size, for *Salamandra*, lies between 4° and 10°. Values for the other salamandrids are of the same order of magnitude.

In experiments of this sort, one cannot tell how much the measured preferences depend upon the animal's previous experience. For this reason, a further experiment was done to determine whether we were dealing with an innate releasing mechanism or whether learning processes are responsible for the selection of certain object sizes. The larvae of *S. Salamandra* are well suited for such experiments. At birth, they are already relatively well developed, with four limbs and mature sense organs. Normally, they soon begin to take food actively.

Group A of the experimental animals was kept after birth in tap water without food. Group B received *Cyclops* and *Daphnia* for 14 days after birth. Animals from each group were then offered a choice between two dummies that differed only in size. The "normal-sized" dummy was a white spot of 2 mm diameter, while the diameter of the "oversized"

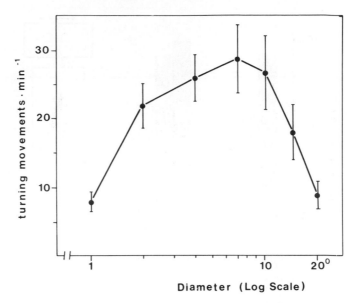

Fig. 2. Dependence of the prey-capture reactions upon the size of the stimulus in *Salamandra salamandra*. Mean and standard deviation for 10 experiments are given in each case.

dummy was 6 mm. A 2-mm object is about the size of a large *Daphnia;* a prey animal measuring 6 mm would be decidedly too large for a newborn salamander larva to swallow. Of the animals without experience, 65% chose the 2-mm dummy, which indicates an innate preference for the proper prey. But the rejection of the oversized stimulus is much more pronounced in larvae with prey experience; 89% of these chose the smaller dummy.

Thus, there appears to be an innate releasing mechanism for prey capture in Salamandra, which uses the parameter "size of prey" as a criterion. Experience with prey capture modifies this mechanism. Similar learning processes are known to occur in newly metamorphosed frogs and toads (Schneider, 1954a). If one uses a dummy with diameter larger than the width of the head of the experimental animal, the prey-capture reactions are not directed at the center of the dummy, but rather at its edge. The releasing stimulus is apparently the moving contour.

Contrast between Stimulus and Background

The dependence of the turning movement upon the contrast of the dummy is shown in Fig. 3. For *Salamandra,* the contrast between dummy and background must be least 0.01 if it is to have a releasing effect.

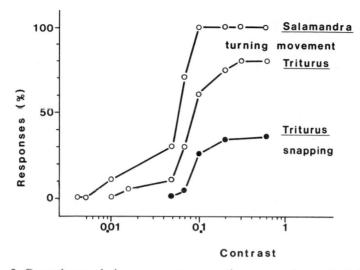

Fig. 3. Dependence of the prey-capture reactions upon the contrast between stimulus and background. At each level of contrast, 25 experiments were done.

(Contrast here is defined as $(I_s - I_b)/(I_s + I_b)$, where I_s = stimulus luminance and I_b = background luminance.) For *Triturus vulgaris*, the contrast must be greater; no reactions are observed until it is increased to 0.015. Further increase in the contrast increases the frequency of positive reactions. Salamanders, in general, react more frequently than newts. At a contrast of 0.1–0.15 a plateau is reached, and further increase of contrast causes no additional increase in number of reactions.

It is noteworthy that when the contrast between stimulus and background is low, only the turning movement can be released, and not the subsequent stages of the prey capture behavior. The snapping reaction appears only when the contrast is appreciable. The data for *Triturus vulgaris* are included in Fig. 3. With a contrast setting of 0.05, there are definite turning movements, but the animal does not snap. The latter reaction appears only at contrasts greater than 0.08. Even when the contrast is further increased, however, the number of snapping reactions remains lower than that of turning movements. For *Salamandra*, with a contrast threshold for the turning movement of 0.01, the minimal contrast releasing the snapping reaction was 0.04.

With "optimal" dummies, the ratio of turning movements to snapping was about 2:1 in the case of terrestrial urodeles. Aquatic animals snapped much more rarely (Fig. 1). The mechanism for release of the snapping reaction, then, always has a higher threshold than the system that releases the first orienting movement.

Velocity of the Stimulus

When the velocity of the dummy is changed (size and contrast being held constant), the frequency of occurrence of the prey-capture reactions is altered. Figure 4 shows the dependence of such responses upon stimulus velocity, for newts and salamanders. Most reactions appeared at angular velocities in the range 5–20 deg sec[-1]. Aquatic animals reacted to higher velocities than terrestrial animals. That the frequency of the responses would be lower, in general, for aquatic animals was to be expected from the data of Fig. 1. The maximal effective stimulus velocity, on the other hand, is remarkable. Turning movements of *Triturus vulgaris* could be released even with stimuli moving at 110 deg sec[-1]—quite a high velocity for urodeles, which are generally considered sluggish animals.

In evaluating these data, one must take into account that the angular velocity values were measured for a distance of 3 cm between animal and dummy. When the animal approaches the prey, the angular velocity of the object of course increases. Accordingly, the object angular velocities releasing snapping reactions are greater. Dummy velocities during snapping have thus not yet been determined precisely. The difficulty lay in the fact that the dummy did not move in a circular path with the eye at its center. Despite these inherent errors, which are greatest at the shorter distances applying in the later stages of the sequence, one can say that for *Salamandra* the optimal velocities for the snapping reaction are about

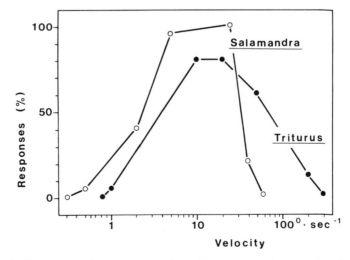

Fig. 4. Frequency of occurrence of turning movements as a function of the velocity of the stimulus.

40–60 deg sec⁻¹, and are thus in the range that represents the maximum velocity eliciting turning movements. The highest object velocities that still release snapping in *Salamandra* lie above 100 deg sec⁻¹. For the velocity parameter, then, it also appears to be true that the first prey-capture reactions have lower thresholds than those that follow.

Visual Acuity in Prey Capture

To test the visual acuity of the animals, a raster of equidistant black and white stripes was presented, moving behind a rectangular window. By using progressively finer patterns of stripes at a constant animal-to-stimulus distance, one can determine the minimal angular separation that produces a turning response. With the pattern 3 cm from the eye, the minimal separation of stripes was 0.1–0.15° for both *Salamandra* and *Triturus*.

A striking result of these experiments was that the newts displayed about the same visual acuity in water and in the air. In water, the refraction between external medium and cornea is nearly eliminated. A pronounced ability to accommodate is therefore required, so that the eye can perform equally in the two media. The urodele eye, however, has only the small ventral m. protractor lentis (Walls, 1942), so that very little accommodation would seem possible.

For this reason, the visual acuity was measured at greater pattern distances, by using a rotating drum with equidistant black and white stripes and the optomotor response. *Triturus vulgaris,* in the aquatic stage, at a pattern distance of 14 cm was found to resolve 0.13° (which represents the width of a single stripe). Land animals of the same species, in contrast, reacted with nystagmus only to coarser rasters. At a distance of 9 cm, the latter resolved a minimum of 0.2°. These results indicate that the newt eye cannot compensate for change of medium by strong accommodation. In the water, the visual acuity even at greater distances is about the same as at 3 cm. In this medium, the eye is emmetropic. In the air, on the other hand, the visual acuity decreases at increased distances. Here the eye appears to be nearsighted. Nevertheless, the myopia of the terrestrial newt may not amount to a serious disadvantage, if the animals restrict themselves to prey that is "within reach."

Newt eyes, because of their almost spherical lenses, tend to have "aquatic optics"—in contrast, for example, to those of the terrestrial *Salamandra,* in which the lenses are flatter. Möller (1951) gives the ratio of lens diameter to lens thickness in *Triturus* 1.06:1, whereas in *Salamandra* it is 1.25:1. The visual acuity of *Salamandra* is unchanged even at considerable distances.

Color Discrimination

For many urodeles it is probably of little importance whether they can distinguish colors. A few species, however, have conspicuous body coloration. The European *Triturus* species in spring assume a "nuptial dress" with markings in a great variety of colors. These make it quite easy to distinguish the different species, as well as the sexes. For example, the belly is either yellow, orange, or red, and may be uniform in color or decorated with dark spots. The back is yellow-brown, blue, or olive-green. On the tail and dorsal crest of the male, there is an additional array of characteristic blue, red, and yellow spots. For these animals, color vision would help in the recognition of a partner.

Experiments to test the ability of urodeles to differentiate color, in which the animals are trained with colored papers (Diebschlag, 1935; Honjo, 1939; Kasperczyk, 1971) have to some extent been successful. But some attempts at training have failed because the experimental animals presented with a choice between a color and gray often displayed a spontaneous preference for the darker of the two stimuli. Birukow (1950) obtained different reactions to different colors in optomotor experiments with drums patterned in colored and gray stripes. Some salamandrids reacted to all colors presented, while others appeared to be color-blind for yellow and yellow-green, or for yellow and red.

Himstedt (1972) employed a novel method to test the ability of urodeles to distinguish wavelength. He used monochromatic "prey" dummies. Of the visually controlled forms of behavior, the prey-capture reactions are particularly consistently released and provide an unambiguous criterion for such experiments. To produce colored dummies, the principle of the shadow photometer was used (Fig. 5). Two lamps (L_1, L_2) illuminate a vertical metal rod, the shadow of which falls on a white translucent paper. This projection surface was mounted on the outside of the glass wall of the animal's container. The distance between rod and projection surface was selected so that the shadows cast by the two lamps were directly adjacent. The shadow of L_1 thus received light only from L_2, and vice versa. When a color filter was placed before one of the lamps and a neutral density filter before the other, adjacent colored and gray surfaces were produced. The brightness of the gray surface could be altered continuously by using different neutral density filters and by changing the distance between lamp and projection surface. To produce the different colors five interference filters (DIL Schott, Mainz) were used: blue (457 nm), green (518 nm), yellow-green (555 nm), yellow (584 nm), and red (635 nm).

Between the rod and the projection surface was an opaque shield with

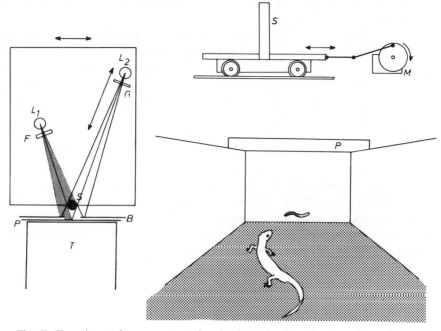

Fig. 5. Experimental arrangement for the investigation of color vision. *B,* shield with worm-shaped opening; *F,* interference filter; *G,* neutral density filter; *L₁* and *L₂,* lamps; *M,* electric motor; *P,* projection screen; *S,* metal rod; *T,* tank containing the animal. (From Himstedt, 1972).

a "worm-shaped" opening cut in the center. The whole optical apparatus, with lamps, filters, and rod, was mounted on a plate that could be moved sideways on steel wheels and rails. This movement was produced by an electric motor. Shield and projection surface were fixed in position. With this arrangement, the animal in its tank viewed a wormlike dummy lying horizontally, which was brighter than its surroundings and within which a colored area was next to a gray area. The boundary between the two areas was oscillated back and forth, so that the colored fraction of the "worm" varied in size.

If the animals could distinguish colored from gray lights, they would always be able to detect the movement of the edge, regardless of which neutral density filter was used, and would react with prey-capture behavior. If the animals have no color vision, there must be a level of brightness at which the gray and the colored surface appear equally bright; then the movement could no longer be detected and would not release a reaction. If identical neutral-density filters are placed before each lamp and the same distance is selected for each, the animals give no reaction. Only if there is a certain degree of contrast, as shown in Fig. 3, do turning movements appear.

Two examples of experiments comparing gray with different colors are shown in Fig. 6. The brightness of the gray surface which was contrasted with a certain wavelength was first varied in steps of 0.1 log unit. At each such step, the frequency of prey-capture reactions was recorded. Eventually, a range of brightness of the gray surface was found such that the reactions became fewer. Within this range, the gray was then changed in smaller steps. The smallest intensity changes available were smaller than the sensitivity of differences in contrast (Fig. 3). Figure 6 shows that there is no intensity at which the reaction disappears altogether.

This method was used to test terrestrial forms of *S. salamandra*, *Triturus vulgaris*, *T. alpestris*, and *T. cristatus* with respect to their ability to distinguish wavelengths. For none of the five colors presented could a step of gray be found that eliminated the reactions. Thus, these urodeles are capable of distinguishing colors from gray.

During the experiments, it became apparent that the animals reacted more frequently to red and blue dummies than to green. The relative stimulus values of the colored dummies were therefore determined more precisely. For each species, that combination of color and gray which had

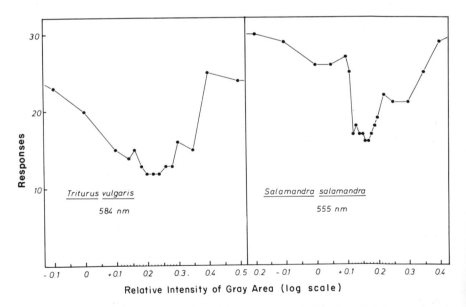

Fig. 6. Two examples of a color vision experiment. Abscissa, brightness of the gray surface in relative logarithmic units; ordinate, number of prey-capture reactions in each of 10 experiments. (From Himstedt, 1972.)

released the fewest reactions in the earlier experiments was presented again to each of 10 animals, and the number of turning movements in 1 min was recorded. In Fig. 7 clear differences can be seen. The green dummy (wavelength 518 nm) releases significantly fewer turning movements in all species than do the blue or yellow and red dummies. That the animals prefer yellow and red dummies perhaps reflects an actual preference for prey of those colors. The animals were fed in the laboratory with red *Tubifex* and yellow mealworms. But blue prey animals are very rare, even in nature, so that the relatively high stimulus value of the blue dummy cannot be explained by an innate or acquired preference for certain prey. Presumably, retinal mechanisms are responsible for this effect.

In these experiments, no differences were found between *Salamandra* and *Triturus*, like those described by Muntz (1963) for phototactic reactions to blue light stimuli. The only observed difference between the two genera was that *Salamandra* is somewhat slower moving and, thus, when reactions per unit time are recorded, gives absolute values lower

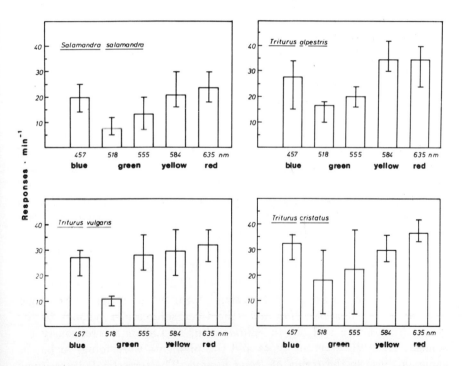

Fig. 7. Releasing efficacy of various colors. The numbers indicate the wavelengths of the stimuli. Mean and scatter of the number of turning movements per minute are given for each of 10 experiments. (From Himstedt, 1972.)

than those for *Triturus*. The suggestion that the retina of *Salamandra* contains no blue receptors is certainly not justified, but, in this nocturnal eye, with its large proportion of red rods, the number of color receptors is probably very low. Under a microscope, about one-tenth of rods on a live retina of *Salamandra* appears to be green rods. However, it is not certain, whether these green rods contain a blue-sensitive pigment.

The question whether the newt can recognize the coloration in the nuptial dress of its partner can be answered in the affirmative. These animals seem to have evolved a system of color recognition that responds particularly well to just those colors—blue and red—which predominate in their body coloration.

ANATOMY AND PHYSIOLOGY OF THE VISUAL SYSTEM

Visual Pigments

Amphibia possess visual pigments with a prosthetic group, retinal, derived either from vitamin A_1 (retinol) or from vitamin A_2 (3-dehydro-retinol). Vitamin A_2 pigments (porphyropsins) are typical of freshwater fish, vitamin A_1 pigments (rhodopsins) occur among terrestrial verte-brates. Wald (1947, 1952) was the first to investigate the retinas of aquatic and terrestrial urodeles. In *Necturus maculosus* and in adult aquatic animals of the species *Diemictylus* (= *Triturus*) *viridescens*, he found vitamin A_2. In metamorphosed terrestrial juveniles of *Triturus virides-cens*, however, he found vitamin A_1. Further investigations of urodeles have, in general, confirmed the rule that aquatic forms have A_2-based porphyropsins as rod pigments, whereas terrestrial forms have A_1-based rhodopsins. Thus, Crescitelli (1958a) found in *Necturus*, $P522_2$ (a pig-ment with maximal absorption at 522 nm, consisting of a protein and retinal$_2$), while in terrestrial *Taricha torosa*, $P502_1$ was present. Brown and co-workers (1963) state that the pigment of the *Necturus* rods is a porphyropsin with maximal absorption at 525 nm.

Liebman (1972) used microspectrophotometry to measure, in living retinas, the absorption not only of rods, but also of other types of recep-tors. He found in *Necturus* a rod pigment, $P527_2$, and only a single cone pigment, $P575_2$. To sample a terrestrial form, he investigated the tiger salamander *Ambystoma tigrinum* (the tiger salamander belongs to the genus *Ambystoma* and not to *Salamandra*, as Liebman erroneously as-sumes). Here the receptor types and the pigments were found to be the same as those in the retina of *Rana pipiens*. The terrestrial *Ambystoma tigrinum* thus has green rods with $P432_1$, red rods with $P502_1$, single cones with $P575_1$, and double cones; the latter have $P575_1$ in the principle member and $P502_1$ in the accessory member.

Himstedt (1973a,b) infers from ERG measurements that in *Triturus* there is evidently a regular alteration of the visual pigments, both during metamorphosis and in an annual rhythm among adult animals. The spectral sensitivities of various species and developmental stages were determined in terms of threshold as measured by the ERG. In Fig. 8 are shown the results from dark-adapted eyes of the alpine newt (*Triturus alpestris*).

The data for larval eyes are an excellent fit to the absorption curve of porphyropsin, $P523_2$ (according to Bridges, 1967). During the metamorphosis the maximum sensitivity is shifted to shorter wavelengths. The data at this stage can be matched to the absorption curve of frog rhodopsin, $P502_1$ (according to Dartnall, 1953). A corresponding conversion of $retinal_2$ to $retinal_1$ in the course of metamorphosis has been described for several species of anurans (for a summary, see, e.g., Crescitelli, 1972). *Triturus*, however, exhibits more than this single change during its ontogeny. When the adult newts are living in the water during the mating season in the spring, they resume the spectral sensitivity of the larvae. The squares in Fig. 8b match the porphyropsin curve. If one studies animals of the same species in summer or fall, when they have left the water and returned to terrestrial life, their spectral sensitivity corresponds to rhodopsin $P502_1$.

In the case of *Triturus*, one can discern an ecological adaptation in the change of spectral sensitivity, occurring simultaneously with a change of habitat. It has been pointed out several times that pools, ponds, and lakes in which amphibians live are characterized by yellowish water (Reuter, 1969; Bridges, 1972; Himstedt, 1973a). This yellow coloration is brought about by organic substances dissolved in the water. Animals living in these waters can make better use of the available light if their receptors are more sensitive to long wavelength light, by virtue of $retinal_2$ pigments.

In *S. salamandra*, however, there is no shift of spectral sensitivity (Himstedt, 1973a). Both before and after metamorphosis, the rods of this species evidently contain rhodopsin $P502_1$. Nor is there any sign in adult animals, which never return to the water, of a seasonal change in the visual pigments.

Morphology of the Visual System

The Eye

The relative size of the eye of most urodeles is smaller than that in the anurans. Predominantly terrestrial urodeles have relatively larger eyes than the aquatic forms. Walls (1942) writes about the members of

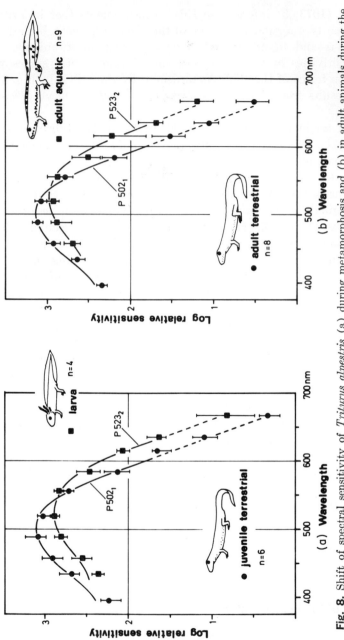

Fig. 8. Shift of spectral sensitivity of *Triturus alpestris* (a) during metamorphosis and (b) in adult animals during the course of the year. P5021, absorption curve of rhodopsin; P523₂, absorption curve of porphyropsin. (From Himstedt, 1973b.)

the families Cryptobranchidae, Amphiumidae, Proteidae, and Sirenidae, which remain in a larval or partly metamorphosed state and which are permanently aquatic, so that their eyes are in a state of "degeneracy or on the ragged edge of it." The eyes are especially small in the cave dwellers *Typhlotriton* and *Typhlomolge* and in the *Sirenidae* and in the *Proteidae* (e.g., *Necturus* and *Proteus*) which live in muddy water.

As the overall size of the eye is reduced during phylogenesis, the size of the individual retinal cells frequently increases. Thus, *Necturus maculosus* has tiny eyes, but large retinal cells. In the retina of this animal, intracellular recordings are therefore much more easily obtained than in other vertebrate eyes. Thus, the retina of Necturus was chosen as an important model for the study of the signal processing within the retinal neuronal network. In *Triturus vulgaris*, *Triturus alpestris*, *Triturus cristatus*, and *Salamandra maculosa*, the size of the eye is negatively correlated relative to the body size (Möller, 1951).

The urodele eye is moved by the six eye muscles common to most vertebrates and a musculus retractor bulbi, which move the eye during swallowing and also during a withdrawal reflex, when the cornea or the head of the animal is touched. Little is known about the other eye movements of urodeles.

As in fish, the *cornea* of the aquatic urodeles contributes less to the overall optical power than does the cornea in the eyes of terrestrial amphibia. In the semiaquatic *Triturus* species, the central part of the cornea is rather flat in relation to the curvature of the sclera. The change in the refractive power of the eye with the change from vision in air to vision in water therefore is less than in animals having a cornea with a stronger curvature.

The *lens* of the eye of many urodeles is relatively thick and in some species (*Triturus*) is nearly spherical. The distance between the posterior surface of the lens and the retina is short. The smaller the eyes, the greater is the relative size of the lens and the thickness of the retina in relation to the diameter of the eye (Möller, 1951). The diameter of the lens (measured along the optimal axis) is between 42% (*Triturus vulgaris*) and 60% (*Salamandra atra* and *Salamandra maculosa*) of the overall diameter of the eye. In older histological studies concerning the vitreous body, a rather regularly organized meshwork of fibrillas was described (e.g., *Salamandra*, Szent-Györgyi, 1914).

Accommodation takes place by a change in the position of the lens within the eye. Accommodation for near objects is accomplished by the contraction of the m. protractor lentis, which moves the lens toward the cornea (Beer, 1899; Hess, 1913). Beer reported that during accommodative movements the lens is also moved somewhat toward the nasal and superior part of the retina and is slightly tilted (*Salamandra atra, Salamandra maculosa,* and *Triturus torosus*). The latter type of movement of the lens might be caused by a combined effect of the m. protractor lentis and the m. tensor chorioideae. The overall effect of the accommodative mechanisms is rather small and less than 5 diopters.

The *pupil* of the urodele eye frequently is oval-shaped with a horizontal longer axis and a small ventral notch. The m. dilatator pupillae, as a rule, is stronger than the m. sphincter pupillae (Franz, 1934). The upper part of the iris in most species is significantly broader than the lower part. During accommodation, the center of the pupil is shifted downward.

After considering the structure of the dioptric apparatus of the urodele eye, it seems to be questionable whether the classical laws of image formation, which are valid for the mammalian eye (Westheimer, 1972), can be easily applied, especially for the small urodele eyes with nearly spherical lenses. Perhaps wave-guide and spatial optical mechanisms, caused by the dense set of paraboloids and ellipsoids ("lenses") seen in the inner segments of the photoreceptors might play a role in the transmission of the light from the posterior surface of the lens to the outer segments of the photoreceptors. Such a mechanism would compensate for the strong spherical aberration of the lens. A considerable loss of light caused by reflection within this spatial optical filter system would accompany such an improvement of the optical image qualities. Brown and co-workers (1963) also concluded from their observations on the transillumination of the whole retina that the outer segment and to a certain degree the whole visual cell could act as a light pipe.

The refractive power of some urodele eyes was measured by Beer (1899). The application of the technique of retinoscopy (Skiascopy) as a tool to measure the refractive power, however, is rather limited for small eyes. The reflecting plane (membrana limitans interna) is not the same as the plane of the photoreceptors' outer segments (Hirschberg, 1882). The smaller the relationship between focal length of the eye and the distance between the reflecting plane and the photoreceptors, the larger the error introduced by this factor. Glickstein and Millodot (1970) have confirmed this recently. If this correction for optical measurements of the refraction is taken into consideration, one can conclude that the animals are either emmetropic or somewhat myopic in their respective main habitats. The change from vision in air to vision in water decreases the refractive power of the eyes, i.e., a terrestrial animal becomes more hyperopic when it moves from land into water, while an aquatic urodele becomes myopic when it changes from vision in water to vision in air.

An additional factor relating to the accommodative range of the small eyes of many urodeles also has to be considered. As in the eye of frogs, in many urodeles the length of the outer segments of the photoreceptors ($25-60\mu$m) is rather large in relation to the focal length of the eye. Therefore (as in the retina of small fish and anurans), without any changes in accommodation, the image of an object remains in focus (at different levels of the outer segments) when the object changes its distance from the eye within a considerable range. This "accommodative neutral range" (5–10 diopters) depends on the relation between the focal length of the optic apparatus and the length of the outer segments. In addition, the gross anatomy of the retina reveals that the inner surface of the retina is not approximately spherical in all urodeles. For example, the inner surface of the retina of *Triturus taeniatus* contains three plicae that divide the retina into a dorsal, central, and anterior part (Ströer, 1940). These different areas of the retina that are at different distances from the cornea may also differ functionally. For example, underwater, the image falling on the more distant parts might be used for visually guided behavior, while the parts of the retina nearer to the lens would receive the best optical image when the refractive power of the eye increases for vision in air.

The Retina

The retina of the urodeles, as in all vertebrates, is composed of 5 neuronal elements: photoreceptors, horizontal cells, bipolar cells, amacrine cells, and ganglion cells, which are embedded in the matrix of glial cells (Müller cells). The neuronal elements are separated from the chorioidal vascular system by the layer of pigment cells. The relative differentiation of the retina of various species can be seen in the overall number and the differentiation of the photoreceptors, the spatial density of the outer segments, the number of cells in the inner nuclear layer, and the number of ganglion cells (Fig. 9). Little is known about the dendritic branching and the synaptic contacts of retinal cells of urodeles except for *Necturus*. We know of no systematic Golgi studies of the urodele retina as have been provided for fish, frogs, and higher vertebrates in the brilliant studies of Ramón y Cajal (1894).

Figure 9 gives examples of retinae of urodeles: That of *Necturus* is in a state of mild phylogenetic degeneration, while that of *Triturus cristatus* is an example of a highly differentiated retina. The state of the retina of *Salamandra salamandra* falls between the retinae of the two other species. Besides rods, cones, and double cones, the retina of many urodeles also contains green rods, which are specific for amphibia. Green rods, for example, were described for the retina of *Salamandra salamandra*, *Triturus vulgaris*, *Triturus alpestris*, and *Triturus cristatus*, while

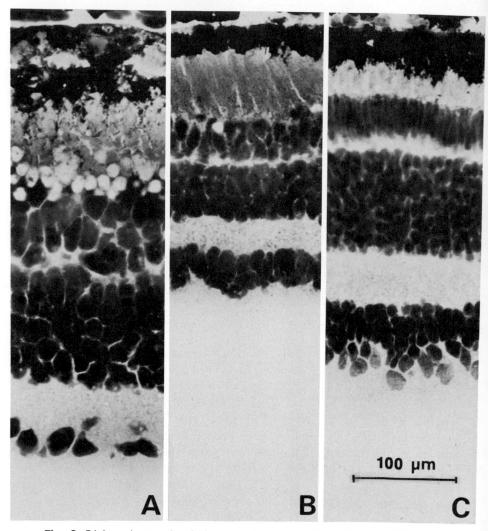

Fig. 9. Light micrograph of the central parts of the retina of (A) *Necturus maculosus*; (B) *Salamandra salamandra*; (C) *Triturus cristatus*. (Courtesy of Professor D. von Keyserlingk, Berlin.)

they were not found in *Necturus maculosus*. The numerical relationship between rods, cones, and double cones is correlated to the relative degree of diurnal and nocturnal behavioral activity (Schultze, 1867a; Landolt, 1871; Hoffmann, 1876; Krause, 1892; Howard, 1908). Quantitative data concerning older histological findings in the retina of urodeles are found in the work of Krause (1892).

Rods. Max Schultze (1867a) described a longitudinal ribbing of the rods' outer segments of *Triturus cristatus* and *Triturus taeniatus,* which was later confirmed for *Necturus maculosus* by Howard (1908). Schultze also saw the discs in the outer segments, which appeared when acetic acid was added to the preparation. He estimated the thickness of the discs to be about 0.3μm. Both aspects of the structure of rod outer segments can be seen in high power electronmicrographs (Brown *et al.,* 1963; Cohen, 1972). The ellipsoid "lens" of the inner segment of rods is, as in the anuran eye, well developed and of convex-concave or plane-concave shape. The ellipsoid forms the outer part of the inner segment. A second structure in the inner segment of the rods which might exert an optical effect is the "paraboloid," which is located proximal to the ellipsoid. The refractive index of both the ellipsoid and the paraboloid is higher than that of the surrounding plasma.

The diameter of the outer and the inner segment of the rods is rather large in many urodeles (*Triturus* and *Salamandra* about 11μm). With respect to the short focal length of the small eyes, a rather low spatial resolution is a necessary consequence of this size. The outer segment of the green rods is usually shorter and thicker than that of the red rods. The green rods are seen much less frequently than the red rods in all retinae investigated thus far. The anisotropia of the rod outer segments, as seen with polarized light, was well known to the nineteenth-century histologists. The polarization axis always corresponds to the main axis of the outer segments.

Cones. Both the diameter of the outer segments ($2–6\mu$m) as well as the length of the single cones and of the double cones are smaller than those of the rods in urodeles. The ellipsoid of single cone inner segments contains oil droplets in many species. Double cones are also present in many species. Frequently, the position of the principal cone's outer segment is at a different level in the retina than the accessory cone's outer segment. The inner segment of the cones contains contractile proteins. In *Triturus cristatus,* the length of the single cone inner segment in the dark-adapted retina (19μm) is considerably larger than in the light-adapted retina (10μm, van Genderen-Stort, 1887). Therefore, in the light-adapted retina, the cone outer segments are much more separated from the rod outer segments and the processes of the pigment cells than in the dark-adapted retina.

Retinal Neurons. Nothing is known about the size of the dendritic fields of bipolar cells and ganglion cells or the extent of the amacrine and horizontal cell processes in well-differentiated urodele retina. The recent studies of the *Necturus* retina by Dowling and Werblin indicate that the principles of the synaptic connections found for the neuronal elements of the anuran retina can also be applied *grosso modo* for the urodele retina. Dowling and Werblin (1969) measured them by the thickness of the different retinal layers in *Necturus* with light microscopy and, in addition, described the extension of dendritic branches of the retinal neurons with the Golgi method. They could easily distinguish rods and cones by their outer segments and found only a few double cones.

The outer nuclear layer of the *Necturus* retina has a thickness of about 1.5 rows of nuclei and contains, in addition to the receptor cell nuclei, some displaced horizontal cells and bipolar cells. The outer plexiform layer is of variable thickness ($2\text{--}10\mu\text{m}$) in different parts of the retina. The inner nuclear layer contains 2–3 layers of cells. The bipolar cells and the horizontal cells are located more distally, the amacrine cells in the more proximal parts of the inner nuclear layer. The processes of a horizontal cell cover a region of about $300\text{--}400\mu\text{m}$. The cell bodies of the bipolar cells are oval shaped and their dendrites branch $80\text{--}100\mu\text{m}$, laterally. Many bipolar cells have a Landolt club, which was discovered by Landolt (1871) in the *Triturus* retina. The Landolt club extends from the bipolar cell layer to the external limiting membrane. Its functional significance is unknown. The amacrine cells frequently have a single, thick process which descends into the inner plexiform layer, where the branches of this process spread laterally.

Electron Microscopic Studies of the *Necturus* Retina

Receptors

The ultrastructure of the *Necturus* photoreceptors was investigated by Brown and co-workers (1963) and by Dowling and Werblin (1969). Figure 10 (top and bottom) are schematic representations of the findings of Brown *et al.* The outer segments of rods and cones differ significantly not only in shape and size, but also in the fine structure of the disc system. The rod discs are about 120 Å thick, the repeating unit (disc plus space) is about 270 Å. The discs contain in their double layer membrane, and probably in a regular array, the photopigment (porphyropsin, $\lambda_{\max} = 525$ nm). The rod discs are separated from the outer plasma membrane. Therefore, three spaces exist: extracellular, intracellular, and intradiscal. The vertical septal divisions of the outer segments are responsible for the vertical striation seen in the light microscope at the outer segment surface. The clefts may allow better diffusion between the extracellular space and the outer segments.

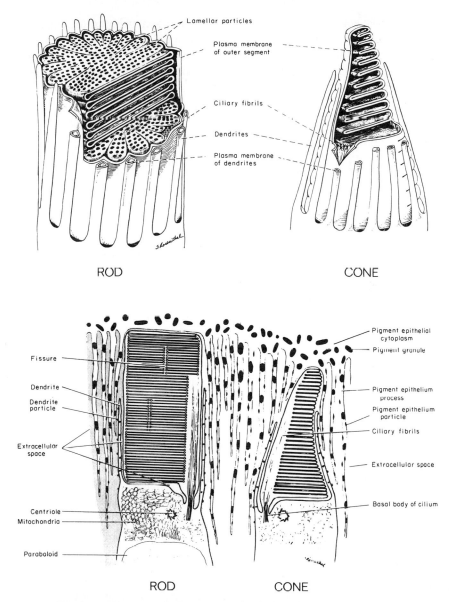

Fig. 10. *Top:* Diagram of the structural relations between rod and cone outer segments in *Necturus. Bottom:* Diagram to show relationships of rod and cone outer segments to the inner segments and the pigment epithelium. (Reproduced from Brown et al., 1963.)

The outer segments of double cones have a somewhat different structure. The common plasma membrane is infolded repeatedly on the side opposite to the cilium to form the double layers (Fig. 10, top). In cones, the space between the double layer (corresponding in rods to the intradiscal space) is directly connected with the extracellular space. The repeating unit in the cone outer segment is about 320 Å.

The inner segments of the photoreceptors are connected with the outer segments by a small cilium. The inner segment contains densely packed mitochondria in the region adjacent to the outer segment, where in the light microscope one sees the ellipsoid (Fig. 10 bottom). The paraboloid can be easily seen in the electron-microscopic photographs.

The Neuronal Network

Dowling and Werblin emphasized the investigation of the synaptic contacts of the retinal neurons and derived a scheme of the connections of the different cells in the retina of Necturus (Fig. 11).

The *outer plexiform layer* varies considerably in thickness (2–10μm). It contains the receptor terminals, which are arranged in 2–3 layers. The distal part of the outer plexiform layer contains more cone synapses, while the proximal part contains more rod synapses. The dendrites of both the bipolar cells and the horizontal cells invaginate into the cone terminals, which contain *ribbon synapses* at the site of invagination (Fig. 11). Ribbon synapses are also formed by the rod terminals, but their contacts with bipolar cell and horizontal cell dendrites are flat. Frequently, rod synapses are displaced laterally from the rest of the inner segment. Some cones also form flat synaptic contacts. The horizontal cells form synapses with other horizontal cell dendrites, but mainly with the dendrites or the cell soma of the bipolar cells. "Feedback synapses" between horizontal cells or bipolar cells to receptor cells were not found. As Fig. 11 shows, the synapses of the horizontal cells are frequently both pre- and postsynaptic structures which occur simultaneously. No conventional synapses have been observed between the horizontal cell and the bipolar cell processes that invaginated into the receptor terminal. It is possible that a nonchemical synaptic interaction occurs between these structures. Contacts containing synaptic vesicles are seen between rod and cone terminals; however, these contacts are not of the ribbon type and no specialization of the pre- and postsynaptic membranes is seen. It seems, therefore, questionable as to whether synaptic signal transmission occurs from receptor to receptor, as described for the photoreceptors for the larval Tiger salamander by Lasansky (1973).

The *inner plexiform layer* is characterized by a greater thickness and density of the synaptic contacts. The terminals of the bipolar cells have

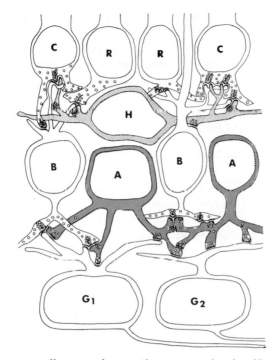

Fig. 11. Summary diagram of synaptic contacts in the *Necturus* retina, as revealed by electron microscopic studies. C, cones; R, rods; H, horizontal cells; B, bipolar cells; A, amacrine cells; G_1 and G_2, ganglion cells. In the diagram, two types of ganglion cells are suggested; one driven primarily by bipolars (G_1), the other driven primarily by the amacrines (G_2). In the latter situation, the amacrine cells involved may be considered as true interneurons, interposed between the bipolar and ganglion cells. For further explanation of the diagram, see description in the text. (Reproduced and slightly modified from Dowling and Werblin, 1969, by permission of the authors.)

ribbon-type synaptic contacts with the dendrites of the ganglion cells and amacrines. These synapses form dyads with a variable combination of postsynaptic elements. About 50% of the dyads are of the amacrine-amacrine type, and 50% are of the amacrine-ganglion cell type. The processes of the amacrine cells, as a rule, form conventional synapses. Dowling and Werblin discriminated two types of synapses. *Reciprocal synapses* appear to transmit signals from the amacrines back to the bipolar cells. The *serial synapses,* on the other hand, are synapses between amacrine cell dendrites which, in turn, have synaptic contacts with the dendrites of ganglion cells.

Two types of ganglion cells exist in *Necturus*, one driven primarily by amacrines, the other driven primarily by direct bipolar cell contacts. From these findings, one can expect that the response of one class of ganglion cells depends closely on the bipolar cell response, while the other class of ganglion cells follows the amacrine cell activity. Physiological evidence for this interpretation is presented later. The class of ganglion cells that receives their main input through the chain—receptors, bipolar cells, amacrine cells—are candidates for movement-sensitive neurons.

Primary Central Visual Pathways

Both the overall organization and the cytoarchitectonics of the brain of the different species of urodeles are well comparable (Herrick, 1941; Jakway and Riss, 1972). With respect to the development of the central visual system, the different species investigated exhibit clear differences in the relative size and differentiation of their "visual brain." Jakway and Riss (1972) see the following main differences in the afferent visual system:

a. The proportion of myelinated to unmyelinated fibers in the optic nerve and the central visual tracts.

b. The presence of a more-or-less developed retinotopic arrangement of the fibers within the optic nerve and the optic tract.

c. The proportional development and the degree of separation of the axial and the marginal parts of the optic tract.

d. The relationship of the axial optic tract to the preoptic nucleus.

e. The differentiation and the sites of the terminal endings of axon collaterals of the optic tract.

The differentiation of the retina and of the central visual structures exhibits a close positive correlation and correlates also with the significance of visual information for the overall behavior of individual species. The differentiation of the visual system increases from *Necturus* to *Cryptobranchus, Ambystoma tigrinum,* and *Salamandra* to *Triturus.* The central visual system of *Triturus* seems to show the highest state of development in urodeles. Investigations show that *Necturus,* on the other side of the rank order, exhibits little differentiation of functionally separate afferent fiber systems and little differentiation of its central visual nuclei as well. Thus, in *Necturus,* the retina and the central visual system seem to have a state of mild degeneration, phylogenetically.

Contralateral Projections

The projection of the retina was investigated, among others,* in the following species: *Necturus maculòsus* (Herrick, 1941), *Cryptobranchus*

* For additional data, see Röthig, 1924 (*Siren lacertina, Cryptobranchus japonicus, Sperlepes fuscus*) and Frey, 1938 (*Proteus*).

allegheniensis (Riss *et al.*, 1963), *Ambystoma tigrinum* (Herrick, 1948; Jakway and Riss, 1972), *Salamandra maculosa* (Röthig, 1924; Kreht, 1930), and *Triturus taeniatus* (Röthig, 1924; Ströer, 1940). In accordance with the findings in other lower vertebrates, the following five projections of the retina were found in the mentioned species (for discussion of homology and nomenclature, see Jakway and Riss, 1972):

1. *The retinotectal pathway*—The overwhelming majority of the optic nerve fibers cross to the contralateral side and form a marginal and an axial fiber bundle behind the chiasma opticum. These bundles traverse the diencephalon and enter the *stratum opticum* of the optic tectum in separate pathways. The degrees of separation of the axial and the marginal portions of the optic tract vary from one species to another. In *Ambystoma*, a medial and a lateral part of the marginal optic tract are visible at the level of the pretectal region. In *Triturus*, several bundles of optic tract fibers, forming the axial and the lateral optic tract respectively, remain separated from each other from the chiasma to their endings in the tectum opticum.

2. *Retinal projections to the ventral and dorsal thalamus*—The fibers entering the thalamic visual nuclei originate mainly from the deeper fiber bundles of the axial part of the optic tract. In *Triturus*, two distinct visual centers were seen in the thalamus by Ströer (1940): The nucleus of Bellonci and the corpus geniculatum laterale, which is a part of the medial dorsal thalamus. The corpus geniculatum laterale is less well developed in the investigated urodele species than in the anuran brain

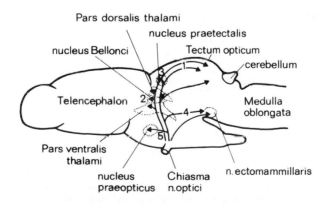

Fig. 12. Diagram of the pathway of the five afferent contralateral optic nerve fiber tracts of the brain of *Ambystoma*. (1) Retinotectal pathway; (2) retino-thalamic pathway; (3) retinopretectal pathway; (4) posterior accessory optic tract; (5) tractus opticus anterior. (Redrawn and modified from Herrick 1948.)

(e.g., *Rana pipiens;* Scalia *et al.*, 1968; and *Bufo marinus;* Rubinson, 1969). In the thalamus of *Ambystoma*, Jakway and Riss (1972) described a clearly separable nucleus of Bellonci located between the ventral and the dorsal thalamic nuclei. Kreht (1930) was not able to find a retinothalamic projection in *Salamandra*, while Röthig (1924) described for the same species a twig of tthe marginal tract running to the dorsolateral part of the thalamus.

3. *The retinopretectal pathway*—The optic tract fibers reaching the pretectal visual region originate from the marginal part of the optic tract in *Ambystoma*. In *Cryptobranchus allegheniensis*, these fibers could either run exclusively with the axial bundle or emerge from the marginal tract.

4. *The posterior accessory (basal) optic tract*—A small tract of optic nerve fibers runs behind the chiasma to the more caudally located *nucleus ectomamillaris*. These optic tract fibers have their respective endings near the root of the oculomotor nerve. It is assumed that this visual input is directly connected with the nerve cells which have axons in the fasciculus longitudinalis medialis and with the cells of the oculomotor nuclei. Fibers of the posterior optic tract are distributed among all optic nerve fiber bundles in *Triturus*, while in *Necturus* these fibers seem to run exclusively in the marginal bundle.

5. *The tractus opticus anterior*—This tract connects the retinal ganglion cell layer with the region of the Nucleus preopticus of the hypothalamus. With the histological techniques applied thus far, it was difficult to localize the endings of this tract with absolute certainty. Also, the question is not yet settled as to whether this tract contains afferent fibers. Jakway and Riss (1972) were able to see endings of degenerating crossed optic nerve fibers running through the marginal optic tract to the preoptic nucleus only in *Ambystoma*. Ströer, on the other hand, found optic tract fibers in *Triturus* which run from the preoptic nucleus toward the main optic tract. He calls these fibers the tractus preoptico-opticus, because they join the optic tract.

While in the older literature, only contralateral projections of the retina had been described for urodeles as well as for anurans, Jakway and Riss have recently obtained clear evidence for the existence of an ipsilateral retinal projection in *Ambystoma*. By using the Fink-Heimer II method, the time of degeneration appeared to be more critical for good staining of the ipsilateral optic tract fibers undergoing anterograde degeneration than for the staining of the contralateral fibers. The ipsilateral fibers are considerably less numerous than the contralateral ones, and have terminals in the neuropil of the ventral and dorsal thalamus and in the pretectal visual region. No direct ipsilateral fibers seem to reach the optic tectum.

The Optic Tectum

In *Ambystoma*, the lateral and the medial parts of the marginal optic tract extend through the anterior three-quarters of the optic tectum (Herrick, 1948; Jakway and Riss, 1972). The same is also true for *Necturus* and *Cryptobranchus allegheniensis*, in which the caudal portion of the tectum is free of optic contributions, while in *Salamandra* the axial and the marginal part of the optic tract can be followed to the most caudal part of the tectal surface (Kreht, 1930). Ströer (1940) describes a very regular retinotopic projection of the optic tract fiber endings in the optic tectum of *Triturus*. The fibers from the nasal, inferior retinal quadrant project to the dorsal optic tectum; the fibers from the superior, nasal retina to the lateral and ventral tectum; the fibers from the upper, temporal retina to the anterior part of the tectum; and finally, the fibers from the lower, temporal retina project to the medial and dorsal tectum. In *Ambystoma*, the tectal terminal field is located between the lateral and medial part of the marginal optic tract, which covers about two-thirds of the superficial *stratum album*. Jakway and Riss (1972) found six layers for the tectal terminal field in *Ambystoma*. Three dense layers alternate with three less dense layers.

These findings are new; a differentiated layering of the superficial tectum opticum has not been previously described in other urodeles. In his review article concerning the visual brain of *Ambystoma tigrinum*, Herrick (1948) emphasizes that the superficial layer of the optic tectum exhibits a rather homogeneous structure. For the description of the overall layering of the optic tectum (fiber and cell layers), Herrick discriminates eight different layers. The six layers of Jakway and Riss mentioned above correspond to layers 1 and 2 of Herrick. In these layers, the synaptic endings of the afferent optic nerve fibers are located and an extensive branching of the dendrites of the tectal cells takes place.

The Efferent Connections of the Optic Tectum

Herrick (1948) found five different efferent connections of the tectum made by myelinated fibers leaving the optic tectum:

1. *Fibers of the posterior commissure*—These fibers run from the optic tectum through the commissura posterior to the nucleus of Darkschewitsch and to the fasciculus longitudinalis medialis. It seems possible that part of optomotor responses are controlled via this fiber system.

2. *Tractus tectothalamicus and tractus tectohypothalamicus cruciatus* —The fibers of this tract extend into the thalamus and the hypothalamus

of both sides and also into the peduncular and tegmental region. Perhaps this system controls visually guided defense mechanisms.

3. *Tractus tectobulbaris and tractus tectospinalis*—The fibers of these tracts contain many thick myelinated axons. They end in the anterior horn region of the lower medulla and the spinal cord. This tract is the direct tectomotor control system. Herrick discriminated two contralateral and one ipsilateral tract. The contralateral tracts cross to the other side at the level of the nuclei of the third and fourth cranial nerves.

4. *Fibers in the brachia of the superior colliculi*—The brachia contain fibers that connect the optic tectum with thalamic nuclei in both directions.

5. *Tractus tectopretectalis*—These fibers pass from the tectum to the pretectum and in the opposite direction.

Nonvisual Input to the Optic Tectum

The optic tectum in the amphibian brain is probably the highest "center" for visual motor-control mechanisms. In the optic tectum of frogs, for example, nonvisual inputs (e.g., somatosensory, auditory, and vibratory stimuli) have a considerable effect on the response pattern of many "visual" cells (Grüsser and Grüsser-Cornehls, 1968b). The same is true for the tectal cells of the salamander (Grüsser-Cornehls and Himstedt, 1973). Frogs without the optic tectum are "blind" to moving small objects and have a very poor general visual orientation; they exhibit, however, a good optokinetic nystagmus (Lázár, 1973).

1. *The general bulbar lemniscal system*—This large tract contains fibers originating in the sensory region of the medulla oblongata. The tract crosses through the ventral commissure and ascends to the mesencephalon. Part of these fibers are distributed rather evenly across the optic tectum, and part of the fibers continue toward the dorsal thalamic nuclei.

2. *Tractus bulbotectalis lateralis*—This tract is closely associated with the bulbar lemniscal system. Its fibers originate in the vestibular nuclei. They end in the most caudal part of the tectum, called the colliculus inferior by Herrick.

3. *Tractus spinotectalis and tractus spinothalamicus* (spinal lemniscus)—This tract originates in the ventral part of the upper spinal cord. The fibers cross in the ventral commissure to the contralateral side and have a widespread distribution of their endings in the cerebellum, in the mesencephalon and, in part, in the pars dorsalis thalami.

4. *Tractus striotectalis*—While the nonvisual input to the optic tectum described in the preceding section may be involved in sensory feedback

and afferent vestibular control mechanisms, the tractus striotectalis might be a tract in which "higher-order, internal control mechanisms" are mediated by the cells of the optic tectum. This tract connects the forebrain with the tectum. According to Herrick, these fibers probably arise from the corpus striatum, though this has not been demonstrated.

The visual nuclei of the posterior thalamus have efferent connections with the peduncular system, the dorsal and the isthmic part of the tegmentum, the hypothalamus and the forebrain. Connections of the pretectal visual region with the hypothalamus are also described (Herrick, 1948).

Electrophysiology of the Visual System

Retina

In this section, only measurements of the responses of single retinal neurons will be discussed. Investigations of the ERG and the "proximal negative response" of urodele retinae have been treated elsewhere (see, e.g., Bortoff, 1964; Himstedt, 1970; Burkhardt, 1972, 1974; Proenza and Burkhardt, 1973).

INTRARETINAL RECORDINGS. Unless otherwise specified, the electrical properties of retinal elements now to be described are based on intraretinal recordings in *Necturus maculosus*. The retina of *Necturus maculosus* is a very favorable preparation for intracellular measurement of the activity of the different retinal neurons, since the cells here are quite large and the isolated eye survives for several hours. But the inferences to be drawn from such recordings are limited by two factors: On the one hand, vision does not play an important role in the normal behavior of *Necturus;* the eye is small and the central visual system poorly developed. On the other hand, the retina is developmentally that of an animal in the larval stage, a condition which in *Necturus* persists throughout life. Because, in other amphibians, a functional change in the retina has been observed to occur at metamorphosis from the larval stage to the adult (Reuter, 1969; Pomeranz, 1972), one must proceed with caution in generalizing from the *Necturus* data to a model for the vertebrate retina.

The individual cell types from which intracellular recordings were made have been identified by intracellular staining with Trypan blue (Bortoff, 1964) and Niagara sky blue (Dowling and Werblin, 1969).

RECEPTORS. *Receptor potential.* When the retina is illuminated, the receptors themselves respond with *hyperpolarization,* usually consisting of a

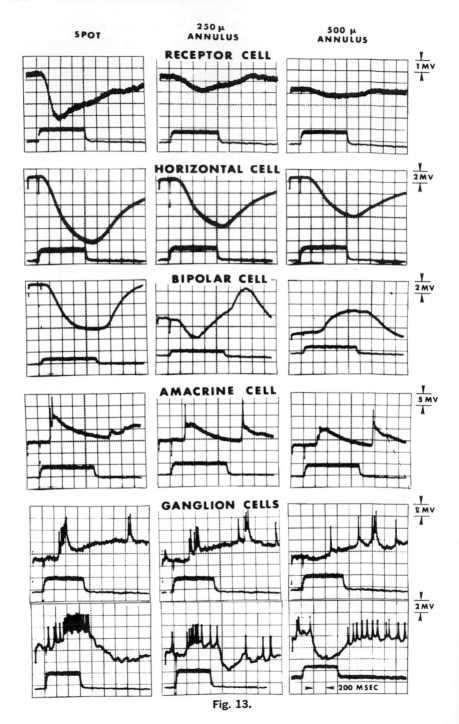

Fig. 13.

transient and a sustained component (Fig. 13) (Bortoff, 1964; Werblin and Dowling, 1969). The latency between stimulus and onset of the potential is about 50 msec for test stimuli, with intensities about one $\log_{10}$ unit above threshold. The rise time to the maximum, in contrast to results obtained from the frog and from the larval tiger salamander (Lasansky and Marchiafava, 1974), is the same for rods and cones and amounts to 50 msec with stimuli one $\log_{10}$ unit above threshold. When the light goes off, a small transient off response is measured. The resting membrane potential (RMP) has been measured at about −30 mV, and the maximal amplitude of the response, after dark adaptation, −6 mV (Norman and Werblin, 1974).

Differences between rods and cones. Rods and cones of the *Necturus* retina exhibit characteristic differences in the time course of the receptor potentials elicited by illumination (Fain and Dowling, 1973; Norman and Werblin, 1974). The same is true for rods and cones of the retina of the larval tiger salamander (Lasansky and Marchiafava, 1974). As compared with the cones, the membrane potential of the rods after illumination with short flashes of light returns much more slowly to the resting level in the dark.

In *Necturus*, the time constant for this return to the RMP amounts to about 1–1.5 sec in the case of the cones (Fig. 14A). The membrane potential of the rods has still not returned to the resting level ten seconds after stimulation, even with low light intensities (Fig. 14B). The initial transient component of the rod response is also more variable in amplitude, from one cell to another, than that of the cones, and it does not appear at all except at saturating light intensities. A possible basis for this phenomenon, discussed by Fain and Dowling (1973), is an interaction between receptors and horizontal cells. Cones and rods in *Necturus*, as in other animals, have different sensitivities to low-intensity light stimuli. Rods are one to one-and-a-half $\log_{10}$ units more sensitive than cones (isolated eye). The minimal stimulus intensity producing a rod response corresponds to an incident photon flux of about 10 quanta (525 nm)/sec/rod. The minimal stimulus intensity required to produce

Fig. 13. Intracellular recordings of the neurons of the *Necturus* retina. The responses were elicited with a spot of light of 100 μm diameter focused on the electrode (left column) and with a small annulus of 250 μm radius and a large annulus of 500 μm radius (center and right columns). The distal retinal neurons respond with slow, graded, mostly hyperpolarizing potentials; the proximal neurons respond with depolarizing, mostly transient potentials. See text for discussion of receptive field properties of the various neurons. (Reproduced from Werblin and Dowling, 1969, by permission of the authors.)

a cone response, however, corresponds to an incident photon flux of 100–200 quanta (575 nm)/sec/cone (Norman and Werblin, 1974). The hyperpolarization by light of the cones (as revealed by intracellular recordings from the retina of Necturus and the larval tiger salamander) is caused by an increase in input resistance of the membrane and a reduction in the permeability of sodium channels which, in darkness, shunt the membrane (Toyoda *et al.*, 1969; Nelson, 1973; Lasansky and Marchiafava, 1974). In rods of the larval tiger salamander, however, the main effect of illumination is an increase of the permeability of the membrane to small ions. The equilibrium potential of these ions (potassium) is more negative than the "resting" membrane potential in darkness (Lasansky and Marchiafava, 1974). Therefore, light induces, according to the Goldman equation, a hyperpolarization of the membrane potential. Fain (1973), however, assumes for the rods of *Necturus* a similar effect of illumination (increase of the membrane resistance) as discussed for the cones. His arguments are deduced from the findings that the maximal membrane potential and the light-evoked hyperpolarization of the membrane of both types of receptors are of the same magnitude.

Intensity dependence. As intensity of the test stimulus increases, so does the amplitude of the receptor potential, in both rods and cones. Also, the response latency decreases, and the initial phase occurs with a more rapid rise. With a flash duration of 180 msec, the transient component of the rod receptor potential first appears at 3.2×10^9 quanta per cm² flash (Fig. 14B). The dependence of amplitude of the rod and cone potentials upon light intensity of the test stimulus is shown in Figure 14C (Fain and Dowling, 1973). Norman and Werblin describe the relationship between amplitude of receptor potential and light intensity as

$$\frac{V_r}{V_{r_{\max}}} = \frac{I^n}{(I^n + k^n)} \tag{1}$$

where V_r is the response amplitude, $V_{r_{\max}}$ is the maximal response amplitude, and I is the stimulus intensity, n is a constant, k corresponds to the intensity required to produce a response of $1/2 V_{r_{\max}}$. The same formula describes the relationship between the response amplitude and the light intensity for the rods of *Ambystoma mexicanum* and for the rods and cones of the larval tiger salamander (Grabowski *et al.*, 1972; Lasansky and Marchiafava, 1974).

The constant n in Equation (1) varies, among different studies, within the range of 0.7 to 1.0. Norman and Werblin (1974) discuss that these differences may be associated with the use of test stimuli of different

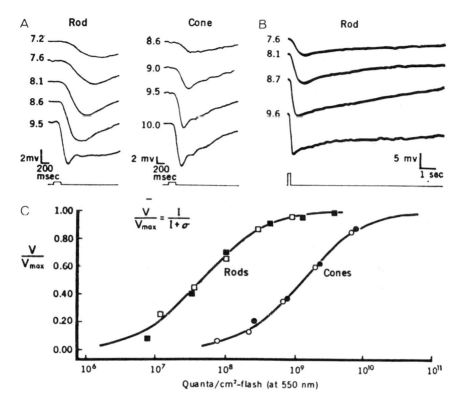

Fig. 14. (A) Comparison of rod and cone responses. Amplitude calibration for rod is twice that for cone. Flashes were 180 msec long and at 510 nm for the rod and 600 nm for the cone. Relative absorbance curves of Fig. 15A were used to convert the quantum intensities of the flashes into equivalent intensities at the λ_{max} of the rod or cone visual pigment. The number to the left of each response gives the equivalent intensity in log quanta/cm²-flash. (B) Responses of a second rod on a much longer time scale. Flashes were 190 msec long at 550 nm and were given at 25-second intervals. (C) Intensity-response curves of mudpuppy photo-receptors. Peak amplitude of response measured as a fraction of the amplitude at saturation for the two most sensitive rods and cones, plotted against the log of the incident quantum intensity at 550 nm. Open and filled symbols are used to refer to the same cells as in Fig. 15. (Reproduced from Fain and Dowling, 1973, by permission of the authors.)

durations. If $n = 1$, Eq. (1) can be rewritten as

$$V_r = \frac{\alpha I}{(1 + k_i)I} \qquad (mV) \qquad (2)$$

With suitable selection of the constants α and k_i, the data available in the literature can be well described by Eq. (2). Equation (2) can be related to a function of the hyperbolic tangent of ln$I$; with a log scaling of I, it simulates the well-known S-shaped curves (see Naka and Rushton, 1967; Lipetz, 1969).

The intensity-response curves of rods and cones extend over about 3.5 log units. For different background illuminations, the curves are displaced along the log-intensity axis. At a given level of adapting light, the cones display a less pronounced sustained hyperpolarization than do the rods. Thus, the range over which the cones can respond is only slightly reduced with increasing background intensity, whereas the operating range of the rods is constantly reduced by adapting light. Accordingly, the characteristic curves for rods become flatter and have a smaller amplitude range when the adapting light intensity is increased (Norman and Werblin, 1974).

Interaction between adjacent receptors. Hyperpolarization of the receptors induced by spot illumination is not affected by additional illumination of an annulus of adjacent receptors (Fig. 14). Stimulation with the annulus alone produces only a slight hyperpolarization, probably resulting from stray light. The receptors of *Necturus*, therefore, have small receptive fields that cannot be influenced by illumination of neighboring receptors (Werblin and Dowling, 1969). These findings differ from the behavior of photoreceptors in the turtle retina, where Baylor and Fuortes (1970) and Baylor *et al.* (1971) found an interaction of neighboring receptors.

Spectral sensitivity of receptors. Measurement of the spectral sensitivity of the rod receptor potential gives a sensitivity maximum at 525 nm, whereas that of cones lies at 572 nm (Fain and Dowling, 1973; Norman and Werblin, 1974). These values are entirely consistent with the respective absorption curves for the photopigments of *Necturus* (Brown *et al.*, 1963; Brown, quoted from Fain and Dowling, 1973, Fig. 15).

HORIZONTAL CELLS. *Response to illumination of the receptive field and spectral sensitivity.* Horizontal cells respond to illumination of the receptive field just as do the receptors, with a *hyperpolarization* (Fig. 14). The RMP has been measured at about −30 mV. The latency from stimulus to response onset amounts to about 100 msec. The initial rise is slower than in the receptors, however. Upon termination of illumination, the potential returns to the resting level with a time constant of about 0.8–1.3 sec (Werblin and Dowling, 1969, Fig. 13). According to the spectral sensitivity curves (Fain, 1973), the responses of *Necturus* horizontal cells appear to be of two kinds: an L-type response, which receives a

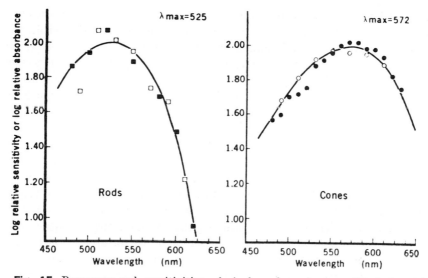

Fig. 15. Responses and sensitivities of single rods and cones. Spectral sensitivities of mudpuppy photoreceptors, plotted against absorbance curves for rod and cone photopigments. (Brown *et al.*, 1963; Brown, 1976.) *Left:* The log relative spectral sensitivities from two cells classified as rods (open and filled squares) and the log relative absorbance of the rod pigment from macrospectrophotometry and whole mudpuppy retinas (curve). *Right:* The log relative spectral sensitivities from two cells classified as cones (open and filled circles) and log relative absorbance of the cone pigment from macrospectrophotometry on whole mudpuppy retinas (curve). (Reproduced from Fain and Dowling, 1973, by permission of the authors.)

hyperpolarizing signal from both rods and cones, and C-type response, which receives a hyperpolarizing signal from rods and a depolarizing signal from cones. The latter is observed when long wavelength stimuli in the presence of blue backgrounds are applied. Among 30 horizontal-cell responses, 29 were found to be from the L-type and one of the C-type. With short wavelength stimuli, or bright flashes of white light, L-type horizontal cells show two components of different frequency properties: a fast decay of the potential probably originated by the cones and a slow decay originated by the rods.

Spatial summation of excitation in the receptive field. The horizontal cells respond with a sustained hyperpolarizing potential, both to a small light spot and to a concentrically positioned ring of light (Fig. 13), which covers the more peripheral parts of the receptive field. With simultaneous stimulation by spot and annulus, the effects combine (Werblin and Dowling, 1969; Burkhardt, 1974). Each horizontal cell thus receives inputs from a large number of receptors, its receptive field being more than 0.5 mm in diameter. One may conclude from the results of Werblin and Dowling that the spatial summation of excitation in the horizontal cells is not linear. It is not yet known whether there is a power-law relationship between the amplitude of the horizontal cell potentials and the area of the light stimulus in the receptive field, as is the case for the horizontal cells in the cat retina (van de Grind et al., 1973).

Intensity dependence. The amplitude of the horizontal-cell potential increases with light intensity, over approximately three $\log_{10}$ units. Here, as in the case of the receptor cells, the relationship can be described by Eq. (1) (Fain, 1973; Burkhardt, 1974; Werblin, 1974). As background illumination is increased, the curves are displaced to the right on the log-intensity axis; however, n is also dependent upon the adapting intensity—it is smaller (0.7) for lower and larger (1.0) for greater background illumination (Werblin, 1974). According to the intensity response curves for flashes of various duration, the cone component of the L-type horizontal cells appear to follow Bloch's law $J \times t = K$ (Bloch, 1885) for flash durations up to 500 msec (Fain, 1973).

BIPOLAR CELLS. *Classes of Bipolar cells.* There are two types of bipolar cells, as defined by their responses to stimulation by a spot of light in the center of the receptive field. Fifty percent of the cells show sustained hyperpolarization and are classified as *off* cells, whereas 50% show a sustained depolarization and are termed *on* cells (Fig. 13). The latency of the bipolar cell response amounts to about 100 msec for light stimuli at intensities three $\log_{10}$ units above threshold. The resting membrane potential, again, measures -30 mV (Werblin and Dowling, 1969). The spectral sensitivity curves for the responses obtained from the RF-center of bipolar cells revealed two classes: one type has only a cone input, the other a rod and a cone input. For both types, *on*-depolarizing and *on*-hyperpolarizing bipolar cells were found (Fain, 1973). The same was reported for the bipolar cell antagonistic surrounds. From Fain's work, however, it is not clear how the spectral sensitivity of the response elicited from the RF-center and that elicited from the RF-periphery are correlated to each other.

Spatial summation of excitation and organization of the receptive fields. If the center of the receptive field is illuminated by a spot and, at the same time, the periphery is stimulated by a concentric annulus of light, the response is less than, or even the reverse of, that produced by the central light spot alone. The *on*-bipolars are not, however, hyperpolarized beyond the resting dark potential when the surrounding of the receptive field is illuminated. Therefore, to determine the effect of illumination of the receptive field periphery, one must depolarize the cell by simultaneous illumination at the center of the field. At the level of the bipolar cells, then, there appears for the first time in the afferent visual system an antagonistic center-surround organization of the receptive field. The response to illumination of the receptive field center always has a shorter latency than the response to illumination of the periphery, even if different stimulus intensities are used (Werblin and Dowling, 1969).

Intensity dependence. In the bipolar cells, too, the relationship between amplitude of membrane potential and intensity of a test stimulus can be described by Eq. (1). The curves are shifted to the right as the background illumination is increased, and n is also dependent on background illumination (Werblin, 1974). The dynamic range of the graded bipolar-cell responses, under constant background illumination, amounts to about two $\log_{10}$ units.

Sensitization and desensitization of the bipolar cell response. The displacement of the intensity-response curves to the right on the log-intensity axis with increased background illumination (that is, the desensitization of the bipolar-cell responses) is thought to be brought about, not by stray light and receptor adaptation, but rather by lateral interaction (Werblin, 1974). Weak background illumination in the center of the receptive field is thought to bring about a sensitization of the bipolar cell response. With stronger background illumination, upon both center and periphery of the receptive field, the effects are found to summate. The shift of the characteristic intensity curve as a result of change in the adapting-light intensity can also be regarded as sensitization. Light stimuli in the center of the receptive field which differ in intensity but are all so strong that, due to saturation, they would ordinarily elicit the same response, can be distinguished by the system when the characteristic curves are shifted by change of the background intensity.

Interaction between horizontal cells and bipolar cells. If a light spot of constant intensity is enlarged from 0.5 to 2 mm diameter, while the center of the receptive field of the cell in question is stimulated with a test spot also of constant intensity, there is a good correlation between the increase in amplitude of the horizontal cell response and the decrease in amplitude of the steady phase of the bipolar cell response. On the basis of this observation, Werblin (1974) suggests that the horizontal cells determine the response from the receptive field periphery of the bipolar cells. The transient part of the bipolar cell response elicited by light stimuli projected to the RF-center is elicited predominantly by receptor-bipolar cell contacts. Because the antagonistic-surround effect is delayed with respect to the response from the center of the receptive field, the early transient part of the response is not affected by the illumination of the RF-periphery.

AMACRINES. *Response to illumination of the receptive field.* Amacrine cells respond *transiently* to illumination of the retina, usually both to "light on" and to "light off," with a short (0.8 to 1.0 sec) *depolarization* with respect to the resting membrane potential (Fig. 13). During this transient response, action potentials of the all-or-none type can appear; but, as a rule, only one or two impulses occur during each depolarizing transient. The latency of the depolarization decreases with increasing light intensity, and amounts to less than 200 msec when light stimuli of intensity three log_{10} units above threshold are given. The resting membrane potential of the amacrines is -30 to -40 mV (Werblin and Dowling, 1969). Since at "on" and at "off," only one or two impulses are produced, one may assume that the slow potentials of the amacrines also play a role in synaptic transmission of signals (i.e., from amacrines to ganglion cells).

Classes of amacrines and organization of the receptive field. Among the amacrines, too, one can distinguish different classes of cells. Some of the amacrines have large receptive fields; these respond with both an *off* and an *on* depolarization, regardless of where within the receptive field the light stimulus is presented. Other cells have receptive fields with small centers (100–200 μm) and peripheries that function antagonistically. Whether the *on* or the *off* response predominates depends on the position and shape of the stimulus within the receptive field (Werblin and Dowling, 1969). Fain (1973) obtained evidence from spectral sensitivity curves of the amacrine cells that, at this level, an interaction of rod and cone signals also occurs. The relative efficiency of these two signals varies from cell to cell.

Intensity dependence. The amplitude of the slow waves of depolarization of the amacrines depends on light intensity, though the dynamic range for this response is less than one log_{10} unit of intensity. With increasing background illumination, the characteristic curves are displaced to the right along the log-intensity axis (Werblin, 1974).

GANGLION CELLS. *Response to illumination of the receptive field.* The ganglion cells respond to illumination of the receptive field center with either a *depolarization* (in the case of *on*-center cells) or a *hyperpolarization* (*off*-center cells) (Fig. 13). The *off*-center ganglion cells become depolarized when the light in the receptive field goes off. Depolarization of the membrane potential above a presumably variable threshold level causes the production of all-or-none impulses (Bortoff, 1964; Werblin and Dowling, 1969). The discharge rate increases with the degree of depolarization. The resting potential in the dark has been measured as −40 mV, but the actual values are probably greater (−60 to −80 mV).

Temporal response properties. In *Necturus*, with respect to the temporal response properties, two types of ganglion cells have been found so far (Werblin and Dowling, 1969; Tuttle, 1974). One type shows *transient on, off,* or *on-off* responses to stimulation with spots of light. The amplitude of the *on* or *off* component of the response depends on the spatial extent of the stimulus within the receptive field and upon the intensity of the light. The characteristic response of these cells resembles that of the amacrines (Fig. 13). Some of these cells show an antagonistic organization of center and periphery of the receptive field, while others do not (Tuttle, 1974).

The other type of ganglion cell has a sustained response to illumination of the receptive field center (*on*-center neurons). This amounts to a sustained depolarization, associated with a corresponding increase in impulse frequency. When the periphery of the receptive field is illuminated with an annulus of light during simultaneous weak illumination of the center, the membrane potential returns to the resting level and an inhibition of the impulse activity occurs. These cells thus have an antagonistic receptive field organization. Their responses, except for the generation of action potentials, resemble those of the bipolar cells both in temporal characteristics and in the antagonistic properties of the receptive fields (Fig. 13). The receptive field organization and the response of the sustained *off*-center ganglion cells are just the reverse of those measured for the *on*-center ganglion cells. The field size of the sustained ganglion cells seems to be larger than that of the transient ganglion cells, as one can conclude from the data and figures published by Tuttle (1974).

Spectral sensitivity. The spectral sensitivity curves of dark-adapted transient ganglion cells also indicate that two components of different spectral sensitivity interact at this level. The spectral sensitivity curves of these cells are very similar to those obtained for the amacrine cells with a maximum mostly around 525 nm. (Fain, 1973). In contrast to the goldfish retina (Spekreijse et al., 1972), antagonistic chromatic responses

were not found in the ganglion cell layer. Due to the rareness of antagonistic chromatic responses in horizontal cells, this finding is not surprising.

Intensity function. The number of extracellularly recorded impulses
of an *on* ganglion cell increases when the intensity of the light stimulus
in the receptive field center increases. The characteristic intensity curves
of the *on* cells extend over a range of two $\log_{10}$ units for the sustained
neurons, while for the transient neurons, the dynamic range is only one
$\log_{10}$ unit. With increasing background illumination, the intensity
curves are displaced to the right on the log intensity axis, without change
of shape. Tuttle (1974) found in his sample of neurons that the sustained
on cells have a lower threshold (0.3 to 1.2 $\log_{10}$ units) than the transient
on-off cells.

Spatial summation of excitation and inhibition. Summation of excitation and inhibition in the receptive fields of ganglion cells has been investigated by illumination of the periphery of the field with intermittent
light stimuli (spots, annuli, or "rotating windmill vanes"), while the
center is illuminated by test stimuli of different intensities (Copenhagen,
1972; Werblin and Copenhagen, 1974). Intermittent illumination of the
receptive field periphery, in the transient *on-off* ganglion cells, induces
a hyperpolarization of the membrane potential and thus leads to an
increase in the threshold for activation by way of the receptive field
center. The curve of response as a function of intensity is displaced to
the right on the log intensity axis by steady light stimuli in the periphery
of the receptive field. If the peripheral light stimuli are intermittent,
there is a further displacement of these curves to the right. The log
intensity-response curves rise less steeply above a certain test-stimulus
intensity (Fig. 16). Because the transient *on-off* ganglion cells are
hyperpolarized by intermittent light stimuli in the periphery of the
field, whereas the amacrines are depolarized, Werblin and Copenhagen
infer that the amacrine cells in the inner plexiform layer transmit a
lateral inhibitory effect to the ganglion cells. Whether this inhibitory
effect is frequency dependent, as was found for the frog retina (Grüsser-
Cornehls, 1968), has not been investigated. That this lateral inhibition
first arises in the inner plexiform layer has been inferred from the
finding that the response of a bipolar cell, though influenced by
stationary light stimuli in the periphery, is not further changed by movement of these light stimuli. In contrast to the transient *on-off* ganglion
cells, the sustained *on* ganglion cells respond in the same way, regardless
of whether the light stimulus in the periphery of the field is moved or
stationary. Therefore, Werblin and Copenhagen assumed that the re-

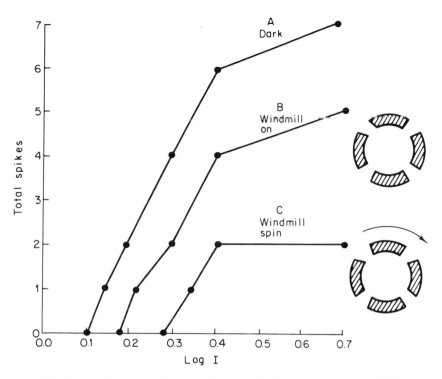

Fig. 16. Effect of the windmill on the *on-off* cell response curves of *Necturus*. Curve A plotted before the presentation of the windmill. Curve B plotted in the presence of the stationary windmill. Curve C plotted with the windmill spinning. (Reproduced from Werblin and Copenhagen, 1974, by permission of the authors.)

sponse of the sustained *on* ganglion cells is not influenced by lateral interaction of the amacrine cells.

Direction-dependent ganglion cells. In a certain fraction of the ganglion cells, the response to moving stimulus patterns is dependent upon the *direction* in which the pattern moves (Norton *et al.*, 1970; Werblin, 1970). By intracellular recording, it has been shown that movement of the stimulus through the excitatory receptive field (ERF) in the null direction leads to a hyperpolarization, whereas movement in the preferred direction causes depolarization of the cell, along with the generation of numerous action potentials (Werblin, 1970). Preferred and null direction are 180° apart.

Comparison between the responses to stationary and moving stimuli. The dependence of the responses of *Necturus* ganglion cells on stimulus intensity and area were determined either by presenting stationary stimuli as flashes of 2-sec duration or by means of stimuli moving at a speed of 260 μm/sec (Tuttle, 1974). The light intensities applied were in the scotopic range. The form and shape of the response-intensity functions, measured for a stimulus range of two $\log_{10}$-units or less, as well as the area functions, are quite similar for both types of stimuli (e.g., stationary or moving) and for both types of ganglion cells (transient and sustained ganglion cells). The response of both types of ganglion cells increases with an increase in intensity of the stimulus, whether stationary or moving. In the same manner, the response of both types of ganglion cells increases with an increase of stimulus area, up to a certain optimal stimulus size. Beyond this optimal size, a further increase in stimulus diameter leads to a decrease in the response strength.

MÜLLER CELLS. The glial cells of the retina (Müller cells) respond to light stimuli with a rather slow depolarization of the membrane potential (Miller and Dowling, 1970). Due to the extension of the glial cells, their responses can be recorded from several retinal layers. The resting membrane potential of the Müller cells is greater than the maximal resting potential found for ganglion cells, though there is pronounced scatter in the values for Müller cells (-20 mV to -85 mV). The receptive fields of the Müller cells are very large (ca. 1–2 mm). The slow potentials are considerably slower than those of the retinal neurons. With respect to latency and time course, the potential elicited from Müller cells by light resembles the b-wave of the ERG. Intensity-response curves also resemble those of the b-wave. In contrast to the intensity-response curve of the retinal neurons, the amplitude of the Müller cell potential increases over a range of 4 to 5 $\log_{10}$ units. Thus, the responses of the Müller cells and the b-wave of the ERG both saturate at higher light intensities than do those of the retinal neurons.

In recordings from the optic nerve of *Necturus*, it has been possible to show that the membranes of glial cells behave like potassium electrodes, changing their membrane potential with change in the extracellular potassium concentration in accordance with the Nernst equation for [K^+] (Orkand et al., 1966). Miller and Dowling assume that the Müller cells behave similarly, and that Müller cell response and the b-wave of the ERG are determined by changes in the extracellular potassium concentration. On the basis of investigations by Faber (1969) on the rabbit retina and their own findings, they suggest that the basis of variation in extracellular potassium concentration is associated with the distal part of the inner nuclear layer, that is, the horizontal and bipolar cells.

The Output Signals of the Retina

Classes of Retinal Ganglion Cells

RETINAL NEURON CLASSES IN *Necturus*. Recordings from fibers in the optic nerve of *Necturus* have indicated the presence of three classes of neurons (Hartline, 1938). (1) fibers that show only a brief activation in response to changing light intensity, (2) fibers that have a prolonged activation (up to 30 sec) at "light on," and (3) fibers that respond only to decrease in illumination. The *"off"* responses of the ganglion cells of *Necturus* were very weak and could be elicited only after at least 10 sec of illumination.

RETINAL NEURON CLASSES IN *Triturus*. In recordings from the optic nerve and the superficial layers of the optic tectum of *Triturus* (Cronly-Dillon and Galand, 1966), some of which were done in the course of investigations of the retinotectal projection after regeneration of the retina (Cronly-Dillon, 1968), four different classes of neurons were found. These could not be assigned to any particular layers in the superficial portion of the optic tectum.

1. *Convexity detectors*—These neurons respond to movement of a small, dark object across a bright background through the excitatory receptive field. The ERF covers 3–6°. It is probably surrounded by an inhibitory field (IRF), like the ERF of the similarly responding Class-2 neurons of the frog retina, for movement of a sufficiently large stimulus pattern over the RF elicits no response from the neurons (see Fig. 17).

2. *Boundary detectors*—These neurons give a prolonged response to the appearance of a stationary light-dark boundary lying within the receptive field. The extent of the ERF here, as in the first class, amounts to 3–6°.

3. *Contrast units*—These cells respond with a *brief*, high-frequency burst to any moving, light-dark boundary within the ERF. The ERF varies between 7° and 12°.

4. *Darkness units*—These neurons are inhibited by light and show a prolonged activation in the dark. The darkness units have large receptive fields; the exact sizes are not given by the authors, but they evidently exceed the RF sizes of the contrast units. The response of the darkness units to moving dark stimulus patterns is to some extent directionally dependent.

RETINAL NEURON CLASSES OF *Salamandra salamandra*. In contrast to those from *Triturus*, recordings of action potentials from afferent axons

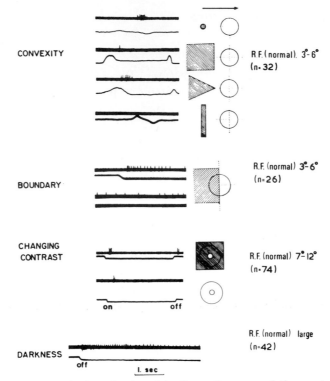

Fig. 17. Types of single units found in the optic nerve of the newt. The number given on the extreme right of each set of records indicates the range of receptive field sizes found for that type of unit; "n" indicates the number of units studied in each case. Lower trace on each record, photocell response. *Convexity unit* responds to a small, black, cardboard lure, or to a convex-pointed edge that is moved through the receptive field. Unit fails to respond to movement of a straight edge. *Boundary unit* responds with a long-lasting tonic discharge to the presence of a sharp stationary boundary that is lying within the unit's receptive field. *Contrast unit* responds with a brief high-frequency burst to any moving boundary that passes through its receptive field. Unit shown here displayed an excitatory *"on"* response (and small *"off"* response) when the center of the receptive field alone was stimulated with a small 1° spot of light that was flashed briefly on and off. Lower record shows how the response to the same spot diminished when the periphery of the receptive field was illuminated with a background light. Hence, this type of unit displays a distinct antagonism between the center and periphery of its receptive field. *Darkness unit* is inhibited by light and responds with a long tonic discharge in the dark. (Reproduced from Cronly-Dillon, 1968, by permission of the author.)

in the superficial layers of the optic tectum of *Salamandra* have indicated a functional layering (Grüsser-Cornehls and Himstedt, 1973).

1. *Layer-1 units*—On penetrating the tectum with a microelectrode, one finds just at its surface a very thin layer of axons that show no response to diffuse illumination (on-off) of the RF. The axons do respond, however, with marked activity when small, black objects more than 1–2° in diameter are moved through the ERF. The response to a black stimulus 7° in diameter, moved in steps through the ERF, lasts 100–200 msec following each change of position. The extent of the receptive field is about 12–16°.

If objects larger than the ERF are moved through the receptive field, the discharge rate is lower the larger the stimulus pattern. This behavior indicates the existence of a very effective inhibitory surround (IRF).

2. *Layer-2 units*—The neurons of the next layer, with diffuse illumination of the whole RF under photopic conditions, exhibit a short *on-off* response, 2–5 impulses both at light on and at light off. The latency to the first impulse is about 100 msec. When a small, black contrasting stimulus 3° in diameter is moved in steps through the ERF, the layer-2 neurons respond briefly, with about 1–4 impulses to each movement (Fig. 18). The ERF of these neurons is oval or round and 6–9° in extent.

3. *Layer-2a neurons*—Subclasses of layer-2 neurons are frequently found with characteristics different from those of the main group of layer-2 cells. In certain penetrations, these *layer-2a neurons* could be located below the main group of layer-2 neurons, though the boundary between the two layers was not very distinct. Layer-2a neurons are characterized by a marked adaptation of the response to repeated diffuse light stimuli (on-off). The number of impulses following the first light stimulus, however, is somewhat greater than in the case of the layer-2 units. Four out of 10 neurons of this group investigated quantitatively had only an *on* response to diffuse light, with a latency to the initial impulse of as much as a second. Some of the layer-2a neurons are activated by small, moving, contrasting stimuli, only if they are moved through the ERF in a certain direction. The null direction differs by about 180° from the preferred direction. The ERF of layer-2a neurons is somewhat larger than that of layer-2 neurons. The diameter of the ERF is 9–12°.

4. *Layer-3 units*—Whereas the layer-2 neurons show only a brief response to the *on* and *off* of diffuse light, the response of layer-3 neurons is sustained. Some of these neurons respond with an *on*-activation, lasting about 0.5–1 sec; but most of them have an *off*-activation, maintained for about 0.5 to 1.5 sec after the light stimulus has been turned off. If a small dark stimulus dot 2.8° in diameter (with contrast −0.94) is moved in small steps through the ERF, the response to each step is

254   URSULA GRÜSSER-CORNEHLS AND WERNER HIMSTEDT

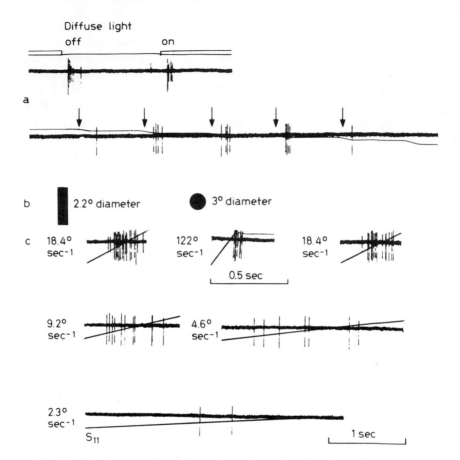

Fig. 18. (a) Response in *Salamandra salamandra* of a layer-2 or short *on-off* neuron to the on-and-off of diffuse light. (b) Response of the same neuron to a black stimulus 3° in diameter moved in steps through the ERF. Arrows indicate where movement begins. (c) Response of the same unit to different velocities of a black bar 2.2° in diameter and 20° in height and a black spot 3° in diameter. Stimulus-background $C = 0.94$. Figure 18 shows a decrease in the discharge rate with a decrease in velocity. (Reproduced from Grüsser-Cornehls and Himstedt, 1973.)

sustained. In the center of the ERF, where the sensitivity is greatest, the response lasts for about 4–6 sec. The size of the ERF of these cells is 10–20°.

Dependence of Retinal Discharge upon Stimulus Parameters

The following discussion is based on the results of quantitative measurements made in *Salamandra salamandra* (Grüsser-Cornehls and Himstedt, 1973). In these experiments, the animals were placed in the perimeter apparatus described by Grüsser and Dannenberg (1965), so that the eye of the animal contralateral to the recording site was centered within the perimeter. The stimuli were stationary or moving objects visible in a $23° \times 23°$ window of the perimeter at a distance of 27 cm from the eye. The following parameters of the stimulus could be varied:

1. The size, A, of the round or rectangular stimuli (black on a white background, contrast -0.94, or white on black background, contrast $+0.94$).

2. The contrast, C, between the moved stimulus and the background (round stimuli of constant size, but different shades of gray on a white background). $C - (I_s - I_b)/(I_s + I_b)$. I_s = stimulus luminance, I_b = background luminance. I_b was about 150 cd/m² for all the experiments to be described.

3. The angular velocity, v, (0.05 to about 120° per sec) for round stimuli of constant size and contrast (black on white).

4. Position of the stimulus pattern in the RF.

ANGULAR SIZE. The dependence of discharge rate upon angular size of the stimulus was investigated in detail only for the layer-2 and -2a neurons. If the size of a stimulus moving through the ERF is varied, it is found that the mean discharge rate is a function of stimulus size, as Hartline (1940b) first described for the ganglion cells of the frog retina applying stationary stimuli. For stimuli smaller than the ERF, it holds that

$$\bar{R} = k_2 \log A/A_s \qquad \text{(impulses sec}^{-1}) \qquad (3)$$

where A_s is the threshold area. For black spots on a white background, A_s amounts to 1–2° for layer-2 and -2a neurons and 0.02° for layer-3 neurons. If the stimulus size exceeds that of the ERF of layer-2 and -2a neurons, the mean discharge rate decreases, indicating the presence of an IRF. In this case, the relationship between $\bar{R}$ and A is given by:

$$\bar{R} = \bar{R}_{max} - k^* \log A/A_s \qquad \text{(impulses sec}^{-1}) \qquad (4)$$

where the declining slope k^*, under our stimulus conditions, was not always identical to k_2 in Eq. (3). k^* is a direct measure of the strength of the inhibitory influences from the surround. As can be seen in Figs 18 and 19, the layer-2 neurons show no marked inhibitory surround; a black stripe, 2.4° wide and 20° high, produces almost the same activation in most neurons as does a black round stimulus 3° in diameter.

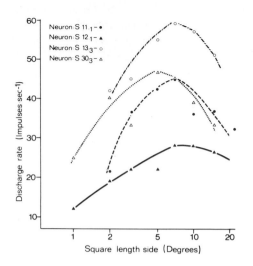

Fig. 19. Relationship in *Salamandra salamandra* between the size of the black square stimulus and the average impulse frequency of four different single layer-2 neurons. Stimulus velocity = 18.5° sec⁻¹, contrast = 0.94.

Figure 19 shows the relationship between the size of black, rectangular stimuli and the mean discharge rate, for three different layer-2 neurons.

CONTRAST BETWEEN STIMULUS AND BACKGROUND. Stimuli of different shades of gray, moved on a white background, were used to measure the contrast-response curve. The threshold of the layer-2 neurons is at a contrast of about 0.25, and that for the layer-3 neurons at a contrast of less than 0.05 when stimulus spots 2.8° in diameter are used. The neuronal discharges increase with increased contrast between the gray, moving stimulus and the white background (Fig. 20).

ANGULAR VELOCITY. If the discharge rate of the neurons is measured at different angular velocities of the stimulus, contrast and stimulus size (smaller than the ERF) remaining constant, the discharge rate can be shown to increase with angular velocity. The relationship between discharge rate and angular velocity can be described by a power-law relationship:

$$\bar{R} = k_1 v^c \qquad \text{(impulses sec⁻¹)} \qquad (5)$$

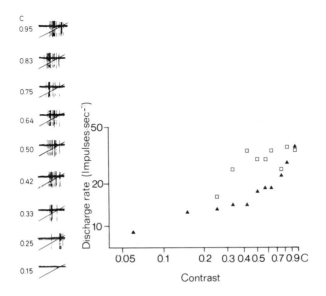

Fig. 20. *Left-hand side.* Original recording in *Salamandra salamandra* of a layer-2 neuron responding to a moving stimulus 3.1° in diameter and of varying shades of gray. Velocity of moving spot, 18.4° sec⁻¹. *Right-hand side:* relationship between the different stimulus-background contrast and the average impulse frequency for the same layer-2 neuron (open square) and for a layer-3 neuron (filled triangle). Stimulus velocity of the layer-3 neuron = 9.6° sec⁻¹. Calculation of contrast: $C = (I_s - I_b)/(I_s + I_b)$; I_s = stimulus luminance, I_b = background luminance.

where $\bar{R}$ is the mean discharge rate, k_1 is a constant, and v is the angular velocity of the stimulus. The exponent c is significantly different for the various classes of neurons. The mean exponent in Eq. 5 for layer-1 units is 0.7; for layer-2 units, 1.4, for layer-2a neurons, 1.1; and for layer-3 neurons, 0.85. The exponent for the layer-2 neurons holds only for angular velocities between 1 and 50°/sec. For angular velocities between 50 and 120°/sec, the response of the layer-2 neurons continues to increase with increasing angular velocity, but the slope of the curve is less. Figure 21 shows the relationship between the angular velocity of a moving stimulus and the discharge rate for the layer-2 and layer-3 neurons.

POSITION OF THE STIMULUS IN THE RECEPTIVE FIELD. It is true of all types of retinal neurons of *Salamandra* that with stepwise movement of a stimulus through the ERF, the activation produced by the stimulus increases, the closer the stimulus approaches the center of the field; that

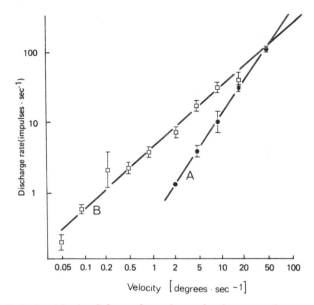

Fig. 21. Relationship in *Salamandra salamandra* between the average impulse frequency and velocity. *Curve A:* Mean value curve with standard deviation for 11 layer-2 neurons. Stimuli: black spot 3.1° in diameter (6 neurons), black square 5° in side length (4 neurons), black bar 20° in height and 2.4° in diameter (1 neuron). The regression line is given by the equation $R = 0.51v^{1.4}$. *Curve B:* Mean value curve with regression line and standard deviation of 5 layer-3 neurons. Stimulus: black spot 3.1° in diameter. Equation of regression line, $R = 4.2v^{0.85}$.

is, the excitation is greatest in the ERF center and declines toward its periphery.

SPECTRAL SENSITIVITY. The spectral sensitivity of layer-2 neurons was determined by measurement of the threshold intensity for the *on* and *off* responses (Himstedt and Fischerleitner, 1974). Sensitivity is expressed as the inverse of the relative number of quanta in a light stimulus which just produces action potentials. The sensitivity maximum of most layer-2 neurons is in the yellow, (at about 560 nm), for both the *off* and the *on* response. In 6 out of 42 neurons, however, dichromatic behavior could be demonstrated. In these fibers, the *on* response had a maximum in the blue, and the *off* response a maximum in the yellow. In green light, at about 510 nm, the two curves intersect (see Fig. 22). It is known from the investigations of Reuter (1969) and Reuter and Virtanen (1972) that the green rods of the frog retina have a spectral sensitivity maximum at 433 nm, while that of the cones is at 560 nm. Thus, one may

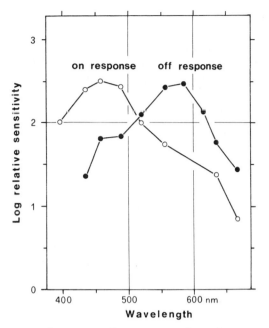

Fig. 22. Responses of a spectrally opponent layer-2 neuron of *Salamandra salamandra*. Open circles: spectral sensitivity of the *on* response; filled circles: spectral sensitivity of the *off* response.

also assume that the dichromatic neurons of the salamander retina receive excitation both from the blue-sensitive green rods and from the yellow-sensitive cones.

Central Visual System: Electrophysiology

Retinotectal Projections

In *Triturus*, there is an orderly topographic projection of the retina upon the optic tectum, similar to that described by Gaze (1958a) for the anurans (Cronly-Dillon and Galand, 1966; Cronly-Dillon, 1968). In *Salamandra salamandra*, too, an orderly retinotopic projection of the fibers from the contralateral retina upon the optic tectum was found (Grüsser-Cornehls and Himstedt, 1973). The lower part of the upper, nasal quadrant of the visual field projects to the lateral part, and the upper part of the upper, temporal quadrant projects to the medial part of the tectum.

In contrast to most of the retinal neurons, the ganglion cells in the tectum frequently show spontaneous activity, especially those cells located in the deeper tectal layers. The following neuron types were found in *Salamandra salamandra* (Grüsser-Cornehls and Himstedt, 1973): In the superficial layers of the optic tectum, between the afferent layers of the layer-2 and layer-3 neurons, action potentials of tectal neurons with very large receptive fields were often recorded. Their ERF extended over about 100–120°, from the nasal border of the visual field toward the temporal side. The ERFs of most of these neurons lay in the lower quadrant, with their upper boundary corresponding about to the horizontal plane of the visual field of the animal. The neurons can be excited both by small, moving stimuli, 1–2° in diameter, and by large stimuli. The sensitivity is uniform over the whole ERF. These "large-field neurons" may be efferent fibers of tectal neurons, or afferent fibers from nontectal regions in the visual centers of the salamander. Because their ERFs are so large, one may rule out with a high degree of probability that the fibers of these neurons come from the retina. Similar neurons have been found in *Triturus*, but these responded to stimulation in the upper half of the visual field (Cronly-Dillon and Galand, 1966). From the reports of Cronly-Dillon and Galand, it is not clear whether these neurons could also be recorded in the lower half of the visual field. These large-field cells of *Triturus* could not be recorded in the optic nerve.

Beneath the three superficial fiber layers, one finds units of the following types: (a) Neurons with receptive fields 10–20° in diameter, activated by stimuli moved from the surround into the RF. Repeated movement within the ERF produces no further reaction, which indicates a rapid neuronal adaptation ("newness" neurons, cf. Lettvin *et al.*, 1959). (b) Neurons that respond especially when an object is moved so as to approach the eye (i.e., along the z-axis), whereas the movement of the stimulus in the z-axis away from the eye elicits little or no response. The response to movement perpendicular to the z-axis is weak, though not as weak as that in similar neurons found in the optic tectum of the frog or toad (Grüsser and Grüsser-Cornehls, 1970). (c) Neurons with very large RFs (larger than 30° in diameter). These neurons respond to all objects larger than 1° moved through the ERF. In some of them, the RF amounts to the entire visual field of the eye (i.e., they are "generalizers"). Others have an oval shaped RF. The neurons frequently display a varying response to diffuse light turned on and off. (d) Binocular neurons, which also respond preferentially to moving stimuli. The ERF spans the entire visual field of the two eyes. (e) Finally, there are neurons reflecting more than one sensory modality, which are located primarily in the deeper tectal layers. Either these cells do not always respond to moving or stationary visual stimuli, or they may require more sophisticated stimulus patterns than those available in our experiments. Such neurons respond to vibration (whole body) and to tactile stimulation of the skin. No auditory influence could be found. This result is in accordance with the fact that the urodeles lack both tympanum and middle ear, but show, like all amphibians, a well-developed musculus opercularis that connects the suprascapula with the operculum and serves to transmit vibrations from the ground via the forelegs to the perilymph (Noble, 1931; Smith, 1968).

All the experiments described in *Salamandra* were done with low-impedance, metal electrodes. It seems probable that, as in the frog's tectum opticum, further classes of tectal neurons exist than those described in the preceding section. Recent studies in our Berlin laboratory indicate that when one records with ultrafine micropipettes, responses of other classes of tectal cells can be measured which are not obtainable with low-impedance metal electrodes (George, 1975; Grüsser and Grüsser-Cornehls, 1976).

URODELES AND COMPARATIVE NEUROBIOLOGY OF THE VISUAL SYSTEM

When one compares the different responses obtained in the retinal neurons of frogs and salamander, one obtains evidence that despite similar, basic principles for the signal processing within the retinal network, different types of retinal ganglion cells are developed during the phylogenesis of the different species. These different neuronal classes appear to serve different filter functions with respect to the visual stimuli present in the natural habitat of each species. However, only restricted information about the multiple mapping of the visual world into the responses of the different classes of retinal ganglion cells and tectal cells of urodeles is available. In addition, important morphological information about the dendritic branching and the distribution of synaptic contacts at the different levels of the inner plexiform layer is missing. This information exists for the anuran retina from the work of Ramón y Cajal (1894), which led to the first attempts to correlate the classes of ganglion cells found in neurophysiological experiments with morphological classes (Maturana *et al.*, 1960; Lettvin *et al.*, 1959).

Responses of Retinal Ganglion Cells in Different Urodeles

In contrast to the members of the family *Rana*, which remain mostly within a very restricted habitat with respect to their prey-catching behavior, the terrestrial urodeles, which are active during darkness or reduced illumination, behave in a manner similar to that of many members of the family *Bufo*. They are active hunters and wander throughout a considerable range of their habitat in search of prey. Urodeles like the *Triturus vulgaris* also seem to have a neuronal organization of their retinal output signals similar to that of toads. Cronly-Dillon and Galand (1966) and Cronly-Dillon, (1968) described four classes of ganglion cells for the Triturus retina which resemble rather closely those found in *Bufo bufo* (Grüsser and Grüsser-Cornehls, 1969, 1970, 1972; see Chapter 5 also): "convexity detectors," "boundary detectors," "changing contrast detectors," and "darkness detectors."

On the other hand, the classes of retinal ganglion cells found in experiments with *Salamandra salamandra* exhibit more similarity in their responses to the classes found in the goldfish retina by Cronly-Dillon (1964) and Jacobson and Gaze (1964). No afferent fibers, which respond similarly to class 1 and class 2 ganglion cells of the anuran retina, were found in the superficial layers of the optic tectum of *Salamandra*, as in the goldfish.

The class 1 and class 2 neuron responses cannot be separated in all anurans. In some anurans even, only one type of these neuronal classes seems to be present. (Grüsser-Cornehls and Lüdcke, 1970; Grüsser-Cornehls and Himstedt, 1973). It seems, therefore, more adequate to assume, as a general framework, three main neuronal classes of the anuran retinotectal input, which might be subdivided in certain species into further subclasses with respect to size or color-contrast specificity (Grüsser-Cornehls, 1973; Grüsser-Cornehls and Saunders, 1975). This "anuran" retinotectal input pattern seems to be present in those urodeles with a highly differentiated retina and exhibits correspondingly differentiated visual behavior. In the more primitive or "degenerate" visual systems of aquatic urodeles (e.g., *Necturus*) and in the salamander, a more "fish-like" retinotectal input pattern seems to be present.

Neuronal Specialization and Morphology

The highly specialized neuronal subsystems in the anuran retina might be explained by the differentiation of the ganglion cells, their dendritic trees (Ramón y Cajal, 1894) and the specialization of the synaptic contacts (Dowling, 1968, 1970). Especially, the type of contacts between bipolar cells, amacrines, and ganglion cells seems to be a good indicator for the degree of retinal subspecialization. Kidd (1961, 1962) and Dubin (1970) also stated, for other vertebrate retinae, that the frequency of conventional synapses increases as the specialization of the retina increases. Dowling repeatedly indicated that the specialization of the retinal network correlates with the frequency of amacrine-amacrine dyads. In the "simple" retina of monkeys, for example, 80% of the dyads are of the amacrine-ganglion cell type, while in the highly specialized frog retina, 75% of the dyads are amacrine-amacrine dyads. The majority of the frog's retinal ganglion cells therefore act as the fourth neuron in the chain: receptor-bipolar-amacrine-ganglion cell and not as the third neuron in the "classical" chain: receptor-bipolar-ganglion cell. This three-neuron chain is typical of the retina in higher mammals.

Similar to the *Necturus* retina, Witkovsky and Dowling (1969) found for the inner plexiform layer of the carp retina 50% amacrine-amacrine dyads and 50% amacrine-ganglion cell dyads. If this correlation between neuronal specificity and the types of dyad synapses in the inner plexiform layer is valid, one should predict for the *Triturus* retina a higher percentage of amacrine-amacrine dyads than for the *Necturus* and salamander retina. We hope that this hypothesis will be tested in the near future.

Comparison of Quantitative Data of the Anuran and the Urodele Retina

Quantitative data about the dependency of the neuronal activity on the different parameters of moving visual stimulus patterns have been thus far obtained in urodeles only for the retinal ganglion cells, which have their endings in the superficial layers of the optic tectum. The essential parameters which were found to determine the neuronal impulse rate of the different classes of anuran retinal ganglion cells determine also the responses of the ganglion cells of the salamander: *Position* of the moving stimulus within the receptive field, *angular size, contrast, angular velocity,* and *rate of repetition* of the movement of the stimulus across the same path through the receptive field. Despite considerable differences in the overall functional organization of the retinal neurons, the quantitative data about the effect of these parameters on the neuronal responses are comparable. An example is given in Table 1. The velocity function of the neuronal response is well described by the power function:

$$\bar{R} = k_1 v^c \quad \text{(impulses sec}^{-1})$$

where $\bar{R}$ is the average neuronal impulse rate and k_1 and c are constants. As Table 1 indicates, the range of the exponent c of this power function found for different classes of ganglion cells of the anuran retina is similar to the range of the exponent c in the salamander retina. In other words, the differentiation of the retina for the detection of the velocity of an object moving in the visual surround of a salamander is, within the behaviorally significant range, no less well developed than in the frog retina.

The data presented in Table 1 are statistically, significantly different, and were obtained with the same set of stimuli. Therefore, the differences between the neuronal classes and individual species, reflect differences in the neuronal signal-processing by the neuronal networks.

Neurophysiological-Behavioral Correlations

As mentioned above, the responses obtained from the fibers of retinal axons in the salamander indicate that the filter function of the retinal network with respect to the visual input is less specific than in the anuran retina. Therefore, it is not surprising that the correlations between retinal, neuronal activity and behavioral findings are less close than for the frogs and toads. For example, the threshold velocity of prey, above which prey-catching is elicited, is significantly higher than the velocity threshold found in single units of layer-3 neurons. On the other hand, one has to assume that the activity of layer-3 neurons of the salamander's retina is involved in the triggering of the first step of prey-catching behavior ("fixation" and "approaching"), because only this class of retinal ganglion cell provides the neurophysiological basis for the visual acuity found in behavioral investigations.

The comparison of the behavioral and the electrophysiological data demonstrates that no class of retinal units performs a selective "recognition" of the main prey of the salamander (slowly moving snails and worms). All types of retinal neurons might be activated by one and the same stimulus. Units of layer 3 might be especially suited for the recog-

Table 1. Comparison of the Exponents of the Velocity Function for Different Classes of Retinal Ganglion Cells and Different Species[a]

Exponent c	Class 1	Class 2	Class 3	Class 4
Rana esculenta	0.5	0.7	0.95[b]	1.0[b]
Bufo bufo		0.7	1.0–1.2[b]	1.1
Hyla septentrionalis		0.5	0.97[b]	0.8–1.0[b]
	layer 1		layer 2	layer 3
Salamandra	0.7[b]		1.1–1.4[b]	0.86[b]

[a] From Grüsser-Cornehls and Himstedt, 1973.
[b] Black stimulus, white background.

nition of small objects (worms) moving slowly at a distance of 10–20 cm. As the salamander approaches its prey, the main group of layer-2 and layer-2a neurons will start to respond to the same stimulus, because the same prey has now a larger angular size and a higher angular velocity. The assumption of such a functional differentiation and sequential neuronal activation is supported by the neurophysiological findings that the contrast and velocity threshold of layer-3 neurons is lower than that of layer-2 neurons. Correspondingly, Himstedt (1967, and unpublished results) found in behavioral experiments a lower contrast and velocity threshold for "fixation" and "approaching" of the prey than for snapping. The steep slope of the velocity function of layer-2 neurons (Fig. 21) indicates narrow filter functions for the discrimination of prey moving slowly at a short distance.

As discussed above, no neurons having a small ERF and a strong IRF comparable to class-2 neurons ("bug detectors") of some species of frogs were found in the salamandra retina. Since the animal's head is constantly moving during its search for prey, however, such a class of neurons would not be a very useful addition to its visual system, because a larger structured pattern in the visual surround would always activate the IRF and, therefore, would prevent the response of such units. Because of the weaker inhibitory effect elicited by stimulus patterns moved across the IRF of the main layers (layer 2, 2a, and 3) of the salamander's retina, a shift of the whole visual world across the retina (for example, by eye or head movement) would activate the retinal neurons and enable the animals to perceive the stationary visual world. However, it would not prevent the perception of a smaller object (snail or worm) moving at a different speed against or with the background. Another good correlation between neurophysiological and behavioral findings is established by the experiments on the spectral sensitivity of layer-2 neurons and the corresponding behavioral measurements of prey-catching elicited by color-contrast stimuli (Himstedt, 1972; Himstedt and Fischerleitner, 1974). The responses of the blue-yellow ganglion cells might be the cause of the poor color discrimination within the green part of the spectrum in the salamander.

In summary, one can draw similar conclusions from the neurophysiological-behavioral correlations found for the retinotectal system of the salamander as for the frog's retina (Grüsser and Grüsser-Cornehls, 1970, 1972, 1973, 1976). The retinal network performs filter functions well adapted to the behavioral demands of the animal. There is, however, no indication that highly specialized pattern recognition such as selective detection of prey and enemy occurs up to the output level of the retina. For the salamander, it is likely that the degree of activation of the single afferent retinal neurons, which have their endings in the different super-ficial tectal layers, varies in the different stages of prey-catching action.

ACKNOWLEDGMENTS

We wish to thank Professor O.-J. Grüsser for his valuable advice on the manu-script, Dr. Ann Biedermann-Thorson for the careful translation of the main parts of Chapter 6, as well as Mrs. J. Dames, Miss E. Krebs and Miss H. Wolynski for their careful technical assistance.

7

The Amphibian Visual System as a Model for Developmental Neurobiology

M. J. Keating and C. Kennard

INTRODUCTION

The processes controlling brain development require, for an adequate description, a fusion of concepts deriving from developmental biology with those emerging from neurobiology. Developmental neurobiology possesses as its base, therefore, the general principles of embryology; but to these must be added special features related to the ontogeny of those aspects of cellular and intercellular organization unique to neural structures.

The generation of cellular diversity, in which different cell types are produced from common precursers, is a dominant feature of development. In no organ is the diversity of cellular differentiation so apparent as in the brain with its large numbers of highly characteristic neuronal populations. Developmental neurobiology must, therefore, face the general problems of differentiation. What mechanisms segregate neural tissue from nonneural tissue? What are the triggers and interactions that commit cells to the differential patterns of gene activity that are reflected in overt cellular differentiation? One of the major thrusts of developmental biology at the present is aimed at the unraveling of the molecular events associated with a particular course of cell differentiation. The dramatic advances in this field have contributed greatly to our understanding of development, but have sometimes given the impression that studies at the molecular level will suffice to explain satisfactorily all developmental phenomena.

Ontogeny, however, is not complete when the requisite number of terminally differentiated cells have been produced. These cells have to occupy the correct parts of the organism and maintain appropriate intercellular relationships with each other. These more complex levels of supracellular organization, therefore, also require explanation. The imposition of spatial order and pattern implicit in the development of all organs reaches its peak in the ordering of neural structure in the brain. Discrete neuronal populations adopt positions in precisely delineated areas of the mature brain as a result of selective proliferation, migration, and even cell death. The anatomic relationships of various neuronal phenotypes and their processes to each other and to the nonneuronal cell types are exquisitely controlled. The principles involved in the cooperative cellular behavior that produces tissues and organs are understood only in the most general terms. Better understanding of spatial ordering, histogenesis, and organogenesis is required before useful questions about these processes can be answered at the molecular level.

An aspect of intercellular relationship that is at once both unique to neural tissue and fundamental to the normal operation of neural function is the formation of specialized contacts, i.e., synapses, between neurons themselves or between neurons and effector structures. A problem specific to developmental neurobiology is the elucidation of the factors responsible for synaptogenesis. Two aspects of synaptogenesis have to be explained. First, there are those features responsible for synaptogenesis itself, the localization and production of the structures associated with the pre- and postsynaptic sites. The second aspect to be accounted for is that of selective synaptic relationships. Neural elements are not randomly interconnected, but instead display a high selectivity in the formation of synaptic contacts. The control mechanisms governing this process must reflect the high degree of spatial order evident in normal synaptic relationships.

A growing brain, the basic synaptic circuits of which have been fashioned by innate epigenetic processes, is capable of a functional interaction with the sensorimotor environment. A second type of developmental control process then becomes operationally feasible. This is a mechanism that could use neural activity, or the products of neural activity, to mold or modulate further neural development. The extent to which this available mechanism is, in fact, utilized in brain maturation is controversial. What cannot be doubted is that, in one sense at least, brain development does not cease with the onset of normal neural function. The existence of memory implies a change in neural function (if not in neural structure) as a result of experience. The way or ways in which environmental stimuli modify the brain either during normal development or during learning situations remains a very active field of neurobiological investigation, the findings in which are, in our opinion, clearly relevant to the discipline of developmental neurobiology.

Experiments carried out on amphibians have played a major role in providing data on which modern developmental biological concepts are based. This is particularly true of studies on neurogenesis in which the amphibian visual system has proved particularly useful. During embryonic and larval stages, the developing brain is accessible to experimental intervention so that the effects of perturbation of the system may be studied. The high degree of spatial order of the synaptic connections linking the eye to the brain and the ability of the optic nerve to regenerate after section made the amphibian visual system the prime model for the study of the genesis of synaptic pattern. This chapter will review some of the ways in which investigations on the amphibian visual system have contributed to present views of neural development.

GENERAL CONCEPTS: INDUCTION, DETERMINATION, AND DIFFERENTIATION; REGULATION, FIELDS, AND POSITIONAL INFORMATION

The point the introduction sought to make was that the development of the brain is merely a special case of organ development. Naturally, therefore, many of the processes involved are merely special examples of general embryological processes. To appreciate some of the issues raised by current work on the amphibian visual system, it is necessary to understand, in general terms, some of the embryological concepts being applied to this special situation.

Unfortunately, embryology abounds with terms coined to describe rather poorly understood events. The terms can, therefore, be defined only loosely if at all and, consequently, are used in different senses by different authors. The sense in which some of these common terms will be used in this chapter is now outlined briefly.

The elaboration of an adult organism from the unicellular zygote involves the production by cell division of a large number of cellular elements and the compartmentalization, among these cellular elements, of discrete properties and functions. Very early proliferative events generate the three "primary germ layers"—ectoderm, mesoderm and endoderm. The further epigenetic events involved in the differential allocation of cellular function involve interactions between these germ layers and between specific subdivisions of them. The term induction is given to those processes by which one tissue interacts with a second, adjacent tissue to influence the developmental pathway followed by the cells of that second tissue. One of the earliest inductive interactions is that between chordamesoderm and the overlying ectoderm that results in the latter producing a sheet of cells, the neural plate, which in turn will give rise to the nervous system. This process has been studied intensively for over 50 years, but is still very inadequately understood. The greater part of this work has been done on amphibians (recently reviewed by Deuchar, 1972), but little more will be said of it here since, although the events taking place are critical to the subsequent production of a visual system, they necessarily predate such a system.

These early inductive phenomena delimit the precursors of neuronal and glial cells. Further degrees of functional specialization gradually emerge among the progeny of the precursors, frequently as the result of more localized inductive interactions. During ontogeny, the developmental capacity of a given cell line, that is, the range of cell types to which the progeny can give rise, is progressively restricted. The process by which a specific pathway of development is singled out from several possible routes has been termed determination. This term refers to a state of commitment of the cell or group of cells to generate, subsequently, a particular class of differentiated cells. The demonstration of such a commitment can be provided only by experimental interference with the system. Isolation experiments, in which a group of cells removed from the embryo nevertheless give rise to a differentiated tissue, provide evidence for such commitment at the time the isolation was performed. Transplantation experiments involve the placing of a group of cells in a foreign part of the embryo and observing whether or not in this situation they generate the same structure they would have produced in the original site. An ability to do so indicates the determined state of the group of cells at the time of transplantation. The difficulty of defining concepts such as determination is illustrated by the fact that a group of cells which appear to be determined in the context of an isolation experiment may show themselves to be undetermined in the context of a transplantation experiment. An example of just this situation will be discussed in a later section on the polarization of the eye.

The end result of determining cellular commitments is the production of the fully differentiated cells themselves. Once again, however, one faces in differentiation a term that can have many meanings. The essence of the concept is that relating to difference—the process of differentiation renders cells overtly different from each other. The problem centers on what one regards as "overt." Does one regard as differentiation the intermediate stages at which overt differences between cell groups are not obvious, but at which time operational differences between the groups demonstrate that separate developmental pathways have already been "determined" for them? Normal usage of the term differentiation, excludes these intermediate stages, and considers only the terminally differentiated state when the developmental pathway is complete. The older criteria of cell differentiation, such as cell size, cell shape, mobility, and mitotic activity (Weiss, 1939) have for most purposes been displaced by more biochemical criteria. These view the terminally differentiated state in terms of the specific macromolecules characteristic of that state; for example, hemoglobin, myoglobin, and chondroitin sulfate as the specific macromolecules of erythrocytes, muscle cells, and cartilage cells, respectively. The difficulty in adopting this type of criterion for neural differentiation is that while it is absolutely clear that, for example, a retinal ganglion cell is quite different from a bipolar cell, the specific macromolecules, if any, characteristic of each type of neuron are not known.

Another aspect of differentiation, which has become part of the concept by general agreement rather than by specific definition, is that which recognizes the process as reflecting differential gene activity. Holtzer *et al.* (1972) wrote that, "The central problem (of differentiation) relates to those endogenous mechanisms that make available in daughter cells genetic information that was not readily available in the mother cell." On this view, differentiation must involve either the selective loss of genetic material or the retention in differentiated cells of the entire genome, large parts of which are functionally repressed. Two types of experiments indicate that the latter view is correct. Thus, Gurdon (1960, 1962) transplanted the nucleus of an intestinal cell into an enucleated oocyte and demonstrated that the genetic material in that nucleus was capable of generating a tadpole. Recent developments in this field have been summarized by Gurdon (1974a,b). The second type of experiment is one which investigates the stability of the differentiated state. An example indicating that the genetic capacity of a differentiated cell is not necessarily restricted to one particular state of differentiation was provided by Stone (1950), who showed that under appropriate conditions the retinal pigment epithelial cells of urodeles were capable of generating neural retinal cells.

The particular differentiative pathway upon which a given cell embarks has been revealed by the techniques of classical embryology to be dependent upon the location of a precursor cell at a critical developmental stage. Those mechanisms governing this spatial ordering of differentiation frequently possess, in early developmental stages, a remarkable property. If material is either removed or added to early embryos, a single embryo nevertheless results (Spemann, 1928). At a similar and later stage, if material that would normally contribute to the formation of a particular organ is removed, adjacent embryonic material, which in the normal course of events would contribute to the formation of another organ, is diverted to constitute the missing parts. Thus, if the presumptive eye region is removed from the neural plate, the remaining neural plate is nevertheless able to constitute an eye (Adelmann, 1929a). The term regulation is given to this ability of embryonic tissue to reconstitute its normal pattern in the face of either deletion or addition. The empirical observations that the site of a precursor determined the future differentiation of its progeny were combined with those showing embryonic regulative behavior, in the observation of Driesch (1908) "Development of a part is a function of its position in relation to the whole." The term embryonic field was used to denote those processes believed to be responsible for this observed spatial ordering of differentiation in regulative systems. A necessary property of these postulated fields was, therefore, the ability to restore themselves, following perturbation, to their original form. The properties of these conceptual entities, fields, have been discussed extensively (Huxley and de Beer, 1934; Weiss, 1939; Child, 1941; Waddington, 1956, 1966; Cooke, 1975).

In those animals, such as echinoderms and amphibians, in which regulative phenomena are easily demonstrable during development (and one has to remember that in annelids, mollusks, and ascidians little regulation can be shown after early segmentation of the egg), the development of the embryo passes through progressive organizational phases. In early phases removal of material is compensated by regulative phenomena with restitution of the complete structure. This early regulative phase is followed by a phase in which removal of material results in permanent defects. This latter developmental period is called the mosaic phase. The transition from regulative to mosaic modes of development, which implies the extinction of the postulated field responsible for the regulative behavior, occurs at different times for different levels of organization within the embryo. Thus, at a time when the overall embryonic field has ceased to exist, regulative phenomena are still demonstrable at the level of future organ formation and, at a later time, when the formation of the particular organ has passed into a mosaic phase, certain substructures within the organ may still display regulative behavior. These empirical observations lead to the concept of a heirarchy of fields, with the spatial extent of successive levels of the heirarchy becoming progressively more local. The time at which regulative development becomes mosaic for any particular structure is usually very early, long before the onset of differentiation in that structure. Thus, although at neural plate stages there is the evidence of regulative capacity already cited, by the succeeding neural tube stage there is considerable evidence that the differentiative pathways open to the constituent neuroblasts are strictly circumscribed (Holtzer, 1951). In other words, the neural tube is strictly mosaic. Similar conclusions to those of Holtzer's amphibian studies were obtained from experiments on the chick neural tube (Wenger, 1950; Watterson and Fowler, 1953; Watterson, 1965). Our purpose in laboring this matter is that a current controversy on the mechanisms controlling synaptogenesis in the retinotectal system centers on the period of development of the structure during which it is reasonable to expect regulative phenomena to operate. Field phenomena occurring in adult vertebrates are restricted to those situations in which ablation of the structure is followed by its regeneration. The ordered regeneration of a limb, for example, requires control mechanisms presumably similar to those operating in early development. Once again, however, regulative phenomena in the regenerating limb bud will cease before overt differentiation of limb structures is apparent.

In an attempt to clarify some of the issues and mechanisms involved in the concept of embryonic field, Wolpert (1969, 1971) has introduced the notion of "positional information," as the information which provides a cell with a knowledge of its spatial position relative to a group of cells within a given boundary. The cell must be capable of interpreting this positional information and, as a result of this interpretation, of setting out upon a particular course of differentiation. The regulative phenomena in development, in the context of this theory, reflect the ability of cells

within a given area to change the positional information so as to reconstitute the boundary and intermediate values of that information. The
interpretation by the individual cells of the changed value of the positional information to which they are exposed will result in that cell
following a different course of development; however, the overall structure generated from the positional information will be normal. Wolpert
felt that the mechanisms specifying positional information might well be
common to the development of many different structures, with morphological diversity resulting from differential interpretation of common
positional information.

The nature and factors controlling the distribution of this positional
information together with the mechanisms by which cells recognize and
interpret the information remain a very challenging field for the whole
of developmental biology.

THE DEVELOPMENT OF THE EYE

Examples of the ways in which studies on the developing amphibian
eye may be used to illustrate some of the concepts discussed in the previous section will now be described.

Induction

An interaction between the mesodermal archenteron roof and the
overlying ectoderm produces, as has been shown, the neural plate. Saxén
(1961) made the intriguing observation that this process could occur even
if the interacting tissues were separated by a Millipore filter. A question
pertinent to the development of an eye is whether further, and perhaps
more local, interactions between the underlying mesoderm and the neural
plate are necessary to produce functional subdivisions of the developing
neural plate into different brain structures. The available evidence seems
to support this view (Dalcq, 1946; Nieuwkoop, 1950; Waddington and
Yao, 1950), and it does seem that the prechordal plate of the mesoderm
is critical to the normal development of the forebrain and paired eyes
(Adelmann, 1937). For further discussion of the nature of the mesoder-
mal-ectodermal interaction responsible for the localization of brain structures in the neural plate, see Saxén and Toivonen (1962), Toivonen and
Saxén (1968), and Toivonen (1972).

The prechordal plate is responsible not only for the actual induction
of presumptive ocular tissue, but also for the suppression of eye formation
in the median plane. In normal development, presumptive eye tissue in

the rostral region of the neural plate separates into two anlage, which come to lie on the lateral aspects of the wall of the primitive forebrain. If the prechordal plate is removed from an early neurula, this process of separation does not occur and a single eye forms in the median position. The suspicion that inductive phenomenon, while specific in their effects, are nonspecific in their mechanisms (Toivonen, 1972) has been supported by the observation that median, cyclopean eyes can also occur by treatment of early embryos with a whole range of chemical agents such as lithium chloride, alcohol, etc. (Adelmann, 1936).

A later tissue interaction of the inductive class that has been extensively investigated is that which occurs when evagination of the optic vesicle brings this structure into contact with the overlying ectoderm. This contact leads to the formation of the lens. Spemann (1901) showed in *Rana fusca* that lens formation did not occur when the eye rudiment was removed prior to contact with the overlying ectoderm. The competence of ectoderm, other than that normally lying above the optic vesicle, to respond to the inductive influence of the vesicle was demonstrated, first, by transplanting eye rudiments beneath the ectoderm in different parts of the body (Lewis, 1904) and, second, by transplanting foreign ectoderm to the region overlying the eye primordium (Mangold, 1931). Conclusions deriving from many such studies (reviewed in Lopashov and Stroeva, 1964; Coulombre, 1965) included (1) that most regions of the early embryonic ectoderm are capable of transformation into lens tissue when appropriately stimulated and (2) that structures other than the eye rudiment are capable of inducing lens formation. Twitty (1955), however, recounts the considerable differences that can be obtained in lens induction between closely related anuran species. McKeehan (1958) showed in the chick that direct contact between the optic vesicle and the overlying ectoderm was not necessary for the inductive interaction.

Although the amphibian visual system has permitted extensive experimental investigation of various aspects of induction and has allowed fairly accurate descriptions of the phenomenon, neither the cellular nor the molecular basis of the interactions have been fully elucidated.

Morphogenetic Movements and Intercellular Affinities

The evagination of the optic vesicle and its subsequent invagination to form the optic cup represents an extensive series of morphogenetic movements. Such movements involve mechanical deformations and changes in affinities between tissue components. Differential cell affinities are now recognized as playing a crucial part in tissue and organ formation (Holtfreter, 1939; Townes and Holtfreter, 1955; Weiss and Taylor,

1960). The view that synaptic recognition is a specialized form of inter-cellular affinity is now widely held.

Mechanisms governing intercellular affinity processes have been studied in experiments in which disaggregated cells selectively reaggregate according to tissue type (Moscona, 1968; Steinberg, 1970). Another class of studies has observed the apparent reassembly of a jumble of different cell types in such a fashion as to simulate their normal histological tissue structure. Boterenbrood (1958) disaggregated the anterior neural plate into single cells which were then mixed and put on an ectodermal membrane. Normal-looking neural structures and isolated eyes formed and not just a mixture of the two structures. This type of histogenesis in tissue culture is a remarkable event, but some of the older descriptions must be viewed with caution (see Gaze, 1967).

Determination and Differentiation

The various steps by which a cell line achieves its final differentiated state are progressive stages in a continuous process. Vogt (1929) showed how the prospective fate of cells of very early embryonic stages may be identified by following the distribution of vital stains placed in different cells. Such a description does not, however, tell us at what stage, for example, a cell becomes committed to taking part in eye formation. If the prospective eye tissue is removed from an early amphibian gastrula and transplanted to, for example, the tail region of an older host, this tissue does not form an eye (Mangold, 1928, 1929). These experiments show that the prospective potency of cells exceed their prospective fate. Transplantation experiments at very early neural plate stages, however, did produce eyes (Adelmann, 1929b; Alderman, 1935). By the criterion of transplantation, then, cells of the newly apparent neural plate are already committed to the formation of an eye and are, therefore, determined. The processes of determination of an organ involve inductive interactions with other tissues, but after this stage the future formation of an organ is under its autonomous control. Thus, it has been shown that a primitive eye rudiment, removed at stage 22 from a *Xenopus* embryo, can be grown in tissue culture and develops into a normal eye (Frank, Hunt, Bergey, and Holtzer, cited in Hunt, 1975a). This does not mean, of course, that complex intertissue interactions have ceased at stage 22; such interactions continue but within the confines of the eye.

Once the lens has been induced, the retina begins to differentiate into its various cell classes. The inner layer of the optic cup is destined to form neural retina while the outer layer will become the pigment epithelium. There is ample evidence that the retinal and pigment layers of the optic cup can interchange their prospective fates (see Twitty, 1955). The inner layer eventually begins to differentiate into neural retina and at this time it loses its capacity to transform into pigment epithelium. This stability of the differentiated state in the neural retina is in marked contrast to that of the pigment epithelium layer. This latter is able to differentiate into retina in anurans until the onset of metamorphosis (Sato, 1953), and in urodeles this capacity exists throughout its whole life (Stone, 1950; Keefe, 1973).

Regulation and Positional Information

The ability of the neural plate to regulate after removal of the presumptive eye region was described in the previous section. The system permits normal eyes to develop after removal of part of the eye anlage at neural plate stages (Spemann, 1912) and also at much later stages, just before neural retinal differentiation begins (Berman and Hunt, 1975; Feldman and Gaze, 1975). Subsequently, more will be said about the regulative properties of the system. The way in which positional information concepts have been applied to the retinotectal system will also be described.

Regeneration of the Amphibian Eye

The urodele eye has the capacity to reconstruct itself after destruction or removal of the greater part of the eye. The attractions that such a regenerating system offers for the analysis of events such as dedifferentiation, redifferentiation, and tissue reorganization and replacement have been emphasized by Reyer (1962).

THE FORMATION OF SYNAPTIC CONNECTIONS BETWEEN THE EYE AND BRAIN

The Concept of Higher-Order Neuronal Specificity

The amphibian visual system has played the paramount role in the study of mechanisms governing the formation of selective neuronal connections. The credit for this must go to R. W. Sperry who, over thirty years ago, first recognized the suitability of the system for investigation of the problem, second, formulated the problem with remarkable clarity, and third, on the basis of simple and elegant experiments, reached conclusions that have dominated thinking on this subject ever since.

The two primary requirements of a preparation on which experimental analysis of selective synaptogenesis may profitably be performed are that it contains a system of spatially ordered synaptic connections and that the system may be perturbed and observed at a time when synaptic connections are forming. Sperry, in the early 1940's realized that the amphibian retinotectal system possessed these necessary attributes. The optic tectum is the neural structure responsible for the initiation of visually guided behavior such as prey localization and prey catching (see Kicliter, 1973b; and other chapters in this volume). A necessary substrate for this sort of behavior is that, in some form, a map of the visual world must be constructed in the optic tectum. This map is constructed by the simple expedient of arranging retinotectal connections in a precise spatial order such that a spatial map of the retina, and hence of the visual field of the eye, is produced across the surface of the optic tectum (Fig. 1). (The anatomic, behavioral, and electrophysiological evidence for this pattern of retinotectal connections is reviewed in other chapters). The requirement that the system permits observations at a time when synaptogenesis is occuring was originally satisfied owing to the remarkable ability to regenerate the optic nerve possessed by lower vertebrates, but lost by higher forms. Koppanyi (1923a,b) argued that optic nerve regeneration occurred after reimplantation and transplantation of amphibian eyes. He based his conclusion on the accurate localization of lures and on the reversal of the skin changes that follow blinding in these animals. The evidence of return of visual function in these papers was equivocal and the histological controls were inadequate. Matthey (1925, 1926) verified Koppanyi's conclusions and described the return of accurately localized visual behavior after optic nerve section or after heteroplastic

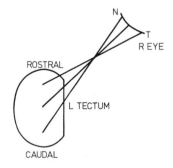

Fig. 1. Diagrammatic representation of the normal pattern of retinotectal connections from the right eye to the left optic tectum in lower vertebrates. The connections across only one axis of the system are shown; the horizontal (nasotemporal) retinal axis projects to the rostrocaudal tectal axis. N, nasal pole of retina; T, temporal pole of retina; R, right; L, left.

eye transplantation in urodeles. It would seem that the pattern of retinotectal connections that occurs during normal development can be restored
after retinal or optic nerve regeneration.

The problem to be explained in this situation of selective synaptic
connections is the differential behavior of the retinal ganglion cells. Why
do cells at the nasal pole of the retina behave so differently from those at
the temporal pole in the matter of selection of their target site in the
tectum? Sperry (1942, 1943a,b) addressed himself to this problem and
argued that this differential behavior of the retinal ganglion cells must
reflect either intrinsic differences between the ganglion cells themselves,
or the action upon a homogeneous population of retinal ganglion cells of
extrinsic influences that cause the axons of these cells to adopt their
normal spatial order. Two possible extrinsic influences, both popular at
the time that Sperry started his investigation of this problem, were the
functionally adaptive value of a connection and contact guidance. Those
who ascribed to function a formative role in the remolding of the nervous
system (e.g., Holt, 1931) suggested that neuronal connections were formed
initially at random; those connections persisted in which activity sub-
served a useful function while the remainder regressed. Sperry (1943a)
examined this hypothesis by rotating the eye of *Triturus viridescens*
through 180°. The immediate effect of this procedure was to cause the
animal to display inverted visuomotor localizing behavior. A lure presented at one point in the visual field, instead of evoking a strike response
aimed at the lure, resulted in a strike response at a point diametrically
opposite the lure position. If the system were capable of a functionally
adaptive reorganization of its connections, however, the animals should
have discarded their normal connections and generated new connections,
the pattern of which would have produced normal visuomotor behavior.
In fact, animals with a rotated eye showed no evidence of such an adjustment even after many months. Sperry concluded that no functionally
adaptive plasticity existed in the intact retinotectal system of urodeles.
It was possible, however, that such a plasticity would be demonstrable
during the formation of connections that would follow section and regeneration of the optic nerve. Sperry (1942; 1943b) therefore, repeated
his experiments on rotation of the eye in the newt, but this time he also
cut the optic nerve and allowed it to regenerate. From an analysis of the
behavioral effects of these procedures, Sperry argued that the character
of the recovered vision conformed in all cases to the orientation of the
retina. Visuomotor reactions were systematically inverted and reversed
in animals in which the eye had been rotated by 180°. Such functionally
maladaptive responses remained totally uncorrected until the death of the
animal. These results indicated that whatever factors governed the forma-

tion of visual synaptic connections after regeneration of the optic nerve, functionally adaptive value was not one of them. Any given retinal locus appeared to reestablish functional contact with its corresponding tectal position, regardless of the functional value to the animal of such contact (Fig. 2).

Sperry (1944) extended such observations to anuran amphibia with similar results. He showed also in that paper that the location of behavioral "scotomata" produced by localized tectal lesions was the same after optic nerve regeneration as it had been prior to optic nerve section. This furnished further evidence that regenerating optic fibers projected to the same tectal areas as those to which they had originally projected. These conclusions, based on behavioral data, have been confirmed electrophysiologically (Gaze, 1959; Maturana et al., 1959).

Various modifications of the eye rotation experiment were performed in amphibians (Stone, 1944; Sperry, 1945) and in teleosts (Sperry, 1948); comparable results were obtained. It was apparent that during ontogenesis functional relationships are established between specific areas of the retina and specific areas of the tectum; furthermore, these same functional relationships are restored during nerve regeneration.

This latter finding also militated against the second possible extrinsic mechanism for the ordering of retinotectal connections—that of mechanical contact guidance of optic nerve fibers to their correct tectal sites along channels in the microenvironment between the eye and the tectum. This view, emphasized by Weiss (1955), attributed the primary role in the

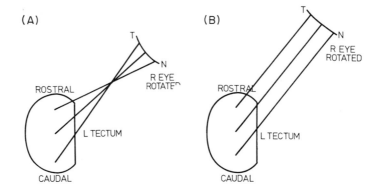

Fig. 2. (A) The pattern of connections, after rotation of the right eye by 180° and section and regeneration of the right optic nerve, that could be predicted on the basis of *either* functionally adaptive value of a connection *or* mechanical guidance. (B) The actual pattern of connections, from the right eye to the left tectum, that is found after rotation of the right eye by 180° and section and regeneration of the right optic nerve.

orientation of nerve fibers to microstructural interfaces in the medium surrounding the nerve fiber. That such general guiding factors are operative in the general orientation of nerve fibers cannot be disputed. Whether they are of sufficient discrimination, however, to produce alone the very highly ordered retinotectal projection must be doubted. In fact, such channels should produce, after eye rotation and optic nerve section, the pattern of connections seen in Fig. 2a, rather than the actual result obtained (Fig. 2b). In urodeles, regeneration is frequently delayed due to the degeneration and subsequent regeneration of the retina. By the time the new optic axons begin to grow toward the brain, there is no trace left of the proximal stump of the optic nerve (Stone, 1930). In anurans, Sperry (1945) emphasized the erratic tortuous course followed by regenerating optic fibers through the region of the scar at the site of section of the optic nerve. For these reasons, mechanical contact guidance mechanisms were discarded as the primary mechanism ordering retinotectal connections.

The elimination of extrinsic influences such as functionally adaptive value and mechanical contact guidance as adequate mechanisms to account for the differential behavior of retinal ganglion cells led Sperry to postulate that ganglion cells and their optic axons must differ intrinsically from each other.

Sperry (1944, 1951, 1963, 1965) suggested that the overt differentiation evident in the retina represented only the tip of the iceberg. Differentiation did not stop at the production of a relatively homogeneous population of retinal ganglion cells. Superimposed upon this was a higher degree of differentiation such that ganglion cells acquired differences from each other, and these differences were spatially ordered according to the position of the ganglion cells in the developing retinal field. Individual retinal ganglion cells were thus highly specific as a result of a process of intrinsic differentiation, with such differences therefore being acquired early in the developmental life of the neuron.

The Chemoaffinity Hypothesis

Using the idea of high-order neuronal specificity as the basis of selective synaptic formation, Sperry speculated, in general terms, on the form this position-dependent differentiation may take and how such differentiation produced selective synaptic connections. As differentiation normally involves synthesis of specific macromolecules, or at least specifically different quantities of a given macromolecular species, it was entirely reasonable for Sperry to suggest that this proposed high-order differentiation similarly reflects the synthesis of cytochemical molecules that label the individual cell. In addition to the labeling of the retinal ganglion cells, a parallel differentiative labeling of the tectal elements to which optic fibers project was also postulated.

Labeled neuronal populations, however, must still interconnect. Sperry suggested that the cytochemical molecules labeling the cells were surface molecules which existed also on the axonal and dendritic processes of the neuron. Synaptic formation occurred only when the molecular interaction between the labels on the putative pre- and post synaptic sites produced a very high affinity between these elements. Incompatibly labeled cells experienced no such affinity and no synapses formed.

Sperry's composite hypothesis to account for selective synaptogenesis is called the chemoaffinity hypothesis (Sperry, 1963; 1965) and consists of four elements. (1) Neurons are intrinsically specific as a result of processes of differentiation. (2) As such, the events responsible for neuronal specification occur very early in the life of the neuron. (3) This difference is manifest by the synthesis of cytochemical labels. (4) The "rule" governing the formation of connections is a "selective and exclusive" one in which a presynaptic neuron ignores all postsynaptic targets other than those that possess the necessary complementary marker.

The way in which more recent work has contributed to our understanding of the processes participating in the various elements of the chemoaffinity hypothesis will now be considered. Although much of this work has been carried out on the amphibian visual system in order to clarify some of the arguments involved, it has been necessary to review work on the fish retinotectal system.

The Rules Governing the Interconnection of Differentiated Neuronal Arrays

Much work purporting to examine the chemoaffinity hypothesis has been performed since it was advanced. Confusion has arisen in some cases since it has not been made clear to which particular element of the hypothesis an experimental question was directed. Thus, the majority of the work has, in fact, been aimed at confirming or denying the proposed "rule of connection," although frequently the experiments have been presented as support, or lack of support, for the whole concept. Attardi and Sperry (1963) introduced a paradigm that seemed entirely appropriate on which to investigate whether the connections between retinal ganglion cells and tectal cells, seen in the normal animal, represented the only possible connections that the participating neurons could tolerate. The basic experimental strategy has been to produce relative size disparities between the retina and the tectum by removing portions of the retina or tectum. In the former case, the reduced number of presynaptic elements have the opportunity of spreading over a greater range of postsynaptic sites than are normally available to them. In the case of tectal deletion, reduced postsynaptic space is available to the innervating neurons. If the "selective and exclusive" rule of connections were correct, then the response of the retinotectal system to this disturbance should be the restitution of those normal retinotectal connections that are still possible. Attardi and Sperry (1963) described just this result after removing a retinal area and cutting the optic nerve in goldfish. Using the Bodian protargol technique to stain regenerating optic fibers, Attardi and Sperry found that after the nerve section fibers regenerating from the remaining retinal areas terminated only in those tectal areas which normally received input from those parts of the retina. Tectal areas corresponding to the ablated portions of retina did not receive optic terminals. It appeared that a retinal ganglion cell would seek out its tectal counterpart and link with it regardless of the presence of large uninnervated areas of the tectum. The same conclusions were reached by Jacobson and Gaze (1965) using electrophysiological mapping techniques on the goldfish retinotectal system. They permitted the optic nerve fibers from only one half of the retina to regenerate and described the restriction of distribution of the fiber termination to the appropriate half of the tectum. The converse experiment of removing half of the tectum and causing the entire optic nerve to regenerate to the remaining half tectum was also carried out by these workers. Only those fibers from the retinal half which normally innervated the remaining tectum established contact. De Long and Coulombre (1965) carried out quadrantic sector removal on developing chick retinae and observed, some days later, deficits of optic innervation in the corresponding tectal quandrants. Although the techniques and findings of De Long and Coulombre have been criticized (Goldberg, 1974), their conclusions have been supported by the recent work of Crossland et al. (1974). This group of experiments on the goldfish and chick retinotectal system thus provided strong support for the selective and exclusive rule of connections proposed by Sperry.

The advent of similar studies on the amphibian retinotectal projection, however, produced results which did not lead to the same general conclusion. In a modification of the experimental design in which half a retina is caused to innervate a whole optic tectum, Gaze et al. (1963) studied the projection from Xenopus eyes which, as a result of operations on the developing eyecup, contained retinal tissue deriving entirely from either nasal or temporal retina. With a technique developed earlier by Székely (1954a), the temporal half of the developing eye of a stage 32/33 Xenopus laevis (Nieuwkoop and Faber, 1956) was removed and

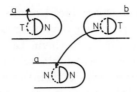

Fig. 3. Construction of a double-nasal eye in a Stage 32 *Xenopus laevis* embryo. The temporal half of the optic cup of the right eye (a) is replaced by a nasal half taken from the left eye of a donor animal (b).

replaced by the nasal half eye from another animal (Fig. 3), generating an eye termed a double-nasal compound eye. A comparable process could produce a double-temporal compound eye. Such eyes developed as normal looking eyes and their projections to the tecta were mapped after metamorphosis. Székely (1954a) had earlier concluded on the basis of rather inadequate behavioral testing on his newts with compound eyes that such eyes restricted their projections to that half of the tectum appropriate to the origin of the compound eye. Thus, double-nasal eyes, he claimed, projected only to caudal tectum, and double-temporal eyes only to rostral tectum. Electrophysiological mapping of *Xenopus* with one compound eye yielded different information. Each half retina of the compound eye projected, in normal retinotopic order, over the whole rostrocaudal extent of the tectum (Fig. 4). Such a finding did not appear to accord with a selective and exclusive rule of connection. For example, central retinal cells in a double-nasal eye (Fig. 4a) project to the most rostral tectum, whereas similar cells in a double-temporal eye project to most caudal tectum (Fig. 4b). Such a result, taken at face value,

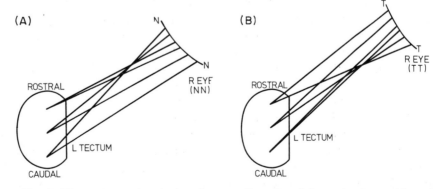

Fig. 4. The pattern of retinotectal connections found in postmetamorphic animals after creation, at stage 32, of (A) a double-nasal eye; (B) a double-temporal eye. (Although, in this figure, the eye is represented as being larger than in Figs. 1 and 2, this was only for clarity of illustration. Such eyes are, in fact, normal in size.)

certainly seems to conflict with the concept of unique affinities between central retinal cells and central tectal elements.

The result obtained on compound eyes was, however, at that time the exceptional class of result, and before using it as a justification for modifying part of the chemoaffinity hypothesis, any alternative explanation of the data that would reconcile it with the hypothesis should be eliminated. Sperry (1965) offered a plausible alternative explanation of the compound eye results. It was known that the arrival of optic fibers at the tectum is necessary for the normal growth and differentiation of that structure (Larsell, 1931; Kollros, 1953; McMurray, 1954) so Sperry suggested that in a tectum which received only nasal retinal fibers only the caudal tectal elements would develop, with the rostral tectum failing to grow. Since a compound eye possesses double the normal complement of nasal fibers, it is entirely conceivable that the caudal tectum should, under the circumstances, hypertrophy. The apparently normal tectum, contralateral to a compound eye, could thus be an overgrown half tectum onto which the fibers from the compound eye project in a manner appropriate to the selective and exclusive rule.

Straznicky et al. (1971a) set out to investigate this suggestion. In animals in which one compound eye was produced as before, they uncrossed the optic chiasma shortly after metamorphosis by inserting into it a piece of Millipore filter. Optic nerve fibers sectioned during this procedure regenerated to find their way to the opposite optic tectum barred by the filter, whereupon they regenerated directly to innervate the ipsilateral tectum (Fig. 5). Fibers from the compound eye thus come to innervate the normal tectum which previously received from the normal eye, while the normal eye innervates the tectum, the nature of which is suspect. If Sperry's suggestion were correct, then the predicted result of such a procedure should be that each half retina of the compound eye would project only to the appropriate half of the tectum, while only half of the retina of the normal eye should project to the suspect tectum. This was not, however, the result obtained by Straznicky et al. (1971a). They found that each half retina of the compound eye projected over the whole of the normal tectum and that the whole of the normal eye projected to the suspect tectum. These authors felt, therefore, that the interpretation of the compound eye results on the basis of selective tectal hypertrophy could not be sustained.

In the meantime size disparity experiments on the goldfish visual system were providing results that seemed to conflict with the earlier conclusions of Attardi and Sperry (1963) and Jacobson and Gaze (1965). Gaze and Sharma (1970) showed that if the caudal half of a goldfish tectum was removed, the whole eye eventually projected to the remaining

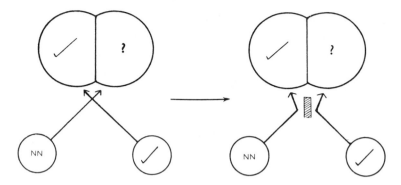

Fig. 5. Diagrams summarizing the experimental procedure adopted to examine the nature of the optic tectum to which a compound eye normally projects. Each diagram shows the two optic tecta above and the two eyes below, seen from the dorsal aspect. Arrows from each eye indicate the optic nerves. The right eye is a compound double nasal (NN) and the left eye (√) is normal. The right tectum is normal (√) and the nature of the left tectum is suspect (?). In the righthand diagram, the hatched area represents the Millipore implant at the chiasma. (From Straznicky *et al.,* 1971a.)

rostral half of the tectum. Yoon (1971) extended these findings to demonstrate compression of the whole visual field onto residual tectal areas after both rostrocaudal and mediolateral tectal deletion. Yoon (1972b) showed, very elegantly, that this compression of the visual field onto a half tectum was a reversible phenomenon. He placed a gelatin barrier transversely across the tectum and observed that the entire retinal projection initially compressed into the rostral tectal area in front of the barrier. The latter was slowly absorbed over a period of several months, and remapping of the animals after the disappearance of the barrier showed that the previously compressed visual field had now spread out again over the entire tectum. Sharma (1972a) also described compression of the visual field onto the remaining tectum following partial tectal ablation. The inverse of compression was also seen in the goldfish retinotectal system after removal of half of the retina. Yoon (1972c) states that, under these circumstances, the connections from the remaining half of a goldfish eye spread across the entire tectal surface. The results of a combination of the retinal removal and tectal removal procedures have been given by both Horder (1971) and Yoon (1972a). In goldfish in which the temporal half of the retina and the caudal half of the tectum had been removed, it was found that the remaining nasal half retina distributed its fibers, in the normal retinotopic order, across the remaining noncorresponding rostral half of the tectum.

These more recent studies seem to illustrate a fundamental plasticity in the mechanisms ordering retinotectal connections. In most of these experimental situations, it does not appear to be absolute retinotectal relationships that are preserved, as would have been required by the concept of uniquely high affinities between appropriately labeled retinal and tectal cells. What was maintained was the relative ordering of the retinotectal relationships. Consideration of this phenomenon led Straznicky *et al.* (1971a) and Gaze and Keating (1972) to propose an alternative to Sperry's exclusive cell-to-cell matching rule. These authors suggested that the important parameter governing the way in which two neuronal arrays interconnect appeared to be the extent of the complement of available retinal ganglion cell fibers projecting to the tectum and the amount of available tectal space. The interaction between pre- and post-synaptic elements must thus involve processes in which the overall extent of the innervating array is recognized, as is also the range of the available innervated array. Interconnection then occurred, within the constraints of the overall polarity of the system that operated to preserve the correct spatial order of connections, in such a fashion that the available boundary cells interconnect while the intermediate cells distribute themselves proportionately between the boundary positions. Competitive interactions for available postsynaptic space were implicit in this model in contrast to the selective and exclusive rule which viewed interconnection between the two arrays as a series of discrete and independent recognition process between a presynaptic cell and its unique postsynaptic site.

In some instances, this hypothesis of "systems matching" has been viewed as an alternative to the entire chemoaffinity hypothesis. This is not necessarily correct. It was offered essentially as a modification of one of the four elements of the chemoaffinity hypothesis. It may be noted, however, that in its broadest form the statement of systems matching was little more than a description of the experimental results on which it was based. It necessarily requires neither acceptance nor rejection of the first three elements of the chemoaffinity hypothesis.

The experiments showing a plasticity in retinotectal connections do, however, admit an interpretation other than that of systems matching. This was recognized by Straznicky *et al.* (1971a) who pointed out that size disparity experiments of the type introduced by Attardi and Sperry (1963) may be fundamentally incapable of revealing unequivocally the rules of connection because of the possibility of "regulative phenomena" following the surgical ablation procedures. Thus, for example, attempts to produce half a retina by partial retinal ablation may fail to achieve the desired object because embryonic regulative phenomena act to restore an entire retina in the remaining tissue. In the case of compound eyes,

each half retina would become a whole retina—the compound eye consisting, therefore, of two eyes. Similarly, attempts to produce half tecta
fail because the remaining tectal tissue regulates to become a whole
tectum. One has to be clear about which aspect of retinal or tectal structure is being regulated. Clearly, since the compound eye looks like a
normal eye and since the half retinae in goldfish do not reconstruct
retinal tissue to fill in the gap left by the removed retina, the proposed
regulation is not a restoration of normal size or of normal form. Feldman
and Gaze (1972) also showed that DNA synthesis in compound retinae
in *Xenopus* occurred only at the ciliary margin. If the mitotic pattern of
each hemiretina had regulated to become that of a normal eye, one would
have expected to also see DNA synthesis in the region of the vertical
midline where the two half retinae join. This was not found, and thus it
appears that it is not spatial distribution of cell division that has been
regulated. The only feature that remains as the candidate for the proposed
regulative modification is the cytochemical "specificity label." The argument runs, therefore, that following the removal of a part of the retina
(tectum) the remaining tissue responds not necessarily by growth or cell
division, but by relabeling the remaining cells to reconstruct the range of
labels associated normally with the whole retina (tectum) (Fig. 6).
Straznicky *et al.* (1971a) considered this argument with reference to the
compound eye situation and regarded it as unlikely, since the proposed
regulation would have had to persist and operate into adult life. Yoon
(1972b) and Meyer and Sperry (1973), on the other hand, regard regulative responses of the divided tissues as the most parsimonious interpretation of those experiments showing an apparent retinotectal plasticity.

Tectal ablation experiments in anuran amphibians have produced

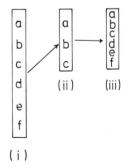

(i)

Fig. 6. Representation of the postulated regulation of specificity labels in the
remaining half tectum after ablation of the other half. (i) Distribution of labels
a–f in a normal tectum; (ii) distribution of labels immediately after removal of
half of the tectum; (iii) the end result of regulative processes in the half tectum,
the reconstitution of labels a–f.

results in apparent conflict with the studies already discussed. Thus, in *Xenopus*, partial tectal removal at either larval stage 54 (Straznicky *et al.*, 1971b) or shortly after metamorphosis (Straznicky, 1973) resulted, when the retinotectal projection was mapped in adult life, not in compression of the visual field onto the remaining tectum, but in a field map containing gaps in those regions normally projecting to the absent tectal tissue. Meyer and Sperry (1973) found the same phenomenon in the tree frog *Hyla regilla*. This different class of results must somehow be incorporated into any general scheme which seeks to account for the formation of selective neuronal connections. Meyer and Sperry (1973) present the issues very cogently. They argued that these results in the anurans demonstrate that the selective and exclusive rule of connection is correct and, therefore, those situations in which it is apparently transgressed are likely to reflect situations in which regulation is occurring. It was pointed out that Sperry (1943b, 1944), in the early presentations of his hypothesis, had postulated a "field-like differentiation" of retinal ganglion cells. Meyer and Sperry (1973) suggested that those such as Straznicky *et al.* (1971a) and Gaze and Keating (1972) who argue that the chemoaffinity theory involves as one of its elements the concept of a unique matching rule, do so only because of a "misinterpretation of these basic concepts in developmental biology." This accusation cannot really be sustained. What is proposed is that the "field" concept applies to adult vertebrate tissues whereas, as discussed earlier, regulative phases of development normally occur very early in ontogeny, certainly prior to the time of normal tissue differentiation. It is conceivable that those operations performed on the developing eyecup to construct a compound eye occur at a time when regulative phenomena are possible. Indeed, results obtained from animals in which just one-half of the developing eye was left *in situ* produced results which could well indicate that under these circumstances regulation has occurred (Berman and Hunt, 1975; Feldman and Gaze, 1975). It would be premature to assume, however, that because regulation occurs in this latter situation when cell division at the cut retinal margin resumes (Horder and Spitzer, 1973), it therefore necessarily occurs in compound eyes in which cell division at the cut edge does not resume (Feldman and Gaze, 1972). It is the proposition of Meyer and Sperry, however, that such field phenomena characteristically occur in adult vertebrate tissues, which strains a basic concept in developmental biology.

Several strands of evidence have emerged suggesting that plastic expansion or compression of retinal projection on the tectum can occur under situations that preclude regulation as the explanatory feature. Sharma (1972a) removed a mediolateral strip of tectal tissue in goldfish so that tectal areas remained on both sides of the strip. This separation of rostral and caudal tectum might have been expected to have caused regulation of the separated areas such that both areas would have accepted a complete visual field. At least the rostral area, by analogy with Yoon's interpretation of his own results, should have regulated. Sharma found, however, that if sufficient time were allowed, the entire visual field distributed itself onto the remaining rostral and caudal tectum, as if the gap in the tectal tissues did not exist. A similar observation was made by Sharma (1972b) after removal of a rostrocaudal strip of tectal tissue (Fig. 7). Those who favor regulation as the explanation of such plastic phenomena would be required to postulate that each tectal area had "partially regulated" and the degree of partial regulation in the two remaining areas was exactly complementary. This is by no means a recognized characteristic of regulative fields. Sharma interpreted his results as support for the systems matching idea, but pointed out that at short intervals after the operation a retinotectal map was frequently obtained that conformed to the normal retinotectal cellular relationships; i.e., a map with a gap in the visual field, corresponding to the deficit in the tectum. The time necessary for this initially normal map to convert to a compressed map could reflect either the time necessary for equilibrium to be reached between the total complement of retinal fibers competing for the available tectal space or the time necessary for the tectal field to regulate the specificity labels of the remaining tectum.

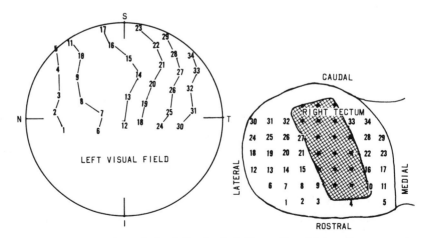

Fig. 7. Representation of the left visual field on the right optic tectum in a goldfish 131 days after removal of the hatched area of the optic tectum. The tectal electrodes are spaced at intervals of 200 μm. The perimetric chart representation of the visual field extends 100° outward from the center of the field. S, superior; T, temporal; I, inferior; N, nasal. (From Sharma, 1972b.)

Cook and Horder (1974) described a similar sequence of events, with sequential recording in the same animal, after section of the optic nerve and removal of the caudal half of the tectum in adult goldfish. The earliest regenerated map obtained consisted only of the nasodorsal field projecting to the rostral tectum, as it does in the normal animal. Over the next two or three months, this initial projection was gradually displaced forward by fibers that would normally have connected with the absent caudal portion of the tectum. Eventually, the whole visual field compressed onto the available rostral tectum. To test whether this latter compression reflected the regulation of the rostral tectum, Cook and Horder, after obtaining field compression, cut the optic nerve again and analyzed the form of the earliest regenerated map. If the remaining tectum had regulated, the earliest map after this second regeneration might be expected to be a whole field mapping into a "whole" tectum. Cook and Horder did not find this. The maps showed a repetition of the process occurring the first time with a partial field initially projecting to rostral tectum and the whole field later compressing in. These authors felt that this finding indicated that no progressive regulative changes were occurring in the lesioned tectum itself. The changes in the optic fiber distribution over the tectum that occurred between one and three months after nerve section were taken to show (a) that there are no terminal cues that uniquely match an incoming fiber with a particular tectal site, since that fiber can terminate, retinotopically, at a series of different tectal sites, (b) that some interaction between the incoming fibers themselves determines the final distribution of fiber terminations over the tectal surface.

The third strand of evidence against the concept of regulation as the explanation of retinotectal plasticity was offered by Feldman et al. (1974). They described an animal in which, as the result of an experimental maneuver, fibers from one eye were directly innervating both tecta. The direct projection of the eye to the ipsilateral tectum contained fibers from the whole eye spread in the normal retinotopic order over the tectal surface. The projection from the eye to its contralateral tectum consisted of fibers only from the nasal portion of the eye, yet these fibers distributed themselves again, in the normal retinotopic order, across the entire contralateral optic tectum (Fig. 8). One cannot reasonably invoke regulation to account for this spreading of the projection from half a retina across the whole tectum, since the half retina concerned is itself part of a normal eye.

These considerations lead us to the view that acceptance of field-type regulation as the mechanism underlying retinotectal plasticity, in the experimental situations that have been discussed in this section, raises

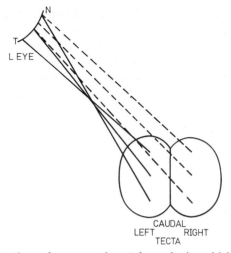

Fig. 8. Representation of an experimental result in which the left eye was caused to innervate, directly, both optic tecta. Fibers from the whole of the eye innervated the left optic tectum. Fibers from only the nasal retina innervated the right optic tectum and spread in order over the whole tectum.

more problems than it solves. The alternative view of a competitive systems matching rule seems more compatible with all the data. This view is, of course, not without its own difficulties. The results of anuran tectal ablation do not appear to fit the scheme. This must be acknowledged as a difficulty, but not necessarily an insuperable one. It is possible, for example, that fibers destined for the removed tectum find an alternative postsynaptic area and do not therefore compete for tectal space with the original complement.

Hunt and Jacobson (1974a) make the point very forcibly that the combination of ablation studies and retinotectal mapping does not logically permit the unequivocal distinction between the view of Meyer and Sperry (1973) and the present authors' position. This is true, but their overcritical attitude to the experimental paradigm leads them to an unnecessary nihilism. Even if logical certainties may not be obtainable from any given experimental situation, strong inferences may be derived from the results of combinations of experiments on the system. It must also be admitted that their proposed solution to the problem, the "three-eyed frog" (Jacobson and Hunt, 1973; Hunt and Jacobson, 1974a) is as subject to logical uncertainties as the other variations of the paradigm that they have criticized. Their definition of "locus specificity" as that property "which enables the axon of each ganglion cell to reach its proper locus in the retinotectal map" (Hunt and Jacobson, 1972b) is carefully couched to embrace both views being considered in this section. The application of this term to the problem of the rules linking neuronal arrays blurs, rather than clarifies, the issues involved (Hunt and Jacobson, 1974a).

If one could find a situation in which, without experimentally perturbing the system, fibers from a given retinal area find available only a tectal area which they do not normally innervate, the response of the system to this situation may shed some light upon the controversy. The differential modes of growth of the retina, which grows in rings at the ciliary margin (Straznicky and Gaze, 1971), and the tectum in which neurogenesis occurs first at the rostrolateral pole and progresses caudomedially (Straznicky and Gaze, 1972; Currie and Cowan, 1974a), means that during early developmental stages in amphibians this situation is obtained. Retinal ganglion cells, which in the adult will occupy central retinal positions and will connect with central tectum at that time, are the first to appear and to send out their axons. When these axons first reach the tectum, only the most rostrolateral tectal cells have begun to differentiate; these cells will, in the adult, receive axons from cells at the temporal retinal pole—retinal cells which at the stage being discussed have not yet been born. If, therefore, at these early stages the optic fibers connect with the tectum in retinotopic order, this would be a result analogous to those of the size disparity paradigm, but in a nonperturbed situation.

Gaze et al. (1972, 1974) mapped the visuotectal projection in Xenopus tadpoles from the early stage 40s through metamorphosis. They showed that retinotopic order existed from stage 48 onward, at a time when the projection was restricted to the rostral third of the tectum. Analysis of the maps obtained, together with the consideration just outlined, led these authors to suggest that during the growth of the retinotectal system in Xenopus synaptic relationships between retinal ganglion cells and tectal cells undergo progressive changes until, after metamorphosis, the adult pattern is achieved. The existence of these ordered, but transitory, connections (Fig. 9) argues against a strict cell-to-cell chemoaffinity view and is more compatible with a systems-matching hypothesis. Chung et al. (1974) demonstrated that at these early transient phases of the retinotectal projection, functional optic synapses are present, thus removing one possible objection to the conclusions of Gaze et al. (1974).

One must always be aware of the danger, when offering one system as a model for a broad subject such as developmental neurobiology, that considerable species differences may exist. For example, studies on the developing retinotectal system of the chick have produced results entirely compatible with the chemoaffinity hypothesis. Thus, after partial retinal

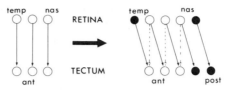

Fig. 9. Representation of the changing pattern of retinotectal synaptic relationships postulated to occur during normal development in *Xenopus*. The closed circles represent new cells appearing at the temporal (temp) and nasal (nas) poles of the retinae and at the posterior (post) aspect of the tectum.

ablation in embryonic chick, the remaining retina projects only to the appropriate part of the tectum and there is no spreading over the whole tectal area (Crossland *et al.*, 1974). Experimental studies on the developing mammalian visual system are just beginning and are, if anything, even more plagued by difficulties of interpretation than are the amphibian studies. Schneider (1973) has described in the Syrian hamster abnormal retinal projections following damage in the neonatal period to the developing superior colliculus. The retinal fibers being denied their normal target site end in areas normally devoid of optic terminations. Schneider made the interesting observation that many of these areas chosen by optic fibers in this abnormal situation were those areas to which the tectum itself normally projects. Even more surprising is the finding that if the brachium of the inferior colliculus, which carries auditory fibers to the medial geniculate nucleus, were sectioned, then subsequently retinofugal axons were found distributed within this medial geniculate nucleus. The significance of this type of finding is that neurons are quite capable of forming connections with target sites other than those with which they normally connect. It can hardly be the case, therefore, that synapses are formed only between uniquely labeled pre- and post-synaptic cells. Some mechanism must account for the absence, during normal development, of fibers from sites with which they are capable of connecting, but normally do not do so. This point is reinforced by a wealth of data showing that if one group of afferent fibers are sectioned, then other nearby intact fibers sprout to innervate part, or all, of the denervated area (Edds, 1953; Liu and Chambers, 1958; Goodman and Horel, 1966; Raisman, 1969; Lund and Lund, 1971; Moore *et al.*, 1971, 1974; Wall and Egger, 1971; Bernstein and Goodman, 1973).

That spatial order may be imposed on abnormal connections in the mammalian as well as the amphibian visual system is suggested by the findings of Jhaveri and Schneider (1974) and Schneider and Jhaveri (1974). They performed partial tectal ablation in the neonatal hamster and claimed that the entire visual field compressed into the remaining portion of the optic tectum. Similarly abnormal, but spatially ordered, synaptic relationships have been described in the visual system of mammals with genetic mutations that result in abnormalities of retinal pigmentation (Guillery and Kaas, 1971; Hubel and Wiesel, 1971; Gaze and Keating, 1972; Kaas and Guillery, 1973; Guillery et al., 1974; Sanderson et al., 1974).

AXIAL POLARIZATION OF THE RETINA

In the previous section, the ways in which spatially ordered neuronal arrays interconnect were examined. Now the manner in which these neuronal arrays acquire spatial order will be discussed. Since the array of retinal ganglion cells and the tectal surface are essentially two dimensional, the positional specification of elements in such surfaces requires organization about two axes. The acquisition of such axes must reflect positional information established at some earlier stage of development. Work on limb development (Harrison, 1921; Swett, 1937), the developing ear (Harrison, 1924, 1936, 1945), and even the neural plate itself (Roach, 1945) had shown that the anteroposterior polarity of these structures was determined before the dorsoventral. Sperry (1943a) predicted that at some early stage of retinal development a similar two-dimensional polarity would be imposed, and he suggested that the anteroposterior (nasotemporal) axis would be determined before the dorsoventral. Both of these predictions were fulfilled. Stone (1944, 1948, 1960) assessed the developmental stage at which the retina becomes functionally polarized by rotation of the optic vesicle and optic cup in *Ambystoma* embryos. Rotation prior to the late tail-bud stage did not prevent the subsequent development of normal visuomotor behavior. Rotation of the developing eye at later stages produced inverted visuomotor function. It was noted that this polarization of the retina occurred just prior to the onset of retinal differentiation. Székely (1954b) found in *Triturus* that what he termed the "local functional specificity" of the retina, was acquired before morphological differentiation of that organ. Székely's behavioral experiments revealed that the polarity of the retina was determined first along the anteroposterior axis and only later along the dorsoventral axis. Jacobson (1968a) rotated the developing eyecup in *Xenopus laevis* larvae at stages 28 to 35. After metamorphosis, electrophysiological mapping of the retinotectal connections showed that rotation of the eye primordium at stage 28 produced maps of normal orientation; rotation at stage 30 resulted in reversal of the anteroposterior axis, but not of the dorsoventral axis; while rotations at stage 31 produced reversal of both axes. The time of retinal polarization in this species is again correlated with the onset of retinal cytodifferentiation. It has been customary to refer to this period as that of "retinal ganglion cell specification" but, as Gaze and Keating (1972) pointed out, the great majority of ganglion cells are not yet born. What is, in fact, determined at this time is the axial polarity according to which a developmental program will subsequently influence the behavior of retinal ganglion cells. The structure that is polarized is not known; the evidence presently available does not compel the popular view that it is the retinal ganglion cells themselves. Nor is it known in what manner the polarity information is transmitted to the retinal ganglion cells. The view that the information influences the terminal differentiation of the ganglion cells is hypothesis, not yet demonstrated fact.

In a recent series of papers, Hunt and Jacobson investigated some of the parameters of the polarization process and some of the constraints under which it operates. Hunt and Jacobson (1973a) showed that the eye anlage, prior to the period of "polarization" demonstrated by rotation procedures, is not *free* of axial information, but does, in fact, possess presumptive reference axes. Eye anlage were removed from the embryo between stages 22 and 28, and either grown in tissue culture or isolated from embryonic axial cues by placing them on the ventral midline of intermediate hosts, until such eyes developed into an eye of stage 37/38. At this stage, the eyes were placed in various orientations in carrier animals and the animals allowed to metamorphose. The retinotectal maps obtained from these eyes were such as to indicate that at the time of transplantation the developing eye contained axial information which it used to organize the tectal projections of the ganglion cells that appeared later. It was necessary to conclude from this observation that what had previously been viewed as the period in which polarity was *established* is really the period in which such polarity becomes *irreversible*. It may be noted in passing that this situation provides an example of the way in which isolation and transplantation experiments can lead to different conclusions as to the time of "determination" of a developmental phenomenon. In the normal course of events, the presumptive reference axes are at this time "locked in" with reference to the general body axis of the embryo. The earlier rotations experiments had, therefore, shown that the presumptive axes could be reversed by periorbital tissue up to stage 30. This repolarization process may take as little as two hours (Hunt and Jacobson, 1974b). The information necessary for this repolarization is not restricted to periorbital tissue, but is more generally distributed throughout the body of the embryo. Hunt and Jacobson (1972a) transplanted eyes of stage 28 embryos to the body, where the eyes remained during the period when the axes are normally locked in. At stage 32 to

34, the eye was transplanted back to a host carrier. After metamorphosis, the retinotectal projection of such eyes revealed that their axes had been locked in with reference to axial information present in the tissues of the body flank of the embryo.

Heterochronic transplantation, a process whereby developing eyes of a given stage are transplanted into hosts of a different stage, showed that irreversible polarization was critically dependent upon the stage of the developing eye, rather than that of the periorbital tissue (Hunt and Jacobson, 1974c). This series of experiments showed, first, that the "trigger" for the locking in came from within the eye anlage itself and, second, that periorbital tissue retained the competence to polarize the retina considerably later than the time at which this process normally occurs.

Wolpert (1969, 1971) has claimed consistently that positional information itself is likely to be universally distributed, with the considerable diversity in morphogenesis reflecting differential responses by developing tissues to common cues. Such a view has been supported by the finding of positional information appropriate to retinal polarization existing on the body flank. It has been reinforced by heteroplastic transplantation of developing *Xenopus* eyes to the orbit of *Ambystoma punctatum* and *Rana pipiens* as intermediate hosts. After transplanation back into a *Xenopus* carrier, mapping of the retinotectal projection from these eyes showed that the "foreign" orbits had been able to irreversibly polarize the developing eye (Hunt and Piatt, cited in Hunt, 1975).

Another question that has been asked about the events occurring at the time of irreversible polarization is whether the stability of the axes shown by the intact eye is also shared by partial retinal fragments. That such might not be the case was suggested by the findings of Straznicky et al. (unpublished results, see Gaze, 1970), who found that removal of half of the developing eyecup sometimes resulted in mirror reduplication of the remaining half. Recently, Feldman and Gaze (1975), Berman and Hunt (1975), and Hunt and Berman (1975) have described a similar phenomenon. Jacobson and Hunt (1973) and Hunt and Jacobson (1974d) found that they could sometimes produce a similar result merely by separating the two retinal halves by a vertical or horizontal cut.

Although each half of a double-nasal and double-temporal eye displayed axial polarity appropriate to that of the fragment at the time of eye construction, Straznicky et al. (1974) found that eyes created by the fusion of two ventral half fragments formed maps which suggested that the polarity of the fragments had undergone some change after fusion. Hunt and Jacobson (1973b) and Hunt and Berman (1975) described similar polarity changes in more bizarre retinal fragment recombinations.

The conclusions reached are that whatever constitutes the functional property known as polarization, it can be modified by interaction between retinal fragments after the time at which, in a normal eye, such axes become irreversible. It is not known whether these interactions represent a normal ongoing process revealed by these abnormal procedures, or an abnormal response to the surgical insult.

Temporal associations between the process of irreversible polarization of the intact eye, the cessation of DNA synthesis in gangliogenic precursor cells, and the disappearance of gap junctions between these cells are considered later in this chapter.

THE ACQUISITION OF TECTAL POLARITY

The ordered matching of two neuronal arrays requires spatial order in both arrays. The degree of order need not necessarily be equal in both, but for the retinal fibers to distribute themselves retinotopically across the tectal surface there must be at least some spatially organized markers on the tectum, with reference to which the optic fiber population orients itself. The only alternative to this view is to propose (Sperry, 1951; Jacobson, 1960) an exquisite temporal control of the arrival of optic fibers and of the maturation of tectal postsynaptic sites, with incoming fibers synapsing with those sites that have just become available. This view, always unlikely for a two-dimensional organization, has been largely discredited by the demonstration that a normal temporal sequence of retinotectal input is *not* a necessary prerequisite for the development of an ordered retinotectal map (Feldman *et al.*, 1971; Hunt and Jacobson, 1972b).

The time at which tectal polarization occurs is not known. An early attempt to provide such information by early tectal rotation experiments in larval Ambystoma was not conclusive (Crelin, 1952). It may be inferred from the presence of an ordered map in *Xenopus* at stage 48 (Gaze *et al.*, 1974) that the tectum possesses the necessary axial information by this stage.

The possibility that the tectal positional information consisted merely of markers at, for example, the most polar regions of the tectum could be examined by performing rotations of small pieces of the tectum. If the polar marker postulate were correct, then the optic fibers should distribute themselves across the tectum normally, unaffected by a small rotated implant. This is not a result obtained (Yoon, 1973; Levine and Jacobson, 1974). Regenerating optic fibers go to their original tectal site on the implant that has now been rotated to a new position, which then produces a distortion in the map. These findings invite the conclusion that there exists a detailed positional specification of the tectal elements which parallels in complexity that of the retina. Once again, the nature of this positional marker and of the tectal structure possessing it is not known.

An extremely interesting analysis of the development of tectal polarity in *Xenopus* has been published recently (Chung and Cook, 1975). These workers observed that the tectal polarity for retinal connections seems to be under the influence of cells in the primitive diencephalon, and also that this polarity may be dissociated from the normal anatomical polarity of the tectum.

THE CELL CYCLE AND DIFFERENTIATION

It is a common view of development biologists that cell division and cell differentiation are mutually exclusive events. By this, they do not mean that differentiated cells cannot divide, although of course fully differentiated vertebrate neurons do not do so. What is meant by the more general proposition is that differentiative events require a preceding DNA replication. Holtzer (1963, 1968, 1970) has suggested that there are two types of cell cycle and that a differentiative event requires a particular type of preceding cell cycle. To this, Holtzer gives the name the quantal cell cycle, from which two daughter cells are produced with synthetic machinery different from that operating in the mother cell. This view that terminal differentiative events in all cell types require a preceding period of DNA synthesis and nuclear division (Holtzer, 1970; Holtzer and Sanger, 1972) has received supporting evidence from studies of myogenesis, chondrogenesis, and erythrogenesis (Holtzer *et al.*, 1972).

An opportunity to examine this intriguing proposition has now been provided by the amphibian visual system. Jacobson (1968b) showed that ganglion cell precursor neuroblasts in the center of the developing retina undergo their final DNA synthesis at stages 28 to 29, just prior to the final locking-in events at stages 29 to 30. An ingenious experiment to investigate further this temporal correlation between terminal differentiation of ganglion cells and the establishment of permanent reference axes in the retina involved the use of 5-bromodeoxyuridine (BUdR). This thymidine analog tends to suppress those events characteristic of the terminally differentiated state while permitting the basic cellular functions, including cell division, to continue. The mechanism of its actions are not yet entirely clear (Holtzer *et al.*, 1972; Levitt and Dorfman, 1974). Bergey *et al.* (1973) found that using this compound they could delay the terminal differentiation of retinal neurons and that administration of BUdR at various developmental stages would block selectively the differentiation of particular retinal neuronal populations. If the developing eye were treated from stage 24, differentiation of all neural types was delayed and final axial polarization was also delayed. Treatment from stage 27 blocked the differentiation of photoreceptors and of the retinal interneurons, but permitted differentiation of ganglion cells. Under these circumstances, final axial polarization occurred at the normal time (Hunt, 1975a,b; Hunt et al., 1976). On the basis of Jacobson's (1968b) observations on final DNA synthesis and these findings in animals treated with BUdR, Hunt et al. (1976) postulated that a specific population of gangliogenic precursor cells, existing in the stage 28/29 Xenopus eye, not only gives rise to ganglion cells but also provides the trigger that evokes the irreversible axial polarization of the eye.

Do these autoradiographic studies of Jacobson (1968b) and the delay of irreversible polarization by the administration of BUdR (Hunt et al., 1976) permit the identification of the ocular structure that is being irreversibly polarized? An entirely reasonable hypothesis, incorporating these findings, would be that irreversible axial polarization involves the retinal ganglion cells themselves. The immediate precursors of the ganglion cells appear to trigger the process. Structural and genetic correlates associated with the development of the differentiated state also appear to occur in these earliest retinal ganglion cells. It could be argued plausibly then that irreversible axial polarization consists of the transmission of positional information to these earliest ganglion cells.

The acquisition of retinal polarity has been studied recently in another anuran amphibian, Rana pipiens. It is interesting to compare the time of irreversible axial polarization and that of final DNA synthesis in the retinal ganglion cell precursors of the central retina in this species to see if, indeed, the correlation observed in Xenopus also holds in Rana. Both Sharma and Hollyfield (1974) and Jacobson et al. (1976) report that the correlation did not hold. Rotation of the developing eyecup at various developmental stages indicated that irreversible axial polarization had occurred at stage 17 (Shumway, 1940). At this time, however, all retinal cells still incorporate tritiated thymidine. Thus, irreversible axial polarization in Rana pipiens is associated with events other than the S phase of the immediate precursor of the retinal ganglion cells. This species difference, if true, and if not due to some trivial factor such as the inability of the rotated eye to establish contact with the surrounding tissues, must call into question the general significance of the correlation observed in Xenopus. The difficulty of examining in the developing retina the correlation of DNA replication with a terminal differentiative event is that, in this system, the nature of the latter is unknown. The suggestion that the terminal differentiation of a retinal ganglion cell goes beyond the separation of ganglion cells from other retinal elements and becomes that spatially dependent process which differentiates a ganglion cell from its fellows is merely a postulate. At the present, no independent evidence exists to verify such a postulate. The presence or absence of a temporal correlation between DNA replication and irreversible axial polarization may not, therefore, be a valid test of the proposition that DNA synthesis and terminal differentiation are related events. The valid test for the proposition in this system is the correlation between final DNA synthesis and the differentiation of recognizable ganglion cells.

CELL COUPLING

Earlier, it was pointed out how the epigenetic processes by which the genome of the zygote is translated into a highly organized multicellular organism require extensive intercellular communication. In particular, the establishment of positional information and the reading of such information by cells presumably involves the intercellular transfer of informational molecules.

Ultrastructural analysis of tissues reveals three types of membrane specialization at points of close contact between cells. Two of these, the *zonula adhaerens* and the *macula adhaerentes diminutae*, are characteristic components of epithelial tissue and are generally regarded as being concerned with intercellular adhesion in tissue construction (Farquhar and Palade, 1963). The third type, the gap junction, is the structure in which the apposing cell membranes are separated by a distance of 30 to 80 Å, and within this space, there appears to be a polygonal lattice-type structure. It is the gap junction that has been advanced as the prime candidate for direct intercellular communication.

There appear to be two modes of intercellular communication: one mediated by ions of low molecular weight and manifested as low resistance electrical pathways between cells, and one mediated by substances of considerably higher molecular weight. Electrical coupling of embryonic cells, first described by Potter, *et al.* (1966), seems to be a common property of developing tissues. It has been found as early as the cleavage stages of *Xenopus* (Slack and Palmer, 1969) and at the blastula stage low resistance junctions appear to exist between all the cells (Ito and Loewenstein, 1969). In most cases where functional studies have demonstrated low resistance junctions, ultrastructural studies have revealed gap junctions, a correlation that supports the identification of the latter as the structure through which the low molecular weight substances transfer from cell to cell (Bennett, 1973).

A more important feature of the gap junction is that molecules up to 10^4 daltons can pass down the aqueous core of the lattice and thus diffuse directly into the intracellular substance of the adjoining cell without access to the intercellular space. This flow of substances, e.g., nucleotides, via gap junctions, may well be, as Loewenstein (1972) suggests, a means of disseminating signals controlling cellular growth and differentiation.

It was, therefore, of considerable interest when Dixon and Cronly-Dillon (1972) described the spatial and temporal distribution of gap junctions in the developing *Xenopus* retina. Between stages 26 and 30, gap junctions were found distributed throughout the developing retina. After stage 31, however, gap junctions were found only in the most peripheral retinal regions, since they disappeared from the central retina. Jacobson and Loewenstein (cited in Jacobson and Hunt, 1973) have shown that small fluorescein-labeled molecules injected into cells in one part of the retina rapidly pass to other retinal areas prior to stage 30, but not at later stages. Thus, there is an interesting temporal correlation between the disappearance of these gap junctions and the stage at which the retinal axes are irreversibly locked in. Since the imposition of axial polarity is a process that probably requires cooperative participation by the cell population being polarized, this correlation is readily understandable.

Reservations were expressed earlier as to whether it was yet established that the retinal ganglion cells themselves were axially polarized. It might be felt that the demonstration that gap junctions between the growing ganglion cells disappeared at the same time as "irreversible polarization" renders such reservations unnecessary. Dixon and Cronly-Dillon (1974) report, however, that gap junctions between pigment epithelial cells also disappear, apart from those at the retinal ciliary margin, at stage 31. This cell population could, therefore, well be the one that is polarized. In the further study of the role of cell-to-cell communication in development, the amphibian visual system holds considerable promise.

THE CURRENT STATUS OF THE CHEMOAFFINITY THEORY

The four elements of the chemoaffinity theory can now be assessed critically in the light of relevant information obtained since the hypothesis was formulated. This exercise is undertaken in the knowledge that no coherent alternative to the overall theory has been advanced and that the recent data can, with certain assumptions, be accommodated by the theory. A risk faced by any such successful theory is, however, that essentially hypothetical components gradually transmute into dogma. Therefore, it seems appropriate to examine separately the constituent elements of the theory to see what status can be afforded to each one. Possible verdicts could include (1) demonstrated fact; (2) very well-supported assertion; (3) plausible hypothesis with no apparent alternative; (4) tenable hypothesis; (5) hypothesis that requires modification; (6) hypothesis that is demonstrably false. The general theory will be discussed in terms of the neuronal population with reference to which it was formulated—the retinal ganglion cells; although once again, this population should be viewed as merely an example of the more general case.

Retinal Ganglion Cells Are Intrinsically Specific as a Result of Processes of Differentiation

This proposition cannot be regarded as proven until the molecular nature of the postulated terminal differentiation is demonstrated. This requires first, the identification of the molecular moiety responsible for selective synaptic formation; second, the demonstration that this moiety is differentially distributed across the retina, and third, that the molecule exists in, or on, the cell as the result of differential gene activity.

Earlier, attention was drawn to the historical background of the proposition that ganglion cells were intrinsically different. This conclusion is forced only if either such an intrinsic difference is demonstrated, or if all possible extrinsic influences have been excluded. Only two extrinsic influences were excluded: those of mechanical guidance and functional adaptation.

For the purposes of argument, let us consider an alternative model which accepts that the differential behavior of retinal ganglion cells reflects chemical differences between ganglion cells, but postulates that these differences are extrinsically imposed and not the product of intrinsic ganglion cell differentiation. This model draws on some ideas of Hughes (1975) and of Marchase et al. (1975). Suppose that the critical molecules involved in synaptic recognition are glycoproteins—a suggestion mooted by Barondes (1970) and Marchase, et al. (1975). Also, suppose that synthesis of these critical glycoproteins involves the participation of surface-membrane located enzymes—the glycosyltransferases—these latter produced by the genetic machinery of the retinal ganglion cells. It could be postulated, however, that all the retinal ganglion cells produce the same glycosyl transferase and the same amount thereof, but that the activity of such transferases is affected by "modifier proteins" (Hughes, 1975) arriving from an external source. As a result of this modification, the nature of the synthesized glycoprotein is changed. If the quantitative or qualitative differential distribution of modifier protein were spatially ordered, the end result of their effects would be a spatially ordered difference in retinal ganglion cell labels, the latter due, however, not to differential gene activity of the retinal ganglion cells, but to a spatially ordered difference in an extrinsic source of modifier protein. Again, purely for the sake of argument, let us suggest that the possible site of synthesis of such a modifier protein might be the pigment epithelial cells. On this model, the population that undergoes a spatially ordered terminal differentiation would be the pigment cell population, the net result of the differentiative process being the spatially ordered differential production of modifier proteins.

Although this model is advanced more for didactic purposes than with any great belief in its validity, one may point out that pigment epithelial cells are capable of regenerating a neural retina endowed with differential retinal ganglion cell behavior (Stone, 1950; Keefe, 1973; Levine and Cronly-Dillon, 1974). In addition, in the mammalian visual system, different mutations that affect retinal pigment cells all share as a common result aberrations in the connectivity of some retinal ganglion cells (Guillery *et al.*, 1974).

Therefore, while it is still probable that retinal ganglion cells are intrinsically specified according to their retinal positions at a certain developmental period, the data available does not compel this view, and thus it is fairly easy to construct an alternative model.

Early Events in Neuronal Life Specify the Terminal Differentiative Pathway of the Retinal Ganglion Cell

The evidence concerning the axial polarization of the retina has previously been discussed. The reasons for preferring that term to the more common one of "retinal ganglion cell specification" were outlined. It was argued that neither the structure being polarized was known, nor the manner in which the polarization influenced the subsequent behavior of retinal ganglion cells. In the context of the chemoaffinity theory, present views identify the early retinal ganglion cell population as the structure being polarized. The effect of polarization is to specify the positional information in these ganglion cells (Hunt and Jacobson, 1972b). Those ganglion cells that are born later receive information in some manner from the older more central ganglion cells (Hunt, 1975a). The correlation of cessation of DNA synthesis in the early retinal ganglion cell precursors with that of the specification of positional information in their progeny is readily explicable. The disappearance of gap junctions between those cells may also indicate their maturing to a differentiated state. The persistence of DNA synthesis and gap junctions at the ciliary margin, when new ganglion cells are appearing, would be expected on the grounds that these new cells would require specification and this itself would demand information transfer, possibly via gap junctions, from older retinal cells. The temporal correlation of ganglion cell differentiation and the intraocular trigger for irreversible axial polarization, shown in the BUdR experiments, is another pointer in the same direction. This portion of the chemoaffinity theory can thus be incorporated into the more recent data to make a very plausible story.

It is not, however, a story to which assent is necessarily compelled. To elaborate on the alternative model just advanced, could it not be that the structure being polarized is the pigment epithelium? The factors identifying the retinal ganglion cell population as the candidate were (a) differentiation begins just after irreversible retinal polarization; (b) DNA synthesis in its precursors ceases just before irreversible axial polarization; (c) gap junctions disappear at the same time except at the periphery; (d) BUdR, which delays their differentiation, delays axial polarization.

Pigment cells in the central retina (a) begin to differentiate just after irreversible polarization (Nieuwkoop and Faber, 1956), (b) gap junctions between pigment epithelial cells disappear at this time except at the periphery (Dixon and Cronly-Dillon, 1974); (c) BUdR administered at times which delay ganglion cell differentiation would, due to its mode of action, probably delay pigment cell differentiation, although definitive information is not available on this point. (d) The authors are aware of no information about DNA synthesis in pigment epithelial cells at this time. It may be seen that the apparently powerful pointers identifying the retinal ganglion cells as the site of axial polarization are not as unique as they might have seemed.

The Differences between Retinal Ganglion Cells Are Cytochemical

For the moment the question about whether the ganglion cells are subject to intrinsic or extrinsic differential influences will be put aside. Can we nevertheless agree that these differences must be manifest as cytochemical cellular labels? The answer, again, must be that such a suggestion is eminently plausible; but since there is no definitive data on this point, alternative interpretations are possible.

It is incontestable that a ganglion cell somehow or other acquires some position-dependent property. Such a property need not, however, be cytochemical; it could, for example, reside in the physical pattern of spontaneous firing of a ganglion cell if the latter could in some sense be spatially coded (see Chung et al., 1970; Chung 1974). It must be remembered that Sperry, in his early experiments, was able to exclude the functionally adaptive value of a connection as a modulating influence, but he did not exclude functional activity within the optic fibers themselves. That alterations in the firing pattern of optic fibers may disturb synaptic connections in the retinotectal system is suggested by the work of Chung, et al. (1973). They showed that if an adult *Xenopus* is reared in a stroboscopically illuminated environment while its sectioned optic nerve regenerates, then although a normal retinotopic map across the surface of the tectum is reconstituted, the normal differential distribution of different optic nerve fiber types in depth in the tectum is not restored. Abnormal visual experience, and hence, perhaps, abnormal firing patterns prevented the formation of a normal pattern of connections.

Although it has just been argued that there is no definitive reason forcing the view that positional labels of retinal ganglion cells must be in the form of macromolecules, such structures remain the most likely candidates for this role. An assay system that may shed some light on the class of interactions involved has been introduced by Barbera *et al.* (1973). Selective affinities in tissue culture between disaggregated retinal cells and tectal fragments in the embryonic chick mimicked the normal pattern of synaptic relationships between the retina and tectum.

The Rule of Connection Is a Selective and Exclusive One

This matter has been discussed in detail in a previous section. The interpretation of investigations aimed at this element is a matter of controversy. The most plausible interpretation appears to be one which requires a modification of this rule in favor of a more competitive process in which neuronal systems match up on the basis of relative affinities rather than absolute ones.

ENDOCRINE INFLUENCES IN NEUROGENESIS

In discussing cellular interactions in neurogenesis, the focus, so far, has been on relatively short-range phenomena. There is, of course, another class of developmental interaction which operates over longer ranges, but nevertheless has profound effects upon the developing brain, and this is the interaction between hormones and their target tissues. The classic example of the importance of hormones during neurogenesis is that revealed by the mental retardation associated with thyroid deficiency. Although the end result of the deficiency is well documented, the role of thyroid hormone in normal brain development is little understood. Other hormones known to effect brain development include the sex hormones, corticosteroids, and growth hormones (Balázs, 1974).

Hormonal activity in the massive morphogenetic rearrangement associated with metamorphosis is well documented both for the insect (Whitten, 1968) and the amphibian (Etkin, 1968). Modification of brain structure is marked during this process (Kollros, 1968; Pipa, 1973). Examination of the mode of operation of metamorphic hormones in these neural changes may provide a model for the more subtle changes occurring in brain development in those animals in which a climactic metamorphosis does not take place. Thyroid hormone has, naturally, been the hormone on which most work has been done, although Hunt and Jacobson (1971) describe some effects of prolactin and somatotrophin upon amphibian brain growth.

The amphibian visual system has not failed to play its customary prominent part in these studies. Schwind (1933) transplanted an eyecup onto the tail region of an early larval frog. During metamorphic resorption of the tail region, while thyroxine was stimulating extensive degeneration of tail cells, the growing eye survived and it eventually rested on the sacral region. This tissue specific response to a circulating hormone provides an example of a well-recognized phenomenon.

A molecular change in the amphibian visual system, triggered by thyroxine, is the metamorphic change in the type of photoreceptor visual pigment. Wald (1946) described the gradual replacement of porphyropsin by rhodopsin while Wilt (1959a,b), by inserting thyroxine pellets into larval eyes, was able to demonstrate a precocious transition from one pigment type to the other. Further analysis of the biochemical change could well contribute to our understanding of the cellular biology of the action of developmental hormones. There are, for example, considerable differences between various anuran species in the precise pigment transition. The transition from porphyropsin to rhodopsin described occurs in *Rana catesbiana* (Crescitelli, 1958), *Rana temporaria* (Muntz and Reuter, 1966), *Rana pipiens* (Liebman and Entine, 1968), and *Hyla regilla* (Crescitelli, 1958). In toads, on the other hand, there appears to be no transition, rhodopsin being the predominant pigment in both larval and adult stages (Crescitelli, 1958; Muntz and Reuter, 1966). *Xenopus* does undergo a transition, but it appears to be in the direction rhodopsin to porphyropin (Crescitelli, 1973).

The functional synaptic relationships of the retina evolve during larval life. This evolution is reflected in changes in receptive field properties of single units recorded from optic nerve fibers (Reuter, 1969; Pomeranz and Chung, 1970; Pomeranz, 1972; Chung *et al.*, 1975). Pomeranz and Chung (1970) and Pomeranz (1972) correlated these receptive field changes with the appearance of different types of dendritic morphology. The appearance during metamorphosis, of the type of unit that shows sustained responses to a standing edge suggests that the maturation of this type of ganglion cell may require thyroid hormone. At the ultrastructural level, Fisher (1972) reported changes in retinal synaptic organization that occurred during metamorphosis. He concentrated on serial-conventional synapses; i.e., a synaptic complex in which a presynaptic amacrine process is also postsynaptic to another amacrine process. This type of synapse, as opposed to other synaptic types of the inner plexiform layer, displays a remarkable increase in number during metamorphosis. Fisher was able to produce this increase before metamorphosis by inserting a thyroxine pellet into one eye.

A further example of the role of thyroxine in neural maturation is the development of the corneal reflex. Kollros (1942) showed that in anuran tadpoles the onset of the corneal reflex (an eye withdrawal in response to corneal stimulation) coincided with the onset of metamorphic climax. If metamorphosis was prevented by hypophysectomy, the corneal reflex did not appear in anurans (although it did do so in urodeles), but could be produced by thyroxine-induced metamorphosis. The introduction of thyroxine-rich agar pellets into the fourth ventricle of midlarval *Rana pipiens* induced the corneal reflex to mature well in advance of other metamorphic phenomena (Kollros, 1943). Subsequent studies (reviewed in Kollros, 1968) monitored the threshold levels of thyroxine required to mediate this effect.

These effects of thyroxine on the maturation of the amphibian visual system thus provide examples of a more generalized effect of thyroid influences on neural maturation. Another amphibian situation in which neural maturation is thyroxine dependent is that of the lateral motor column (Beaudoin, 1956), while in the case of the Mauthner cells, it is their atrophy and degeneration that is thyroxine-dependent (Stefanelli, 1951; Pesetsky, 1962). In mammals, work on maturation of dendritic patterns (Eayrs, 1971; Balázs and Richter, 1973) and on cerebellar development (Hajós *et al.*, 1973) illustrates the ubiquitous influence of thyroxine in vertebrate neurogenesis.

TROPHIC INFLUENCES

The most obvious signs of neural communication are those electrochemical events associated with rapid information transfer from one neuron to another. These transitory phenomena are, however, only one aspect of the intercellular relationships obtaining in the brain. There are many other relationships of longer-term nature in which an interaction between two neural cells or between a neural cell and its periphery influences the structure and function of one or both of the two participants. This broad and poorly defined area is usually given the general term neurotrophic. It includes the striking relationships in which each member of the pair is vital for the continued integrity of the partner—in the absence of one, the other will die. The vital dependence of skeletal muscle upon its motor innervation is an example of this class of trophic interaction. Less striking, but hardly less important, is another class in which some metabolic properties of the target cell are modulated. In its broadest sense, the term trophic could cover those mechanisms which establish and maintain patterns of synaptic connections.

Most work on trophic influences has, of course, concentrated on the neuromuscular relationship. On the sensory side, the effects of severance of an afferent input upon the continued integrity of either the peripheral receptor or the central neuron have been described. As an example of the former, the dependence of taste buds upon their nerve supply has been extensively detailed (May, 1925; see Guth, 1968). The visual system has provided the classical example of "transneuronal degeneration" in the degeneration of lateral geniculate neurons deprived of their optic input (see Cowan, 1970a). The same neurons illustrate clearly the bidirectional nature of the trophic relationship, since they also degenerate if deprived of their terminations in the visual cortex (Cowan, 1970a).

Some of the early evidence that optic nerve fibers may influence the development of visual centers was presented by Harrison (1929). He studied the effect on proliferation and differentiation of tectal cells after heteroplastic transplantation of developing eyes between embryos of different species of *Amblystoma*. The larger eye of *A. tigrinum* in an *A. punctatum* host produced cellular hyperplasia in the enlarged optic tectum contralateral to the transplanted eye. Conversely, a small hypoplastic tectum was a result of transplanting the small *A. punctatum* eye into a large *A. tigrinum* host. Two points emerge from this study. First, it seems that the control of the size of the eye is autonomous to the transplant; second, neural development of the optic tectum is dependent upon the extent of the optic fiber input that it receives.

The work on this relationship since then has sought to monitor those aspects of tectal development susceptible to alterations in optic afferent input, usually adopting the rather extreme reduction in optic input consequent upon eye enucleation. Such a procedure reduces the tectal thickness (Terry and Gordon, 1960), reduces the number of cells in most tectal layers (Larsell, 1929, 1931; Kollros, 1953; McMurray, 1954; Eichler, 1971), and leads also to actual cell loss (Kollros, 1953). The earlier the enucleation was performed, the more devastating were the effects upon tectal development. Kollros (1953) believed that the primary effect of optic deafferentation was upon the process of tectal cell proliferation and that the greater part of the tectal hypoplasia reflected reduced mitotic activity. These conclusions were strengthened by the results of subsequent work, cited before, showing reduction in tectal cell numbers. McMurray (1954) showed that temporary interruption of the optic nerve, by crushing, yielded an almost immediate reduction in mitotic activity in the contralateral optic tectum. Regeneration of the crushed optic nerve, however, increased the mitotic activity to normal and in some cases, supranormal levels.

Currie and Cowan (1974a), in their critical appraisal of this field, suggest that there are a number of features in the earlier work which do not accord with this interpretation. It is difficult to explain why the reduction in mitotic number is most marked in the rostral portion of the tectum at a time when the main wave of tectal cell proliferation is occurring in the caudal tectal areas. Currie and Cowan confirmed a reduction of some 16% in mitotic figures following enucleation in *Rana pipiens*, but from the distribution of this reduction, they argued that deafferentation limits gliogenesis, not neurogenesis. In other species, optic deafferentation causes tectal hypoplasia not by affecting cellular proliferation, but by a delayed degeneration of differentiated neurons. This appears to be the case in the chick (Cowan *et al.*, 1968; Kelly and Cowan, 1972) and in a teleost fish (Schmatolla and Erdman, 1973). Perhaps this is also the case in *Rana*.

The nature of the factor from an optic fiber that is capable of sustaining a tectal cell is not known. In other neurotropic situations, the nature of the trophic message is also unclear. The general aspect of neuronal trophic functions has been considered recently (Drachman, 1974a) and Drachman (1974b) points out that the trophic messages could be either any link in the chain of events involved in normal synaptic transmission or some special trophic substances that he appropriately called mysterines. In considering trophic phenomena, one tends to concentrate on interneuronal relationships. The amphibian visual system displays such trophic relationships, but offers, in addition, the intriguing dependence of glial cell proliferation upon neuronal fiber input (Currie and Cowan, 1974a). That the relationship between optic fiber input and tectal glial cells is more than just a simple dependence of the latter upon the former is shown by the work of Gaze and Watson (1968) who described a rapid division of glial cells after *section* of the optic nerve in a newt.

CELL DEATH

It is strange, at first sight, that during embryogenesis, which is a time of unparalleled cellular proliferation and growth, a normal feature of organ development is frequently massive death of cellular elements. The importance of these degenerative processes for normal morphogenesis is well illustrated in the development of the sex organs. In both sexes, the selective degeneration of Müllerian and Wolffian derivatives is a necessary step in the formation of normal sex organs. Another example of cell death, that has already been mentioned briefly, occurs during resorption of the tail during anuran metamorphosis. Not only tail cells die, but neurons in the spinal cord innervating the tail also die, as do the Mauthner neurons.

Although cell death is thus a common occurrence and one which has aroused considerable interest, neither the causative mechanism nor the developmental significance of these processes is obvious (Saunders, 1966; Saunders and Gasseling, 1968). Ernst (1926) detailed various morphogenetic events involving cell death, and the next worker to treat extensively this topic was Glücksmann (1940, 1951), who described waves of cell death during the maturation of the amphibian eye. Glücksmann discerned three different ontogenetic roles for this degeneration: (1) morphogenetic—when cell death in selective areas changes the form of a structure; (2) histiogenetic—which seems to occur at critical stages in the differentiation of a tissue; and (3) phylogenetic—which produces regression of a transient or vestigial tissue.

Dying cells may be seen in the amphibian eye during invagination of the eyecup, but the first major episode occurs soon after induction of the lens from the overlying ectoderm and seems to involve ectodermal cells subjected to the inducing influence of the neural retina, but which are not actually incorporated into the lens. Why such cells should die rather than participate in the proliferating lens is not apparent.

Histiogenetic cell death occurs in three separate waves of cell degeneration during retinal differentiation in *Rana temporaria* (Glücksmann, 1940). The first cell-death wave occurs in the central retina, just prior to the appearance of the first retinal ganglion cells. The second wave, occurring some 40 hours later, involves again central retinal cells, but this time in the inner nuclear layer. Sixty hours later, a wave of degeneration involving the outer nuclear layer occurs. Glücksmann noted this temporal relationship between a wave of cell death and the subsequent appearance of a new layer in central retinal regions. The causal nature, if any, of this relationship has not yet been elucidated.

Källén (1965) viewed this cell death as a mechanism that "mops-up" defective cells. Thus, cells survive until the arrival of some intrinsic or extrinsic trigger to further differentiation. The defective cells do not respond adequately to the trigger and for some reason die. This is, of course, a teleological rather than a mechanistic explanation of the phenomena.

Another view of cell death in the developing nervous system, that has received both favor and some experimental support, is the redundancy hypothesis (Hamburger and Levi-Montalcini, 1949). They suggested that much of the cell death seen in the anterior motor columns and spinal ganglia could be explained by the postulate that neurogenic mechanisms generate an excess of cells to ensure adequate innervation of the periphery. Those cells unable to reach or to maintain contact with the periphery die. Studies on cell death in the ventral horn of *Xenopus* after limb extirpation supports the view that at a certain stage of its development the motor neuron requires contact with the periphery to survive (Prestige, 1967, 1974).

This and other examples of cell death in vertebrate neurogenesis are considered in more depth in a recent review by Cowan (1973). He comes to the sober conclusion that while it is relatively easy to pose some very interesting questions about the phenomenon, it is much more difficult to provide substantial answers.

THE ROLE OF FUNCTION IN NEUROGENESIS

The process of neural development is a continuous one from the time of neurulation until death. Most attention in developmental neurobiology tends to be directed to unraveling those embryonic mechanisms that convert a sheet of undifferentiated neural precursor cells into a functioning brain. Development does not, however, stop at that point. Indeed, the ability of a functioning brain to react to the environment and to initiate behavior permits a whole new class of interactions to modify the further development of the brain. Considerable interest centers on the possibility that experience modifies or molds neural structure in early life. It is only in the last decade or so that the functional characteristics of specific neuronal systems have been shown to be susceptible to manipulation of the early environment. The most dramatic advances have involved observations on neuronal connections subserving binocular vision in cats (Hubel and Wiesel, 1963, 1965; Blakemore, 1974; Pettigrew, 1974).

The amphibian visual system also offers evidence of a system of connections, whose function appears to be susceptible to the early visual environment. This work will be described only in outline, since it has recently been reviewed elsewhere (Keating, 1974, 1976). The system of connections relates to the binocular visual field of anuran amphibians, that is, the portion of the visual field seen by both eyes of these animals.

In amphibians, the primary tectal projection of the optic nerve fibers is entirely crossed, so that the whole visual field of one eye maps to the contralateral optic tectum. In anurans, a secondary system of connections links the rostral areas of the two tecta so that the binocular portion of the visual field of each eye projects not only to the contralateral optic tectum, but also, through this indirect pathway, to the ipsilateral optic tectum (Gaze, 1958b; Gaze and Jacobson, 1962, 1963a; Keating and Gaze, 1970b). The pattern of connections in this intertectal system is precisely ordered in such a fashion that the projection of the binocular visual field through both eyes to each tectum is in register. Thus, in these rostral tectal regions, any one point in binocular visual space projects to a tectal point directly through the contralateral eye and to the same tectal point through the ipsilateral eye by way of the intertectal system. A feature of this system that aroused interest was its response, in *Xenopus*, to surgical manipulation of one eye. Such a procedure alters the projection of the visual field through the manipulated eye to its contralateral optic tectum. The surprising finding following this procedure, hinted at by Gaze *et al.* (1965) and later confirmed by Gaze *et al.* (1970), was that the intertectal connections changed to maintain the registration of binocular visual input through the two eyes to each tectum. Keating (1968) and Gaze *et al.*, (1970) suggested that this plasticity of intertectal connections was functionally mediated, requiring binocular visual experience. This prediction has been supported by the demonstration that binocular visual deprivation following surgical manipulation of one eye in *Xenopus* larvae prevents the plastic rearrangement of intertectal connections that normally follows this procedure (Keating, 1974; Keating and Feldman, 1975). The role of binocular visual function in the normal development of the intertectal connections has been examined by rearing normal animals in darkness (Keating and Feldman, 1975) or with just one eye (Feldman and Keating, 1976). Both procedures reduced the precision of organization in the intertectal system, but a normal overall pattern of connections still appeared. It seemed that processes independent of binocular visual experience can mold the general pattern of intertectal connections, but the "fine tuning" of the system requires visual experience.

It has been suggested (Keating, 1974) that the role of this functionally dependent "tuning" is to maintain the congruence of visual input from the two eyes throughout the life of the animal. A frontal binocular overlap in the visual fields of the two eyes first appears during meta-morphosis, but the geometry of the interocular relationships changes continuously throughout life. In *Xenopus,* these changes are quite con-siderable and occur rapidly during, and just after, metamorphosis, and more slowly during subsequent juvenile and adult life. If, as seems prob-able (Keating, 1976), binocular inputs are to be maintained in register in the face of a changing interocular geometry, then a continuous change in the detailed connections of the intertectal system is required. This change could be mediated by a mechanism utilizing binocular visual ex-perience. The plasticity required of the system would decrease in extent from the time of first appearance of the intertectal responses at stage 61 (Beazley *et al.,* 1972). The capacity of the intertectal system to re-spond to experimentally induced changes in interocular relationships re-flects this normal requirement. Keating *et al.* (1975) showed that during early metamorphic climax the system has the capacity to respond to very large changes in interocular geometry, that by late metamorphic climax the capacity is reduced, and by late adult life not even relatively small changes in interocular geometry evoke a plastic response from the inter-tectal system. Keating and Feldman (1976) have confirmed this impres-sion of a gradually reduced capacity of the intertectal system to respond to changes in visual input.

The susceptibility of these intertectal connections to visual experience will prove, probably, to be a rather complex phenomenon. Attempts to demonstrate a similar plasticity in *Rana pipiens* have failed (Jacobson, 1971; Jacobson and Hirsch, 1973; Skarf, 1973; Skarf and Jacobson, 1974). Whether this reflects a true species difference, or whether the different recording techniques selects two populations of intertectal response which react differently to visual experience remains to be elucidated.

The demonstration of functionally dependent changes in systems of visual connections as diverse as those of the anuran intertectal system and the cat geniculocortical system suggests that this class of develop-mental mechanism is widely utilized during the later phases of vertebrate neural development.

SUMMARY

The amphibian visual system has provided an experimental substrate for the investigation of a wide range of problems in developmental neuro-biology. These extend from the factors involved in the earliest events of neural development, through short- and long-range cellular interactions which participate in brain maturation, to those areas in which the functioning of the brain may modulate its own further development. Some of the fields on which study of the amphibian visual system has illuminated our understanding of developmental neurobiology have been considered.

Developmental neurobiology as a discipline is moving rapidly from a descriptive to an analytical mode. Its requirement for a clear conceptual framework on which to base further experimental strategies is thus greater than ever. The incorporation of ideas deriving from general embryology into such a framework is vital, but such an incorporation must proceed with caution. The sense in which the embryological concepts are being used must be stated rigorously, and their suitability in the neural situation to which they are being applied must be carefully examined.

Much of the excitement in the field, and its hope for the future, lies in the belief that the molecular mechanisms responsible for the observed phenomena are now amenable to study. It is, however, necessary in many situations first to unravel the principles of supracellular organization that are operating, for it is only in the light of such information that the most profitable questions may be asked about the molecular mechanisms. It is not unreasonable to believe that in this rapidly growing field the amphibian visual system will continue to play a major part in the elucidation of the cellular and molecular events underlying the various aspects of neural development.

Standards for Laboratory Amphibians

George W. Nace

INTRODUCTION

The investigator concerned with biological processes, such as those involving the nervous system, has always sought animal models that most clearly illustrate the point in question and are thus most amenable to the investigative effort. Too frequently, however, investigators do not thoroughly familiarize themselves with the biology of the whole animal, and consequently encounter difficulties with the biology and the laboratory maintenance of the species they select.

As amply illustrated in this volume, an amphibian is often selected by the neurobiologist as his model. It is evident why this selection is made. As typical tetrapods, amphibians possess most of the features of higher vertebrates, yet retain many simplifying characteristics that facilitate analysis. Furthermore, they may be readily studied at all stages from the time of fertilization through maturity. As ectothermic animals, their use simplifies the experimental procedures by eliminating the need for the complex metabolic support systems required when working with endotherms. Finally, amphibians have traditionally been ubiquitous and readily accessible by local collection or from commercial suppliers (Nace *et al.*, 1971). To appreciate the potential and past contributions of amphibians to neurobiology, one need only be reminded of the classical work of Harrison (1907) who used amphibian embryos and the tissue culture technique to determine that the axon is not produced by the tandem assembly of fragments of peripheral cells.

317

Research in all of the biological sciences, including neurobiology, faces the dilemma that techniques and concepts have reached such sophistication that the questions to be answered are often more precise than are the biological systems available on which to test the hypotheses. It is no longer enough to place a neurological preparation on a device and make some measurements. The precision of current equipment demands objects of study which meet high standards of quality and reliability (Nace, 1968, 1975). Investigators who use mice understand well that funding or publication cannot be expected if the genetic, nutritional, and health standards of their animals are not specified; but unfortunately, experimental biologists who use other animals tend to treat these matters in a much more cavalier manner. It must be appreciated that standards of quality are not met by using a nerve preparation from any amphibian which may be fortuitously available. Neurological functions differ not only between species, but also between populations and individuals of a species and from season to season. The use of a particular species, or even individuals, simply for reasons of convenience, is no longer adequate. Neither the strictures of specimen quality nor of science are satisfied: improper quality yields unreliable results; the choice of materials for reasons of availability or simple experimental design in the aggregate yields hypotheses based on a conceptual animal that is nonexistent. The neurobiologist who fails to consider these biological truths seriously underestimates the degree to which the parts of an animal are integrated to derive a functional whole.

To the practicing experimental biologist, these considerations would seem to pose insuperable problems because the concept of biological standards should apply not only to amphibians, but to any animal model selected. It is additionally difficult for those using amphibians because the need for standardized, high-quality animals has been complicated by the increasing difficulty of obtaining any kind of satisfactory amphibian material.

THE BIOLOGICAL STANDARD

The general problem of biological standards as it relates to the variability of species, populations, and individuals at different seasons may be illustrated by considering the animal popularly referred to as the leopard frog. For years, it has been recognized that this designation covered a wide variety of forms from an extensive geographical range, yet it was common to call any spotted frog *Rana pipiens* or, if the investigator was especially careful, to call it a member of the *R. pipiens* complex. There is, however, evidence that, on occasion even a different but related spotted species, *R. palustris,* the pickerel frog, has been inadvertently included in this designation.

Such confusion of taxonomy and its deleterious influence on the goal of standardization must now change! Pace (1974), as summarized below, has published an extensive, but still incomplete, revision of the taxonomy of the leopard frog within the limits of the United States. Species names have been defined for members of the group which possess a variety of distinguishing characteristics. The experimental biologist would do well to become acquainted with this new classification of one of the most frequently used groups of experimental frogs. This situation typifies many groups of animals. The study of animal systematics is far from complete, and populations of animals which, at any point in time, are classified as members of one or of several species may later be reclassified among several species or lumped into a single species.

Evidence for differences between populations within the several species of the leopard frogs is not fully documented, but many observations suggest a high degree of pond specificity and, therefore, of discreteness of their populations. The careful investigator will be cautious of this source of variability. And this is in addition to the variability expected between any heterozygous individuals.

Another source of variability arises from the differing physiological states of leopard frogs at different seasons of the year and at different latitudes and altitudes. The reasons for this are evident when it is recalled that ectothermic animals must be finely adapted to climatic and topographical features of their environment. For example, in the summer, *R. pipiens* are active and capable of a wide variety of spacial movements (Rittschof, 1975). The males engage in growth and self-preservation and the females, in addition to these activities, engage in specialized functions concerned with egg production. In the northern environment, changes occur in the fall to prepare both sexes for prolonged hibernation under ice, while in the southern environment they remain active throughout the year, with short intervals of dormancy to escape frost. In addition, changes occur at the mating season, which takes place at different times, depending on both latitude and altitude.

It is evident that the use of frogs from different sources or at different phases in their life cycle may yield highly variable results, and this is true of all species which might be selected as models. It is not enough to transfer a hibernating frog to room temperature in the hope that it will revert to a summer physiology, or to refrigerate a summer frog in the hope that it will assume a hibernation physiology. These physiological states are not controlled by temperature alone, but by complex neurological and hormonal systems which are responsive to many circumstantials such as photoperiod, temperature, moisture, and nutritional state.

THE SUPPLY OF AMPHIBIANS

The Quantity

It is important to realize that, with the exception of the Mexican axolotl, until very recently, all amphibians used for experimental or commercial purposes were collected from the wild and were obtained either directly from the collectors or from dealers (Gibbs *et al.*, 1971). It was predicted that regardless of the supply of animals in nature, this source would be inadequate to the need (Nace, 1968), since changing conditions were producing a decrease in the population of people willing to collect these animals, whether they be urodeles or anurans. This situation could be corrected only by fundamental changes in the sociology of the populations from which collectors are recruited and by a return of the dealerships which market these animals from the impersonal corporations that now function to the more personal organizations that were able to recruit and retain these collectors. These problems of collector availability and dealer organization have common causes and do not seem amenable to modification.

More recently, however, a second factor has become more serious. This is the unavailability of commercially significant concentrations of the animals in the natural environment. Although as recently as five to eight years ago, one midwestern dealer processed 96–100 *tons* of frogs per year for educational and research purposes, the current yield is only a fraction of this. Indeed, one western state which as recently as 1969–1970 produced 10 *tons* of leopard frogs produced only 250 *pounds* in 1974–1975. Efforts to increase this productivity have included increasing the pay, but even collectors with 30 to 40 years experience were unsuccessful in finding the animals (R. G. McKinnell, personal communication).

The Quality

Concurrent with the reduced quantity, there has been a reduction in the quality of the animals. Several dealers, using techniques which for years were successful in maintaining animals on their premises, recently lost tons of frogs in their holding facilities. This condition is further signaled by reports of windrows of dead frogs found in hibernacula in the springs of 1972, 1973, and 1974. It is also indicated by a report that on a field expedition to isolated breeding ponds in a western state, whereas normally 90% of the eggs in a clutch develop, only 10% of the eggs were found to be developing in the spring of 1974 (R. G. McKinnell, personal communication). Thus, not only are the animals in short supply, but many suffer from pathologies that are not well understood, which may arise from nutritional deficiency, environmental contamination, or stress (Rittschof, 1975).

Although the full geographic range of these conditions, the reasons behind them, and the extent to which species other than the leopard frogs have been affected are not well known and are not documented, informal evidence of many kinds suggests the conditions are widespread and involve many species. Such animals from the wild are clearly unsuitable for high-quality experimental work.

SOLUTIONS TO THE PROBLEMS

Tactical

Good Handling

The first step in improving the use of those animals available is to practice good care and management. A guide of such practices was recently prepared by the Subcommittee on Amphibian Standards of the Committee on Standards of the Institute of Laboratory Animal Resources of the National Research Council (Nace et al., 1974).* Space limitations do not allow the inclusion of substantive information concerning the sources, housing, husbandry, and practices of the kind covered in this guide. Although the guide contains a chapter on the classification of amphibians commonly used for laboratory research, it was prepared prior to the taxonomic revision of the R. pipiens complex (Pace, 1974). Since this group of frogs is so important to neurophysiologists and since the literature describing them is not readily accessible to neurophysiologists, it is appropriate here to present a key to the adult males. It must also be noted, however, that some populations of this complex, particularly in the southwestern states, require additional definition. The following description and key is quoted from Pace (1974):

* It is available as ISBN 0-309-02210-X from the Printing and Publishing Office, National Academy of Sciences, 2101 Constitution Avenue N.W., Washington, D.C. 20418.

Rana pipiens Schreber

This is probably the most widely ranging member of the species complex. It is the only leopard frog known in Canada. In the United States it is found in New England, in New York and Pennsylvania, in most of Ohio and northern Kentucky, in northern and central Indiana, in northern Illinois, in Iowa and west to and through the Rocky Mountains. In the Far West it is found in the Snake River Valley, the Columbia River Valley, and in Lake Tahoe and other areas of California and Nevada. It is also found at higher elevations at least as far south as Alpine, Arizona, and may occur in at least the northern part of Mexico as well.

Rana utricularia Harlan

Found throughout most of the Atlantic Coastal Plain from southern New York and northern New Jersey and through the Gulf Coastal Plain to somewhere between Corpus Christi and Victoria, Texas. It is found in southern Missouri, southern Illinois, southwestern Indiana, most of Kentucky, and extreme southern Ohio. It is found in southeastern Kansas and eastern Oklahoma and is the only leopard frog known from Tennessee, Arkansas, Louisiana, Mississippi, Alabama, Georgia Florida, South Carolina, North Carolina, Virginia and Delaware.

Rana berlandieri Baird

In the United States this species is known only from southern Texas. It is known from as far north as Johnson County, in central Texas, and San Patricio County, along the Gulf Coast. It may also occur west of the Pecos River (known from Ward County, Texas, whose western border lies along the Pecos River).

Rana blairi Mecham, Littlejohn, Oldham, Brown and Brown

Found in the central plains and prairie regions of the United States, from eastern Colorado, northeastern New Mexico, northern Texas, Oklahoma (except the southeastern third of the state), most of Kansas, part of Nebraska and Iowa, and in northern Missouri, central Illinois, and in scattered localities further east (western Indiana) and south (southern Illinois).

KEY TO ADULT MALES IN THE *Rana pipiens* COMPLEX FROM THE UNITED STATES (from Pace, 1974)

1.   Skin at angle of jaw overlying internal vocal sac not differentiated in texture or color from surrounding skin (may be somewhat stretched); no distinct white spots on centers of tympana; dorsolateral folds continuous and not displaced, usually wide and low, but discernible to the point where the leg joins the body; dorsal spots usually ringed with light coloration . . . . *Rana pipiens*

1'.   Skin at angle of jaw overlying internal vocal sac differentiated from surrounding skin in some way (e.g., texture or pigmentation); tympanal spots, dorsolateral folds, and dorsal spots variable 2

2(1'). Mullerian ducts absent, or specimen from Florida 3

2'.   Mullerian ducts present and specimen from Texas . . . *Rana berlandieri*

3(2). External vocal sacs large, spherical, apparently thin-skinned, lying loose at angle of jaw when not inflated or from Florida; dorsolateral folds usually continuous and not displaced . . . . *Rana utricularia*

3'.   External vocal sacs small, usually visible only because skin at angle of jaw is conspicuous when internal vocal sac is not inflated owing to texturings of the skin below the labial stripe; dorsolateral folds usually discontinuous and displaced medially . . . . *Rana blairi*

In addition to classification as a species, it is important for the experimental biologist to identify the quality of the animals used in each protocol. Terminology for the quality of research amphibians is given by Nace *et al.* (1974). This terminology is based on nine criteria of quality which are used to define several categories of animals falling under the general headings of "wild," "wild caught," "laboratory reared," and "laboratory bred." This source also contains appendices which give the status of "endangered" amphibians and detail the laws controlling amphibian use. The experimental biologist should be particularly cautious to avoid violating the regulations which other biologists have developed to protect endangered amphibians and to guide the use of those not on the endangered list. Treanor (1975) is particularly useful as a presentation of the problems which face those responsible for regulating amphibian use.

Several areas of amphibian management are underdeveloped. These are the control of reproductive cycles, the regulation of growth, the evaluation of nutritional regimens, and the management of disease. Better understanding of the endocrine control of oogenesis and egg maturation, with emphasis on the roles of photoperiod, temperature cycles, and climatic changes in timing this control and on the involvement of nutrition is badly needed. The regulation of growth involves similar factors. The problem of nutritional regimens is inseparable from the fact that to date few amphibians can be maintained on nonliving diets. Indeed, the choice of *Xenopus* for many studies is based less on its "scientific merit" than on the fact that it is one of the few amphibians which thrive on nonliving diets. Mechanisms for presenting nonliving diets have yet to be perfected, but are under study and will be followed by analyses of dietary requirements. Epidemic diseases need not constitute a problem in amphibian management, since most of them are related to stress on the animals. Current handling, housing, and feeding recommendations minimize the stress that underlies such epidemics. However, the prevention, diagnosis, and management of specific diseases that afflict individual animals must be greatly improved in order to prevent losses of valuable individuals in experimental or breeding regimens.

Note that an amphibian may show many symptoms of distress, such as ulcered skin, clouded cornea, inflamed ventral surface, a drooping countenance, high concentrations of parasites and survive for a prolonged period, or may show no external symptoms, yet be dead the following day. Although many organisms are found in association with amphibians

(Glorioso *et al.*, 1974; van der Waaij *et al.*, 1974), the relationship between these and the pathological state is poorly understood. Because amphibians are an ancient vertebrate, many symbiotic and successful parasitic relationships have been established and their influence on the host has not been adequately defined.

Although adequate procedural recommendations are made, Nace and co-workers (1974) do not compile the handling and housing errors perpetrated by users of amphibians. Such a compilation would have included hosing newly arrived warm animals with cold water, placing aquatic animals in chlorinated water, refrigerating summer frogs, "hibernating" animals at the wrong temperature or in an inadequate quantity of water, being satisfied to keep animals at room temperature without food for many days because they don't die rapidly, placing frogs in a mouse cage with mouse litter and little water or toads in an aquarium with much water, failing to change water frequently enough to avoid fouling, and many others.

Good Practices

In addition to the good handling required to maintain healthy animals, the investigator has the responsibility to meet the standards of animal identification just described. He must make use of the best resources available for the classification of his animals. Note, however, that, as illustrated by the case of *R. pipiens*, it is never possible to adequately evaluate reports that identify species without giving geographic data. The citation of a dealer who sells animals collected over the range from Canada to Mexico and from Nebraska to Michigan does not help.

The careful biologist must take three precautions: (1) collect all the information required for each experimental grade of animal as described in Nace and co-workers (1974); (2) submit representative animals to an appropriate specialist for classification (see Wake *et al.*, 1975, for information on guides to such specialists); and (3) keep "voucher" specimens.

The carcasses of voucher specimens from which preparations for critical experiments were taken should be preserved (see Wake *et al.*, 1975, for guides to the techniques). Such specimens may be used at any time to assure correct classification should the systematics of an animal group be revised. They are also a source of information on such matters as gender and reproductive state and nutritional and disease status which may not seem important in the context of a given experiment until other data or reports from other laboratories demand reinterpretation of data. Provided the observational data are accurate, such reinterpretation could well avoid the repetition of many studies and thus serve importantly in conserving the animal resources.

Strategic

Develop Sources of Standard Animals

The support of all biologists is needed for the long-term solution of the problems that have been discussed. This is to encourage the development of cultured amphibians and to make use of the cultured amphibian resources which are available. By so doing, standard animals can be used and natural resources are spared (Nace, 1975). The progress that has resulted from the use of mammalian models since defined strains of laboratory mice became available is known to all. Similar advances can be expected when defined amphibians become readily available.

At the present time, cultured anurans are available in the United States from the Amphibian Facility of the University of Michigan and from Louisiana State University. The most readily available animals at the Amphibian Facility are leopard frogs, *Bombina orientalis*, *Xenopus laevis*, and several species of the reed frog, *Hyperolius*. These represent, respectively, the Ranidae, Discoglossidae, Pipidae, and Hyperoliidae, each with distinctive and useful characteristics. The Louisiana State University colony specializes in *R. catesbeiana*.

Among urodeles, the only readily available cultured species is *Ambystoma mexicanum*, the Mexican axolotl. The best developed colony of these is at Indiana University, although some are also maintained at the University of Michigan. The only other cultured urodele is *Pleurodeles waltlii*, some of which are maintained in the laboratory of Joseph Bagnara of the University of Arizona, but whose major source is from the laboratory of Professor Gallien at the University of Paris.

The development of amphibian culture procedures and colonies is expensive, however, and these efforts have been retarded by modest support and by the failure of investigators to express their needs to those who establish funding priorities. As a consequence, it is necessary to assess charges for these cultured animals. Neurobiologists who have much at stake in the quality of their experimental model should be outspoken in expressing their needs. At the operating level, those who desire cultured animals should obtain current price lists, determine the availability of the animals required, and adequately budget for these animals during the planning phases of their investigations.

If neurobiologists and other biologists insist upon the quality of animals appropriate to the significance of their work, there seems a reasonable likelihood that during the coming years resources will become adequate to the need and capable of providing amphibians with full definition of their physiological and genetic properties. Already numerous mutations of interest to neurobiologists have been discovered in the axolotl (Malacinski and Brothers, 1974), and a few have been observed in the leopard frog.

ACKNOWLEDGMENTS

Contribution No. 63 from the Amphibian Facility. Supported by a National Institutes of Health resources grant (P06 RR 00572) and the Grass Foundation.

Bibliography

Adams, J. C., and Warr, W. B. (1974). The use of horseradish peroxidase (HRP) in identifying neuronal connections. *28th Ann. Meeting Cajal Club* (unpublished).

Abramov, I. (1972). Retinal mechanisms of colour vision. *In* "Handbook of Sensory Physiology" (M. G. F. Fuortes, ed.), Vol. VII, Part 2, pp. 567–607. Springer-Verlag, Berlin and New York.

Adelmann, H. B. (1929a). Experimental studies on the development of the eye. I. The effect of the removal of median and lateral areas of the anterior end of the urodelan neural plate on the development of the eyes (*Triton taeniatus* and *Amblystoma punctatum*). *J. Exp. Zool.* **54**, 249–291.

Adelmann, H. B. (1929b). Experimental studies on the development of the eye. II. The eye-forming potencies of the median portions of the urodelan neural plate (*Triton taeniatus* and *Amblystoma punctatum*). *J. Exp. Zool.* **54**, 201–317.

Adelmann, H. B. (1936). The problem of cyclopia. *Q. Rev. Biol.* **11**, 161–182 and 284–304.

Adelmann, H. B. (1937). Experimental studies on the development of the eye. IV. The effect of partial and complete excision of the prechordal substrata on the development of the eyes of *Amblystoma punctatum*. *J. Exp. Zool.* **75**, 199–227.

Adler, K., and Taylor, U. H. (1973). Extraocular perception of polarized light by orienting salamanders. *J. Comp. Physiol.* **87**, 203–212.

Adrian, E. D., and Matthews, R. 1927a. The discharge of impulses in the optic nerve and its relation to the electric changes in the retina. *J. Physiol. (London)* **63**, 378–414.

Adrian, E. D., and Matthews, R. (1927b). The process involved in retinal excitation. *J. Physiol. (London)* **64**, 279–301.

Adrian, E. D., and Matthews, R. (1928). The interaction of retinal neurones. *J. Physiol. (London)* **65**, 273–298.

Alderman, A. L. (1935). The determination of the eye in the anuran, *Hyla regilla*. *J. Exp. Zool.* **70**, 205–232.

Ariens Kappers, C. U., Huber, C. G., and Crosby, E. C. (1936). "The Comparative Anatomy of the Nervous System of Vertebrates, Including Man," Vol. II. Macmillan, New York.

Attardi, D. G., and Sperry, R. W. (1963). Preferential selection of central pathways by regenerating optic fibers. *Exp. Neurol.* **7**, 46–64.

Autrum, H. (1959). Das Fehlen unwillkürlicher Augenbewegungen beim Frosch. *Naturwissenschaften* **46**, 435.

Bajandurow, B. I., and Pegel, W. A. (1933). Der bedingte Reflex bei Fröschen. *Z. Vergl. Physiol.* **18**, 284–297.

Balázs, R. (1974). Influence of metabolic factors on brain development. *Br. Med. Bull.* **30**, 126–134.

Balázs, R., and Richter, D. (1973). Effects of hormones on the chemical maturation of the brain. *In* "Biochemistry of the Developing Brain" (W. Himwich, ed.), pp. 253–299. Dekker, New York.

Barbera, A. J., Marchase, R. B., and Roth, S. (1973). Adhesive recognition and retinotectal specificity. *Proc. Nat. Acad. Sci. U.S.A.* **70**, 2482–2486.

Barlow, H. B. (1953). Summation and inhibition in the frog's retina. *J. Physiol. (London)* **119**, 69–88.

Barlow, H. B. (1957). Increment thresholds at low intensities considered as signal/noise discriminations. *J. Physiol. (London)* **136**, 469–488.

Barlow, H. B., Hill, R. M., and Levick, W. R. (1964). Retinal ganglion cells responding selectively to direction and speed of image motion in the rabbit. *J. Physiol. (London)* **173**, 377–407.

Barondes, S. H. (1970). Brain glycomacromolecules and interneuronal recognition. *In* "The Neurosciences: Second Study Program" (F. O. Schmitt, ed.), pp. 747–760. Rockefeller Univ. Press, New York.

Barrio, A. (1964). Especies cripticas dei género *Pleurodema* que conviven en una misma area, identificadas por el canto nupcial (*Anura, Leptodactylidae*). *Physis* **24**, 471–489.

Barrio, A. (1970a). Caracteristicas del cariotipo de los pseudidos (Amphibia, Anura). *Physis* **29**, 505–510.

Barrio, A. (1970b). *Insuetophrynus acarpicus,* un nuevo leptodactilio firmisternio, Sudamericano (Amphibia, Anura). *Physis* **30**, 331–341.

Barrio, A., and Pistol de Rubel, D. (1972). Encuesta cariotípica de poblaciones Argentino-Uruguayas de *Odontophrynus americanus* (*Anura, Leptodactylidae*) relacionada con otros rasgos taxonomicos. *Physis* **31**, 281–291.

Barrio, A., and Rinaldi de Chieri, P. (1970a). Estudios citogenéticos sobre el genero *Pleurodema* y sus consecuencias evolutivas (*Amphibia, Anura, Leptodactylidae*), *Physis* **30**, 309–319.

Barrio, A., and Rinaldi de Chieri, P. (1970b). Relaciones cariosistemáticas de los Ceratophryidae de la Argentina. *Physis* **30**, 321–329.

Baumann, C. (1967). Sehpurpurbleichung und Stäbchenfunktion in der isolierten Froschnetzhaut. III. Die Dunkeladaptation des skotopischen Systems nach partieller Sehpurpur bleichung. *Pfluegers Arch. Gesamte Physiol. Menschen Tiere* **298**, 70–81.

Baumann, C. (1970). Regeneration of rhodopsin in the isolated retina of the frog (*Rana esculenta*). *Vision Res.* **10**, 627–637.

Baumann, C., and Scheibner, H. (1968). The dark adaptation of single units in the isolated frog retina following partial bleaching of rhodopsin. *Vision Res.* **8**, 1127–1138.

Baylor, D. A., and Fuortes, M. G. F. (1970). Electrical responses of single cones in the retina of the turtle. *J. Physiol. (London)* **207**, 77–92.

Baylor, D. A., Fourtes, M. G., and O'Bryan, P. M. (1971). Receptive fields of cones in the retina of the turtle. *J. Physiol. (London)* **214**, 265–294.

Beaudoin, A. R. (1956). The development of lateral motor column cells in the lumbo-sacral cord in *Rana pipiens*. II. Development under the influence of thyroxin. *Anat. Rec.* **125**, 247–259.

Beazley, L., Keating, M. J., and Gaze, R. M. (1972). The appearance during development of responses in the optic tectum following visual stimulation of the ipsilateral eye in *Xenopus laevis*. *Vision Res.* **12**, 407–410.

Beçak, M. L., Beçak, W., and Vizotto, L. D. (1970a). A diploid population of the polyploid amphibian *Odontophrynus americanus* and an artificial intra-specific triploid hybrid. *Experientia* **26**, 545–546.

Beçak, M. L., Denaro, L., and Beçak, W. (1970b). Polyploidy and mechanisms of karyotypic diversification in Amphibia. *Cytogenetics* **9**, 225–238.

Bechterev, W. (1884). Uber die Function de Vierhugel. *Arch. Gesamte Physiol. Menschen Tiere* **33**, 413–439

Beer, T. (1899). Die Akkomodation des Auges bei Amphibien. *Pflügers Arch. Gesamte Physiol. Menschen Tiere* **73**, 501–534.

Bennett, M. V. L. (1973). Function of electronic junctions in embryonic and adult tissues. *Fed. Proc., Fed. Am. Soc. Exp. Biol.* **32**, 65–75.

Bergey, G. K., Hunt, R. K., and Holtzer, H. (1973). Selective effects of bromodeoxyuridine on developing Xenopus laevis retina. *Anat. Rec.* **175**, 271.

Berman, N., and Hunt, R. K. (1975). Visual projections to the optic tecta in *Xenopus* after partial extirpation of the embryonic eye. *J. Comp. Neurol.* **162**, 23–42.

Bernstein, J. J., and Goodman, D. C. (1973). Overview of neuromorphological plasticity. *Brain, Behav. Evol.* **8**, 162–164.

Birukow, G. (1938). Untersuchungen über den optischen Drehnystagmus und über die Sehschärfe des Grasfrosches (*Rana temporaria* L.). *Z. Vergl. Physiol.* **25**, 92–142.

Birukow, G. (1939). Pukinjesches Phänomen und Farbensehen beim Grasfrosch (*Rana temporaria*). *Z. Vergl. Physiol.* **27**, 41–79.

Birukow, G. (1950). Vergleichende Untersuchungen über das Helligkeits- und Farbensehen bei Amphibien. *Z. Vergl. Physiol.* **32**, 348–382.

Birukow, G., and Meng, M. (1955). Eine neue Methode zur Prüfung des Gesichtssinnes bei Amphibien. *Naturwissenschaften* **42**, 652–653.

Bishop, S. C. (1943). "Handbook of Salamanders." Cornell Univ. Press (Comstock), Ithaca, New York.

Blair, W. F. (1955). Size difference as a possible isolation mechanism in *Microhyla*. *Am. Nat.* **89**, 297–302.

Blair, W. F. (1956). The species as a dynamic system. *Southwest. Nat.* **1**, 1–5.

Blair, W. F. (1958). Mating call in the speciation of anuran amphibians. *Am. Nat.* **92**, 27–51.

Blair, W. F. (1962). Non-morphological data in anuran classification. *Syst. Zool.* **11**, 72–84.

Blair, W. F. (1964). Isolating mechanisms and interspecies interactions in anuran amphibians. *Q. Rev. Biol.* **39**, 334–344.

Blair, W. F. (1969). Especiación en los sapos (género *Bufo*). *Acta Zool. Lilloana* **24**, 317–326.

Blair, W. F. (1972). "Evolution in the Genus Bufo." Univ. of Texas Press, Austin.

Blair, W. F. (1973). Major problems in anuran evolution. *In* "Evolutionary Biology of the Anurans" (J. L. Vial, ed.), pp. 1–8. Univ. of Missouri Press, Columbia.

Blair, W. F. (1976). Adaptation of anurans to equivalent desert scrub of South and North America. *In* "Evolution of Desert Biota" (D. W. Goodall, ed.), Univ. of Texas Press, Austin (in press).

Blakemore, C. (1974). Development of functional connexions in the mammalian visual system. *Br. Med. Bull.* **30**, 152–157.

Bloch, A. M. (1885). Expériences sur la vision. *C. R. Hebd. Seances Acad. Sci.* **37**, 493–495.

Bogart, J. P. (1967). Chromosomes of the South American amphibian family Ceratophridae with a reconsideration of the taxonomic status of *Odontophrynus americanus. Can. J. Genet. Cytol.* 9, 531–542.

Bogart, J. P. (1970). Cromosomas en algunos géneros de anuros. *Act. Conqr. Latin. Zool., 4th, 1970,* Vol. 1, pp. 79–86.

Bogart, J. P. (1971). Afinidades entre los géneros de anuros en las familias Pelobatidae y Ceratophrynidae comose muestra por analisis cromosomico. *Acta Zool. Lilloana* 28, 19–29.

Bogart, J. P. (1972). Karyotypes. *In* "Evolution in the Genus Bufo" (W. F. Blair, ed.), pp. 171–195. Univ. of Texas Press, Austin.

Bogart, J. P. (1973). Evolution of anuran karyotypes. *In* "Evolutionary Biology of the Anurans" (J. L. Vial, ed.), pp. 337–349. Univ. of Missouri Press, Columbia.

Bokermann, W. C. A. (1966). "Lista Anotada das Localidades Tipo de Anfíbios Brasilieros." Servico de Documentacão-RUSP, São Paulo.

Boll, F. (1876). Zur Anatomie und Physiologie der Retina. *Monatsber. Dtsch. Akad. Wiss. Berlin* 44, 783–787.

Bortoff, A. (1964). Localization of slow potential responses in the *Necturus* retina. *Vision Res.* 4, 627–635.

Boterenbrood, E. C. (1958). Organisation in aggregates of anterior neural plate cells of *Triturus alpestris. Proc. K. Ned. Akad. Wet., Ser. C* 61, 470–481.

Boycott, B. B., and Dowling, J. E. (1969). Organization of the primate retina: Light microscopy. *Proc. R. Soc. London, Ser. B* 255, 109–184.

Boycott, B. B., Mrosovsky, N., and Muntz, W. R. A. (1964). Black and white preferences in the frog, *Rana temporaria* and other anura. *J. Exp. Biol.* 41, 865–877.

Boynton, R. M. (1973). Implications of the minimally distinct border. *J. Opt. Soc. Am.* 63, 1037–1043.

Boynton, R. M., and Whitten, D. N. (1970). Visual adaptation in monkey cones: Recordings of late receptor potentials. *Science* 170, 1423–1426.

Bragg, A. N. (1964). Further study of predation and cannibalism in spadefoot tadpoles. *Herpetologica* 20, 17–24.

Branston, N. M., and Fleming, D. G. (1968). Efferent fibers in the frog optic nerve. *Exp. Neurol* 20, 611–623.

Bridges, C. D. B. (1967). Spectroscopic properties of porphyropsin. *Vision Res.* 7, 348–369.

Bridges, C. D. B. (1972). The rhodopsin-porphyropsin visual system. *In* "Handbook of Sensory Physiology" (H. J. A. Dartnall, ed.), Vol. VII, Part I, pp. 417–480. Springer-Verlag, Berlin and New York.

Brown, H. A. (1969). The heat resistance of some anuran tadpoles (Hylidae and Pelobatidae). *Copeia* pp. 138–147.

Brown, K. T. (1968). The electroretinogram: Its components and their origins. *Vision Res.* 8, 633–677.

Brown, J. T. (1976). (In preparation.)

Brown, K. T., and Crawford, J. M. (1967). Melanin and the rapid light-evoked responses from pigment epithelium cells of the frog eye. *Vision Res.* 7, 165–178.

Brown, P. K., Gibbons, I. R., and Wald, G. (1963). The visual cells and visual pigment of the Mudpuppy *Necturus. J. Cell Biol.* 19, 79–106.

Brown, W. T., and Ingle, D. (1973). Receptive field changes produced in frog thalamic units by lesions of the optic tectum. *Brain Res.* 59, 405–409.

Bruesch, S. R., and Arey, L. B. (1942). The number of myelinated and unmyelinated fibers in the optic nerve of vertebrates. *J. Comp. Neurol.* **77**, 631–665.

Burkhardt, D. A. (1970). Proximal negative response of frog retina. *J. Neurophysiol.* **33**, 405–420.

Burkhardt, D. A. (1972). Sensitization in the *Necturus* retina. *J. Opt. Soc. Am.* **62**, 1377.

Burkhardt, D. A. (1974). Sensitization and centre-surround antagonism in *Necturus* retina. *J. Physiol. (London)* **236**, 593–610.

Burkhardt, D. A., and Berntson, C. G. (1972). Light adaptation and excitation: Lateral spread of signals within the frog retina. *Vision Res.* **12**, 1095–1112.

Burkhardt, D. A., and Whittle, P. (1973). Intensity coding in the frog retina. Quantitative relations between impulse activity and graded activity. *J. Gen. Physiol.* **61**, 305–322.

Butenandt, E., and Grüsser, O.-J. (1968). The effect of stimulus area on the response of movement detecting neurons in the frog's retina. *Pfluegers Arch. Gesamte Physiol. Menschen Tiere* **298**, 238–293.

Byzov, A. L., and Utina, I. A. (1971). Centrifugal effects on the amacrine cells in the frog's retina. *Neirofiziligiya* **3**, 293–300.

Carey, R. (1975). A quantitative analysis of the distribution of the retinal elements in frogs and toads with special emphasis on the *Areae retinalis.* Unpublished Master's Thesis, University of Massachusetts, Amherst.

Cei, J. M. (1949). Costumbres nupciales y reproducción de un batracio caracteristico chaqueño (*Leptodactylus bufonius* Boul.). *Acta Zool. Lilloana* **8**, 105–110.

Cei, J. M. (1955). Chacoan batrachians in central Argentina. *Copeia* pp. 291–293.

Cei, J. M. (1962a). Mapa preliminar de la distribución continental de las "sibling species" del grupo ocellatus (género Leptodactylus). *Rev. Soc. Argent. Biol.* **38**, 258–265.

Cei, J. M. (1962b). *"Batracios de Chile."* Ediciones de la Univ. de Chile, Santiago.

Cervetto, L., and MacNichol, E. F., Jr. (1972). Inactivation of horizontal cells in the turtle retina by glutamate and aspartate. *Science* **178**, 767–768.

Chapman, R. M. (1961). Spectral sensitivity of single neural units in the bullfrog retina. *J. Opt. Soc. Am.* **51**, 1102–1112.

Chapman, R. M. (1966). Light, wavelength, and energy preferences of the bullfrog: Evidence for color vision. *J. Comp. Physiol. Psychol.* **61**, 429–435.

Child, C. M. (1941). *"Patterns and Problems of Development."* Univ. of Chicago Press, Chicago, Illinois.

Chung, S. H. (1974). In search of the rules for nerve connections. *Cell* **3**, 203–207.

Chung, S. H., and Cooke, J. (1975). Polarity of structure and of ordered nerve connection in the developing amphibian brain. *Nature* (London) **258**, 126–132.

Chung, S. H., Raymond, S. A., and Lettvin, J. Y. (1970). Multiple meaning in single visual units. *Brain, Behav. Evol.* **3**, 72–101.

Chung, S. H., Gaze, R. M., and Stirling, R. V. (1973). Abnormal visual function in *Xenopus* following stroboscopic illumination. *Nature (London), New Biol.* **154**, 186–189.

Chung, S. H., Keating, M. J., and Bliss, T. V. P. (1974). Functional synaptic relations during the development of the retinotectal projection in amphibians. *Proc. R. Soc. London, Ser.* **187**, 449–459.

Chung, S. H., Stirling, R. V., and Gaze, R. M. (1975). The structural and functional development of the retina in larval *Xenopus. J. Embryol. Exp. Morphol.* **33**, 915–940.

Cintrón, G. (1970). Niche separation of tree frogs in the Luquillo forest. *In* "A Tropical Rain Forest: A Study of Irradiation and Ecology at El Verde, Puerto Rico" (H. T. Odum, ed.). US At. Energy Comm., Oak Ridge, Tennessee.

Cleland, B. G., and Levick, W. R. (1974). Brisk and sluggish concentrically organized ganglion cells in the cat's retina. *J. Physiol. (London)* **240**, 421–456.

Cohen, A. I. (1972). Rods and cones. *In* "Handbook of Sensory Physiology" (M. G. F. Fuortes, ed.), Vol. VII, Part 2, pp. 63–110. Springer-Verlag, Berlin and New York.

Colbert, E. H. (1955). "Evolution of the Vertebrates." Wiley, New York.

Cone, R. A. (1964). Early receptor potential of the vertebrate retina. *Nature (London)* **204**, 736–739.

Cone, R. A. (1965). The early receptor potential of the vertebrate eye. *Cold Spring Harbor Symp. Quant. Biol.* **30**, 483–491.

Cone, R. A., and Cobbs, W. H. (1969). Rhodopsin cycle in the living eye of the rat. *Nature (London)* **221**, 820–822.

Cook, J. E., and Horder, T. J. (1974). Interactions between optic fibres in their regeneration to specific sites in the goldfish tectum. *J. Physiol. (London)* **241**, 89P–90P.

Cooke, J. (1975). The Emergence and regulation of spatial organization in early animal development. *Annu. Rev. Biophys. Bioeng.* **4**, 185–217.

Copenhagen, D. A. (1972). The Role of Interneurons in Controlling Sensitivity in the Retina. Ph.D. Thesis, University of California, Berkeley.

Corben, C. J., Ingram, G. J., and Tyler, M. J. (1974). Gastric brooding: Unique form of parental care in an Australian frog. *Science* **186**, 946–947.

Coulombre, A. J. (1965). The eye. *In* "Organogenesis" (R. L. De Haan and H. Ursprung, eds.). Holt, New York.

Cowan, W. M. (1970a). Anterograde and retrograde transneuronal degeneration in the central and peripheral nervous system. *In* "Contemporary Research Methods in Neudoanatomy" (W. J. H. Nauta and S. O. Ebbesson, eds.), pp. 217–251. Springer-Verlag, Berlin and New York.

Cowan, W. M. (1970b). Centrifugal fibers to the avian retina. *Br. Med. Bull.* **26**, 112–118.

Cowan, W. M. (1973). Neuronal death as a regulative mechanism in the control of cell number in the nervous system. *In* "Development and Aging in the Nervous System" (M. Rockstein, ed.). Academic Press, New York.

Cowan, W. M., and Powell, T. P. S. (1963). Centrifugal fibers in the avian visual system. *Proc. R. Soc. London, Ser. B* **158**, 232–252.

Cowan, W. M., Adamson, L., and Powell, T. P. S. (1961). An experimental study of the avian visual system. *J. Anat.* **95**, 545–563.

Cowan, W. M., Martin, A. H., and Wenger, E. (1968). Mitotic patterns in the optic tectum of the chick during normal development and after early removal of the optic vesicle. *J. Exp. Zool.* **169**, 71–92.

Crelin, E. S. (1952). Excision and rotation of the developing *Amblystoma* optic tectum and subsequent visual behavior. *J. Exp. Zool.* **120**, 547–578.

Crescitelli, F. (1958). The natural history of visual pigments. *In* "Photobiology," Biol. Colloq., pp. 30–51. Oregon State College, Corvallis.

Crescitelli, F. (1972). The visual cells and visual pigments of the vertebrate eye. *In* "Handbook of Sensory Physiology" (H. J. A. Dartnall, ed.), Vol. VII, Part I, pp. 245–363. Springer-Verlag, Berlin and New York.

Crescitelli, F. (1973). The visual pigment system of *Xenopus laevis:* Tadpoles and adults. *Vision Res.* **13**, 855–865.

Crescitelli, F., and Sickel, E. (1968). Delayed off-responses recorded from the isolated frog retina. *Vision Res.* **8,** 801–816.

Cronly-Dillon, J. R. (1964). Units sensitive to direction of movement in the goldfish optic tectum. *Nature (London)* **203,** 214–215.

Cronly-Dillon, J. R. (1968). Pattern of retinotectal connections after retinal regeneration. *J. Neurophysiol.* **31,** 410–418.

Cronly-Dillon, J. R., and Galand, G. (1966). Analyse des résponses visuelles unitaires dans le nerf optique et le tectum du Triton, *Triturus vulyuris. J. Physiol. (London)* **58,** 502–503.

Crossland, W. J., Cowan. W. M., Rogers, A., and Kelly, J. P. (1974). The specification of the retino-tectal projection in the chick. *J. Comp. Neurol.* **155,** 127–164.

Currie, J., and Cowan, W. M. (1974a). Some observations on the early development of the optic tectum in the frog (*Rana pipiens*), with special reference to the effects of early eye removal on mitotic activity in the larval tectum. *J. Comp. Neurol.* **156,** 123–142.

Currie, J., and Cowan, W. M. (1974b). Evidence for the late development of the uncrossed retinothalamic projections in the frog, *Rana pipiens. Brain Res.* **71,** 133–139.

Czeloth, H. (1931). Untersuchungen über die Raumorientierung von Triton. *Z. Vergl. Physiol.* **13,** 74–163.

Dalcq, A. (1946). Recent experimental contributions to brain morphogenesis in amphibia. *Growth* **10,** 85–119.

Dartnall, H. J. A. (1953). The interpretation of spectral sensitivity curves. *Br. Med. Bull.* **9,** 24–30.

Dartnall, H. J. A. (1957). "The Visual Pigments." Wiley, New York.

Dartnall, H. J. A. (1962). The photobiology of visual processes. *In* "The Eye" (H. Davson, ed.), 1st ed., Vol. 2, pp. 321–533. Academic Press, New York.

Dartnall, H. J. A. (1967). The visual pigment of the green rods. *Vision Res.* **7,** 1–16.

Dartnall, H. J. A. (1972). Photosensitivity. *In* "Handbook of Sensory Physiology" (H. J. A. Dartnall, ed.), Vol. VII, Part 1, pp. 122–145. Springer-Verlag, Berlin and New York.

De Long, G. R., and Coulombre, A. J. (1965). Development of the retinotectal projection in the chick embryo. *Exp. Neurol.* **13,** 351–363.

Deuchar, E. M. (1972). *Xenopus laevis* and developmental biology. *Biol. Rev. Cambridge Philos. Soc.* **47,** 37–112.

De Valois, R. L. (1965). Behavioral and electrophysiological studies of primate vision. *In* "Contributions to Sensory Physiology" (W. D. Neff, ed.), Vol. 1, pp. 137–138. Academic Press, New York.

De Valois, R. L., Abramov, I., and Jacobs, G. H. (1966). Analysis of response patterns of LGN cells. *J. Opt. Soc. Am.* **56,** 966–977.

De Vito, J. L., Clausing, K. W., and Smith, O. A. (1974). Uptake and transport of horseradish peroxidase by cut end of the vagus nerve. *Brain Res.* **82,** 269–271.

Diebschlag, E. (1935). Zur Kenntnis der Grosshirnfunktion einiger Urodelen und Anuren. *Z. Vergl. Physiol.* **21,** 343–394.

Dixon, J. S., and Cronly-Dillon, J. R. (1972). The fine structure of the developing retina of *Xenopus laevis. J. Embryol. Exp. Morphol.* **28,** 659–666.

Dixon, J. S., and Cronly-Dillon, J. R. (1974). Intercellular gap junctions in pigment epithelium cells during retinal specification in *Xenopus laevis. Nature (London)* **241,** 505.

Dodt, E., and Jessen, K. H. (1961). Das adaptive Verhalten der Froshnetzhaut untersucht mit der Methode der konstantan electrischen Antwort. *Vision Res.* 1, 228–243.

Donner, K. O. (1950). The spike frequencies of mammalian retinal elements as a function of wavelength of light. *Acta Physiol. Scand.* 21, Suppl. 72, 1–59.

Donner, K. O. (1958). The spectral sensitivity of vertebrate elements. In "Visual Problems of Colour," pp. 541–563. Natl. Phys. Lab. Symp., London.

Donner, K. O. (1959). The effect of a coloured adapting field on the spectral sensitivity of frog retinal elements. *J. Physiol. (London)* 149, 318–326.

Donner, K. O. (1973). Rod dark-adaptation and visual pigment photoproducts. In "Biochemistry and Physiology of Visual Pigments" (H. Langer, ed.), pp. 205–208. Springer-Verlag, Berlin and New York.

Donner, K. O., and Reuter, T. (1962). The spectral sensitivity and photopigment of the green rods in the frog's retina. *Vision Res.* 2, 357–372.

Donner, K. O., and Reuter, T. (1965). The dark-adaptation of single units in the frog's retina and its relation to the regeneration of rhodopsin. *Vision Res.* 5, 615–632.

Donner, K. O., and Reuter, T. (1967). Dark-adaptation processes in the rhodopsin rods of the frog's retina. *Vision Res.* 7, 17–41.

Donner, K. O., and Reuter, T. (1968). Visual adaptation of the rhodopsin rods in the frog's retina. *J. Physiol. (London)* 199, 59–87.

Donner, K. O., and Rushton, W. A. H. (1959a). Retinal stimulation by light substitution. *J. Physiol. (London)* 149, 288–302.

Donner, K. O., and Rushton, W. A. H. (1959b). Rod-cone interaction in the frog's retina analysed by the Stiles-Crawford effect and by dark adaptation. *J. Physiol. (London)* 149, 303–317.

Dowling, J. E. (1960). Chemistry of visual adaptation in the rat. *Nature (London)* 188, 114–118.

Dowling, J. E. (1963). Neural and photochemical mechanisms of visual adaptation in the rat. *J. Gen. Physiol.* 46, 1287–1301.

Dowling, J. E. (1968). Synaptic organization of the frog retina: An electron microscopic analysis comparing the retinas of frogs and primates. *Proc. R. Soc. London, Ser. B* 170, 205–228.

Dowling, J. E. (1970). Organization of vertebrate retinas. The Jonas M. Friedenwald Memorial Lecture. *Invest. Ophthalmol.* 9, 655–680.

Dowling, J. E., and Boycott, B. B. (1966). Organization of the primate retina: Electron microscopy. *Proc. R. Soc. London, Ser. B* 166, 80–111.

Dowling, J. E., and Cowan, W. M. (1966). An electron microscopy study of normal and degenerating centrifugal fiber terminals in the pigeon retina. *Z. Zellforsch. Mikrosk. Anat.* 170, 205–228.

Dowling, J. E., and Ripps, H. (1970). Visual adaptation in the retina of the skate. *J. Gen. Physiol.* 56, 491–520.

Dowling, J. E., and Ripps, H. (1972). Adaptation in skate photoreceptors. *J. Gen. Physiol.* 60, 698–719.

Dowling, J. E., and Ripps, H. (1973). Effect of magnesium on horizontal cell activity in the skate retina. *Nature (London)* 242, 101–103.

Dowling, J. E., and Wald, G. (1958). Vitamin A deficiency and night blindness. *Proc. Natl. Acad. Sci. U.S.A.* 44, 648–661.

Dowling, J. E., and Werblin, F. S. (1969). Organization of retina of the Mudpuppy, *Necturus maculosus. J. Neurophysiol.* 32, 315–338.

Drachman, D. B., ed. (1974a). Trophic functions of the neuron. *Ann. N.Y. Acad. Sci.* **228**.

Drachman, D. B. (1974b). Trophic actions of the neuron: An introduction. *Ann. N.Y. Acad. Sci.* **228**, 3–5.

Driesch, H. (1908). "Science and Philosophy of the Organism," 1st ed. Black, London.

Dubin, M. W. (1970). The inner plexiform layer of the vertebrate retina: A quantitative and comparative electron microscopic analysis. *J. Comp. Neurol.* **140**, 479–506.

Dunn, E. R. (1926). "The Salamanders of the Family Plethodontidae." Smith College, Northampton, Massachusetts.

Easter, S. S. (1968). Excitation in the goldfish retina: Evidence for a non-linear intensity code. *J. Physiol. (London)* **195**, 253–271.

Eayrs, J. T. (1971). Thyroid and developing brain. Anatomical and behavioral effects. *In* "Hormones in Development" (M. Hamburgh and E. J. W. Barrington, eds.). Appleton, New York.

Ebbesson, S. O. E. (1972). A proposal for a common nomenclature for some optic nuclei in vertebrates and the evidence for a common origin of two such cell groups. *Brain, Behav. Evol.* **6**, 75–91.

Ebbesson, S. O. E., Jane, J. A., and Schroeder, D. M. (1970). On the organization of central visual pathways in vertebrates. *Brain, Behav. Evol.* **3**, 178–194.

Edds, M. V., Jr. (1953). Collateral nerve regeneration. *Q. Rev. Biol.* **28**, 260–276.

Eibl-Eibesfeldt, I. (1951). Nahrungserwerb und Beuteschema der Erdkröte (*Bufo bufo* L.). *Behaviour* **4**, 1–35.

Eibl-Eibesfeldt, I. (1967). "Grundriss der vergleichenden Verhaltensforschung—Ethologie." R. Piper, Munich.

Eichler, V. (1971). Neurogenesis in the optic tectum of larval *Rana pipiens* following unilateral enucleation. *J. Comp. Neurol.* **141**, 375–396.

Eikmanns, K. H. (1955). Verhaltensphysiologische Untersuchungen über den Beutefang und das Bewegungssehen der Erdkröte (*Bufo bufo* L.). *Z. Tierpsychol.* **12**, 229–253.

Endler, J. (1970). Kinesthetic orientation in the California newt (*Taricha torosa*). *Behaviour* **37**, 15–23.

Enroth-Cugell, C., and Robson, J. G. (1966). The contrast sensitivity of retinal ganglion cells of the cat. *J. Physiol. (London)* **187**, 517–552.

Enroth-Cugell, C., and Shapley, R. M. (1973). Flux, not retinal illumination is what cat retinal ganglion cells really care about. *J. Physiol. (London)* **233**, 311–326.

Ernst, M. (1926). Ueber Untergang von Zellen während der normalen Entwicklung bei Wirbeltieren. *Z. Anat. Entwicklungsgesch.* **79**, 228–262.

Ernst, W., and Kemp, C. M. (1972). The effects of rhodopsin decomposition on PIII responses of isolated rat retinae. *Vision Res.* **12**, 1937–1946.

Estes, R. (1970a). Origin of the Recent North American lower vertebrate fauna: An inquiry into the fossil record. *Forma Functio* **3**, 139–163.

Estes, R. (1970b). New fossil pelobatid frogs and a review of the genus Eopelobates. *Bull. Mus. Comp. Zool.* **139**, 293–339.

Estes, R., and Reig, O. A. (1973). The early fossil record of frogs: A review of the evidence. *In* "Evolutionary Biology of the Anurans" (J. L. Vial, ed.), pp. 11–63. Univ. of Missouri Press, Columbia.

Estes, R., and Wake, M. H. (1972). The first fossil record of caecilian amphibians. *Nature (London)* **239**, 228–231.

Etkin, W. (1968). Hormonal control of amphibian metamorphosis. *In* "Metamorphosis: A Problem in Developmental Biology" (W. Etkin and L. I. Gilbert, eds.). Appleton, New York.

Evans, E. M. (1966). On the ultrastructure of the synaptic region of visual receptors in certain vertebrates. *Z. Zellforsch. Mikrosk. Anat.* **71**, 499–516.

Ewert, J.-P. (1965). "Der Einfluss peripherer Sinnesorgane und des Zentralnervensystems auf die Antwortbereitschaft bei der Richtbewegung der Erdkröte (*Bufo bufo* L.)." Math. Nat. Dissertation, Göttingen.

Ewert, J.-P. (1967a). Der Einfluss von Störreizen auf die Antwortbereitschaft bei der Richtbewegung der Erdkröte (*Bufo bufo* L.). *Z. Tierpsychol.* **24**, 298–312.

Ewert, J.-P. (1967b). Aktivierung der Verhaltensfolge beim Beutefang der Erdkröte (*Bufo bufo* L.) durch elektrische Mittelhirnreizung. *Z. Vergl. Physiol.* **54**, 455–481.

Ewert, J.-P. (1967c). Elektrische Reizung des retinalen Projektionsfeldes im Mittelhirn der Erdkröte (*Bufo bufo* L.). *Pfluegers Arch., Gesamte Physiol. Menschen Tiere* **295**, 90–98.

Ewert, J.-P. (1967d). Untersuchungen über die Anteile zentralnervöser Aktionen an der taxisspezifischen Ermüdung beim Beutefang der Erdkröte (*Bufo bufo* L.). *Z. Vergl. Physiol.* **57**, 263–298.

Ewert, J.-P. (1968a). Verhaltensphysiologische Untersuchungen zum "stroboskopischen Sehen" der Erdkröte (*Bufo bufo* L.). *Pfluegers Arch. Gesamte Physiol. Menschen Tiere* **299**, 258–166.

Ewert, J.-P. (1968b). Der Einfluss von Zwischenhirndefekten auf die Visuomotorik im Beute- und Fluchtverhalten der Erdkröte (*Bufo bufo* L.) *Z. Vergl. Physiol.* **61**, 41–70.

Ewert, J.-P. (1969a). Das Beutefangverhalten Zwischenhirn-defekter Erdkröten (*Bufo bufo* L.) gegenüber bewegten und ruhenden visuellen Mustern. *Pfluegers Arch.* **306**, 210–218.

Ewert, J.-P. (1969b). Quantitative Analyse von Reiz-Reaktionsbeziehungen bei visuellem Auslösen der Beutefang-Wende-reaktion der Erdkröte (*Bufo bufo* L.). *Pflüegers Arch.* **308**, 225–243.

Ewert, J.-P. (1970a). Neural mechanisms of prey-catching and avoidance behavior in the toad (*Bufo bufo* L.). *Brain, Behav. Evol.* **3**, 36–56.

Ewert, J.-P. (1970b). Aufnahme und Verarbeitung visueller Informationen im Beutefang- und Fluchtverhalten der Erdkröte *Bufo bufo* (L.). *Verh. Dtsch. Zool. Ges.* pp. 218–226.

Ewert, J.-P. (1971). Single-unit response of the toad (*Bufo americanus*) caudal thalamus to visual objects. *Z. Vergl. Physiol.* **74**, 81–102.

Ewert, J.-P. (1972). Zentralnervöse Analyse und Verarbeitung visueller Sinnesreize. *Naturwiss. Rundsch.* **25**, 1–11.

Ewert, J.-P. (1973). Lokalisation und Identifikation im visuellen System der Wirbeltiere. *In* "Orientierung der Tiere im Raum" (M. Lindauer, ed.) Part 1, p. 307. G. Fischer Verlag, Stuttgart.

Ewert, J.-P. (1974). The neural basis of visually guided behavior. *Sci. Am.* **230**, 34–42.

Ewert, J.-P., and V. Becker (1976). Invariants in the visual prey recognition system of the common toad. (In preparation.)

Ewert, J.-P., and Birukow, G. (1965a). Über den Einflus des Zentralnervensystems auf die Ermüdbarkeit der Richtbewegung im Beuteschema der Erdkröte *Bufo bufo* (L.). *Naturwissenschaften* **52**, 68–69.

Ewert, J.-P., and Birukow, G. (1965b). Aufmerksamkeitsverschiebungen durch

Begleitreize bei der Beutefanghandlung der Erdkröte (*Bufo bufo* L.). *Kurz-nachr. Akad. Wiss. Goettingen*, Heft 6, 27–31.

Ewert, J.-P., and Borchers, H.-W. (1971). Reaktionscharakteristik von Neuronen aus dem Tectum opticum und Subtectum der Erdkröte *Bufo bufo* (L.) *Z. Vergl. Physiol.* 71, 165–189.

Ewert, J.-P., and Borchers, H.-W. (1974a). Inhibition of toad (*Bufo bufo* L.) retinal "on-off" and "off"-ganglion cells via active eye closing. *Vision Res.* 14, 1275–1276.

Ewert, J.-P., and Borchers, H.-W. (1974b). Antworten retinaler Ganglienzellen bei freibeweglichen Kröten. *J. Comp. Physiol.* 92, 117–130.

Ewert, J.-P., and H. Burghagen (1976a). Visual pattern recognition in different anuran species. (In preparation.)

Ewert, J.-P., and H. Burghagen (1976b). Ontogenetic aspects of size-constancy phenomena in the prey-catching behavior of the common toad *Bufo bufo* (L.). (In preparation.)

Ewert, J.-P., and Gebauer, L. (1973). (Grössenkonstanzphänomene im Beutefang-verhalten der Erdkröte (*Bufo bufo* L.). *J. Comp. Physiol.* 85, 303–315.

Ewert, J.-P., and Härter, H.-A. (1968). Inhibitionsphänomene im visuellen System der Erdkröte. *Naturwissenschaften* 55, 235.

Ewert, J.-P., and Härter, H.-A. (1969). Der hemmende Einfluss gleichzeitig bewegter Beuteattrappen auf das Beutefangverhalten der Erdkröte (*Bufo bufo* L.). *Z. Vergl. Physiol.* 64, 135–153.

Ewert, J.-P., and Hock, F. J. (1972). Movement sensitive neurones in the toad's retina. *Exp. Brain Res.* 16, 41–59.

Ewert, J.-P., and Ingle, D. (1971). Excitatory effects following habituation of prey-catching activity in frogs and toads. *J. Comp. Physiol. Psychol.* 77, 369–374.

Ewert, J.-P., and W. Kehl (1976). Recognition of complex visual patterns via storage processes in the toad's brain. (In preparation.)

Ewert, J.-P., and Kleinlogel, H. (1971). Jahreszeitliche Anderung der Wich-Aktivität bei der Erdkröte *Bufo bufo* (L.). *Z. Tierpsychol.* 28, 479–486.

Ewert, J.-P., and Rehn, B. (1968). Wirksamkeit optischer Reizmuster beim Auslösen des Fluchtverhaltens der Wechsel-Kröte. *Naturwissenschaften* 55, 351.

Ewert, J.-P., and Rehn, B. (1969). Quantitative Analyse der Reiz-Reaktions-beziehungen bei visuellem Auslösen des Fluchtverhaltens der Wechselkröte (*Bufo viridis* Laur.). *Behavior* 35, 212–234.

Ewert, J.-P., and B. Rehn (1976). Functional description of avoidance zones in the toad's brain by electrical point stimulation. (In preparation.)

Ewert, J.-P., and E. Schuchardt (1976). Electron microscope studies on synaptic organisation of the toad's optic tectum. (In preparation.)

Ewert, J. P., and Siefert, G. (1974a). Neuronal correlates of seasonal changes in contrast-detection of prey-catching behavior in toads (*Bufo bufo*). *Vision Res.* 14, 431–432.

Ewert, J.-P., and Siefert, G. (1974b). Seasonal change of contrast-detection in the toad's (*Bufo bufo* L.) visual system. *J. Comp. Physiol.* 94, 177–186.

Ewert, J.-P., and R. Traud (1976). The enemy picture of the toad (*Bufo bufo* L.). (In preparation.)

Ewert, J.-P., and von Seelen, W. (1974). Neurobiologie and System-Theorie eines visuellen Muster-Erkennungsmechanismus bei Kröten. *Kybernetik* 14, 167–183.

Ewert, J.-P., and von Wietersheim, A. (1974a). Ganglienzellklassen in der retino-tectalen Projektion der Kröte (*Bufo bufo* L.). *Acta Anat.* 88, 56–66.

Ewert, J.-P., and von Wietersheim, A. (1974b). Musterauswertung durch Tectum-
und Thalamus/Praetectum-Neurone im visuellen System der Kröte (Bufo bufo
L.). J. Comp. Physiol. 92, 131–148.

Ewert, J.-P., and von Wietersheim, A. (1974c). Der Einfluss von Thalamus/
Praetectum-Defekten auf die Antwort von Tectum-Neuronen gegenüber visuellen Mustern bei der Kröte (Bufo bufo L.). J. Comp. Physiol. 92, 149–160.

Ewert, J.-P., Speckhardt, I., and Amelang, W. (1970). Visuelle Inhibition und
Excitation im Beutefangverhalten der Erdkröte (Bufo bufo L.). Z. Vergl.
Physiol. 68, 84–110.

Ewert, J.-P., Hock, F., and von Wietersheim, A. (1974). Thalamus/Praetectum/
Tectum: Retinale Topographie und physiologische Interaktionen bei der
Kröte (Bufo bufo L.). J. Comp. Physiol. 92, 343–356.

Ewert, J.-P., Borchers, H.-W., Hock, F. J., and von Wietersheim, A. (1975). In
"Biokybernetik V, Mustererkennung im visuellen System der Kröte. (H. Dris-
dhel and P. Dettmar, eds.) p. 243. Veb G. Fischer Verlag, Jena.

Eysel, U. T., and Grüsser, O.-J. (1971). Neurophysiological basis of pattern recognition in the cat's visual system. In "Zeichenerkennung durch biologische und
technische Systeme" (O.-J. Grüsser and R. Klinke, eds.). Springer-Verlag, Berlin
and New York.

Faber, D. S. (1969). "Analysis of the Slow Transretinal Potentials in Response to
Light." Ph.D. Thesis, University of New York, Buffalo.

Fain, G. L. (1973). "Responses of Rods and Cones and the Interaction of Rod and
Cone Signals in the Mudpuppy Retina." Doctoral Dissertation, Johns Hopkins
University, Baltimore, Maryland.

Fain, G. L., and Dowling, J. E. (1973). Intracellular recordings from single rods
and cones in the mudpuppy retina. Science 180, 1178–1180.

Farquhar, M. G., and Palade, G. E. (1963). Junctional complexes in various epi-
thelia. J. Cell Biol. 17, 373–393.

Feldman, J. D., and Gaze, R. M. (1972). The growth of the retina in Xenopus
laevis. II. Retinal growth in compound eyes. J. Embryol. Exp. Morphol. 27,
381–387.

Feldman, J. D., and Gaze, R. M. (1975). The development of half-eyes in Xenopus
tadpoles. J. Comp. Neurol. 162, 13–22.

Feldman, J. D., and Keating, M. J. (1976). (In preparation.)

Feldman, J. D., Gaze, R. M., and Keating, M. J. (1971). Delayed innervation of
the topic tectum during development in Xenopus laevis. Exp. Brain Res. 14,
16–23.

Feldman, J. D., Keating, M. J., and Gaze, R. M. (1974). Retino-tectal mismatch:
A serendipitous experimental result. Nature (London) 253, 445–446.

Fernandez de Molina, A., and Hunsperger, R. W. (1962). Organization of the subcortical system covering defense and flight reactions in the cat. J. Physiol.
(London) 160, 200–213.

Fisher, L. J. (1972). Changes during maturation and metamorphosis in the synaptic
organization of the tadpole retina inner plexiform layer. Nature (London) 235,
391–393.

Fite, K. V. (1969). Single-unit analysis of binocular neurons in the frog optic
tectum. Exp. Neurol. 24, 475–486.

Fite, K. V. (1973). The visual fields of the frog and toad: A comparative study.
Behav. Biol. 9, 707–718.

Fite, K. V., and Carey, R. (1973). "The Photoreceptors of the Frog and Toad: A

Quantitative Study." Paper presented at Association for Research in Vision and Ophthalmology, Annual Meeting.

Fite, K. V., and Rego, M. (1974). "Binocular Vision and Prey-catching Behavior in the Leopard Frog, *Rana pipiens*." Paper presented at Neurosciences Meeting, St. Louis, Missouri.

Frank, R. N. (1969). Photoproducts of rhodopsin bleaching in the isolated, perfused frog retina. *Vision Res.* 9, 1415–1433.

Frank, R. N. (1971). Properties of "neural" adaptation in components of the frog electroretinogram. *Vision Res.* 11, 1113–1123.

Franz, V. (1934). Höhere Sinnesorgane. Vergleichende Anatomie des Wirbeltierauges. *In* "Handbuch der vergleichenden Anatomie der Wirbeltiere," (L. Bolk, E. Göppert, E. Kallius, and W. Lubosch, eds.) Vol. II, Part 2, pp. 989–1292. Urban E. Schwarzenberg, Berlin.

Frey, E. (1938). Studien über die hypothalamische Optikuswurzel der Amphibien. II. Proteus anguineus und die phylogenetische Bedeutung der hypothalamischen Optikuswurzel. *Proc. K. Ned. Akad. Wet.* 41, 1015–1021.

Frontera, J. G. (1952). A study of the anuran diencephalon. *J. Comp. Neurol.* 96, 1–69.

Furukawa, T., and Hanawa, I. (1955). Effects of some common cations on electro retinogram of the toad. *Jpn. J. Physiol.* 5, 289–300.

Fusco, R. R., and Hood, D. C. (1974). "Locus of Light Adaptation in the Frog's Rod System." Paper presented at Eastern Psychological Association Meeting.

Fusco, R. R., and Hood, D. C. (1976). A comparison of adaptational changes at the rod receptors and ganglion cells of *Rana pipiens*. In preparation.

Gaillard, F., Liege, B., and Galand, G. (1975). Remarks on the frog's binocular visual field: Existence of a horopter. (In preparation.)

Gallardo, J. M. (1961). On the species of Pseudidae (Amphibia, Anura). *Bull. Mus. Comp. Zool.* 125, 111–134.

Gaupp, E. (1899), *In* "Anatomie des Frosches" (Ecker and Wiederschein, eds.). Vieweg, Braunschweig.

Gaze, R. M. (1958a). The representation of the retina on the optic lobe of the frog. *Q. J. Exp. Physiol. Cogn. Med. Sci.* 43, 209–214.

Gaze, R. M. (1958b). Binocular vision in frogs. *J. Physiol. (London)* 143, 20P.

Gaze, R. M. (1959). Regeneration of the optic nerve in *Xenopus laevis. Q. J. Exp. Physiol. Cogn. Med. Sci.* 44, 290–308.

Gaze, R. M. (1967). Growth and differentiation. *Annu. Rev. Physiol.* 29, 59–86.

Gaze, R. M., ed. (1970). "Formation of Nerve Connections." Academic Press, New York.

Gaze, R. M., and Jacobson, M. (1962). The projection of the binocular visual field on to the optic tecta of the frog. *Q. J. Exp. Physiol. Cogn. Med. Sci.* 47, 273–280.

Gaze, R. M., and Jacobson, M. (1963a). The path from the retina to the ipsilateral tectum in the frog. *J. Physiol. (London)* 165, 73P–74P.

Gaze, R. M., and Jacobson, M. (1963b). 'Convexity detectors' in the frog's visual system. *J. Physiol. (London)* 169, 1–3.

Gaze, R. M., and Keating, M. J. (1970). Receptive field properties of single units from the visual projection to the ipsilateral tectum in the frog. *Q. J. Exp. Physiol. Cogn. Med. Sci.* 55, 143–152.

Gaze, R. M., and Keating, M. J. (1972). The visual system and "neuronal specificity." *Nature (London)* 237, 375–378.

Gaze, R. M., and Sharma, S. C. (1970). Axial differences in the reinnervation of the goldfish optic tectum by regenerating optic nerve fibres. *Exp. Brain Res.* **10**, 171–181.

Gaze, R. M., and Watson, W. E. (1968). Cell division and migration in the brain after optic nerve lesions. *Growth Nerv. Syst., Ciba Found. Symp.* pp. 53–67.

Gaze, R. M., Jacobson, M., and Székely, G. (1963). The retinotectal projection in *Xenopus* with compound eyes. *J. Physiol. (London)* **165**, 484–499.

Gaze, R. M., Jacobson, M., and Székely, G. (1965). On the formation of connections by compound eyes in *Xenopus*. *J. Physiol. (London)* **176**, 409–417.

Gaze, R. M., Keating, M. J., Székely, G., and Beazley, L. (1970). Binocular interaction in the formation of specific intertectal neuronal connexions. *Proc. R. Soc. London, Ser. B* **175**, 107–147.

Gaze, R. M., Chung, S. H., and Keating, M. J. (1972). Development of the retinotectal projection in *Xenopus*. *Nature (London)* **236**, 133–135.

Gaze, R. M., Keating, M. J., and Chung, S. H. (1974). The evolution of the retinotectal map during development in *Xenopus*. *Proc. R. Soc. London, Ser. B* **185**, 301–330.

George, A. (1975). Mikroelektroden ableitung einzelner neurone im tectum opticum von *R. esculenta*. *Med. Diss. Berlin*.

Gibbs, E. L., Nace, G. W., and Emmons, M. B. (1971). The live frog is almost dead. *Bioscience* **21**, 1027–1034.

Gibson, J. J. (1966). "The Senses Considered as Perceptual Systems." Houghton, Boston, Massachusetts.

Glickstein, M., and Millodot, M. (1970). Retinoscopy and eye size. *Science* **168**, 605–606.

Glorioso, J. C., Amborski, R. L., Larkin, J. M., Amborski, G. F., and Culley, D. D., Jr. (1974). Laboratory identification of bacterial pathogens. *Am. J. Vet. Res.* **35**, 447–450.

Glücksmann, A. (1940). Development and differentiation of the tadpole eye. *Br. J. Ophthalmol.* **24**, 153–178.

Glücksmann, A. (1951). Cell deaths in normal vertebrate ontogeny. *Biol. Rev. Cambridge Philos. Soc.* **26**, 59–86.

Goin, C. J., and Goin, O. B. (1962). "Introduction to Herpetology." Freeman, San Francisco, California.

Goldberg, S. (1974). Studies on the mechanics of development of the visual pathway in the chick embryo. *Dev. Biol.* **36**, 24–43.

Goldstein, E. B. (1967). Early receptor potential of the isolated frog (*Rana pipiens*) retina. *Vision Res.* **7**, 837–845.

Goldstein, E. B. (1968). Visual pigments and the early receptor potential of the isolated frog retina. *Vision Res.* **8**, 953–964.

Goldstein, E. B. (1970). Cone pigment regeneration in the isolated frog retina. *Vision Res.* **10**, 1065–1068.

Goldstein, E. B., and Wolf, B. M. (1973). Regeneration of the green-rod pigment in the isolated frog retina. *Vision Res.* **13**, 527–534.

Goodman, D. C., and Horel, J. A. (1966). Sprouting of optic tract projections in the brain stem of the rat. *J. Comp. Neurol.* **127**, 71–88.

Gordon, J., and Graham, N. (1973). Early light and dark adaptation in frog on-off retinal ganglion cells. *Vision Res.* **13**, 647–659.

Gordon, J., and Graham, N. (1975). "Effects of Light Adaptation on the Sensitivity and Time Course of the Frog Proximal Negative Response." Paper presented at Association for Research in Vision and Ophthalmology Meeting, Sarasota.

Gouras, P. (1965). Primate retina: Duplex function of dark-adapted ganglion cells. *Science* **147**, 1593–1594.

Grabowski, S. R., Pinto, L. H., and Pak, W. L. (1972). Adaptation in retinal rods of axolotl: Intracellular recordings. *Science* **176**, 1240–1243.

Graham, C. H., and Bartlett, N. R. (1939). The relation of size of stimulus and intensity in the human eye. II. Intensity thresholds for red and violet light. *J. Exp. Psychol.* **24**, 574–587.

Graham, C. H., Brown, R. H., and Moto, F. A. (1939). The relation of size of stimulus and intensity in the human eye. I. Intensity thresholds for white light. *J. Exp. Psychol.* **24**, 555–573.

Graham, N., and Ratliff, F. (1974). Quantitative theories of the integrative action of the retina. *In* "Contemporary Developments in Mathematical Psychology" (D. H. Krantz *et al.*, eds.), Vol. II, pp. 306–371. Freeman, San Francisco, California.

Granit, R. (1933). The components of the retinal action potential in mammals and their relation to the discharge in the optic nerve. *J. Physiol. (London)* **11**, 207–239.

Granit, R. (1938). Processes of adaptation in the vertebrate retina in the light of recent photochemical and electrophysiological research. *Doc. Ophthalamol.* **1**, 7–77.

Granit, R. (1942). Colour receptors of the frog's retina. *Acta Physiol. Scand.* **3**, 137–151.

Granit, R. (1947). "Sensory Mechanisms of the Retina." Oxford Univ. Press, London and New York.

Granit, R., and Riddell, H. A. (1934). The electrical responses of light- and dark-adapted frogs' eyes to rhythmic and continuous stimuli. *J. Physiol. (London)* **81**, 1–28.

Grant, D., Anderson, O., and Twitty, V. (1968). Homing orientation by olfaction in newts (*Taricha rivularis*). *Science* **160**, 1354–1356.

Green, D. G., Dowling, J. E., Ripps, H., and Siegel, I. M. (1975). Retinal mechanisms of visual adaptation in the skate. *J. Gen. Physiol.* **65**, 483–502.

Gruberg, E. R., and Ambros, V. R. (1974). A forebrain visual projection in the frog (*Rana pipiens*). *Exp. Neurol.* **44**, 187–197.

Grüsser, O.-J., and Dannenberg, H. (1965). Eine Perimeter-Apparatur zur Reizung mit bewegten visuellen Mustern. *Pflüegers Arch. Gesamte Physiol. Menschen Tiere* **285**, 373–378.

Grüsser, O. J., and Grüsser-Cornehls, U. (1968a). Neurophysiologische Grundlagen visueller angeborener Auslosemechanismen beim Frosch. *Z. Vergl. Physiol.* **59**, 1–24.

Grüsser, O.-J., and Grüsser-Cornehls, U. (1968b). Die Informationsverarbeitung im visuellen System des Frosches. *In* "Kybernetik 1068" (H. Marko and G. Färber, eds.), pp. 331–360. Oldenbourg, Munich.

Grüsser, O.-J., and Grüsser-Cornehls, U. (1969). Neurophysiologie des Bewegungssehens. Bewegungsempfindlicheund richtungsspezifische Neurone im visuellen System. *Ergeb. Physiol., Biol. Chem. Exp. Pharmakol.* **61**, 178–265.

Grüsser, O.-J., and Grüsser-Cornehls, U. (1970). Die Neurophysiologie visuell gesteuerter Verhaltensweisen bei Anuren. *Verh. Dtsch. Zool. Ges.* **64**, 201–218.

Grüsser, O.-J., and Grüsser-Cornehls, U. (1972). Comparative physiology of movement-detecting neuronal systems in lower vertebrates (Anura and Urodela). *Bibl. Ophthalmol.* **82**, 260–273.

Grüsser, O.-J., and Grüsser-Cornehls, U. (1973). Neuronal mechanisms of visual

movement perception and some psychophysical and behavioral correlations. *In*
"Handbook of Sensory Physiology" (H. Autrum *et al.,* eds.), Vol. VII, pp.
333–429. Springer-Verlag, Berlin and New York.

Grüsser, O.-J., and Grüsser-Cornehls, U. (1976). Physiology of the anuran visual
system. *In* "Neurobiology of the frog," (R. Llinas and W. Precht, eds.).
Springer-Verlag, Berlin and New York.

Grüsser, O.-J., and Klinke, R., eds. (1971). "Zeichenerkennung durch biologische
und technische Systeme." Springer-Verlag, Berlin and New York.

Grüsser, O.-J., Grüsser-Cornehls, U., Finkelstein, D., Henn, V., Patutschnik, M., and
Butenandt, E. (1967). A quantitative analysis of movement detecting neurons
in the frog's retina. *Pfluegers Arch. Gesamte Physiol. Menschen Tiere* **293**,
100–106.

Grüsser, O.-J., Finkelstein, D., and Grüsser-Cornehls, U. (1968a). The effect of
stimulus velocity on the response of movement-sensitive neurons of the frog's
retina. *Pfluegers Arch. Gesamte Physiol. Menschen Tiere* **300**, 49–66.

Grüsser, O.-J., Grüsser-Cornehls, U., and Licker, M. D. (1968b). Further studies on
the velocity function on movement-detecting class 2 neurons in the frog retina.
Vision Res. **8**, 1173–1185.

Grüsser-Cornehls, U. (1968). Response of movement detecting neurons of the frog's
retina to moving patterns under stroboscopic illumination. *Pfluegers Arch.* **303**,
1–13.

Grüsser-Cornehls, U. (1973). Bewegungsempfindliche Neuronensysteme im visuellen
System von Amphibien. Eine vergleichende neurophysiologische Untersuchung.
Nova Acta Leopold. **37**, 117–136.

Grüsser-Cornehls, U., and Himstedt, W. (1973). Responses of retinal and tectal
neurons of the salamander (*Salamandra salamandra* L.) to moving visual
stimuli. *Brain, Behav. Evol.* **7**, 145–168.

Grüsser-Cornehls, U., and Lüdcke, M. (1970). Vergleichende neurophysiologische
Untersuchungen zur Signalverarbeitung in der Netzhaut der Anuren. *Pfluegers
Arch. Gesamte Physiol. Menschen Tiere* **148**, 319.

Grüsser-Cornehls, U., Grüsser, O.-J., and Bullock, T. H. (1963). Unit response in
the frog's tectum to moving and non-moving visual stimuli. *Science* **141**,
820–822.

Grüsser-Cornehls, U., and Saunders, R. McD. (1975). The spectral properties of
class 1, 2, 3 and 4 neurons of the frog's optic tectum. *Pfluegers Arch.,* Suppl.
vol. **359**, R101.

Guillery, R. W., and Kaas, J. H. (1971). A study of normal and congenitally
abnormal retino-geniculate projection in cats. *J. Comp. Neurol.* **143**, 73–100.

Guillery, R. W., Casagrande, V. A., and Oberdorfer, M. O. (1974). Congenitally
abnormal vision in Siamese cats. *Nature (London)* **252**, 195–199.

Gurdon, J. B. (1960). The developmental capacity of nuclei taken from differentiating endoderm cells of *Xenopus laevis. J. Embryol. Exp. Morphol.* **8**,
505–526.

Gurdon, J. B. (1962). Adult frogs derived from the nuclei of single somatic cells.
Dev. Biol. **4**, 256–273.

Gurdon, J. B. (1974a). The genome in specialized cells, as revealed by nuclear transplantation in Amphibia. *In* "The Cell Nucleus" (H. Busch, ed.), Vol. 1,
Academic Press, New York.

Gurdon, J. B. (1974b). "The Control of Gene Expression in Animal Development."
Oxford Univ. Press (Clarendon), London and New York.

Guth, L. (1968). "Trophic" influences of nerve on muscle. *Physiol. Rev.* **48,** 645–687.

Hailman, J. P., and Jaeger, R. G. (1974). Phototactic responses to spectrally dominant stimuli and use of color vision by adult anuran amphibians: A comparative survey. *Anim. Behav.* **22,** 757–795.

Hajós, F., Patel, A. J., and Balázs, R. (1973). Effect of thyroid deficiency on the synaptic organization of the rat cerebellar cortex. *Brain Res.* **50,** 387–401.

Hamburger, V., and Levi-Montalcini, R. (1949). Proliferation, differentiation and degeneration in the spinal ganglia of the chick embryo under normal and experimental conditions. *J. Exp. Zool.* **111,** 457–501.

Harrison, R. G. (1907). Observations on the living, developing nerve fiber. *Anat. Rec.* **1,** 116–118.

Harrison, R. G. (1921). On relations of symmetry in transplanted limbs. *J. Exp. Zool.* **32,** 1–136.

Harrison, R. G. (1924). Experiments on the development of the internal ear. *Science* **59,** 448.

Harrison, R. G. (1929). Correlation in the development and growth of the eye studied by means of heteroplastic transplantation. *Wilhelm Roux' Arch. Entwicklungs Mech. Org.* **120,** 1–55.

Harrison, R. G. (1936). Relations of symmetry in the developing ear in *Amblystoma punctation. Proc. Natl. Acad. Sci. U.S.A.* **22,** 238–247.

Harrison, R. G. (1945). Relations of symmetry in the developing embryo. *Trans. Conn. Acad. Arts Sci.* **36,** 277–330.

Hartline, H. K. (1938). The response of single optic nerve fibers of the vertebrate eye to illumination of the retina. *Am. J. Physiol.* **121,** 400–415.

Hartline, H. K. (1940a). The receptive fields of optic nerve fibers. *Am. J. Physiol.* **130,** 690–699.

Hartline, H. K. (1940b). The effects of spatial summation in the retina on the excitation of the fibers of the optic nerve. *Am. J. Physiol.* **130,** 700–711.

Hartline, H. K. (1941–1942). The neural mechanisms of vision. *Harvey Lect.* **37,** 39–68.

Hecht, M. K. (1963). A reevaluation of the early history of the frogs. Part II. *Syst. Zool.* **12,** 20–35.

Hecht, S., Shlaer, S., and Pirenne, M. H. (1942). Energy, quanta, and vision. *J. Gen. Physiol.* **25,** 819–840.

Herrick, C. J. (1925). The amphibian forebrain. III. The optic tracts and centers of amblystoma and the frog. *J. Comp. Neurol.* **39,** 433–489.

Herrick, C. J. (1941). Optic and postoptic systems of the fibres in the brain of *Necturus. J. Comp. Neurol.* **75,** 487–544.

Herrick, C. J. (1948). "The Brain of the Tiger Salamander *Ambystoma tigrinum.*" Univ. of Chicago Press, Chicago, Illinois.

Herter, K. (1930). Weitere dressurversuche an Fischen *Z. Vergl. Physiol.* **11,** 730–748.

Hess, C. (1913). Gesichtssinn. *In* "Handbuch der vergleichenden Physiologie" (H. Winterstein, ed.), Fischer, Jena.

Heusser, H. (1958). Zum geruchlichen Beutefinden und Gähnen der Kreuzkröte (*Bufo calamita* L.). *Z. Tierpsychol.* **15,** 94–98.

Heyer, R. W. (1969). The adaptive ecology of the species groups of the genus *Leptodactylus* (Amphibia; Leptodactylidae). *Evolution* **23,** 421–428.

Himstedt, W. (1967). Experimentelle Analyse der optischen Sinnesleistungen im Beutefangverhalten der einheimischen Urodelen. *Zool. Jahrb., Abt. Allg. Zool. Physiol. Tiere* **73,** 281–320.

Himstedt, W. (1969). Zur Funktion eines Reizfiltermechanismus im visuellen System der Urodelen. *Z. Vergl. Physiol.* **62**, 197–204.

Himstedt, W. (1970). Das Elektroretinogramm des Feuersalamanders (*Salamandra salamandra L.*) vor und nach der Metamorphose. *Pfluegers Arch.* **318**, 176–184.

Himstedt, W. (1971). Die Tagesperiodik von Salamandriden. *Oecologia* **8**, 194–208.

Himstedt, W. (1972). Untersuchungen zum Farbensehen von Urodelen. *J. Comp. Physiol.* **81**, 229–274.

Himstedt, W. (1973a). Die spektrale Empfindlichkeit von Urodelen in Abhängigkeit von Metamorphose, Jahreszeit und Lebensraum. *Zool. Jahrb., Abt. Allg. Zool. Physiol. Tiere* **77**, 246–274.

Himstedt, W. (1973b). Die spektrale Empfindlichkeit von Triturus alpestris (Amphibia, Urodela) während des Wasser- und Landlebens. *Pfluegers Arch.* **341**, 7–14.

Himstedt, W., and Fischerleitner, E. (1974). Farbencodierung in Retinaneuronen von Salamandern. *Naturwissenschaften* **61**, 220.

Himstedt, W., Freidank, U., and Singer, E. (1976). Die Veränderung eines Auslösemechanismus im Beutefangverhalten während der Entwicklung von *Salamandra salamandra* (L.). *Z. Tierpsychol.* (in press).

Hinde, R. A. (1954). Changes in responsiveness to a constant stimulus. *Behaviour* **2**, 41–54.

Hinsche, G. (1935). Ein Schnappreflex nach "Nichts" bei Anuren. *Zool. Anz.* **111**, 113–122.

Hirschberg, J. (1882). Zur Dioptrik und Ophthalmoskopie der Fisch- und Amphibienaugen. *Arch. Anat. Physiol., Physiol. Abt.* 493–526.

Hock, P. A. (1975). "Adaptation of the Frog's 580 Cone System: A Comparison of Receptor and Ganglion-cell Sensitivity Changes." Ph.D. Dissertation, Columbia University, New York.

Hock, P. A., Fusco, R. R., and Hood, D. C. (1975). "Comparison of Receptor and Ganglion-cell Sensitivity Changes During Steady-state Light Adaptation." Paper presented at Association for Research in Vision and Ophthalmology Meeting, Sarasota.

Hoffmann, K.-P. (1970). Retinotopische Beziehungen und Struktur Rezeptiver Felder im Tectum opticum und Praetectum der Katze. *Z. Vergl. Physiol.* **67**, 26–57.

Hoffmann, K.-P. (1973). Conduction velocity in pathways from retina to superior colliculus in the cat: A correlation with receptive-field properties. *J. Neurophysiol.* **36**, 409–424.

Hoffmann, C. K. (1876). Zur Anatomie der Retina. *Niederl. Arch. Zool.* **3**, 1–45.

Holmgren, F. (1870–71). Om retinaströmmen. *Upsala läkaref. Förh,* **6**, 419–455.

Holt, E. B. (1931). "Animal Drive and the Learning Process." Holt, New York.

Holtfreter, J. (1939). Gewebeaffinitat, ein Mittel der embryonalen Formbildung. *Arch. Exp. Zellforsch. Besonders Gewebezuecht.* **23**, 169–209.

Holtzer, H. (1951). Reconstitution of the urodele spinal cord following unilateral ablation. Part 1. Chronology of neuron regulation. *J. Exp. Zool.* **117**, 523–558.

Holtzer, H. (1963). Comments on induction during cell differentiation. *Colloq. Ges. Physiol. Chem.* **13**, 171–176.

Holtzer, H. (1968). Induction of chondrogenesis: A concept in quest of mechanisms. *In "Epithelial-mesenchymal Interactions"* (R. Fleischmajer and R. E. Billingham, eds.), pp. 152–164. Williams & Wilkins, Baltimore, Maryland.

Holtzer, H. (1970). Myogenesis. *In* "Cell Differentiation" (O. Schjeide and J. de Villis, eds.), pp. 476–503. Van Nostrand-Reinhold, Princeton, New Jersey.

Holtzer, H., and Sanger, J. W. (1972). Myogenesis: Old views rethought. *In* "Research in Muscle Development and the Muscle Spindle" (B. Banker and R. Pryzbalski, eds.), pp. 122–133. Exerpta Med. Found., Amsterdam.

Holtzer, H., Weintraub, H., Mayne, R., and Mochan, B. (1972). The cell cycle, cell lineages, and cell differentiation. *Curr. Top. Dev. Biol.* **7**, 229–256.

Honjo, I. (1939). Farbensinn der Feuersalamandorlarven. *Mem. Coll. Sci., Univ. Kyoto, Ser. B* **15**, 207–235.

Hood, D. C. (1972a). Adaptational changes in the cone system of the isolated frog retina. *Vision Res.* **12**, 875–888.

Hood, D. C. (1972b). Suppression of the frog's cone system in the dark. *Vision Res.* **12**, 889–907.

Hood, D. C., and Grover, B. G. (1974). Temporal summation by a vertebrate photoreceptor. *Science* **184**, 1003–1005.

Hood, D. C., and Hock, P. A. (1972). Where do the frog's rods go when the lights come on? *Am. J. Optom.* **49**, 888.

Hood, D. C., and Hock, P. A. (1973). Recovery of cone receptor activity in the frog's isolated retina. *Vision Res.* **13**, 1943–1951.

Hood, D. C., and Hock, P. A. (1975). Light adaptation of the receptors: Increment threshold functions for the frog's rods and cones. *Vision Res.* **15**, 545–553.

Hood, D. C., and Mansfield, A. F. (1972). The isolated receptor potential of the frog: Action spectra before and after bleaching. *Vision Res.* **12**, 2109–2119.

Hood, D. C., Hock, P. A., and Grover, B. G. (1973). Dark adaptation of the frog's rods. *Vision Res.* **13**, 1953–1963.

Horder, T. J. (1971). Retention, by fish optic nerve fibres regenerating to new terminal sites in the tectum, of "chemospecific" affinity for their original sites. *J. Physiol. (London)* **216**, 53P–55P.

Horder, T. J., and Spitzer, J. L. (1973). Absence of cell mobility across the retina in *Xenopus laevis* embryos. *J. Physiol. (London)* **233**, 33P–34P.

Howard, A. D. (1908). The visual cells in vertebrates, chiefly in the *Necturus maculosus. J. Morphol.* **19**, 561–631.

Hubel, D. H., and Wiesel, T. N. (1959). Receptive fields of single neurones in the cats striate cortex, *J. Physiol.* (London) **148**, 574–591.

Hubel, D. H., and Wiesel, T. N. (1902). Receptive fields, binocular interaction, and functional architecture in the cat's visual cortex. *J. Physiol.* (London) **160**, 106–154.

Hubel, D. H., and Wiesel, T. N. (1963). Receptive fields of cells in striate cortex of very young visually inexperienced kittens. *J. Neurophysiol.* **26**, 994–1002.

Hubel, D. H., and Wiesel, T. N. (1965). Binocular interaction in striate cortex of kittens reared with artificial squint. *J. Neurophysiol.* **28**, 1041–1059.

Hubel, D. H., and Wiesel, T. N. (1971). Aberrant visual projections in the Siamese cat. *J. Physiol. (London)* **218**, 33–62.

Hughes, R. C. (1975). "Membrane Glycoproteins: A Review of Structure and Function." Butterworth, London.

Humphrey, N. K. (1970). What the frog's eye tells the monkey's brain. *Brain, Behav. Evol.* **3**, 324–337.

Hunt, R. K. (1975a). The cell cycle, cell lineage, and neuronal specificity. *In* "The Cell Cycle and Cell Differentiation" (H. Holtzer and J. Reinart, eds.), pp. 43–62. Springer-Verlag, Berlin and New York.

Hunt, R. K. (1975b). Developmental programming for retinotectal patterns. *In* "Cell Patterning" (R. Porter and J. Rivers, eds.), Ciba Found. Symp. (New Series), No. 29 (New Ser.), pp. 131–159. Assoc. Sci. Publ., Amsterdam.

Hunt, R. K., and Berman, N. (1975). Patterning of neuronal locus specificities in retinal ganglion cells after partial extirpation of embryonic eyes. *J. Comp. Neurol.* **162**, 43–70.

Hunt, R. K., and Jacobson, M. (1971). Neurogenesis in frogs after early larval treatment with somatotrophin or prolactin. *Dev. Biol.* **26**, 100–124.

Hunt, R. K., and Jacobson, M. (1972a). Development and stability of positional information in *Xenopus* retinal ganglion cells. *Proc. Natl. Acad. Sci. U.S.A.* **69**, 780–783.

Hunt, R. K., and Jacobson, M. (1972b). Specification of positional information in retinal ganglion cells in *Xenopus:* Stability of the specified state. *Proc. Natl. Acad. Sci. U.S.A.* **69**, 2860–2864.

Hunt, R. K., and Jacobson, M. (1973a). Specification of positional information in retinal ganglion cells of *Xenopus:* Assay for analysis of the unspecified state. *Proc. Natl. Acad. Sci. U.S.A.* **70**, 507–511.

Hunt, R. K., and Jacobson, M. (1973b). Neuronal locus specificity: Altered pattern of spatial deployment in fused fragments of embryonic *Xenopus* eyes. *Science* **180**, 509–511.

Hunt, R. K., and Jacobson, M. (1974a). Neuronal specificity revisited. *Curr. Top. Dev. Biol.* **8**, 203–259.

Hunt, R. K., and Jacobson, M. (1974b). Rapid reversal of retinal axes in embryonic *Xenopus* eyes. *J. Physiol. (London)* **241**, 90P–91P.

Hunt, R. K., and Jacobson, M. (1974c). Specification of positional information in retinal ganglion cells of *Xenopus:* Intra-ocular control of the time of specification. *Proc. Natl. Acad. Sci. U.S.A.* **71**, 3616–3620.

Hunt, R. K., and Jacobson, M. (1974d). Development of neuronal locus specificity in *Xenopus* retinal ganglion cells after surgical eye transection or after fusion of whole eyes. *Dev. Biol.* **40**, 1–15.

Hunt, R. K., Bergey, G. K., and Holtzer, H. (1976). Bromodeoxyuridine: Localisation of a developmental program in *Xenopus* optic cup. *Dev. Biol.* (in press).

Hurvich, L. M., and Jameson, D. (1957). An opponent-process theory of color vision. *Psychol. Rev.* **64**, 384–404.

Huxley, J. S., and de Beer, G. R. (1934). "The Elements of Experimental Embryology." Cambridge Univ. Press, London and New York.

Inger, R. F. (1967). The development of a phylogeny of frogs. *Evolution* **21**, 369–384.

Ingle, D. (1968a). Visual releasers of prey-catching behavior in frogs and toads. *Brain, Behav. Evol.* **1**, 500–518.

Ingle, D. (1968b). Spatial dimensions of vision in fish. *In* "The Central Nervous System and Fish Behavior" (D. Ingle, ed.), pp. 51–60. Univ. of Chicago Press, Chicago, Illinois.

Ingle, D. (1970). Visumotor functions of the frog optic tectum. *Brain, Behav. Evol.* **3**, 57–71.

Ingle, D. (1971a). Prey-catching behavior of anurans toward moving and stationary objects. *Vision Res., Suppl.* **3**, 447–456.

Ingle, D. (1971b). The experimental analysis of visual behavior. *Fish Physiol.* **5**, 59–71.

Ingle, D. (1971c). Discrimination of edge-orientation by frogs. *Vision Res.* **11**, 1365–1367.

Ingle, D. (1972). Depth vision in monocular frogs. *Psychon. Sci.* **29**, 37–38.

Ingle, D. (1973a). Selective choice between double prey-objects by frogs. *Brain, Behav. Evol.* **7**, 127–144.

Ingle, D. (1973b). Evolutionary perspectives on the function of the optic tectum. *Brain, Behav. Evol.* **8**, 211–237.

Ingle, D. (1973c). Disinhibition of tectal neurons by pretectal lesions in the frog. *Science* **180**, 422–424.

Ingle, D. (1973d). Two visual systems in the frog. *Science* **181**, 1053–1055.

Ingle, D. (1973e). Size-preference for prey catching in frogs: Relationship to motivational state. *Behav. Biol.* **9**, 485–491.

Ingle, D. (1973f). Spontaneous shape discrimination by frogs during unconditioned escape behavior. *Physiol. Psychol.* **1**, 71–73.

Ingle, D. (1975). The frogs visual system as a model for studies in selective attention. *In* "Model Systems in Biological Psychiatry" (D. Ingle and H. Shein, eds.). MIT Press, Cambridge, Massachusetts.

Ingle, D. (1976a). Central visual mechanisms in Anurans. *In* "Neurobiology of the Frog" (R. Llinas and W. Precht, eds.) Springer-Verlag, Berlin and New York.

Ingle, D. (1976b). Cine analysis of snapping accuracy in monocular frogs. (Submitted for publication.)

Ingle, D. (1976c). Preference of frogs for horizontal contours in a visual-cliff test. (Submitted for publication.)

Ingle, D., and Cook, J. (1976). Size-constancy experiments in the frog. (Submitted for publication.)

Ingle, D., and Sprague, J. (1975). Sensorimotor function of the midbrain tectum. *Neurosci. Res. Prog. Bull.* **13**, 169–288.

Ingram, G. J., Anstis, M., and Corben, C. J. (1975). Observations on the Australian leptodactylid frog, *Assa darlingtoni. Herpetologica* **31**, 425–429.

Ito, S., and Loewenstein, W. R. (1969). Ionic communication between early embryonic cells. *Dev. Biol.* **19**, 228–243.

Jacobson, M. (1960). "Studies in the Organisation of Visual Mechanisms in Amphibians." Ph.D. Thesis, Edinburgh University.

Jacobson, M. (1962). The representation of the retina on the optic tectum of the frog. Correlation between retinotectal magnification factor and retinal ganglion cell count. *Q. J. Exp. Physiol.* **47**, 170–178.

Jacobson, M. (1968a). Development of neuronal specificity in retinal ganglion cells of *Xenopus. Dev. Biol.* **17**, 202–218.

Jacobson, M. (1968b). Cessation of DNA synthesis in retinal ganglion cells correlated with the time of specification of their central connections. *Dev. Biol.* **17**, 219–232.

Jacobson, M. (1971). Absence of adaptive modification in developing retinotectal connections in frogs after visual deprivation or disparate stimulation of the eyes. *Proc. Natl. Acad. Sci. U.S.A.* **68**, 528–532.

Jacobson, M., and Gaze, R. M. (1964). Types of visual response from single units in the optic tectum and optic nerve of the goldfish. *Q. J. Exp. Physiol.* **49**, 199–209.

Jacobson, M., and Gaze, R. M. (1965). Selection of appropriate tectal connections by regenerating optic nerve fibres in adult goldfish. *Exp. Neurol.* **13**, 418–430.

Jacobson, M., and Hirsch, H. V. B. (1973). Development and maintenance of connectivity in the visual system of the frog. I. The effects of eye rotation and visual deprivation. *Brain Res.* **49**, 47–65.

Jacobson, M., and Hunt, R. K. (1973). The origins of nerve-cell specificity. *Sci. Am.* **228**, 26–35.

Jacobson, M., Hirsch, H. V. B., Duda, M., and Hunt, R. K. (1976). Dynamics of retinal specification in *Rana pipiens*. (Submitted for review.)

Jaeger, R. G., and Hailman, J. P. (1971). Two types of phototactic behavior in anuran amphibians. *Nature (London)* **230**, 189–190.

Jakway, J. S., and Riss, W. (1972). Retinal projections in the tiger salamander, *Ambystoma tigrinum. Brain, Behav. Evol.* **5**, 401–442.

Jhaveri, S. R., and Schneider, G. E. (1974). Retinal projections in Syrian hamsters: Normal topography, and alterations after partial tectum lesions at birth. *Anat. Rec.* **178**, 383.

Johnson, F. C. (1959). Genetic incompatibility in the call races of *Hyla versicolor* Le Conte in Texas. *Copeia* pp. 327–335.

Johnstone, J. R., and Mark, R. F. (1971). The efference copy neurone. *J. Exp. Biol.* **54**, 403–414.

Joly, J. (1963). La sédentarité et le retour au gite chez la salamandre tachetée. *C. R. Hebd. Seances Acad. Sci.* **256**, 3510–3512.

Joly, J. (1968). Données écologiques sur la salamandre tachetée *Salamandra salamandra (L.). Ann. Sci. Nat., Zool. Biol. Anim.* [12] **10**, 301–366.

Kaas, J. H., and Guillery, R. W. (1973). The transfer of abnormal visual field representations from the dorsal lateral geniculate nucleus to the visual cortex in Siamese cats. *Brain Res.* **59**, 61–95.

Källén, B. (1965). Degeneration and regeneration in the vertebrate central nervous system during embryogenesis. *Prog. Brain Res.* **14**.

Kaneko, A. (1970). Physiological and morphological identification of horizontal bipolar, and amacrine cells in goldfish retina. *J. Physiol. (London)* **207**, 623–633.

Kanno, Y., and Loewenstein, W. R. (1966). Cell-to-cell passage of large molecules. *Nature (London)* **212**, 629.

Karamian, A. I., Vesselkin, N. P., Belekhova, M. G., and Zagorulko, T. M. (1966). Electrophysiological characteristics of tectal and the thalmo-cortical divisions of the visual system in lower vertebrates. *J. Comp. Neurol.* **127**, 559–576.

Kasperczyk, M. (1971). Comparative studies on colour sense in Amphibia (*Rana temporaria* L., *Salamandra salamandra* L. and *Triturus cristatus* L.). *Folia Biol.* (Kraków) **19**, 241–288.

Keating, M. J. (1968). Functional interaction in the development of specific nerve connexions. *J. Physiol. (London)* **198**, 75P–77P.

Keating, M. J. (1974). The role of visual function in the patterning of binocular visual connexions. *Br. Med. Bull.* **30**, 145–151.

Keating, M. J. (1976). Early visual experience and the development of the visual system. *Prog. Neurobiol.* (in press).

Keating, M. J. (1976). (In preparation.)

Keating, M. J., and Feldman, J. D. (1975). Visual deprivation and intertectal neuronal connections in *Xenopus laevis. Proc. R. Soc. Lond. Ser. B* **191**, 467–474.

Keating, M. J., and Feldman, J. D. (1976). (In preparation.)

Keating, M. J., and Gaze, R. M. (1970a). Observations on the surround properties of the receptive fields of frog retinal ganglion cells. *Q. J. Exp. Physiol. Cogn. Med. Sci.* **55**, 129–142.

Keating, M. J., and Gaze, R. M. (1970b). The ipsilateral retinotectal projection in the frog. *Q. J. Exp. Physiol. Cogn. Med. Sci.* **55**, 284–292.

Keating, M. J., Beazley, L., Feldman, J. D., and Gaze, R. M. (1975). Binocular interaction and intertectal neuronal connections: Dependence upon developmental stage. *Proc. R. Soc. Lond. Ser. B* **191**, 445–466.

Keefe, J. R. (1973). An analysis of urodelian retinal regeneration. IV. Studies of the cellular source of retinal regeneration in *Triturus cristatus carnifex* using H³-thymidine. *J. Exp. Zool.* **184**, 239–258.

Kelly, J. P., and Cowan, W. M. (1972). Studies on the development of the chick optic tectum. III. Effects of early eye removal. *Brain Res.* **42**, 263–288.

Kicliter, E. (1973a). Flux, wavelength and movement discrimination in frogs: Forebrain and midbrain contributions. *Brain, Behav. Evol.* **8**, 340–365.

Kicliter, E. (1973b). "An Anatomical Connection Between the Anterior Thalamus and the Telencephalon in the Frog." Paper presented at the Society for Neurosciences Annual Meeting.

Kicliter, E., and Northcutt, R. G. (1975). Ascending afferents to the telencephalon of Ranid frogs: An anterograde degeneration study. *J. Comp. Neurol.* **161**, 239–254.

Kidd, M. (1961). Electron microscopy of the inner plexiform layer of the retina. *In* "Cytology of Nervous Tissue," pp. 88–91. Taylor & Francis, London.

Kidd, M. (1962). Electron microscopy of the inner plexiform layer of the retina in the cat and the pigeon. *J. Anat.* **96**, 179–187.

Kirschfeld, K., and Reichardt, W. (1962). Die Verarbeitung stationaärer optischer Nachrichten im Komplexauge von Limulus. *Kybernetik* **1**, 155–163.

Kleinschmidt, J. (1973). Adaptation properties of intracellularly recorded gecko photoreceptor potentials. *In* "Biochemistry and Physiology of Visual Pigments" (H. Langer, ed.), pp. 219–224. Springer-Verlag, Berlin and New York.

Kluge, A. G., and Farris, J. S. (1969). Quantitative phyletics and the evolution of anurans. *Syst. Zool.* **18**, 1–32.

Klüver, H., and Bucy, P. C. (1938). Analysis of certain effects of bilateral temporal lobectomy in the Rhesus monkey with special reference to "psychic blindness." *J. Psychol.* **5**, 33–54.

Knapp, H., Scalia, F., and Riss, W. (1965). The optic tracts of *Rana pipiens*. *Acta Neurol. Scand.* **41**, 325–355.

Kolb, H., and Famiglietti, E. V. (1974). Rod and cone pathways in the inner plexiform layer of cat retina. *Science* **186**, 47–49.

Kollros, J. J. (1942). Experimental studies on the development of the corneal reflex in Amphibia. I. The onset of the reflex and its relationship to metamorphosis. *J. Exp. Zool.* **89**, 36–67.

Kollros, J. J. (1943). Experimental studies on the development of the corneal reflex in Amphibia. II. Localized maturation of the reflex mechanism effected by thyroxin-agar implants into the hindbrain. *Physiol. Zool.* **16**, 269–279.

Kollros, J. J. (1953). The development of the optic lobes in the frog. *J. Exp. Zool.* **123**, 153–187.

Kollros, J. J. (1968). Endocrine influences in neural development. *Growth Nerv. Syst., Ciba Found. Symp.* pp. 179–193.

Koppanyi, T. (1923a). Die replantation von augen. II. Haltbarkeit und funktionsprufung bei verscheidenen wirbeltierklassen. *Arch. Mikrosk. Anat. Entwicklungs mech.* **99**, 15–42.

Koppanyi, T. (1923b). Die replantation von augen. III. Die physiologie der replantierten saugeraugen. *Arch. Mikrosk. Anat. Entwicklungs mech.* **99**, 43–60.

Korn, A., and von Seelen, W. (1972). Dynamische Eigenschaften von Nervennetzen im visuellen System. *Kybernetik* **10**, 64–77.

Krause, W. (1892). Die Retina. III. Die retina der Amphibien. *Int. Monatsschr. Anat. Physiol.* **9**, 197–236.

Kreht, H. (1930). Über die Faserzuge im Zentralnervensystem von *Salamandra maculosa* L. *Z. Mikrosk.-anat. Forsch.* **23**, 239–320.

Kuffler, S. W. (1953). Discharge patterns and functional organization of mammalian retina. *J. Neurophysiol.* **16**, 37–68.

Kühlhorn, F. (1959). Beitrag zur Kenntnis der Ernährungsbiologie unserer heimischen Amphibien. *Veröeff. zool. Staatssamml. Muenchen* **5**, 145–188.

Kühn, A. (1929). Phototropismus und Phototaxis der Tiere. *In* "Handbuch der normalen und pathologischen Physiologie" (A. Bethe *et al.*, eds.), Vol. 12, pp. 17–35 Springer-Verlag, Berlin and New York.

Kühne, W. (1878). "On the Photochemistry of the Retina and on Visual Purple." Macmillan, New York.

Kuznetsova, L. P. (1963). Effect of dark adaptation on the sensitivity of single elements of the frog retina to various monochromatic radiations. *Biofizika* **8**, 234–237.

Landolt, E. (1871). Beitrag zu Anatomie der Retina vom Frosch, Salamander und Triton. *Arch. Mikrosk. Anat.* **7**, 81–100.

Landreth, H. F., and Ferguson, D. E. (1967). Newt orientation by sun-compass. *Nature (London)* **215**, 516–518.

Larsell, O. (1929). The effect of experimental excision of one eye on the development of the optic lobe and opticus layer in larvae of the tree frog (*Hyla regilla*). *J. Comp. Neurol.* **48**, 331–353.

Larsell, O. (1931). The effect of experimental excision of one eye on the development of the optic lobe and opticus layer in larvae of the tree-frog (*Hyla regilla*). II. The effect on cell size and differentiation of cell processes. *J. Exp. Zool.* **58**, 1–20.

Lasansky, A. (1973). Organization of the outer synaptic layer in the retina of the larval tiger salamander. *Phil. Trans. R. Soc. London* **265**, 471–489.

Lasansky, E., and Marchiafava, P. L. (1974). Light-induced resistance changes in retinal rods and cones of the tiger salamander. *J. Physiol. (London)* **236**, 171–191.

Laufer, M., Svaetichin, G., Mitarai, G., Fatechand, R., Vallecalle, E., and Villegas, J. (1961). The effect of temperature, carbon dioxide, and ammonia on the neuron-glia unit. *In* "The Visual System: Neurophysiology and Psychophysics" (R. Jung and H. Kornhuber, eds.), pp. 454–463. Springer-Verlag, Berlin and New York.

LaVail, H. H., and LaVail, M. M. (1972). Retrograde axonal transport in the central nervous system. *Science* **176**, 1416–1417.

Lázár, G. (1969). Efferent pathways of the optic tectum in the frog. *Acta Biol. (Szeged)* **20**, 171–183.

Lázár, G. (1971). The projection of the retinal quadrants on the optic centers in the frog. A terminal degeneration study. *Acta Morphol. Acad. Sci. Hung.* **19**, 325–334.

Lázár, G. (1973). Role of the accessory optic system in the optokinetic nystagmus of the frog. *Brain, Behav. Evol.* **5**, 443–460.

Lázár, G., and Székely, G. (1967). Golgi studies on the optic center of the frog. *J. Hirnforsch.* **9**, 329–344.

Lázár, G., and Székely, G. (1969). Distribution of optic terminals in the different optic centers of the frog. *Brain Res.* **16**, 1–14.

Lettvin, J. Y., Maturana, H. R., McCulloch, W. S., and Pitts, W. H. (1959). What the frog's eye tells the frog's brain. *Proc. IRE* **47**, 1940–1951.

Lettvin, J. Y., Maturana, H. R., McCulloch, W. S., and Pitts, W. H. (1961). Two remarks on the visual systems of the frog. *In* "Sensory Communication" (W. Rosenblith, ed.), pp. 757–776. MIT Press, Cambridge, Massachusetts.

Levine, M. W., and Abramov, I. (1975). An analysis of spatial summation in the receptive fields of goldfish retinal ganglion cells. *Vision Res.* **15**, 777–789.

Levine, R. L., and Cronly-Dillon, J. R. (1974). Specification of regenerating retinal ganglion cells in the adult newt, *Triturus cristatus*. *Brain Res.* **68**, 319–329.

Levine, R. L., and Jacobson, M. (1974). Deployment of optic nerve fibres is determined by positional markers in the frog's tectum. *Exp. Neurol.* **43**, 527–538.

Levitt, O., and Dorfman, A. (1974). Concepts and mechanisms of cartilage differentiation. *Curr. Top. Dev. Biol.* **8**, 103–151.

Lewis, W. H. (1904). Experimental studies on the development of the eye in amphibia. I. On the origin of the lens in *Rana palustris*. *Am. J. Anat.* **3**, 505–530.

Liberman, E. A. (1957). The nature of the information arriving at the brain by one nerve fiber from two retinal receptors in the frog. **2**, 427–430.

Liebman, P. A. (1972). Microspectrometry of photoreceptors. In "Handbook of Sensory Physiology" (M. G. Fuorter, ed.), Vol. VII, Part 1, pp. 481–528. Springer-Verlag, Berlin and New York.

Liebman, P. A., and Entine, G. (1968). Visual pigments of frog and tadpole (*Rana Pipiens*). *Vision Res.* **8**, 761–775.

Liebman, P. A., Rice, R., Carroll, S., Entine, G., and Laties, A. (1967). Triggers for C wave and pigment migration. *Invest. Ophthalmol.* **6**, 214.

Liege, B., and Galand, G. (1972). Single-unit visual responses in the frog's brain. *Res. Vision* **12**, 609–622.

Liege, B., Gaillard, F., and Galland, G. (1973). Peut-on parler d'horoptere chez la Grenouille? *J. Physiol. (Paris)* **67**, 290A.

Liem, S. S. (1970). The morphology, systematics, and evolution of the Old World tree frogs (Rhacophoridae and Hyperoliidae). *Fieldiana, Zool.* **57**, 1–145.

Liem, S. S. (1973). A new genus of frog of the family Leptodactylidae from SE Queensland, Australia. *Mem. Queensl. Mus.* **16**, 459–470.

Lipetz, L. E. (1961). Mechanism of light adaptation. *Science* **133**, 639–640.

Lipetz, L. E. (1969). The transfer functions of sensory intensity in the nervous system. *Vision Res.* **9**, 1205–1234.

Littlejohn, M. J. (1968). Frog calls and the species problem. *Aust. Zool.* **14**, 259–264.

Littlejohn, M. J., and Oldham, R. S. (1968). *Rana pipiens* complex: Mating call structure and taxonomy. *Science* **162**, 1003–1005.

Liu, C. N., and Chambers, W. W. (1958). Intraspinal sprouting of dorsal root axons. *AMA Arch. Neurol. Psychiatry* **79**, 46–61.

Loewenstein, W. R. (1972). Cellular communication through membrane junctions. *Arch. Intern. Med.* **129**, 299–305.

Loewenstein, W. R. (1973). Membrane junctions in growth and differentiation. *Fed. Proc., Fed. Am. Soc. Exp. Biol.* **32,** 60–64.

Lopashov, G. V., and Stroeva, O. G. (1964). "Development of the Eye: Experimental Studies." Israel Program Sci. Transl., Jerusalem.

Lorenz, K. (1939). Vergleichende Verhaltensforschung. *Zool. Anz.* **12,** 69–102.

Lund, R. D., and Lund, J. S. (1971). Synaptic adjustment after deafferentation of the superior colliculus of the rat. *Science* **171,** 804–807.

Lutz, B. (1973). "Brazilian Species of Hyla." Univ. of Texas Press, Austin.

Lynch, J. D. (1971). Evolutionary relationships, osteology, and zoogeography of leptodactyloid frogs. *Univ. Kans. Mus. Nat. Hist., Misc. Publ.* **53,** 1–238.

Lynch, J. D. (1973). The transition from archaic to advanced frogs. *In* "Evolutionary Biology of the Anurans" (J. L. Vial, ed.), pp. 133–182. Univ. of Missouri Press, Columbia.

Lythgoe, R. J. (1940). The mechanism of dark-adaptation. *Br. J. Ophthalmol.* **24,** 21–43.

McClanahan, L. J. (1964). Osmotic tolerance of the muscles of two desert-inhabiting toads, *Bufo cognatus* and *Scaphiopus couchi. Comp. Biochem. Physiol.* **12,** 501–508.

McClanahan, L. J. (1967). Adaptations of the spadefoot toad, *Scaphiopus couchi,* to desert environments. *Comp. Biochem. Physiol.* **20,** 73–99.

McClanahan, L. J. (1972). Changes in body fluids of burrowed spadefoot toads as a function of soil water potential. *Copeia* pp. 209–216.

McClanahan, L. J., Shoemaker, V., and Ruibal, R. (1973). Evaporative water loss in a cocoon-forming South American anuran. *Abstr. Pap., 53rd Annu. Meet. Am. Soc. Ichthyol. Herpetol., 1973.*

McDiarmid, R. W. (1971). Comparative morphology and evolution of frogs of the neotropical genera *Atelopus, Dendrophryniscus, Melanophryniscus* and *Oreophrynella. Bull. Los Angeles County Mus. Sci.* **12,** 1–66.

McGill, J. I., Powell, T. P. S., and Cowan, W. M. (1966a). The retinal representation upon the retina and isthmo-optic nucleus in the pigeon. *J. Anat.* **100,** 5–33.

McGill, J. I., Powell, T. P. S., and Cowan, W. M. (1966b). The organization of the projection of the centrifugal fibers to the retina in the pigeon. *J. Anat.* **100,** 35–49.

McIlwain, J. T. (1972). Central vision: Visual cortex and superior colliculus. *Annu. Rev. Physiol.* **34,** 291–314.

McKeehan, M. S. (1958). Induction of portion of the chick lens without contact with the optic cup. *Anat. Rec.* **132,** 297–305.

McMurray, V. M. (1954). The development of the optic lobes in *Xenopus laevis.* The effect of repeated crushing of the optic nerve. *J. Exp. Zool.* **125,** 247–263.

Madison, D. M. (1969). Homing behaviour of the red-cheeked salamander, *Plethodon jordani. Anim. Behav.* **17,** 25–39.

Malacinski, G. M., and Brothers, A. J. (1974). Mutant genes in the Mexican axolotl. *Science* **184,** 1142–1147.

Mangold, O. (1928). Das Determinations problem. I. Das Nerven system und die Sinnesorgane der Seitenlinie unter spezieller Berücksichtigung der Amphibien. *Ergeb. Biol.* **3,** 152–227.

Mangold, O. (1929). Experimente zur analyse der dermination und induktion der medullarplatte. *Wilhelm Roux' Arch. Entwicklungsmech. Org.* **117,** 586–696.

Mangold, O. (1931). Das determinations problem. III. Das Wirbeltierange in der Entwichlung und Regeneration. *Ergeb. Biol.* **7,** 193–403.

Marchase, R. B., Barbera, A. J., and Roth, S. (1975). A molecular approach to retinotectal specificity. *In* "Cell Patterning" (R. Porter and J. Rivers, eds.), pp. 315–327. Ciba Found. Symp. No. 29 (New Ser.). Assoc. Sci. Publ., Amsterdam.

Marg, E., and Adams, J. E. (1970). Evidence for a neurological zoom system in vision from angular changes in some receptive fields of single neurons with changes in fixation distance in the human visual cortex. *Experientia* **26**, 270–271.

Marler, P. R., and Hamilton, W. J. (1966). "Mechanisms of Animal Behavior." Wiley, New York.

Martin, A. A. (1967). Australian anuran life histories: Some evolutionary and ecological aspects. *In* "Australian Inland Waters and their Fauna: Eleven Studies" (A. H. Weatherley, ed.), pp. 175–191. Aust. Natl. Univ. Press, Canberra.

Martin, A. A. (1971). Life history as an aid to generic delimitation in the family Hylidae. *Copeia* pp. 78–89.

Matsumoto, N., and Naka, K. (1972). Identification of intracellular responses in the frog retina. *Brain Res.* **42**, 59–71.

Matthes, E. (1924). Die Rolle des Gesichts-, Geruchs- und Erschütterungssinnes für den Nahrungserwerb von Triton. *Biol. Zentralbl.* **44**, 72–87.

Matthey, R. (1925). Récupération de la vue après resection des nerfs optique chez le Triton. *C. R. Soc. Biol.* **93**, 904–906.

Matthey, R. (1926). Récupération de la vue après greffe de l'oeil chez le triton adulte. *C. R. Seances Soc. Biol. Ses Fil.* **94**, 4–5.

Maturana, H. R. (1958a). "The Fine Structure of the Optic Nerve and Tectum of Anurans: An Electron Microscope Study." Doctoral Dissertation, Harvard University, Cambridge, Massachusetts.

Maturana, H. R. (1958b). Efferent fibers in the optic nerve of the toad (*Bufo bufo*). *J. Anat.* **92**, 21–27.

Maturana, H. R. (1959). Number of fibers in the optic nerve and the number of ganglion cells in the retina of Anurans. *Nature* (*London*) **183**, 1406–1407.

Maturana, H. R., and Frenk, S. (1965). Synaptic connections of the centrifugal fibers in the pigeon retina. *Science* **150**, 359–361.

Maturana, H. R., Lettvin, J. Y., McCulloch, W. S., and Pitts, W. H. (1959). Physiological evidence that cut optic nerve fibres in the frog regenerate to their proper places in the tectum. *Science* **130**, 1709–1710.

Maturana, H. R., Lettvin, J. Y., McCulloch, W. S., and Pitts, W. H. (1960). Anatomy and physiology of vision in the frog (*Rana Pipiens*). *J. Gen. Physiol.* **43**, Suppl. 2, 129–175.

May, R. M. (1925). The relation of nerves to degenerating and regenerating taste buds. *J. Exp. Zool.* **42**, 371–410.

Mayhew, W. W. (1962). *Scaphiopus couchi* in California's Colorado Desert. *Herpetologica* **18**, 153–161.

Mayhew, W. W. (1965). Adaptations of the amphibian, *Scaphiopus couchi,* to desert environments. *Am. Midl. Nat.* **74**, 95–109.

Mecham, J. S., Littlejohn, M. J., Oldham, R. S., Brown, L. E., and Brown, J. R. (1973). A new species of leopard frog (*Rana pipiens* complex) from the plains of the central United States. *Occas. Pap. Mus. Tex. Tech. Univ.* **18**, 1–11.

Meng, M. (1958). Untersuchungen zum Farben- und Formsehen der Erdkröte (*Bufo bufo* L.) *Zool. Beitr.* **3**, 313–363.

Mertens, R., and Wermuth, H. (1960). "Die Amphibien und Reptilien Europas." Frankfurt am Main.

Meyer, R. L., and Sperry, R. W. (1973). Tests for neuroplasticity in the anuran retinotectal system. *Exp. Neurol.* **40**, 525–539.

Michael, C. R. (1970). Integration of retinal and cortical information in the superior colliculus of the ground squirrel. *Brain, Behav. Evol.* **3**, 205–209.

Miles, F. A., and Rogers, C. F. (1972). Centrifugal control of the avian retina, I-V. *Brain Res.* **48**, 65–156.

Miller, R. F., and Dowling, J. E. (1970). Intracellular responses of the Müller (Glial) cells of mudpuppy retina: Their relation to b-wave of the electro-retinogram. *J. Neurophysiol.* **33**, 323–341.

Milstead, W. W. (1972). Toward a quantification of the ecological niche. *Am. Midl. Nat.* **87**, 346–354.

Möller, A. (1951). Die Struktur des Auges bei Urodelen verschiedener Körpergröβe. *Zool. Jahrb., Abt. Allg. Zool. Physiol. Tiere* **62**, 138–182.

Moore, J. A. (1961). The frogs of eastern New South Wales. *Bull. Am. Mus. Nat. Hist.* **121**, 149–386.

Moore, R. Y., Björklund, A., and Stenevi, V. (1971). Plastic changes in the adrenergic innervation of the rat septal areas in response to denervation. *Brain Res.* **33**, 13–35.

Moore, R. Y., Björklund, A., and Stenevi, V. (1974). Growth and plasticity of adrenergic neurones. *In* "The Neurosciences: Third Study Program" (F. O. Schmitt and F. G. Worden, eds.), pp. 961–977. MIT Press, Cambridge, Massachusetts.

Morescalchi, A. (1967). The close karyological affinities between a *Ceratophrys* and *Pelobates* (*Amphibia Salientia*). Experientia **23**, 1–4.

Moscona, A. (1968). Cell aggregation: Properties of specific cell-ligands and their role in the formation of multicellular systems. *Dev. Biol.* **18**, 250–277.

Motozikawa, F. (1974). Olfactory input to the thalamus: Electrophysiological evidence. *Brain Res.* **67**, 334–337.

Müller, H. (1851). Zur Histologie der Netzhaut. *Z. Wiss. Zool.* **3**, 234–237.

Muntz, W. R. A. (1962a). Microelectrode recordings from the diencephalon of the frog, (*Rana pipiens*) and a blue-sensitive system. *J. Neurophysiol.* **25**, 699–711.

Muntz, W. R. A. (1962b). Effectiveness of different colors of light in releasing the positive phototactic behavior of frogs, and a possible function of the retinal projection to the diencephalon. *J. Neurophysiol.* **25**, 712–720.

Muntz, W. R. A. (1963). Phototaxis and green rods in Urodeles. *Nature (London)* **199**, 620.

Muntz, W. R. A., and Reuter, T. (1966). Visual pigments and spectral sensitivity in *Rana temporaria* and other European tadpoles. *Vision Res.* **6**, 601–618.

Murakami, M., and Kaneko, A. (1966). Differentiation of PIII subcomponents in cold-blooded vertebrate retinas. *Vision Res.* **6**, 627–636.

Nace, G. W. (1968). The amphibian facility at the University of Michigan. *Bioscience* **18**, 767–775.

Nace, G. W. (1975). The need for biological standards. *Fed. Proc., Fed. Am. Soc. Exp. Biol.* **34**, 2197–2198.

Nace, G. W., Waage, J. K., and Richards, C. M. (1971). Sources of amphibians for research. *Bioscience* **21**, 768–773.

Nace, G. W., Culley, D. D., Emmons, M. B., Gibbs, E. L., Hutchison, V. H., and McKonnell, R. G. (1974). "Amphibians: Guidelines for the Breeding, Care, and Management of Laboratory Animals." Nat. Acad. Sci., Washington D.C.

Naka, K. I., Inoma, S., Kosugi, Y., and Tong, C. W. (1960). Recording of action potentials from single cells in the frog retina. *Jpn. J. Physiol.* **10**, 436–442.

Naka, K. I., and Rushton, W. A. H. (1966). S-potentials from colour units in the retina of fish (*Cyprinidae*). *J. Physiol.* (*London*), **185**, 536–555.

Naka, K. I., and Rushton, W. A. H. (1967). The generation and spread of S-potentials in fish (*cyprinidae*). *J. Physiol.* (*London*) **192**, 437–461.

Nelson, C. E., and Miller, G. A. (1971). A possible case of mimicry in frogs. *Herp. Rev.* **3**, 109.

Nelson, R. (1973). A comparison of electrical properties of neurons in *Necturus* retina. *J. Neurophysiol.* **36**, 519–535.

Nevo, E. (1968). Pipid frogs from the early Cretaceous of Israel and pipid evolution. *Bull. Mus. Comp. Zool.* **136**, 255–318.

Niewkoop, P. D. (1950). Neural competence and neural fields. *Rev. Suisse Zool.* **57**, 23–40.

Niewkoop, P. D., and Faber, J. (1956). "A Normal Table of Xenopus laevis (Daudin)." North-Holland Publ., Amsterdam.

Nilsson, S. E. G. (1964a). An electron microscopic classification of the retinal receptors of the leopard frog (*Rana pipiens*). *J. Ultrastruct. Res.* **10**, 390–416.

Nilsson, S. E. G. (1964b). Receptor cell outer segment development and ultrastructure of the disk membranes in the retina of the tadpole (*Rana pipiens*). *J. Ultrastruct. Res.* **11**, 581–620.

Noble, G. K. (1931). "The Biology of the Amphibia." McGraw-Hill, New York.

Noble, G. K. (1955). "The Biology of the Amphibia." Dover Publication, New York.

Noell, W. K. (1954). The origin of the electroretinogram. *Am. J. Ophthalmol.* **38**, 78–90.

Norman, R. A., and Werblin, F. S. (1974). Control of retinal sensitivity. I. Light and dark adaptation of vertebrate rods and cones. *J. Gen. Physiol.* **63**, 37–61.

Norton, A. S., Spekreijse, H., Wagner, H. G., and Wolbarsht, M. L. (1970). Responses to directional stimuli in retinal preganglionic units. *J. Physiol.* (*London*) **206**, 93–107.

Nye, P. W., and Naka, K. I. (1971). The dynamics of inhibitory interaction in a frog receptive field: A paradigm of paracontrast. *Vision Res.* **11**, 377–392.

Olds, J., and Milner, P. (1954). Positive reinforcement produced by electrical stimulation of septal area and other regions of rat brain. *J. Comp. Physiol. Psychol.* **47**, 419–427.

Orkand, R. K., Nicholls, J. G., and Kuffler, S. W. (1966). Effect of nerve impulses on the membrane potential of glial cells in the central nervous system of amphibia. *J. Neurophysiol.* **29**, 788–806.

Orton, G. L. (1953). The systematics of vertebrate larvae. *Evolution* **2**, 63–75.

Pace, A. E. (1974). Systematic and biological studies of the leopard frogs (*Rana pipiens* complex) of the United States. *Misc. Publ., Mus. Zool. Univ. Mich.* **148**, 1–140.

Pak, W. L. (1965). Some properties of the early electrical response in the vertebrate retina. *Cold Spring Harbor Symp. Quant. Biol.* **30**, 493–499.

Parsons, T. S., and Williams, E. E. (1963). The relationships of the modern amphibia: A re-examination. *Q. Rev. Biol.* **38**, 26–53.

Pesetsky, I. (1962). The thyroxine-stimulated enlargement of Mauthner's neuron in anurans. *Gen. Comp. Endocrinol.* **2**, 229–235.

Pettigrew, J. O. (1974). The effect of visual experience on the development of stimulus specificity by kitten cortical neurones. *J. Physiol.* (*London*) **237**, 49–74.

Pickering, S., and Varju, D. (1967). Ganglion cells in the frog retina: Inhibitory receptive field and long latency response. *Nature (London)* **215**, 545–546.

Pigarev, I. N., Zenkin, G. M., and Girman, S. V. (1971). Activity of the retina's detectors in unrestrained frogs. *Sechenov Physiol. J. USSR* **57**, 1448–1453.

Pipa, R. L. (1973). Proliferation, movement, and regression of neurons during the post-embryonic development of insects. *In* "Developmental Neurobiology of Arthropods" (D. Young, ed.). Cambridge Univ. Press, London and New York.

Platz, J. E., and Platz, A. L. (1973). *Rana pipiens* complex: Hemoglobin phenotypes of sympatric and allopatric populations in Arizona. *Science* **179**, 1334–1336.

Ploog, D., and Gottwald, P. (1974). "Verhaltensforschung." Urban & Schwarzenberg, Berlin.

Pomeranz, B. (1972). Metamorphosis of frog vision: Changes in ganglion cell physiology and anatomy. *Exp. Neurol.* **34**, 187–199.

Pomeranz, B., and Chung, S. H. (1970). Dendritic-tree anatomy codes form—vision physiology in tadpole retina. *Science* **170**, 983–984.

Popashava and Stroeva (1964).

Porter, K. R. (1972). "Herpetology." Saunders, Philadelphia, Pennsylvania.

Post, D. D., and Pettus, D. (1966). Variation in *Rana pipiens* (Anura: Ranidae) of eastern Colorado. *Southwest. Nat.* **11**, 476–482.

Potter, D. D., Furshpan, E. J., and Lennox, E. S. (1966). Connections between cells of the developing squid as revealed by electrophysiological methods. *Proc. Natl. Acad. Sci. U.S.A.* **55**, 328–336.

Potter, H. D. (1969). Structural characteristics of cell and fiber populations in the optic tectum of the frog (*Rana catesbieana*). *J. Comp. Neurol.* **136**, 203–232.

Potter, H. D. (1972). Terminal arborizations of retinotectal axons in the bullfrog. *J. Comp. Neurol.* **144**, 269–284.

Prestige, M. C. (1967). The control of cell number in the lumbar ventral horns during the development of *Xenopus laevis* tadpoles. *J. Embryol. Exp. Morphol.* **18**, 359–387.

Prestige, M. C. (1974). Axon and cell numbers in the developing nervous system. *Br. Med. Bull.* **30**, 107–111.

Proenza, L. M., and Burkhardt, D. A. (1973). Proximal negative response and retinal sensitivity in the mudpuppy, *Necturus maculosus*. *J. Neurophysiol.* **36**, 502–518.

Pyburn, W. F. (1961). The inheritance and distribution of vertebral stripe color in the cricket frog. *In* "Vertebrate Speciation" (W. F. Blair, ed.), pp. 235–261. Univ. of Texas Press, Austin.

Pyburn, W. F. (1975). A new species of microhylid frog of the genus *Synapturanus* from southeastern Columbia. *Herpetologica* 31:439–443.

Rabb, G. B. (1960). On the mating and egg-laying behavior of the Surinam toad, *Pipa pipa. Copeia* pp. 271–276.

Raisman, G. (1969). Neuronal plasticity in the septal nuclei of the adult rat. *Brain Res.* **14**, 25–48.

Ramon, P. (1894). "Investigaciones micrograficas en el encephalo de los batraceos y reptiles." Facultad de Medicina de Zaragoza.

Ramón y Cajal, S. (1892). "The Structure of the Retina" (transl. by S. A. Thorpe and M. Glickstein. Thomas, Springfield, Illinois, 1972).

Ramón y Cajal, S. (1894). "Die Retina der Wirbeltiere" (Obersetzt von R. Gréeff). Bergmann, Wiesbaden.

Ray, J. A. (1970). Instrumental avoidance learning by the tiger salamander *Ambystoma tigrinum. Anim. Behav.* **18**, 73–77.

Raybourn, M. S. (1975). A spatio-temporal analysis of the binocular input to the optic tectum of the frog. *Brain Beh. Evol.* 11, 161.

Reig, O. A. (1964). El problema del origen monofiletico y polifiletico de los anfíbios, con consideraciones sobre las relaciones entre anuros, urodelos y ápodos. *Ameghiniana* 3, 191–211.

Reig, O. A. (1972). *Macrogenioglottus* and the South American bufonid toads. *In* "Evolution in the Genus Bufo" (W. F. Blair, ed.), pp. 14–36. Univ. of Texas Press, Austin.

Reig, O. A., and Cei, J. M. (1963). Elucidación morfologico-estadistica de las entidades del género *Lepidobatrachus* Budgett (Anura, Ceratophrynidae) con consideraciones sobre la extensión del distrito chaqueño del dominio zoogeofrafico subtropical. *Physis* 67, 181–204.

Reuter, T. (1969). Visual pigments and ganglion cell activity in the retinae of tadpoles and adult frogs (*Rana temporaria*). *Acta Zool. Fenn.* 122, 1–64.

Reuter, T., and Virtanen, K. (1972). Border and colour coding in the retina of the frog. *Nature (London)* 239, 260–263.

Reuter, T. E., White, R. H., and Wald, G. (1971). Rhodopsin and porphyropsin fields in the adult bullfrog retina. *J. Gen. Physiol.* 58, 351–371.

Reyer, R. W. (1962). Regeneration in the Amphibian eye. *Symp. Soc. Study Dev. Growth* 20, 211–265.

Richards, W. (1968). Spatial re-mapping in the primate visual system. *Kybernetik* 4, 146–156.

Riggs, L. A. (1937). Dark adaptation in the frog eye as determined by the electrical response of the retina. *J. Cell. Comp. Physiol.* 9, 491–510.

Riss, W., and Jakway, J. S. (1970). A perspective on the fundamental retinal projections of vertebrates. *Brain, Behav. Evol.* 3, 30–35.

Riss, W., Knapp, H., and Scalia, F. (1963). Optic pathways in *Cryptobranchus alleghceniensis* as revealed by the Nauta technique. *J. Comp. Neurol.* 121, 31–43.

Riss, W., Pedersen, R. A., Jakway, J. S., and Ware, C. B. (1972). Levels of function and their representation in the vertebrate thalamus. *Brain, Behav. Evol.* 6, 26–41.

Rittschof, D. (1975). "Some Aspects of the Natural History and Ecology of the Leopard Frog, *Rana pipiens.*" Doctoral Thesis, The University of Michigan, Ann Arbor.

Roach, F. C. (1945). Differentiation of the central nervous system after axial reversals of the medullary plate of *Amblystoma*. *J. Exp. Zool.* 99, 53–77.

Romer, A. S. (1966). "Vertebrate Paleontology." Univ. of Chicago Press. Chicago Illinois.

Röthig, P. (1924). Beiträge zum Studium des Zentralnervensystems der Wirbeltiere. IX. Ober die Faserzüge im Zwischenhirn der Urodelen. *Z. Mikrosk. Anat. Forsch.* 1, 5–40.

Rubinson, K. (1968). Projections of the tectum opticum of the frog. *Brain, Behav. Evol.* 1, 529–561.

Rubinson, K. (1969). Retinal projections in the toad, *Bufo marinus*. *Anat Rec.* 163, 254.

Rushton, W. A. H. (1959). Excitation pools in the frog's retina. *J. Physiol. (London)* 149, 327–345.

Rushton, W. A. H. (1961). Rhodopsin measurement and dark-adaptation in a subject deficient in cone vision. *J. Physiol. (London)* 156, 193–205.

Rushton, W. A. H. (1965). The Ferrier Lecture: Visual adaptation. *Proc. R. Soc. London, Ser. B* **162**, 20–46.

Rushton, W. A. H., and Cohen, R. D. (1954). Visual purple level and the course of dark adaptation. *Nature (London)* **173**, 301.

Rushton, W. A. H., and Powell, D. S. (1972). The rhodopsin content and the visual threshold of human rods. *Vision Res.* **12**, 1073–1081.

Saez, F. A., and Brum, N. (1959). Citogenética de anfibios anuros de América del Sur. Los cromosomas de *Odontophrynus americanus* y *Ceratophrys ornata*. *An. Fac. Med., Univ. Repub. Montevideo* **44**, 414–423.

Saez, F. A., and Brum, N. (1960). Chromosomes of South American amphibians. *Nature (London)* **185**, 945.

Sanderson, K. J., Guillery, R. W., and Shackelford, R. M. (1974). Congenitally abnormal visual pathways in mink (*Mustela vision*) with reduced retinal pigment. *J. Comp. Neurol.* **154**, 225–248.

Sato, T. (1953). Über die Ursachen des Ausbleibens der Linsenregeneration und zugleich über die linsenbildendeFähigkeit des Pigment-epithels bei den Anuren. *Wilhelm Roux' Arch. Entwicklungs Mech. Org.* **146**, 487–514.

Saunders, J. W. (1966). Death in embryonic systems. *Science* **154**, 604–612.

Saunders, J. W., and Gasseling, M. T. (1968). Ectodermal-mesodermal interactions in the origin of limb symmetry. *In* "Epithelial-mesenchymal Interactions" (R. Fleischmajer and R. E. Billingham, eds.). Williams & Wilkins, Baltimore, Maryland.

Savage, J. M. (1966). An extraordinary new toad (*Bufo*) from Costa Rica. *Rev. Biol. Trop.* **14**, 153–167.

Savage, J. M. (1973). The geographic distribution of frogs: Patterns and predictions. *In* "Evolutionary Biology of the Anurans" (J. L. Vial, ed.), pp. 351–445. Univ. of Missouri Press, Columbia.

Saxén, L. (1954). The development of the visual cells. Embryological and physiological investigations on Amphibia. *Ann. Acad. Sci. Fenn., Ser. A4* **23**, 1–93.

Saxén, L. (1956). The initial formation and subsequent development of the double visual cells in Amphibia. *J. Embryol. Exp. Morphol.* **4**, 57–65.

Saxén, L. (1961). Transfilter neural induction of amphibian ectoderm. *Dev. Biol.* **3**, 140–152.

Saxén, L., and Toivonen, S. (1962). "Primary Embryonic Induction." Prentice-Hall, Englewood Cliffs, New Jersey.

Scalia, F. (1973). Autoradiographic demonstration of optic nerve fibers in the stratum zonale of the frog's tectum. *Brain Res.* **58**, 484–488.

Scalia, F. (1976). The optic pathway of the frog: Nuclear morphology and connections. *In* "The Neurobiology of the Frog" (R. Llinas and W. Precht, eds.). Springer-Verlag, Berlin and New York. (in press).

Scalia, F., and Colman, D. R. (1974). Aspects of the central projection of the optic nerve in the frog as revealed by anterograde migration of horseradish peroxidase. *Brain Res.* **79**, 496–504.

Scalia, F., Colman, D. R. (1975). Identification of telencephalic-afferent thalamic nuclei associated with the visual system of the frog. *Neuroscience* (Abstract).

Scalia, F., and Fite, K. (1974). A retinotopic analysis of the central connections of the optic nerve in the frog. *J. Comp. Neurol.* **158**, 455–478.

Scalia, F., and Gregory, K. (1970). Retinofugal projections in the frog: Location of the postsynaptic neurons. *Brain, Behav. Evol.* **3**, 16–29.

Scalia, F., Knapp, H., Halpern, M., and Riss, W. (1968). New observations on the retinal projection in the frog. *Brain, Behav. Evol.* **1**, 324–353.

Schacher, S. M., Holtzman, E., and Hood, D. C. (1974). Uptake of horseradish peroxidase by frog photoreceptor synapses in the dark and the light. *Nature (London)* **249**, 261–263.

Schacher, S. M., Holtzman, E., and Hood, D. C. (1975). "Synaptic Activity of Frog Photoreceptors." Paper presented at the Association for Res. in Vision and Ophthalmology Meeting, Sarasota.

Scheibner, H. and Baumann, C. (1970). Properties of the frog's retinal ganglion cells as revealed by substitution of chromatic stimuli. *Vision Research* **10**, 829–836.

Scheich, H., and Th. H. Bullock (1974). The detection of electric fields from electric organs. In "Handbook of Sensory Physiology" (H. Autrum *et al.*, eds.) Vol. III/3; Electroreceptors and other specialized receptors in lower vertebrates (A. Fessard, ed.) p. 201. Springer-Verlag, Berlin, New York.

Schipperheyn, J. J. (1963). Respiratory eye movements and perception of stationary objects in the frog. *Acta Physiol. Pharmacol. Neerl.* **12**, 157–159.

Schipperheyn, J. J. (1965). Contrast detection in frog's retina. *Acta Physiol. Pharmacol. Neerl.* **13**, 231–277.

Schleidt, W. (1962). Die historische Entwicklung der Begriffe "Angeborenes auslösendes Schema" und "Angeborener Auslösemechanismus" in der Ethologie. *Z. Tierpsychol.* **19**, 697–722.

Schmatolla, E., and Erdman, G. (1973). Influence of retino-tectal innervation on cell proliferation and cell migration in the embryonic teleost tectum. *J. Embryol. Exp. Morphol.* **29**, 697–712.

Scheich, H., and Th. H. Bullock (1974). The detection of electric fields from electric organs. In "Handbook of sensory physiology." (H. Autrum *et al.*, eds.) Vol. III/3; Electroreceptors and other specialized receptors in lower vertebrates (A. Fessard, ed.) p. 201. Springer-Verlag, Berlin, New York.

Schneider, C. W. (1968). Avoidance learning and the response tendencies of larval salamander *Ambystoma punctatum* to photic stimulation. *Anim. Behav.* **16**, 492–495.

Schneider, D. (1954a). Beitrag zu einer analyse des Beute- und Fluchtuerhaltens einheimischer Anuren. *Biol. Zentralbl.* **73**, 225–282.

Schneider, D. (1954b). Das Gesichtsfeld und der Fixiervorgang bei einheimischen Anuren. *Z. Vergl. Physiol.* **36**, 147–164.

Schneider, G. E. (1969). Two visual systems: Brain mechanisms for localization and discrimination are dissociated by tectal and cortical lesions. *Science* **163**, 895–902.

Schneider, G. E. (1970). Mechanism of functional recovery following lesions of visual cortex or superior colliculus in neonate and adult hamsters. *Brain, Behav. Evol.*, **3**, 295–323.

Schneider, G. E. (1973). Early lesions of superior colliculus: Factors affecting the formation of abnormal retinal projections. *Brain, Behav. Evol.* **8**, 73–109.

Schneider, G. E., and Jhaveri, S. R. (1974). Neuro-anatomical correlates of spared or altered function after brain lesions in the newborn hamster. In "Plasticity and Recovery of Function in the Central Nervous System." Academic Press, New York.

Schultze, M. (1867a). Über Stäbchen und Zapfen der Retina. *Arch. Mikrosk. Anat.* **3**, 215–247.

Schultze, M. (1867b). Bemerkungen iiber Bau und Entwicklung der Retina. *Arch. Mikrosk. Anat.* (1867b). **3**, 371–382.

Schwind, J. L. (1933). Tissue specificity at the time of metamorphosis in frog larvae. *J. Exp. Zool.* **66,** 1–14.

Sharma, S. C. (1972a). Reformation of retinotectal projections after various tectal ablations in adult goldfish. *Exp. Neurol.* **34,** 171–182.

Sharma, S. C. (1972b). Redistribution of visual projections in altered optic tecta of adult goldfish. *Proc. Nat. Acad. Sci. U.S.A.* **69,** 2637–2639.

Sharma, S. C., and Hollyfield, J. G. (1974). Specification of retinal central connections in *Rana pipiens* before the appearance of the first post-mitotic ganglion cell. *J. Comp. Neurol.* **155,** 395–408.

Shen, S. C., Greenfield, P., and Boell, E. J. (1955). The distribution of cholinesterase in the frog brain. *J. Comp. Neurol.* **102,** 717–743.

Shoemaker, V. H., Balding, D., and Ruibal, R. (1972). Uricotelism and low evaporative water loss in a South American frog. *Science* **175,** 1018–1020.

Shoop, C. R. (1965). Orientation of *Ambystoma maculatum:* Movements to and from breeding ponds. *Science* **149,** 558–559.

Shortess, G. K. (1963). Binocular interaction in the frog retina. *J. Opt. Soc. Am.* **53,** 1423–1429.

Shumway, W. (1940). Stages in the anatomical development of *Rana pipiens. Anat. Rec.* **78,** 138–147.

Sillman, A. J. (1974). Rapid dark-adaptation in the frog cone. *Vision Res.* **14,** 1021–1027.

Sillman, A. J., Ito, H., and Tomita, T. (1969). Studies on the mass receptor potential of the isolated frog retina. I. General properties of the response. *Vision Res.* **9,** 1435–1442.

Sillman, A. J., Owen, W. G., and Fernandez, H. R. (1973). Rapid dark adaptation in the frog rod. *Vision Res.* **13,** 393–402.

Siminoff, R., Schwassmann, H. O., and Kruger, L. (1966). An electrophysiological study of the visual projection to the superior colliculus of rat. *J. Comp. Neurol.* **127,** 435–444.

Sirovich, L., Abramov, I., Gordon, J., and Levine, M. (1973). "Photopigments and Pseudopigments." Paper presented at the Association for Research in Vision and Ophthalmology Meeting, Sarasota.

Sivak, J. G. (1973). Interrelation of feeding behavior and accomodative lens movements in some species of North America freshwater fishes. *J. Fish. Res. Board* **30,** 1141–1145.

Skarf, B. (1973). Development of binocular single units in the optic tectum of frogs raised with disparate stimulation to the two eyes. *Brain Res.* **51,** 352–357.

Skarf, B., and Jacobson, M. (1974). Development of binocularly driven single units in frogs raised with asymmetrical visual stimulation. *Exp. Neurol.* **42,** 669–686.

Slack, C., and Palmer, J. F. (1969). The permeability of intercellular junctions in the early embryo of *Xenopus laevis,* studied with a fluorescent tracer. *Exp. Cell Res.* **55,** 416–419.

Smith, J. J. B. (1968). Hearing in terestrial urodeles: A vibration-sensitive mechanism in the ear. *J. Exp. Biol.* **48,** 191–205.

Snyder, M., and Diamond, T. (1968). The organization and function of the visual cortex in the tree shrews. *Brain Behav. Evol.* **1,** 244–288.

Spekreijse, H., Wagner, H. G., and Wolbarsht, M. L. (1972). Spectral and spatial coding of ganglion cell responses in goldfish retina. *J. Neurophysiol.* **35,** 73–86.

Spemann, H. (1901). Ueber Korrelationen in der Entwicklung des Auges. *Verh. Anat. Ges.* **15,** 61–79.

BIBLIOGRAPHY 361

Spemann, H. (1912). Über die Entwicklung umgedrehter Hirnteile bei Amphibienen bryonen. *Zool. Jahrb.* **3**, Suppl. 15, 1–48.

Spemann, H. (1928). Die Entwicklung seitlucher und dorso-ventraler Keimhälften bei verzögerten Kemversorgung. *Z. Wiss. Zool.* **132**, 105–134.

Sperry, R. W. (1942). Reestablishment of visuomotor coordinations by optic nerve regeneration. *Anat. Rec.* **84**, 470.

Sperry, R. W. (1943a). Effect of 180 degree rotation of the retinal field on visuomotor coordination. *J. Exp. Zool.* **02**, 263 279.

Sperry, R. W. (1943b). Visuomotor coordination in the newt (*Triturus viridescens*) after regeneration of the optic nerve. *J. Comp. Neurol.* **79**, 33–55.

Sperry, R. W. (1944). Optic nerve regeneration with return of vision in anurans. *J. Neurophysiol.* **7**, 57–70.

Sperry, R. W. (1945). Restoration of vision after crossing of optic nerves and after contralateral transplantation of eye. *J. Neurophysiol.* **8**, 15 28.

Sperry, R. W. (1948). Patterning of central synapses in regeneration of the optic nerve in Teleosts. *Physiol. Zool.* **21**, 351–361.

Sperry, R. W. (1951). Mechanisms of neural maturation. *In* "Handbook of Experimental Psychology" (S. S. Stevens, ed.), pp. 236–280. Wiley, New York.

Sperry, R. W. (1963). Chemoaffinity in the orderly growth of nerve fibre patterns and connections. *Proc. Natl. Acad. Sci. U.S.A.* **50**, 703–710.

Sperry, R. W. (1965). Embryogenesis of behavioral nerve nets. *In* "Organogenesis" (R. L. De Haan and H. Ursprung, eds.), pp. 161–186. Holt, New York.

Sprague, J. M., Berlucchi, G., and Bernadino, A. (1970). The superior colliculus and pretectum in visually guided behavior and visual discrimination in the cat. *Brain, Behav. Evol.* **3**, 285–294.

Stefanelli, A. (1951). The Mauthnerian apparatus in the Ichthyopsida; its nature and function and correlated problems of neurohistogenesis. *Rev. Biol.* **26**, 17–34.

Steinberg, M. S. (1970). Does differential adhesion govern self-assembly processes in histogenesis? Equilibrium configurations and the emergence of a hierarchy among populations of embryonic cells. *J. Exp. Zool.* **173**, 395–434.

Stell, W. K. (1967). The structure and relationship of horizontal cells and photoreceptor-bipolar synaptic complexes in goldfish retina. *Am. J. Anat.* **121**, 401–424.

Stevens, R. J. (1973). A cholinergic inhibitory system in the frog optic tectum: Its role in visual electrical responses and feeding behavior. *Brain Res.* **49**, 309–321.

Stewart, M. M. (1967). "Amphibian of Malawi." State Univ. of New York Press, Albany.

Stiles, W. S. (1959). Color vision: The approach through increment-threshold sensitivity. *Proc. Natl. Acad. Sci. U.S.A.* **45**, 100–114.

Stone, J., and Hoffman, K.-P. (1972). Very slow-conducting ganglion cells in the cat's retina: A major, new functional type? *Brain Res.* **43**, 610–616.

Stone, L. S. (1930). Heteroplastic transplantation of eyes between the larvae of two species of *Amblystoma*. *J. Exp. Zool.* **55**, 193–261.

Stone, L. S. (1944). Functional polarization in retinal development and its reestablishment in regenerating retinae of rotated grafted eyes. *Proc. Soc. Exp. Biol. Med.* **57**, 13–14.

Stone, L. S. (1948). Functional polarization in developing and regenerating retinae of transplanted eyes. *Ann. N.Y. Acad. Sci.* **49**, 856 865.

Stone, L. S. (1950). The role of retinal pigment cells in regenerating neural retina of adult salamander eyes. *J. Exp. Zool.* **113**, 9–32.

Stone, L. S. (1960). Polarization of the retina and development of vision. *J. Exp. Zool.* **145**, 85–96.

Straschill, M., and Hoffmann, K.-P. (1969). Functional aspects of localization in the cat's tectum opticum. *Brain Res.* **13**, 274–283.

Straznicky, K. (1973). The formation of the optic fibre projection after partial tectal removal in *Xenopus. J. Embryol. Exp. Morphol.* **29**, 397–409.

Straznicky, K., and Gaze, R. M. (1971). The growth of the retina in *Xenopus laevis:* An autoradiographic study. *J. Embryol. Exp. Morphol.* **26**, 67–79.

Straznicky, K., and Gaze, R. M. (1972). The development of the tectum in *Xenopus laevis:* An autoradiographic study. *J. Embryol. Exp. Morphol.* **28**, 87–115.

Straznicky, K., Gaze, R. M., and Keating, M. J. (1971a). The retinotectal projections after uncrossing the optic chiasma in *Xenopus* with one compound eye. *J. Embryol. Exp. Morphol.* **26**, 523–542.

Straznicky, K., Gaze, R. M., and Keating, M. J. (1971b). The establishment of retinotectal projections after embryonic removal of rostral or caudal half of the optic tectum in *Xenopus laevis* toad. *Proc. Int. Union Physiol. Sci.* **9**, 540.

Straznicky, K., Gaze, R. M., and Keating, M. J. (1974). The retinotectal projection from a double-ventral compound eye in *Xenopus laevis. J. Embryol. Exp. Morphol.* **31**, 123–137.

Ströer, W. F. H. (1940). Das optische System beim Wassermolch. *Acta. Neerl. Morphol. Norm. Pathol.* **3**, 178–195.

Swett, F. H. (1937). Determination of limb-axes. *Q. Rev. Biol.* **12**, 322–339.

Szabó, I. (1962). Nahrungswahl und Nahrung des gefleckten Feuersalamanders. *Acta Zool. Acad. Sci. Hung.* **8**, 459–477.

Székely, G. (1954a). Untersuchung der Entwicklung optischer Reflexmechanismen an Amphibienlarven. *Acta Physiol. Acad. Sci. Hung. Suppl.* **6**, 18.

Székely, G. (1954b). Zur ausbildung der lokalen funktionellen spezifität der retina. *Acta Biol. (Szeged)* **5**, 157–167.

Székely, G. (1973). Anatomy and synaptology of the optic tectum. *In* "Handbook of Sensory Physiology" (R. Jung, ed.), Vol. VII, Part 3, pp. 1–26. Springer-Verlag, Berlin and New York.

Székely, G., Setalo, G., Lázár, G. (1973). Fine structure of the frog's optic tectum: Optic fiber termination layers. *J. Hirnforsch.* **14**, 189–225.

Szent-Györgyi, A. (1914). Untersuchungen über den Glaskörper der Amphibien und Reptilien. *Arch. Mikrosk. Anat.* **85**, 303–359.

Tandy, M., and Keith, R. (1972). *Bufo* of Africa. *In* "Evolution in the Genus Bufo" (W. F. Blair, ed.), pp. 119–170. Univ. of Texas Press, Austin.

Terry, R. J., and Gordon, J. Jr. (1960). The effects of unilateral and bilateral enucleation on optic lobe development and pigmentation of the skin in *Rana catesbieana* larvae. *J. Exp. Zool.* **143**, 245–257.

Therman, P. O. (1939). Rod and cone electroretinograms in relation to pigment migration in normal and adrenalized frogs. *J. Cell. Comp. Physiol.* **14**, 253–259.

Tihen, J. A. (1960). Two new genera of African bufonids, with remarks on the phylogeny of related genera. *Copeia* pp. 225–233.

Tinbergen, N. (1972). "Instinktlehre, vergleichende Erforschung angeborenen Verhaltens." Parey, Berlin.

Toivonen, S. (1972). Heterotypic tissue interactions in the segregation of the central nervous system (CNS). *In* "Cell Differentiation" (R. Harris, P. Allin and D. Viza, eds.), pp. 30–34. Munksgaard, Copenhagen.

Toivonen, S., and Saxén, L. (1968). Morphogenetic interacton of presumptive neural and mesodermal cells mixed in different ratios. *Science* **159**, 539–540.

Tomita, T. (1963). Electrical activity in the vertebrate retina. *J. Opt. Soc. Am.* **53**, 49–57.

Tomita, T. (1965). Electrophysiological study of the mechanisms subserving color coding in the fish retina. *Cold Spring Harbor Symp. Quart. Biol.* **30**, 559–566.

Tomita, T., Murakami, M., Hashimoto, Y., and Sasaki, Y. (1961). Electrical activity of single neurons in the frog's retina. *In* "The Visual System: Neurophysiology and Psychophysics" (P. Jung and H. Kornhuber, eds.), pp. 24–31. Springer-Verlag, Berlin, and New York.

Townes, P. S., and Holtfreter, J. (1955). Directed movements and selective adhesion of embryonic amphibian cells. *J. Exp. Zool.* **128**, 53–120.

Toyoda, J. (1973). Membrane resistance changes underlying the bipolar cell response in the carp retina. *Vision Res.* **13**, 283–294.

Toyoda, J., Nosaki, H., and Tomita, T. (1969). Light induced resistance changes in single photoreceptors of *Necturus* and *Gekko*. *Vision Res.* **9**, 453–463.

Toyoda, J., Hashimoto, H., Anno, H., and Tomita, T. (1970). The rod response in the frog as studied by intracellular recording. *Vision Res.* **10**, 1093–1100.

Toyoda, J., Hashimoto, H., and Ohtsu, K. (1973). Bipolar-amacrine transmission in the carp retina. *Vision Res.* **13**, 295–307.

Trachtenberg, M. C., and Ingle, D. (1974). Thalamo-tectal projections in the frog. *Brain Res.* **79**, 419–430.

Treanor, R. R. (1975). "Management of the Bullfrog (*Rana catesbieana*) Resource in California," Inland Fish. Admin. Report 75-1, p. 30. California Dept. of Fish & Game, Sacramento.

Trevarthen, C. B. (1968a). Two mechanisms of vision in primates. *Psychol. Forsch.* **31**, 299–337.

Trevarthen, C. B. (1968b). Vision in fish: The origins of the visual frame for action in vertebrates. *In* "The Central Nervous System and Fish Behavior." (D. Ingle, ed.). Univ. of Chicago Press, Chicago, Illinois.

Trueb, L. (1970). Evolutionary relationships of casque-headed tree frogs with co-ossified skulls (Family Hylidae). *Univ. Kans. Publ. Mus. Nat. Hist.* **18**, 547–716.

Tuttle, J. R. (1974). "An Analysis and Comparison of the Responses of *Necturus* Retinal Ganglion Cells to Stationary and Moving Stimuli." Ph.D. Thesis, Rockefeller University, New York.

Twitty, V. (1955). Eye. *In* "Analysis of Development" (B. H. Willier, P. A. Weiss, and V. Hamburger, eds.). Saunders, Philadelphia, Pennsylvania.

Tyler, M. J. (1971). The phylogenetic significance of vocal sac structure in hylid frogs. *Univ. Kans. Publ. Mus. Nat. Hist.* **19**, 319–360.

Uexküll, J. V. (1909). "Umwelt and Innenwelt der Tiere." Berlin.

Uttal, W. R. (1973). "The Psychobiology of Sensory Coding." Harper, New York.

Valenstein, E. S. (1969). Biology of drives. *Neurosci. Res. Symp. Summ.* **3**, 1–107.

van de Grind, W. A., Grüsser, O.-J., and Lunkenheimer, H. U. (1973). Temporal transfer properties of the afferent visual system. Psychophysical, neurophysiological and theoretical investigations. *In* "Handbook of Sensory Physiology" (R. Jung, ed.), Vol. VII, Part 3, pp. 431–573. Springer-Verlag, Berlin and New York.

van der Waaij, D., Cohen, B. J., and Nace, G. W. (1974). Colonization patterns of aerobic gram negative bacteria in the cloaca of *Rana pipiens*. *Lab. Anim. Sci.* **24**, 307–317.

van Genderen-Stort, (1887). Über form-und Orlsveränderungen der Netzhaut elemente unter Eintlub von Licht und Dunkel.

Varju, D. (1969). Functional classification and receptive-field organization of retinal ganglion cells in the frog. In "Processing of Optical Data by Organisms and by Machines" (W. Reichardt, ed.), pp. 366–383. Academic Press, New York.

Vesselkin, N. P., Agayan, A. L., and Nomokonova, L. M. (1971). A study of the thalamo-telencephalic afferent system in frogs. Brain, Behav. Evol. 4, 295–306.

Vogt, W. (1929). Gestaltungsanalyse am Amphibienkeim mit örtlicher Vitafärbung. II. Gastrulation und Mesodermbildung bei Urodelen und Anuran. Wilhelm Roux' Arch. Entwicklungs mech. Org. 120, 384–706.

von Holst, E., and Mittelstaedt, H. (1950). Das Reafferenzprinzip. Naturwissenschaften 37, 464–476.

von Holst, E., and St. Paul, U. (1960). Vom Wirkungsgefüge der Triebe. Naturwissenschaften 47, 409–422.

von Seelen, W. (1968). Informationsverarbeitung in homogenen Netzen von Neuronenmodellen. Kybernetik 5, 133–148.

von Seelen, W. (1970). Zur Informationsverarbeitung im visuellen System der Wirbeltiere. I. II. Kybernetik 7, 43–60.

Vullings, H. G. B., and Kers, J. (1973). The optic tracts of Rana temporaria, and a possible retino-preoptic pathway. Z. Zellforsch. Mikrosk. Anat. 139, 179–200.

Waddington, C. H. (1956). "Principles of Embryology." Allen & Unwin, London.

Waddington, C. H. (1966). Fields and gradients. In "Major Problems in Developmental Biology" (M. Lock, ed.), pp. 105–124. Academic Press, New York.

Waddington, C. H., and Yao, T. (1950). Studies on regional specificity within the organization centre of urodeles. J. Exp. Biol. 27, 126–144.

Wager, V. A. (1965). "The Frogs of South Africa." Purnell & Sons, Cape Town.

Wagner, H. G., MacNichol, E. F., Jr., and Wolbarsht, M. L. (1960). The response properties of single ganglion cells in the goldfish retina. J. Gen. Physiol. 43, Suppl. 6, Part 2, 45–62.

Wake, D. B. (1966). Comparative osteology and evolution of the lungless salamanders, family Plethodontidae. Mem., South. Calif. Acad. Sci. 4, 1–111.

Wake, D. B., Zweifel, R. C., Dessauer, H. C., Nace, G. W., Pionka, E. R., Rabb, G. B., Ruibal, R., Wright, J. W., and Zug, G. R. (1975). Report of the Committee on Resources in Herpetology. Copeia pp. 391–404.

Wald, G. (1946-1947). The chemical evolution of vision. Harvey Lect. 41, 117–160.

Wald, G. (1952). Biochemical evolution. In "Modern Trends in Physiology and Biochemistry" (E. S. Guzman Barrón, ed.), pp. 337–376. Academic Press, New York.

Wald, G. (1953). The biochemistry of vision. Annu. Rev. Biochem. 22, 497–526.

Wald, G. (1959). The photoreceptor process in vision. In "Handbook of Physiology" (Am. Physiol. Soc., J. Field, ed.), Sect. 1, Vol. I, pp. 671–692. Williams & Wilkins, Baltimore, Maryland.

Wald, G. (1968). Molecular basis of visual excitation. Science 162, 230–239.

Wall, P. D., and Egger, M. D. (1971). Formation of new connexions in adult rat brains after partial deafferentation. Nature (London) 232, 542–545.

Walls, G. L. (1942). "The Vertebrate Eye and its Adaptive Radiation." Hafner, New York.

Wasserman, A. O. (1957). Factors affecting interbreeding in sympatric species of spadefoots (Scaphiopus). Evolution 11, 320–338.

Wasserman, A. O. (1970). Polyploidy in the common tree toad, Hyla versicolor. Science 167, 385–386.

Watterson, R. L. (1965). Structure and mitotic behaviour of the early neural tube. *In* "Organogenesis" (R. L. De Haan and H. Ursprung, eds.), pp. 129–159. Holt, New York.

Watterson, R. L., and Fowler, (1953). Regulative development in lateral halves of chick neural tubes. *Anat. Rec.* **117**, 773–803.

Weinstein, G. W., Hobson, R. R., and Dowling, J. E. (1967). Light and dark adaptation in the isolated rat retina. *Nature (London)* **215**, 134–138.

Weiss, P. (1939). "Principles of Development. A text in Experimental Embryology." Holt, New York.

Weiss, P. (1955). The nervous system. *In* "Analysis of Development," (B. H. Williev, P. A. Weis, and V. Hamburg, eds.) pp. 346–401. Saunders, Philadelphia.

Weiss, P., and Taylor, A. C. (1960). Reconstitution of complete organs from single-cell suspensions of chick embryos in advanced stages of differentiation. *Proc. Natl. Acad. Sci. U.S.A.* **46**, 1177–1185.

Wenger, E. L. (1950). An experimental analysis of relations between parts of the brachial spinal cord of the embryonic chick. *J. Exp. Zool.* **114**, 51–81.

Werblin, F. S. (1970). Response of retinal cells to moving spots: Intracellular recordings in *Necturus maculosus. J. Neurophysiol.* **33**, 342–350.

Werblin, F. S. (1974). Control of retinal sensitivity. II. Lateral interactions at the outer plexiform layer. *J. Gen. Physiol.* **63**, 62–87.

Werblin, F. S., and Copenhagen, D. R. (1974). Control of retinal sensitivity. III. Lateral interactions at the inner plexiform layer. *J. Gen. Physiol.* **63**, 88–110.

Werblin, F. S., and Dowling, J. E. (1969). Organization of the retina of the mudpuppy *Necturus maculosus.* II. Intercellular recordings. *J. Neurophysiol.* **32**, 339–355.

Westheimer, G. (1972). Optical properties of vertebrate eyes. *In* "Handbook of Sensory Physiology" (M. G. F. Fuortes, ed.), Vol. VII, Part 2, pp. 449–482. Springer-Verlag, Berlin and New York.

Whitten, J. (1968). Metamorphic changes in insects. *In* "Metamorphosis: A Problem in Developmental Biology" (W. Etkin and L. I. Gilbert, eds). Appleton, New York.

Wiens, J. A. (1970). Effects of early experience on substrate pattern selection in *Rana aurora* tadpoles. *Copeia* No. 3, pp. 543–548.

Wiens, J. A. (1972). Anuran habitat selection: Early experience and substrate selection in *Rana cascadae* tadpoles. *Anim. Behav.* **20**, 218–220.

Wilt, F. H. (1959a). The differentiation of visual pigments in metamorphosing larve of *Rana catesbieana. Dev. Biol.* **1**, 199–233.

Wilt, F. H. (1959b). The organ specific action of thyroxin in visual pigment differentiation. *J. Embryol. Exp. Morphol.* **7**, 556–563.

Witkovsky, P., and Dowling, J. E. (1969). Synaptic relationship in the plexiform layers of carp retina. *Z. Zellforsch. Mikrosk. Anat.* **100**, 60–82.

Witkovsky, P., Nelson, J., and Ripps, H. (1973). Action spectra and adaptation properties of carp photoreceptors. *J. Gen. Physiol.* **61**, 401–423.

Wlassak, R. (1893). Die optischern heitungs—bahnen des Frosches. *Arch. Anat. Physiol., Physiol. Abt., Suppl.* pp. 1–28.

Wolpert, L. (1969). Positional information and the spatial pattern of cellular differentiation. *J. Theor. Biol.* **25**, 1–47.

Wolpert, L. (1971). Positional information and pattern formation. *Curr. Top. Dev. Biol.* **6**, 183–224.

Yoon, M. G. (1971). Reorganization of retinotectal projection following surgical operations on optic tectum of goldfish. *Exp. Neurol.* **33,** 395–411.

Yoon, M. G. (1972a). Transposition of the visual projection from the nasal hemi-retina onto the foreign rostral zone of the optic tectum in goldfish, *Exp. Neurol.* **37,** 451–462.

Yoon, M. G. (1972b). Reversibility of the reorganization of retinotectal projections in goldfish. *Exp. Neurol.* **35,** 565–577.

Yoon, M. G. (1972c). Synaptic plasticities of the retina and of the optic tectum in goldfish. *Am. Zool.* **12,** 106.

Yoon, M. G. (1973). Retention of the original topographic polarity by the 180° rotated tectal reimplant in young adult goldfish. *J. Physiol. (London)* **233,** 575–588.

Young, R. W. (1970). Visual cells. *Sci. Am.* **223,** 80–91.

Subject Index

A 6
B 7
C 8
D 9
E 0
F 1
G 2
H 3
I 4
J 5